Matthew Arnold

Matthew Arnold

❧❧❧❧

BY

LIONEL TRILLING

NEW YORK: COLUMBIA UNIVERSITY PRESS

LONDON: GEORGE ALLEN and UNWIN, LTD.

TO DIANA

—»» «««—

PREFACE TO THE SECOND EDITION

THIS BOOK was first published ten years ago. The demand for it during this time, although certainly not large, has been steady enough to have exhausted the last printing of the original publisher; this is naturally a satisfaction to me, and no less gratifying is the action of the Press of my own University in making the book again available. Because of technical considerations a revision of the text was not possible. I have been able to correct certain literal inaccuracies, although probably not all. But I have not been able to let my pencil follow its strong, irritable impulse to alter phrases, sentences, and paragraphs, or to modify and make juster the statements that now cause me uneasiness. For this I am very glad. One's sense of style does, I think, improve with the years and one is likely to acquire stricter notions of how prose should sound and of what is due one's readers; and possibly one even does also acquire more precise notions of the way things are, of what the object really is. But were I able to undertake incidental revisions I should certainly be led on to fundamental ones, and I am relieved that circumstance protects me from this temptation. Leaving aside the question of whether or not it is proper to impose a present self on a former self, I know that ten years ago I had the advantage of a much more intimate connection with Matthew Arnold than I have now, and of much more knowledge of certain aspects of 19th-century thought. When the book was done, I quite intentionally turned away from the subject, knowing that my absorption in it had inevitably had its effect on my mind, one that on the whole I thought beneficial, but having no wish to be, as one says in the academic profession, "an Arnold man." Were I now to undertake any fundamental revision, I should be tampering with the work of a writer who, whatever the lapses of his knowledge, knew more about certain matters than I do now and, whatever the failures of his judgment, had the considerable advantage of a deep involvement with his subject.

I may, however, without encroachment, mention two faults of the book of which I became aware soon after its publication. Mr. Edmund Wilson remarked in a review that in my narrative of Arnold's youthful stress the figure of Arthur Hugh Clough is not sufficiently clear and solid; I think that this is so, and it is indeed a fault, and an opportunity missed. Then I am in agreement with the reviewers who said that I did not pay enough attention to the aesthetics of Arnold's poetry. I speak in particular of these two insufficiencies because they are of a kind which the reader can supply if once he has been put in mind of them.

The ten years have of course seen a continuing production of scholarly and critical work on Arnold. I could certainly have derived benefit from this work had it been available to me as I was writing; but, so far as I know, nothing has as yet appeared which would lead me to change in any essential way my account of Arnold's thought. The two most considerable publications of the decade are *The Poetry of Matthew Arnold: A Commentary,* by Chauncey Brewster Tinker and Howard Foster Lowry (Oxford University Press, 1940), which is mentioned in my original preface as not yet published, and *Matthew Arnold, Poète: Essai de biographie psychologique,* by Professor Louis Bonnerot (Paris, Didier, 1947). The new edition of Arnold's poems by Professor Tinker and President Lowry is on the point of publication and Dr. Lowry's edition of Arnold's notebooks may now be expected shortly.

At first with every year that I worked on this book, then with every month, eventually with every week, I felt increasingly that its subject had an intense relevance to the cultural and political situation of the world, and I tried to give expression to this sense in an Introductory Note. Ten years later the substance of that Note seems dreadfully to need no modification. The Third Reich has fallen, but the assault on mind which the Nazis made has not failed. What the Minister of Education said about science in German we can now hear being said in Russian, and as the accompaniment of the same absolutism that, ten years ago, horrified us in Germany. And now, although we perhaps fear the force of that absolutism even more than we formerly did, we are rather less sensitive than we were a decade ago to the perversions of mind it necessarily makes. It is wrong to suppose that these perversions of mind occur only where absolutism exerts its actual physical force; absolutism has the power both to attract and to weary what seems to oppose it. Our liberals and intellectuals, almost as if at the behest of the external force, have become even less eager than ten years ago to see the object as it really is, less willing to believe that in a time of change and danger openness and flexibility of mind are, as Arnold said, the first of virtues. Pride in mind and a true conception of the nature of mind seem to go from them. A very able scholar recently wrote a book chiefly to show that Arnold did not in actual practice always exemplify the virtues of mind he praised in his writing—despite all his talk of disinterestedness, he himself was often passionate and unfair, and so on. But does this matter and is it not a symptom of our confusion to remark it—an evidence of our losing the sense of human limits, therefore of human powers, therefore of human processes, of our turning to the desperate absolute, thus to make it a reproach to a man that he did not achieve the perfection of his ideal?

Were I writing of Arnold now I should not say the same things I said ten years ago. I should not, I think, write quite so much as Arnold's advocate on certain particular points, and my feeling of intimacy with him would undoubtedly have a different quality. But I should write of him with an even enhanced sense of his standing for the intellectual virtues that are required by a complex society if it is to survive in real and not in merely simulated life; and also with an enhanced sense of two other things: of how difficult it is to make

Preface to the Second Edition

these virtues seem attractive and necessary, and of Arnold's personal fortitude in carrying out his chosen task of making them appear so.

L. T.

New York City

‐≫≫‐ ‐≪≪‐

PREFACE

THE writing of this book has put me under many happy obligations. Of the members of the Columbia University faculty who have furthered this work, I am especially indebted to Professor Emery Neff, who fostered and guided it through its development and put at my disposal his wide knowledge of the 19th century. The late Ashley H. Thorndike read only a single chapter in a primitive draft but I remember with gratitude and affection our conversations about Arnold. Professor Jefferson Butler Fletcher and Professor Hoxie Neale Fairchild gave me criticism of the greatest value. Professor George Sherburn, Professor Horatio Smith, Professor William York Tindall and Dr. Henry Wells helped preserve me from inaccuracies of fact and expression. I am grateful to Professor Mark Van Doren and Professor James Gutmann for reading the work in manuscript, to Professor Otto P. Schinnerer and Professor Henry H. L. Schulze for their help in German matters, to Mr. H. Theodric Westbrook for aiding me in matters of the classics, and to Mr. Alan W. Brown for his generous assistance with the proofs. Professor Jacques Barzun helped me with the material on race in Chapter VIII and, with the most friendly forbearance, went over more drafts of the work than I dare remember.

I am very grateful to Professor Sidney Hook of New York University for giving me the advantage of his criticism. Dr. Chilson Leonard of Phillips Exeter Academy graciously permitted me to use material from his admirable *Matthew Arnold in America,* a manuscript work in the Sterling Memorial Library at Yale. Professor Howard Foster Lowry was most generous in his willingness to answer questions from his great knowledge of Arnold. It was through his kindness, too, that I procured the photograph reproduced in the frontispiece. I regret that the edition of Arnold's notebooks which Professor Lowry is preparing with Professor Karl Young and Professor Waldo H. Dunn and the edition of and commentary on Arnold's poems which he is preparing with Professor Chauncey Brewster Tinker were not published in time for me to make use of them as—with the permission of the Oxford University Press—I have made use of his edition of Arnold's letters to Clough.

The librarians of the Pierpont Morgan Library, the Sterling Memorial Library at Yale, the Union Theological Seminary Library and the Columbia University Library have been most helpful. Many publishers and individuals have allowed me to quote from works of which they hold the copyright; their names are given on the page following the reference notes. For time spent at Yaddo when this work was first begun I thank the Yaddo Corporation, and I am most grateful to Mr. John Slade of Saratoga, member of the Corporation, for his interest in the book and for several useful references.

My friend Bettina Sinclair generously read the proof in the midst of her own pressing work. My sister Harriet Trilling Schwartz gave me valuable aid in the preparation of the manuscript. Without the devotion which my sister-in-law Cecelia Rubin gave to the typing I should have been quite lost. My friends Elsa and James Grossman not only helped me with linguistic and historical matters and with literary advice but they made the writing easier by their affectionate concern for the task. My debt to my wife Diana Trilling is greatest of all; I cannot calculate its full sum, for it amounted to collaboration; at every stage of the book she was my conscience, and there is scarcely a paragraph that was not bettered by her unremitting criticism and her creative editing.

L. T.

New York City.

INTRODUCTORY NOTE

I HAVE undertaken in this book to show the thought of Matthew Arnold in its complex unity and to relate it to the historical and intellectual events of his time. I have consulted almost no unpublished material and whatever biographical matter I have used is incidental to my critical purpose. However, because I have treated Arnold's ideas in their development, this study may be thought of as a biography of Arnold's mind.

A writer's reputation often reaches a point in its career where what he actually said is falsified even when he is correctly quoted. Such falsification—we might more charitably call it mythopoeia—is very likely the result of some single aspect of a man's work serving as a convenient symbol of what other people want to think. Thus it is a commonplace of misconception that Rousseau wanted us to act like virtuous savages or that Milton held naive, retrograde views of human nature. In a world where action presses and where it is believed that the coexistence of two ideas must keep us from acting on either, it is very easy for Arnold's subtle critical dialectic to be misrepresented and for his work to be reduced to a number of pious and ridiculous phrases about "the grand style," "culture," "sweetness and light." My critical intention has been to make clear what, in my opinion, Arnold as poet and as critic of literature, politics and religion actually said and meant.

I speak of the complex unity of Arnold's thought: to some, unity might suggest system and Arnold had a passionate dislike of system; an exposition of his ideas that seemed to systematize them would be

directly contrary to his spirit. Arnold's thought, nevertheless, has a
logic and architecture which is none the less strict for being organic
and not mechanical. He cherished the modulation of his opinions—
but the modulation cannot be seen unless the unity of his thought
is understood.

Only less intense than Arnold's fear of systematic criticism was
his fear of historical criticism. By historical criticism Arnold meant
criticism which goes on the "scientific" assumption that when we
have learned a great deal about the age in which a writer lived,
when we have catalogued the books he read and the events he witnessed, we must inevitably come to an understanding of the man
and his thought. I have not, I hope, made any such assumption in
giving so much attention to the historical background of Arnold's
work. On the other hand, Arnold himself always insisted that the
act of criticism requires that we suspend our absolute standards and
look at events or ideas, whether past or present, in the light of their
historical determinants. He believed that the critic must be the *"undulating and diverse* being of Montaigne" and that one of the ways
to achieve this flexibility is through the use of the *proper* historical
method. Arnold's judgment of the French Revolution is an example of this method at work. Was he a partisan of the Revolution or
its vigorous opponent? We might show by quotation that he was
either or both, but actually he was neither; his feeling about the
Revolution was determined, first, by his notion of the historical context in which it had occurred and, second, by the particular historical
moment in which he was writing. What determined him to speak
for or against the Revolution at any particular time was his conception of how much of the Revolutionary principle England at *that*
time required. Certainly to miss the historical and dialectical nature
of Matthew Arnold's own way of thinking is to misinterpret him
entirely.

E. M. Forster recalls Arnold's line, "Who prop, thou ask'st, in
these bad days, my mind?" and smiles to think how halcyon were
the days of '48 compared with our own. He says (erroneously) that

Arnold was chiefly worried by problems of faith, doubt and personal survival, and goes on: "but the collapse of all civilization, so realistic for us, sounded in his ears like a distant and harmonious cataract, plunging from Alpine snows into the eternal bosom of the Lake of Geneva. . . . If public violences increase and Geneva itself disappears—who is going to prop our minds? They? The great minds of the past? They, who imagined, at the worst, a local or a philosophic catastrophe?"

Well, since Mr. Forster wrote, public violences have increased and certainly Geneva, the Geneva of the League of Nations, has disappeared. And with it has vanished faith in a certain kind of liberalism. It was in some part Arnold's liberalism, and surely the liberalism of Mr. Forster's friend, G. Lowes Dickinson, who was, if anyone was, Arnold's spiritual descendant. "Practical politics," Dickinson said, explaining his own *Modern Symposium,* "involves fighting, and the object of such a book as mine, as it was Plato's object long ago, is to raise the mind above the fighting attitude. There lies obscurely the great problem of the relation of ideals to passion and interests which I do not seem able clearly to formulate." Highminded and sweetly reasonable, Dickinson, like Arnold, fought against Anarchy—International Anarchy, as he called it; he is said to have given the League of Nations its name, certainly he gave it his faith and energy. But history moved aside what seemed the instrument of his "ideal" and disclosed the ugly "passion and interests" which it hid.

Ideals, however, do not fail because they are ideal, and liberalism does not fail because it follows Arnold's idealism; rather, it fails because it does *not* follow Arnold's realism. When Mr. Forster dismisses Arnold the prose writer he does not mean to dismiss Arnold the poet; the poet, he believes, is secure, propping us in bad days, not because art is a "weapon" stronger than parks of artillery—that is foolish to suppose—but because Arnold's poetry can remind us of a world where will is not everything and can suggest the ideal life of man. But the poet's vision gave the prose writer his goal. *To see the object as it really is* is no less the aim of the poet than of the practical man; Arnold the poet saw first the problems Arnold the practical man tried to solve. *To see the object as it really is* was the essence of Arnold's teaching; and where he failed it was because he could not himself achieve sufficient objectivity.

The beginning student of politics, the beginning student of philosophy, will explain at once the impossibility of ever seeing the object as it really is; nor was Arnold so naive as to think that in practical life, let alone in the metaphysics he hated, it could easily, or always, or completely, be seen. But the limitations of men exist in varying degrees; surely it is not the limitation itself but the worship of limitation which is degrading. In our time we read the address of Germany's Minister of Science, Education and People's Education on the occasion of the 550th anniversary of the University of Heidelberg: "The charge of [our] enmity to science is true . . . if the complete absence of preconceptions and predispositions, unrestrained objectivity, are to be taken as characteristics of science. . . . The old idea of science based on the sovereign right of abstract intellectual activity has gone forever. The new science is entirely different from the idea of knowledge that found its value in an unchecked effort to reach the truth." In a time when to the duplicity of nations is added a shrewd madness denying that words have any meaning at all, Arnold, with his insistence on objectivity and the powers of human reason, may well prop our minds.

The German Minister's pronouncement is, of course, the extreme of a false position, and Arnold was not especially concerned with such extremes; he was not so much concerned with combating vile positions as with refining relatively good ones: as a critic he would rather harry his friends than destroy his enemies. If, he was always saying, you hold this opinion, do you really know what consequent opinions you must hold and what actions you must perform? Are you sure that it is really to your own true interest to hold them and perform them? He looked with coolness upon action, it is true, but not because he had any quarrel with action itself, only because he knew that action is not always itself—that it goes beyond itself, becomes a means of faith, a way of escaping thought and what seem to be the humiliations of necessary doubt. Now, in a day when intellectual men are often called upon to question their intellect and to believe that thought is inferior to action and opposed to it, that blind partisanship is fidelity to an idea, Arnold has still a word to say—not against the taking of sides but against the belief that taking a side settles things or requires the suspension of reason.

Arnold's failures in judgment were many, as they must have been with a man who took upon himself his peculiarly ungrateful task. T. S. Eliot tells us that Arnold was not a revolutionary and not a reactionary, but that does not mean he was neutral: rather, he tried to make the past of Europe march with the future. Arnold did not believe that he lived in the period of stasis which Mr. Eliot says was his; indeed, he saw it as a time when all the old orders were breaking up, the order of the Reformation and of the French Revolution as well as the order of ecclesiastic feudalism. From each he desired to conserve the best, and consequently he gets his drubbings from all parties, many of them deserved. He sought to conciliate epochs and that is something that history but no single man can successfully do. Yet Arnold's eclectic and dialectical method has its vitality exactly because it is the method of history.

Arnold's vision is said to be too simple, too genteel, incomplete; he lacked—to quote T. S. Eliot yet again—the vision of the horror and the glory of life. He was, indeed, too much inclined to believe that the art of Periclean Athens was obviously the highest, and all else either a falling away from or a striving toward it; and that the placid, perspicacious Anglicanism of Bishop Wilson was the sum of modern morality. But he did not really, as we are sometimes led to believe, see life through a haze of bland gentility. It is truly life that he sees—a life in which Wragg, poor thing, had her existence in a ditch, a life which included the horrors of St. Helens and Spitalfields, the hideous schools, the hymns of the chapel and the lucubrations of the episcopal study, the lowness and meanness of the forms the human spirit can take. Of the "masters of reality," as Bernard Shaw calls them, he was not one of the greatest. But he was one of them—with an ideal of order, of peace and of unity which would develop the truly human in man, and his words are still fresh:

Undoubtedly we are drawing on towards great changes; and for every nation the thing most needful is to discern clearly its own condition, in order to know in what particular way it may best meet them. Openness and flexibility of mind are at such a time the first of virtues. . . . Perfection will never be reached; but to recognise a period of transformation when it comes, and to adapt themselves honestly and rationally to its laws, is perhaps the nearest approach to perfection of which men and nations are capable. No habits or attachments should prevent their trying to do this; nor indeed, in the long run, can they. Human thought, which made all institutions, inevitably saps them, resting only in that which is absolute and eternal.

It goes without saying that admiration for a writer does not mean agreement. Indeed, I believe it will be apparent that it is much more with Arnold's method that I am in agreement than with his conclusions. But where I have disagreed with Arnold's conclusions, I have not attempted to supply other answers to the problems with which he dealt, although it would scarcely be possible not to indicate the direction in which I felt the right answer lay. Where I disagree, as where I agree, my chief effort has been to draw out and make clear the full implications of Arnold's positions.

CONTENTS

Chapter One

»»» «««

"A"

*No virtue can be conceived as prior to this virtue
of endeavoring to preserve oneself.*—SPINOZA

THE secretary of old Lord Lansdowne, the Liberal peer,
was a singularly handsome young man whose manners
were Olympian and whose waistcoats were remarkable.
He was most ironic; his very serious university friends were often
annoyed with him because he laughed too much. As the protégé
of a political peer and of his father's friend, the Prussian Minister
von Bunsen, he had entry to a society of talent and power and was
much in demand for dinner parties. "A very gentlemanly young
man," said Henry Crabb Robinson, another friend of his father,
who had him to breakfast, "with a slight tinge of the fop that does
no harm when blended with talents, good nature & high spirits."

When a volume of verse called *The Strayed Reveller* appeared in
1849 and it became an open secret that the signature "A" hid the
authorship of Matthew Arnold, everyone who knew him was astonished at the temper of the volume. Those who were acquainted
with his father, Dr. Thomas Arnold, were amazed that any poetry
at all should come from an Arnold, and Matthew's friends and
family were puzzled that a book so gaily titled and by so gay a
young man should be so sad. His sister Mary wrote of the volume
and of her brother as he was at this time: "I used to breakfast with
him sometimes, and then his Poems seemed to make me know Matt
so much better than I had ever done before. Indeed it was almost

like a new Introduction to him . . . I felt there was so much more of . . . practical questioning in Matt's book than I was at all prepared for; in fact that it showed a knowledge of life and conflict which was *strangely like experience* if it was not the thing itself; and this with all Matt's great power I should not have looked for."

But in less intimate circles the impression he created was a different one. When, for instance, he went abroad and visited George Sand, she said that he made on her "l'effet d'un Milton jeune et voyageant" and although she meant, perhaps, nothing more than that he was English, handsome, conceited and on his travels, she might have meant, too, that she saw the invincible gravity of a Milton and the unmistakable air of a self-dedicated man.

As we look now at the two prize poems, the Rugby *Alaric at Rome* and the Newdigate *Cromwell,* the only published work of Matthew Arnold before the 1849 volume, it is surprising that his friends were not better prepared for the tone of *The Strayed Reveller.* True, the emotions of prize poems are not too firmly based; perhaps the schoolboy who had won a declamation prize with the Doge's magnificent curse of Venice from *Marino Faliero* was only "Byronizing" when he drew his picture of doomed Rome. But *Alaric,* despite its naivety and frequent triteness, is a real poem:

> Hast thou not marked on a wild autumn day
> When the wind slumbereth in a sudden lull,
> What deathlike stillness o'er the landscape lay,
> How calmly sad, how sadly beautiful;
> How each bright tint of tree, and flower, and heath
> Were mingling with the sere and withered hues of death?

> And thus, beneath the clear, calm vault of heaven
> In mournful loveliness that city lay,
> And thus, amid the glorious hues of even
> That city told of languor and decay:
> Till what at morning's hour lookt warm and bright
> Was cold and sad beneath that breathless, voiceless night.

And *Cromwell* is even more indicative of the temper of the Arnold the world was to know. Its epigraph was taken from Schiller—

> Schrecklich ist es, deiner Wahrheit
> Sterbliches Gefäss zu seyn.

"It is awful to be the mortal vessel of Thy truth." Cromwell, of course, was an attractive subject for a young man in an age unsure of the future of democracy, especially a young man concerned with the problems of laissez-faire and the Ten Hours' Bill, whose father was a friend of Carlyle and the champion of the non-priestly church for which Cromwell had fought. Nevertheless, the real significance of the poem was neither political nor religious, but profoundly personal; it is young Matthew himself who is aghast at the awfulness of being the mortal vessel of truth.

Cromwell is in the heroic couplets the Newdigate rules then prescribed but the couplets make no attempt at classical strictness and the poem's spirit is pure romanticism—from the invocation, in Coleridge's vein, to the moral powers of ocean and mountain, "cradles of freedom," through the Wordsworthian defense of childish ambition ("Say not such dreams are idle: for the man Still toils to perfect what the child began") to the Byronic burst at the end, when Cromwell gives up his intention of an easeful life in America and dedicates himself to his terrible destiny in cadences that foretell "Sohrab and Rustum:"

> Then all his vision faded, and his soul
> Sprang from its sleep! and lo, the waters roll
> Once more beneath him; and the fluttering sail,
> Where the dark ships rode proudly, woo'd the gale;
> And the wind murmur'd round him, and he stood
> Once more alone beside the gleaming flood.

Meditation on themes like these comes strangely from a young man whom everyone thinks a dandy. But this dandy, after all, had been reared in the tradition of men who felt themselves mortal vessels of truth. His boyhood had been spent in the Lake Country and under Wordsworth's affectionate eye. He had roamed Loughrigg, skated on Rydal Water and boated on Windermere. He had never seen Coleridge, but the memory of the great man and the sight of that pitiable memento of his life, Hartley Coleridge, were often before him. It was awful to have been the mortal vessel of truth—and to leave behind the derelict Hartley to mock all the grand words that had been addressed to him in "Frost at Midnight." "What do I care for Society? I am all for the individual Citizen," said the brilliant wrecked Hartley, and when he asked for a drink it was not water that he wanted, as the good Dr. Arnold had supposed. "Tintern Abbey" was even more grimly mocked: on fine days young Matthew had seen Dorothy Wordsworth in her wheelchair, "the shooting lights" of her "wild eyes" extinguished in the blankness of idiocy. And once he had been taken by his father to call at Greta Bank to meet Southey, who shook hands and said, "So, now you've seen a live poet!"

Yet to all outward appearance the boy had been untouched by the tradition in which he was bred; it was generally admitted that he was literary, but it was much more generally observed that he was a dandy. The "Fox How Magazine," which the Arnold children wrote among themselves, took frequent occasion to comment on Matthew's elegance of dress and deportment and on his supercilious disdain of the dress and deportment of his kin. At Winchester, where his father had sent him at the age of fourteen to experience the tough discipline of his own old school, Matthew had coolly said to the Headmaster that the work of his form was quite light; his fellows heard of the remark with natural horror and at a commination ritual known as "cloister peelings" had dragged him before the school to be pelted with "pontos." While at Winchester he had walked to Hursley to visit his godfather Keble; he was very polite but he irreverently noted Keble's "flibbertigibbet, fanatical, twinkling expression." And when, after a year of Winchester, he had come to Rugby, he behaved as neither of the two prize Arthurs of Rugby, Stanley and Clough, would have thought of behaving; when as a member of the Sixth Form he displeased Dr. Arnold and was stood behind the Doctor's chair, he gratified his friends by making faces over his father's head.

Nor did the dignity of Oxford impress Arnold with the need for greater gravity of manner or purpose. He came to Balliol, as a classmate's commemorative poem said, "wide-welcomed for a father's fame," but he

> Entered with free bold step that seemed to claim
> Fame for himself.

Indeed, far from relying upon his father, he seemed to cultivate as great a divergence as possible from his father's "line." Dr. Arnold had once been astonished at the conversation of a group of footloose young Englishmen at a Milanese inn; they had been ribald and it therefore seemed strange to him that they could be so intelligent; but Matthew had a genial amount of ribaldry which he gracefully exhibited in his letters to Clough. He was everything of which his father would have disapproved—jaunty, indolent, debonair, affected. His banter and lack of seriousness became proverbial among his friends. The poets of his choice, led by Béranger, were unorthodox and epicurean. He read Spinoza, an atheistic philosopher, and Emerson, who taught him the dangers of conformity and the need for preserving in oneself the glow of life. In his first year he won a Hertford scholarship, but thereafter he was casual about his work. "M. has gone out fishing when he ought properly to be working," wrote Clough in the summer of 1844 from a reading party which Arnold had joined and was doing his best to ignore or disrupt.

And at times his activities were Jorrocksesque. "We arrived here on Friday evening," wrote his friend Hawker during a trip with young Matthew in 1843, "after sundry displays of the most consummate coolness on the part of our friend Matt, who pleasantly induced a belief into the passengers of the coach that I was a poor mad gentleman, and that he was my keeper."

A trip to Paris in 1846, in part motivated by a desire to follow the actress Rachel through her Paris season, only exaggerated his passion for gaiety, fantasy and flamboyance. He visited George Sand at Nohant (he had long been devoted to her novels) and came back with the wondrous waistcoats and a conscious indifference to church-going. "Matt is full of Parisianism," Clough wrote; "Theatres in general, and Rachel in special: he enters the room with a chanson of Béranger's on his lips—for the sake of French words almost conscious of tune: his carriage shows him in fancy parading the Rue de Rivoli; and his hair is guiltless of English scissors: he breakfasts at 12, and never dines in Hall, and in the week or 8 days rather (for 2 Sundays must be included) he has been to chapel *once."*

In 1845, to the disappointment but not to the surprise of his friends, Arnold took a second at Balliol and retired to a temporary post as classical undermaster at Rugby while he stood for a fellowship at Oriel. He seems to have been unchastened by his scholastic defeat, his pedagogic duties, or by the Rugby tradition. A young colleague at the school had got an ugly reputation for being "fast:" he kept a horse and it had been said, falsely, that he was a hunting man; he was worried about his good name. One day he entertained at tea the straitlaced parents of a pupil and young Arnold entered, casual, tall, black-whiskered. Languidly he waved aside the food that was offered him. "No thank you, my darling," he said, "I've just bitten off the tails of those three bull-pups of yours, and that does take the edge off one's appetite." And he continued, disregarding the horror of the guests and the alarm of his host, "By the way, I had a look at that mare of yours when I was in the stable. I'd advise you to have her vetted before you ride her to hounds again."

The pietistic tone never failed to raise all his impish dander. "I do not give satisfaction at the Masters Meetings," he writes to

Clough. "For the other day when Tait [the head-master] had well observed that strict Calvinism devoted 1000s of mankind to be eternally,—and paused—I, with, I trust the true Xtian Simplicity suggested '——'." And he goes on, in a parody of pious "self-examination:" "True, I give satisfaction—but to whom? True, I have yet been late on no Morning, but do I come behind in no thing? True, I search the Exercises, but the Spirits?—For which Reason it seems not clear why I should stand at Oriel [for the fellowship]: for wisdom I have not, nor skilfulness—after the Flesh—no, nor yet Learning: and [who] will see a delicate Spirit tossed on Earth, opossum like, with the down fresh upon him, from the maternal Pouches of nature, in the grimed and rusty coalheaver, sweating and grunting

> with the Burden of an honour
> Unto which he was not born.—

I have other ways to go." And, suddenly: "But, my dear Clough, have you a great Force of Character? That is the true Question. For me, I am a reed, a very whoreson Bullrush: yet such as I am I give satisfaction."

He won, of course, the fellowship at Oriel and recouped his Balliol debacle, as Clough had done before him. He was elected exactly thirty years after his father had received the same honor, and old Wordsworth was very pleased. He was now in the university tradition of the Doctor and of Newman.

But Arnold himself was unmoved. His insouciance continued through the fellowship days and through his removal in 1847 to London to become secretary to Lord Lansdowne.

He had been trained to every sober virtue in one of the most pious households of England, taught everlastingly by precept and example that life was serious, yet every act that his friends record of Matthew Arnold at this time is a denial of his training, every word that he writes in his letters is an assertion of his own pleasant difference from other men. He is intent upon making himself a Disraelian dandy—gay, careless, cocky. His friends found that Arnold's cool gaiety made him remote, that he seemed untouched by the doubts and worries which made their intellectual lives, that he might call them "my love" and "my darling" as his habit was, but that he seemed always at a distance, separated from them by irony and laughter, and their affection for him was touched with bitterness. Yet out of this cool, aloof gaiety come the brooding verses of *The Strayed Reveller* and, shortly after, in 1852, of *Empedocles on Etna.*

Is the paradox a simple one? Probably not, but all the pitfalls of interpretive biography warn us away from the attempt to explore its complexity. Simplicity, however, will not serve; it is impossible to believe that this cockiness is merely the high spirit of youth— or a literary young man's emulation of two of his literary idols, the arrogant Byron and the lordly Goethe—or simply the rebellion of a young man against his father's "line." If we are to understand the relation of Arnold's poetry to his life we must understand the relation of the cockiness to his philosophy; for when the dandyism was at work, Arnold produced poetry, but when the dandyism failed, poetry failed too.

Reading Arnold's letters to Clough through the years 1845-1853 one becomes increasingly certain that his friends were right when they felt that Arnold's gaiety kept them at a distance; one becomes equally certain that he intended it to do just that. James Anthony Froude was irritated that Arnold seemed remote from their problems—largely of personal religion; John Duke Coleridge felt that he could announce his marriage to Arnold only with constraint and misgiving, and Arnold himself feels the necessity of disclaiming to him any "want of interest in my friends;" it is, he says, "an old subject" and should have been cleared up by now. "The accusation, as you say, is not true. I laugh too much and they make one's laughter mean too much." But the fact is that

Arnold feared his friends and kept them off—feared even Clough
at times nearly as much as any of them and as early as 1848 considered attenuating the friendship. He gave up the idea at the time
but the relationship certainly grew less and less fertile until by
1853 it was an affectionate formality. "Thyrsis" is the lament for a
dead friend but also for a dead friendship.

What Arnold feared in all his friends, and especially in Clough
as the most intimate, was a thing that he feared in himself. He
perceived in his friends the driving restless movement of the
critical intellect trying to solve the problems of the 19th century.
He perceived in himself the poetic power, but knew that his genius
was not of the greatest, that the poetic force was not irresistible in
him, that it might not be able to carry before it all else in his personality. He knew he had the right power to make poetry but that
it lacked something in assertiveness, that it was only delicately
rooted in him. He believed that the critical intellect, seizing the
whole personality, splitting it into segments, making it doubtful,
incapacitating it for poetry, was the force against which his poetic
gifts must be protected.

The long sad personal battle with Clough is fought under a
cloak of aesthetic discussion. Arnold does not like Clough's
poetry and tells him so, now mitigating his criticism, now roaring
it out with humorous exaggeration; Clough, he says, has mistaken the whole function and method of poetry. True, he has a
sincerity so manifest that it "always produces a powerful effect
on the reader" and this is no slight virtue, for "the spectacle of a
writer striving evidently to get breast to breast with reality is always
full of instruction and very invigorating." But it is not enough.
"More and more," he writes to his sister "K," "I feel bent against the
modern English habit (too much encouraged by Wordsworth) of
using poetry as a channel for thinking aloud, instead of making
anything." Clough's is the way of the admirable *man* but not the
way of the artist; and "I doubt your being an *artist,*" says Arnold.
In the end, we gather, it is even not enough for a man.

It is no easy task, Arnold is willing to concede, to be a poet in the 19th century, and he himself has considered giving up the attempt. It is an age which, though moving and profound, he finds deeply unpoetical—not because it is ugly but because it is without unity. Arnold is sure that, poetical age or unpoetical, poetry must be beautiful, must give pleasure or it is not poetry, and Clough's poetry, whatever its virtues of sincerity or of fine thought, is not beautiful and gives no pleasure. It is perfectly apparent where the trouble lies in Clough: he has made too great a commitment to the critical intellect. "I often think," Arnold writes, "that even a slight gift of poetical expression which in a common person might have developed itself easily and naturally, is overlaid and crushed in a profound thinker so as to be of no use to him to help him to express himself."

It is the problem of the antagonism between the creative imagination and the critical intellect which lies at the very heart of the romantic philosophy. "I hope, Philosophy and Poetry will not neutralize each other, and leave me an inert mass," Coleridge said. And again, writing of the same difficulty that Arnold was discovering in Clough: "Imagination which if it be a Jack o'Lanthorn to lead us out of [the] way is however—at the same time a Torch to light us whither we are going. A whole Essay might be written on the Danger of *thinking* without Images." Arnold is impatient with Clough, calls him "a mere d——d depth hunter in poetry," because Clough cannot see the charm in *Phèdre;* he finds no "message" in it and is insensitive to its surface, to its grouping of objects, to its style, which is in itself a meaning and a "message." In short, so far as Arnold can see, Clough is simply not a poet. However admirably sincere, devotional, rhetorical, metaphysical, Clough's poems may be, they are, says Arnold, never "natural." Clough's poetry is of the head. But the antithesis to the head is not the heart but the *whole being*. Arnold urges Clough to try a therapeutic reading of the Bhagavad Gita because "the Indians distinguish between meditation or absorption—and knowledge." Clough, the complete Westerner, does not like the book.

Every poet, of course, knows what Arnold wanted Clough to learn from the Bhagavad Gita.* Schopenhauer, who was deeply influenced by it, gives us, in his definition of genius, a good approximation of what it intends:

Only through the pure contemplation . . . which ends entirely in the object, can Ideas be comprehended; and the nature of *genius* consists in preeminent capacity for such contemplation. Now, as this requires that a man should entirely forget himself and the relations in which he stands, *genius* is simply the completest *objectivity* ["you poor subjective, you," Arnold called Clough], *i.e.,* the objective tendency of the mind, as opposed to the subjective, which is directed to one's own self—in other words, to the will. Thus genius is the faculty of continuing in the state of pure perception, of losing oneself in perception, and of enlisting in this service the knowledge which originally existed only for the service of the will; that is to say, genius is the power of leaving one's own interests, wishes, and aims entirely out of sight, thus of entirely renouncing one's own personality for a time, so as to remain *pure knowing subject,* clear vision of the world; and this not merely at moments, but for a sufficient length of time, and with sufficient consciousness, to enable one to reproduce by deliberate art what has thus been apprehended, and "to fix in lasting thoughts the wavering images that float before the mind."

Poetry, then, is a precipitation of the whole personality, of the non-conscious as well as the conscious, a distillation of the complete being. It is not to be produced by a restless effort of the will—which was what Coleridge meant when he said that the creative power was not known to "the sensual and the proud." It is the spontaneous integration of body and mind: for Shelley the "elo-

* The complex and hazy discussion of the Self which the Bhagavad Gita contains is touched on in Chapter III, though lightly even there. Arnold had at his disposal several translations of the Gita. None, apparently, has the approval of modern scholarship. The first English translation was that of Sir Charles Wilkins (1785). I suspect that Arnold read the essay of W. von Humboldt on the Gita (Berlin 1826) and the improved and amplified Latin version made by Lassen in 1846 from the Latin rendering of A. W. von Schlegel (1823). There was no new English translation until that of J. Cockburn Thomson in 1855 and Arnold speaks of the Gita before that date.

quent blood" tells "an ineffable tale;" for Wordsworth the poet sees into the life of things with "the power of harmony," the "deep power of joy;" Keats speaks of proving the axioms of philosophy on his pulses; Coleridge makes Joy the source of the creative power, "not mirth or high spirits, or even happiness, but a consciousness of entire and therefore well being, when the emotional and intellectual faculties are in equipoise—"

> Joy that ne'er was given,
> Save to the pure, and in their purest hour,
> Life, and Life's effluence, cloud at once and shower,
> Joy, Lady! is the spirit and the power,
> Which, wedding Nature to us, gives in dower *
> A new Earth and new Heaven,
> Undreamt of by the sensual and the proud—
> Joy is the sweet voice, Joy the luminous cloud—
> We in ourselves rejoice!
> And thence flows all that charms or ear or sight,
> All melodies the echoes of that voice,
> All colours a suffusion from that light.

But poor Clough, however eloquent and sincere his mind, does not have eloquent blood; however great his capacity for high spirits, he does not have the deep power of joy. "We in ourselves rejoice" —but Clough did not rejoice in himself, and above all things Arnold desired to do just that. He knew that the power of joy could fade, the poetic power vanish. Coleridge had quoted to Tom Wedgwood the lines from "Dejection: An Ode" on the loss of his "shaping power of imagination" which had sprung from joy and vanished with it; "I give you these lines for the Truth and not for the Poetry," he had written.

Arnold knew his own weakness and he feared the contamination of a friend in whom the poetic joy was absent. By 1848 he was

---

* The punctuation of this line is that suggested by H. W. Garrod in his *Wordsworth* (2nd Edition, 1927) p. 132, n. "Joy is the spirit which weds Nature to us, and in so doing gives us an earth and heaven," he says, and supplies the commas. With Mr. Garrod's book, I. A. Richards' *Coleridge On Imagination* (1935) greatly illuminates the psychological problem Arnold was facing.

quite explicit to himself about the matter and formulated a "theory of intellectual dietetics" which involved "intellectual seclusion, and . . . the barring out all influences that [he] felt troubled [him] without advancing [him]." Clough was at first to be among the influences barred out; he was readmitted, but the rift was a real one and in 1853, when Clough is explicit about the failure of the friendship and importunes Arnold with accusations of coldness, Arnold reviews the relationship, translating into the language of personality what he had hitherto said only in the language of literary criticism. "You certainly do not seem to me sufficiently to desire and earnestly strive towards—assured knowledge—activity —happiness. You are too content to *fluctuate*—to be ever learning, never coming to the knowledge of the truth. This is why, with you, I feel it necessary to stiffen myself—and hold fast my rudder." And again: "You ask me in what I think or have thought you going wrong: in this: that you would never take your assiette as something determined final and unchangeable for you and proceed to work away on the basis of that: but were always poking and patching and cobbling at the assiette itself—could never finally, as it seemed—'resolve to be thyself'—but were looking for this and that experience, and doubting whether you ought not to adopt this or that mode of being of persons qui ne vous valaient pas because it might possibly be nearer the truth than your own: you had no reason for thinking it *was,* but it *might* be."

" 'Resolve to be thyself:' " Arnold quotes the words from one of his own poems; they are the words that Nature speaks to the poet when he is "weary of [himself], and sick of asking What I am, and what I ought to be."

> "Resolve to be thyself: and know, that he
> Who finds himself, loses his misery."

The advice is not *know* thyself but *be* thyself, and this it would seem is not easy for a young man in the 19th century.

"No virtue," said Spinoza, "can be conceived as prior to this virtue of endeavoring to preserve oneself." And all of Arnold's youthful affectation is directed toward the preservation of himself, toward allowing himself to be himself. If he wanted to protect his power of joy he had to keep off his friends by setting between them and him the barrier of his eccentricity. The fight with Clough might be painful; with other, less intimate, friends the dandyism was an easier weapon: "Our friend Matt utters as many absurdities as ever," wrote Hawker, the victim of the lunacy hoax in 1843, "with as grave a face, and I am afraid wastes his time considerably, which I deeply regret." Misunderstood, hiding behind a mask of irresponsibility, Arnold is free to cultivate that internal, meditative, slowly-precipitating part of himself which is to produce poetry. He is free from the questioning moralism and the restless intellectual drive of Rugby and Oxford: *"Es bildet ein Talent sich in der Stille"* —behind the high wall of his mockery.

But the fight was not merely a personal one and Arnold is not, on the whole, inclined to speak of it as personal at all. He believes that he is resisting the whole of turbulent contemporary Europe. When he speaks of the age as unpoetical he is not being precious and "aesthetic;" the depth of his seriousness may be seen in the passionate letter he wrote to Clough in 1848. "I have been at Oxford the last two days and hearing Sellar and the rest of that clique who know neither life nor themselves rave about your poem* gave me a strong almost bitter feeling with respect to them, the age, the poem, even you. Yes I said to myself something tells me I can, if need be, at last dispense with them all, even with him [i.e., Clough]: better that, than be sucked for an hour even into the Time Stream in which they and he plunge and bellow. I became calm in spirit, but uncompromising, almost stern. [They are] more English than European, I said finally, more American than English:

---

* The poem is *The Bothie of Tober-na-Vuolich; A Long-Vacation Pastoral,* which Clough wrote in September 1848. Sellar raved in praise but Clough records in a letter to Emerson that "in Oxford though there has been a fair sale and much talk of it, the verdict is 'indecent & profane, immoral & (!) Communistic.' "—Letter 8, *Emerson-Clough Letters,* edited by H. F. Lowry and R. L. Rusk, Cleveland, 1934.

and took up Obermann, and refuged myself with him in his forest against your Zeit Geist." More English than European, more American than English: that is, more restlessly energetic, more Protestantly intellectualistic, more Calvinistically self-examining in the striving for truth. And the musings of Senancour's *Obermann* with which Arnold "refuged himself" are devoted to the sufferings of a modern man whose personality has been split by this modern habit of thought, who has lost his personal integration and the power to feel surely; he spends his days in the Alpine forest, the victim of an icy (if verbose) despair.

To the modern reader, Senancour's *Obermann* is probably comprehensible only by a strenuous effort and it is sometimes a wonder how Arnold, with his humor and urbane proportion, could have given the book so important a place in his life. Yet for all his surface fatuity, Obermann is no fool and as a cultural symbol he is invaluable. He understood, before most and better than many, that there are conditions of modern life which check and invalidate the emotions and induce a miserable frigidity.

It is this catastrophe that Arnold fears for himself. Let a poet of strong mind, he says, be exposed to the influences of modern intellectual men and of modern intellectual popularity and he is doomed. For what Arnold calls all "the born-to-be-tight-laced of my friends and acquaintance"—all the world-betterers and problem-solvers of Oxford—knowing nothing of the world, of man's mind and of poetry, will seize him and make him "talk of his usefulness and imagine himself a Reformer, instead of an Exhibition." And when he has thus misconceived himself he will lose the deep, sure insight which is the prime power of the poet, which comes from integration, proportion and joy but, above all, from a certain unconsciousness; the poet will become a system-maker. The system-maker can lie, but the true poet cannot lie; for his poetry is experience and as such must have its own truth.

And Arnold contrasts the bright sunny genius of George Sand with the pious system-making morality of Hannah More and

Mrs. Trimmer; "What hideosities [,] what Solecisms, what Lies, what crudities, what distortions, what Grimaces, what affectations, what disownments of that Trimmer-X-Hannah-More-typed spirit." The mention of George Sand is sufficient to dispel the thought that Arnold was prescribing an ivory tower for the poet; George Sand's scope of social, political and religious interest is broad and active.

It is in the year 1848 that Arnold lays down his program of "intellectual dietetics:" the year of revolution in France, of riots, mass-meetings and the threat of revolution in England. It is in this year that Matthew Arnold is so concerned about style in literature that he speaks of giving up his best friend for not conforming to his ideas of what style should be. Yet Arnold, perhaps the most serious poet of his time, stood among the Chartist crowds and went to Chartist meetings and was deeply impressed by them; nor is there the slightest contradiction in these two facts. For to young Arnold the problem of style is inevitably bound up with the events and problems of '48. "The style," he says, "is the expression of the nobility of the poet's character, as the matter is the expression of the richness of his mind." And continues: "But on men character produces as great an effect as mind." He reads an article by Carlyle (still his political guide, though later he is to speak of him as a "moral desperado"), and investigates what makes the article different from a newspaper article. The ideas are much the same, but "it is the style and feeling by which the beloved man appears. Apply this, Infidel, to the Oriental Poem"—the Bhagavad Gita. And he clinches the argument with, "How short could Mill write Job?" Morality, he is saying, is not a matter of the reason alone, but of the emotions as well; he might have quoted from Spinoza whom at this time he was reading: "A true knowledge of good and evil cannot restrain any emotion in so far as the knowledge is true, but only in so far as it is considered as an emotion." Style is character, it is the quality of a man's emotion made apparent; then, by an inevitable extension, style is ethics, style is government.

"There are two offices of Poetry," Arnold writes in 1849, "—one

to add to one's thoughts and feelings—another to compose and
elevate the mind by a sustained tone, numerous allusions, and a
grand style." It is the *style* of Sophocles as much as the philosophical
validity of his ideas that makes his work spiritually satisfying. At
times Arnold seems to imply that one of the offices of poetry is to
create that golden world of which Sir Philip Sidney spoke, which
stands as the silent criticism of our actual world of brass. "If one
loved what was beautiful and interesting in itself *passionately*
enough, one would produce what was excellent without troubling
oneself with religious dogmas at all." Yet this almost musical
conception of poetry is by no means abstract. Content, judged by
the standards of social usefulness and by the critical intellect, is
basic. If Arnold attacks Clough for writing poetry which tries to
"*solve* the Universe," he also attacks Tennyson because, with all
his exquisite skill, he "dawdl[es] with its painted shell." Goethe
had said, "I honor both the rhythm and the rhyme, by which poetry
first becomes poetry; but what is really deeply and fundamentally
effective—what is truly educative and inspiring, is what remains
of the poet when he is translated into prose," and Arnold, already
Goethean, so far from setting up the goal of style for its own sake,
declares that "modern poetry can only subsist by its *contents*." The
complete personality is not merely an end in itself; it is a social
end. Poetry, the product of the complete personality, is a social
thing, dictated by society to serve society. "For in a *man* style is the
saying in the best way *what you have to say*. The *what you have
to say* depends on your age."

But the age of the 19th century offered material with which it
was difficult to cope: "the poet's matter being *the hitherto experience of the world, and his own,* increases with every century"—it
is too vast. The 17th century had offered a smaller harvest, easier
to gather and easier to stow "more finely and curiously." Yet despite its vastness and despite its seemingly unpoetical nature, the
present age *must* be coped with; if the poet evades the contemporary experience, he says nothing: "Burbidge lives quite beside the

true poetical life, under a little gourd," says Arnold of the man with whom Clough had published the joint volume, *Ambarvalia*—"so much for him." As for Arnold himself—"for me you may often hear my sinews cracking under the effort to unite matter. . . ." The manuscript is incomplete but the meaning is clear: to unite matter into the integral whole which is the true aim of poetry. Poetry must, in modern times, serve as "a complete magister vitae," as did the poetry of the ancients. True, he had warned Clough he must not try to *solve* life in poetry—but there is a difference between solving life and integrating and unifying it. In short, modern poetry must assume something of the character of religion, as did the poetry of the ancients—not of dogmatic religion, not even of religious morality, but of religion as an agency which binds life into a whole, for the great problem of modern life is disunity. At this point style and content merge perfectly.

Later Arnold will attack the problem of disunity at its social source but now he is concerned only with its reflection in art. He is dissatisfied with contemporary poetry because it gets lost "in parts and episodes and ornamental work," is unable to "press forwards to the whole." The achievement of an aesthetic wholeness depends upon the achievement of a philosophical wholeness—and when Arnold writes his famous sonnet to his spiritual masters and says of Sophocles that he saw life whole, he does not mean that Sophocles saw all of life, every part of it, but that what he did see he saw as *a* whole,* an infinitely difficult task for the poet of the multitudinous 19th century, whose life is reflected in poetry of "exquisite bits and images." Keats, Shelley, Browning, men of admirable though unequal talent, fall victims to multitudinousness, for they do not understand that "they must begin with an Idea of the world in order not to be prevailed over by the world's multi-

---

* John Chamberlain (in *The New York Times* of April 29, 1935) speaks of "that Arnoldian phrase which denies that literature can make use of a division of labor." This is the common interpretation of the phrase but it is contrary to Arnold's critical beliefs.

tudinousness." In some part their failure is the result of going back
to the Elizabethan poets—"those d—d Elizabethan poets"—for their
models. Arnold saw the Renaissance as a period in which unity
was being shattered, the exuberance of expression and the richness
of imagery of the Elizabethan poets as the attractive symptoms of
a disorganizing culture. At a time when life demands integration
above all else, and therefore a poetry marked by plainness of speech
and by a driving towards the whole, the vogue of the Elizabethans,
of Shelley, Keats and Browning with their atomism and their
"multitudinousness" seems a calamity. The Greeks of the great
period, with their high social organization, should far rather be the
modern model. "Those who cannot read G[ree]k sh[ou]ld read
nothing but Milton and parts of Wordsworth: the state should see
to it." The last clause is illuminating.

Integration—this is the obsessive theme of Arnold's youthful
letters to Clough, the integration of the individual, the integration of the work of art, the integration, finally, of the social order.
Paradoxically, Arnold sought the way to his own personal integration through an Elizabethan eccentricity of conduct. In the end,
however, the fate he feared and fought overtook him; the poetic
power passed away. It passed with youth and the ability to maintain the youthful dandyism. He was always to retain a reasoned
admiration of gaiety and high spirits, and a light insouciance to
use against the pointless sobriety of English culture; he was everlastingly elegant and perhaps not annoyed at being called a Jeremiah
in kid gloves. But the youthful quality which had sustained his
poetry disappears.

He seems always, in the Romantic fashion, to have been awaiting
its inevitable end. Few poets can have been more conscious of their
youth. "But be bustling about it; we are growing old, and advancing towards the deviceless darkness: it would be well not to reach
it till we had at least tried *some* of the things men consider desirable." The theme recurs so often. "How life rushes away, and youth.

One has dawdled and scrupled and fiddle faddled—and it is all over." "What a difference there is between reading in poetry and morals of the loss of youth, and experiencing it!"

The tone of the gloriously excited letters to Clough becomes calmer and sinks to the flat, almost desperate, coolness of the letters which G. W. E. Russell edited—letters so dull that their appearance after Arnold's death, Gosse tells us, gave a severe setback to his enviable reputation.* Arnold became the man whom Jowett was to praise by saying that "he was the most sensible man of genius whom I have ever known and the most free from personality." Arnold of the untrimmed hair † and the gay waistcoats, the elaborate hoaxes and the flourishing opinion! He himself knows it. "I am past thirty," he says, "and three parts iced over."

He himself knows it and with the utmost pain. He is frozen over but he is fearfully conscious of what lies beneath the ice. He is reconciled, he would have himself believe, to the course of his life; for there is, he fancies hesitantly, a power which, by shaping the impulses even against our conscious will, works out to the individual's good, even though, to him, it does not seem good. And yet

> . . . Often, in the world's most crowded streets,
> But often, in the din of strife,
> There rises an unspeakable desire
> After the knowledge of our buried life,
> A thirst to spend our fire and restless force
> In tracking out our true, original course;
> A longing to inquire
> Into the mystery of this heart that beats
> So wild, so deep in us, to know
> Whence our thoughts come and where they go.
> And many a man in his own breast then delves,
> But deep enough, alas, none ever mines:

---

* The opinion of Arnold Bennett dissents charitably: "His letters make very good quiet reading."

† He never lost his pride in his hair, however: "that perpetual miracle, my hair," he said, and he offered to let a friend pull it to scotch any suspicion that it might be a wig.

And we have been on many thousand lines,
And we have shown on each talent and power,
But hardly have we, for one little hour,
Been on our own line, have we been ourselves.

He is only forty-five when his last volume appears. It is very slim, though it is the product of fifteen years. It is very admirable, but undoubtedly, as Arnold himself says, the Muse has gone away. The poet looks back to "the joy, the bloom, the power" and after this volume he writes no more poetry in the twenty-one years that yet remain to him. But in 1849 he is twenty-seven and still joyous and his friends are puzzled by *The Strayed Reveller* that has just appeared.

Chapter Two

✤✤✤

HIS FATHER AND HIS ENGLAND

. . . The age [is] the force which hurries him, whether willing or unwilling, along with it, guiding him, moulding him; so that one may venture to pronounce that the fact of being born ten years earlier or later would have made a man an entirely different person as regards his own development and his influence on others.—GOETHE.

IF THE press of conflicting ideas, the struggle between irreconcilable ideals, the sense of the intellect's everlasting necessity to choose,—if these are inimical to the meditative poise of the whole personality which makes the true poet, then it is remarkable that Matthew Arnold was a poet at all. For, from his first hours, he lived between two worlds. He was born on Christmas eve, 1822, and the representatives of the two worlds stood with him at the christening font. His baptismal sponsor was John Keble who called himself Misoneologus, Hater of New Ideas; Keble's world was dead. His father was Thomas Arnold who desired a world of the future; it was a world powerless to be born.

At Matthew's christening there was peace and deep friendship between his father and his godfather; the two young clergymen continued the intimacy of their college days and, although of widely different temperaments, found a common ground in their devotion to the Church. But the year in whose last days Matthew Arnold was born brought events which were to be fatal to the friendship.

For several months before the August of 1822, the servants of

36

Castlereagh, the Foreign Secretary, had been careful to remove their master's razors lest he commit a rash act on himself, for he suffered from a pathological depression of spirit—the melancholia which the French used to call the English malady. On the 12th of August, they overlooked his penknife and he cut his throat. Castlereagh was a more complex man and perhaps personally more decent than could be admitted by Shelley and Byron in their just hatred and by a repressed lower class in its just resentment. But if he was not the most ruthless member of a reactionary cabinet, he was the member most talented in the execution of its repressive policy and he had become for the world the embodiment of Tory tyranny. As his funeral cortège passed out of the rain into West-minster Abbey, a grim crowd greeted his casket with cheers.

Castlereagh's suicide marked the end of Tory absolutism. For twenty years before his death it had held the nation in an iron grip; the Terror in France had frightened the Tory rulers of England to hysteria, and every manifestation of popular will had been met with Treasonable Practices Bills, Combination Acts, press censor-ships, suspensions of Habeas Corpus, Seditious Meetings Bills, "Six Acts" and Peterloo massacres. Now, after 1822, the rigor was to relax and in the next decade the forces of the new industrialism would be free to struggle for the political establishment of a power already established in economic fact.

But in the time between the crumbling of the feudal dyke and the full tide of industrial power at the first Reform Bill, the Church of England was faced with a momentous choice. During the pre-ceding years it had traveled a political road which had not been exactly quiet but at least had been clearly marked; in effect the Church had agreed with the sentiment of Lord Braxfield, delivered in his charge to the jury at one of the sedition trials of 1794: "Two things must be attended to which require no proof. First, that the British Constitution is the best that ever was since the creation of the world, and [second, that] it is not possible to make it better." With revolution in France and threatened revolution in England the

Church had defended this sentiment, often with more than spiritual force. The clergy was closely allied with the landowning class by bonds of blood and interest; it had much to lose from reform. The pulpits consequently rang with praise of the old order and condemnation of change; and some of the mobs that attacked the homes of Nonconformist radicals during the last years of the 18th century did so in the Church's name and, it is even suspected, at the Church's instigation. There was a clergyman among the magistrates who, in 1819, called out the cavalry to charge the crowd protesting against the Corn Laws on "Peterloo" field.

Yet to a few realistic and imaginative churchmen it was apparent that the tides of industrialism and democracy were not to be stemmed. The course of the Church was then no longer as clear as it had once been; industrialism and democracy as they grew placed the Church in a danger which seemed to allow not one course but two. The Church might choose to remain what it was, part of the crumbling feudal dyke, perhaps to be swept away forever; or it might attempt to cut the channels for the flood of a new age—and to do this it would have to move in the direction of the tide.

Thomas Arnold advocated the latter course, attempting to shape the new age to the Church, even though this meant reshaping the Church to receive the new age. But John Keble gave his allegiance neither to Liberals nor to Tories but to the martyred Charles. Misoneologus would have none of the new age. So far from considering the possibility of recasting the Church to modernity, he desired to win it away from its renegade allegiance to the House of Hanover, back to its 17th century Stuart character, then to lead an arrogant and stiff-necked England once more into its fold. The divergent aspirations of the two men broke their friendship.

The ideals of these two friends were profoundly significant. Their positions bounded all that was vigorous in the thought of the English Church; and the problems of the State in their modern aspect had first appeared in the religious quarrels of the 16th century and did

not wholly lose their religious character until the 19th century had
nearly passed. The Church comprised the elements of both feudalism and monopolism. The philosophical defenders of the old political order—Burke, Coleridge, Wordsworth—took refuge in its ideals,
and the prophets of the new order made it the object of their attack.
But though its feudal and monopolistic elements were strong, the
Church nevertheless contained the seeds of a democratic ideal which
a few men nurtured. While the Church as a whole represented to
the nation the principle of dogmatic authority standing in opposition
to the principle of liberal democracy, certain parties within the
Church were rising to oppose dogmatic authority with a kind of
popular liberalism.

Matthew Arnold, then, had his baptism between the ideals of ecclesiastical dogmatism and ecclesiastical democracy. Keble named
him and stood responsible for his sins until confirmation, and Matthew Arnold in his youth was to echo Keble's yearning to escape
from the rationalistic and industrial present to a past that had never
been. But Thomas Arnold had engendered and was to train him;
Matthew in his maturity was to look from past and present to a
future that could never be.

II

Modernity has not been kind to Matthew Arnold's father. Men
who have had the ear of our time have made his name something of
a mockery. Bertrand Russell has used him as the symbol of all that
was repressive in the old education. Lytton Strachey has represented
him as intellectually dishonest and emotionally warped.

It is, indeed, not easy to represent him truly. For Thomas Arnold
to emerge as what he really was, a man singularly honest in conduct
and greatly vital in thought, many preconceptions must be put aside
and the light of history must be turned on him. He concerned himself with a nation in transition and he dealt with problems old to our
time, if still unsolved, but relatively new to his: the problems of

changing social codes and values. His mistakes were many, sometimes absurd, sometimes even vicious. He could not always escape from the preconceptions of class and profession, though he tried and often succeeded. He refused, as his son was to refuse, to grant himself the comfort of an absolute commitment to any party; he said in approval of Falkland, whom he greatly admired, that he protested "so strongly against the evil of his party, that he had rather die by their hands than in their company."

The Arnolds were of the middle class, originally of Suffolk but settled on the Isle of Wight where Thomas was born in 1795. From his father, a collector of customs, he inherited the cardiac weakness which was to take him off at the age of forty-seven and which he was to bequeath to his son Matthew. Educated first at home, then at a small Wiltshire school, he completed his pre-university training at Winchester. He won a scholarship to Corpus Christi and went to Oxford in 1811. His university career was sound rather than brilliant and his election to an Oriel fellowship in 1815 was a tribute more to his promise than to his achievement.

At Corpus Christi Thomas Arnold's intimate friends were Keble and J. T. Coleridge, the nephew of the poet. From young Coleridge Arnold acquired an enthusiasm for the poetry and Tory politics of the Lake group, and from both friends, but especially from Keble, who was already confirmed in his apostolic and mystical conception of the Church, he derived the strong pietism of his early days. However, the years at Oriel modified the Corpus attitude. The two colleges represented the two tendencies which were to struggle for supremacy in the Church—Corpus standing for the dogmatic view, Oriel for the liberal. (Of course Keble and Newman were both Fellows of Oriel but they were grieved by the hostility of the intellectual environment.) The so-called Noetics of Oriel—the group that included Copleston, Hawkins, Whately and Hampden—were certainly not religious radicals; it did not, for example, occur to them to raise the fundamental doubts of religion that were agitating the clergy of the Continent. But, defending religion, they continued the

18th century tradition of ecclesiastical rationalism, refused to accept
the mystical authority of dogma, and were willing to raise questions
which might be rationally answered. Newman, who for a time came
within the orbit of the group, saw that the inevitable result of its
position was to represent dogma as merely the product of limited
human reason and withdrew from the dangerous association.

But it was neither the mystical charm of dogma nor the rigor
of logic that chiefly attracted Thomas Arnold. Far more than either,
history established his faith, having first, however, shaken it. At
eight he had read Priestley's *Lectures on History* and through his
boyhood he was deep in Russell, Gibbon and Mitford. He had been
called "Poet Arnold" at Winchester because he had written a play
about Simon de Montfort and a poem about Piercy, Earl of North-
umberland, but a poet he certainly was not, nor even a reader of
the finest taste; he thought the Greek tragedians overrated and
shrank for moral reasons from Aristophanes, Tibullus, Propertius
and Juvenal. He was, however, poetically in love with history. And
now, at Oriel, history began to be integral with his religion. Indeed,
it might almost be said that his devotion to religion was to become a
devotion to a concept of history. He was disturbing his friends with
certain doubts about the doctrine of the Trinity as taught by the
Thirty-Nine Articles. "Do not start, my dear Coleridge," Keble
wrote; "I do not believe that Arnold has any serious scruples of the
understanding about it, but it is a defect of his mind that he cannot
get rid of a certain feeling of objections." Years later, Coleridge, recalling the incident, explained that Arnold's doubts "were not low
nor rationalistic in their tendency, according to the bad sense of that
term; there was no indisposition in him to believe merely because
the article transcended his reason; he doubted the proof and the
interpretation of the textual authority." The matter that was disturbing Arnold, and that his friends were trying to explain away
with what the Reverend James Martineau (but he was a Unitarian)
called "sacerdotal sophistries," was the question of the influence of
events upon dogma. What, Arnold wanted to know, had happened

in the 17th century to cause the makers of the Articles to promulgate the doctrine of the Trinity in its existing form? If the doctrine had arisen from the necessities of the time and not from an absolute truth, it could legitimately be interpreted and reformulated to fit the changed attitudes of the 19th century. At a later time he was to apply the same reasoning, more fully developed, to the Ten Commandments themselves: "It is not that we may pick and choose what commandments we like to obey, but as all the commandments have no force upon us *as such*—that is, as positive and literal commands addressed to ourselves—it is only a question how far each commandment is applicable to us—that is, how far we are in the same circumstances with those to whom it was given." It is a sentence which contains in essence the historical relativism which was to play so important a part in Matthew Arnold's criticism of literature, politics and religion.

At the end of 1818, Thomas Arnold took deacon's orders and in the beginning of the next year removed to the little town of Laleham with his mother, his aunt and his invalid sister, Susannah. In 1820 he married Mary Penrose and for the next nine years he enjoyed a self-imposed rustication, supporting himself by tutoring young men for the universities.

Laleham lies on the Thames in Middlesex, some eighteen miles from London, near the mill and brewery town of Staines at the juncture of the Thames and the Colne. Staines is an old town but most of its tradition lies in the river, for the island of Runnymede is close by. Across from Laleham, on the Surrey side of the Thames, lies Chertsey—the "poetic town of our childhood," Matthew called it, "as opposed to the practical historical Staines"—where the poet Cowley had spent his last years and where Charles James Fox had lived. Laleham itself was a good place for a poet to be born in, beautiful on its green bank, surrounded by trees. The family lived in a big solid house of red brick, "semi-Dutch" in architecture, with a wide lawn. The children came in rapid clerical succession and the father ruled them firmly. He was stern, but young and athletic; he loved to play games with them, gave each a dog's name and drew up for their discipline an elaborate set of kennel rules. Matthew answered to "Crab." *

Thomas Arnold was twenty-four when he settled at Laleham; his letters make him seem older than his years, though much later he was to surprise the boy Arthur Stanley with his youthful appearance. He was of great physical vigor—"I want absolute play," he said— and he loved his body and its energy. "His character—a living whole —cannot be analyzed without being lost from view," said James Martineau. "Its beauty is not of form, like a statue, or of color, like a picture, but of *movement,* like—what he simply was—a man." His athleticism was matched by an intellectual pugnacity that seldom abated. He was not subtle, almost a virtue in a profession whose members so often make truth lie on a hair over an abyss; subtlety was almost consciously repressed by a dramatic sense of the tough reality of life, too pressing to allow him to temper his weapon as fine as he might: let Newman be subtle! Above all, he was ambitious, "one of the most ambitious men alive," he said of himself, with an ambition that could only be satisfied by a great administrative post —like Wordsworth, he "always fancied that he had talents for command"—or by great literary fame. For him, he said, it was "aut Caesar aut nullus" and Laleham, despite the protests of friends who esteemed his abilities, was the nullity he chose.

He was happy at Laleham, worked hard in the morning with

* Matthew was the only remarkably gifted child of the family, though several of his brothers and sisters were notable. William Delafield Arnold won admiration, and an early death, as an administrator of education in the Punjab; he was the author of *Oakfield,* one of the few novels of Anglo-Indian life that attempts a realistic portrayal of the English bureaucracy. The younger Thomas Arnold, the father of Mrs. Humphry Ward, a man of no very remarkable intellect or achievement, is yet interesting for his two Catholic conversions. Two other brothers, Walter and Edward, are rather shadowy; Walter in his youth was in the Navy; Edward entered the Church and the Education Office. Of the girls, Jane, the oldest child and Matthew's favorite sister, the beloved "K," was intelligent and well educated; a strong partisan of liberalism, she was the wife of William Forster, a Quaker manufacturer who played a prominent part as a Liberal member of Parliament and was associated with Matthew as a proponent of popular education. A sister, Mary, after the tragic end of her first marriage, studied in London, where she carried on the family's liberal tradition by becoming an adherent to the theories of Maurice and Kingsley. Of two other sisters, Susan married and Frances did not.

his young men, exercised strenuously with them, watched their morals with a hypersensitive eye, taught in the town Sunday School and disliked it. He loved family life passionately. His wife, some five years older than he, was a woman of charm and intellect, though during the Laleham years we get glimpses of her only as a harassed mother and devoted wife, copying her husband's letters and recording his conversations in notebooks. But she flowered when, after Arnold's Rugby appointment, they built a vacation home at Fox How in the Lake Country; she became a favorite of the tight-knit intellectual society of the place, whose animating spirit was Wordsworth, not at all the grim man of tradition but gay and sociable; the poet had a special affection for her and her relation with Mrs. Wordsworth was said to be filial. Advancing years increased her charm and activity and when her husband died their home was scarcely less the intellectual center it had been during the Doctor's life. Whately and Julius Hare continued to visit Mrs. Arnold; the young men of the Church were devoted to her; it was said of Matthew's friend, Arthur Lake, that he became a different man when he spoke of her; and for Henry Crabb Robinson she was one of the last refuges for liberal talk on Church and State that his beloved Lakes could offer and, after Wordsworth's death, one of the few people who could bring him to visit the memory-laden district. Her large family grown and dispersed, Mrs. Arnold remained at Fox How and bore an old woman's grateful burden of excessive family visiting:—"How the good hospitable old Lady stands it all surprises everyone." She never lost her intimate touch with the intellectual life of the day and Matthew's letters to her are to one he considered his intellectual equal.*

* Her granddaughter, Mary Arnold (Mrs. Humphry Ward), with that predilection of the literary English for explaining qualities of personality by "racial" strains—a predilection which so admirable a writer as Havelock Ellis has canonized with the paraphernalia of science in his *A Study of British Genius*—ascribes Matthew's poetic temperament to his mother. "Both [Matthew and his brother Thomas] had derived from some remoter ancestry—possibly through their Cornish mother, herself the daughter of a Penrose and a Trevenen—elements and qualities which were lacking in the strong personality of their father. Imagination, 'rebellion against fact,' spirituality, a tendency to dream, unworldliness, the passionate love of beauty and charm, 'inef-

Laleham was quiet and removed but England was not quiet and Thomas Arnold was not removed. Great changes were taking place; men believed that revolution threatened. Arnold broke his seclusion to travel on the Continent; the relics of imperial Rome and the landmarks of the hated Revolution in France disturbed him. He was haunted by history. He learned German to read Niebuhr, the first of the modern historians to see antiquity in the realistic light of social conflict, and he himself saw the struggle of Roman patricians and plebeians matched by the Tories and Liberals. As he worked on notes and on a lexicon to his favorite Thucydides he was disturbed by the problems of democracy. His studies were in antiquities but not antiquarian.

In 1827, the trustees of an ancient but decayed public school declared the headmastership vacant. Arnold applied, though without much hope of success. But there was enough uneasiness about all the public schools to make the trustees attend seriously the prophecy made by Hawkins, Provost of Oriel and Arnold's friend and former teacher, that if Arnold were elected "he would change the face of education all through the public schools of England." In August 1828, Thomas Arnold entered upon his duties as headmaster of Rugby.

The Rugby appointment was the beginning of Arnold's public career but it was a career that was not primarily pedagogical and Arnold himself would have been hurt and his friends puzzled if they could have foreseen that, a hundred years later, he would be remembered chiefly as a schoolmaster. He himself wished to be known for his writings: "I have," he said, "a testimony to deliver.

---

fectualness' in the practical competitive life—these, according to Matthew Arnold . . . were and are the characteristic marks of the Celt. . . . Imagination in my father led to a lifelong and mystical preoccupation with religion; it made Matthew Arnold one of the great poets of the nineteenth century."—*A Writer's Recollections*, vol. i, p. 53. Dr. Arnold, according to Ellis (pp. 37–50), shared the traits of the "race" of East Anglia, a race "more remarkable for force of character than force of intellect," a race of great statesmen and ecclesiastics, notable for patience, deliberate flexibility, grasp of detail, love of liberty and independence, not too ready for abstract thought but apt for martyrdom. Cornwall, however, is included by Ellis in "the most conspicuous center of English intellect."

I must write or die." Yet he wrote formally on education but twice. Rugby was only the scene and Rugby School was only the detail—even though the most loved and intimate detail—of Arnold's far broader activity. Throughout the Rugby years Thomas Arnold was a leader in the religious and political conflict of England, the conflict between the old and the new. In that struggle he forged the attitudes which were to be the greater part of his intellectual legacy to Matthew.

III

In 1833 John Keble preached the sermon at the Oxford assize. He spoke of the apostasy of the English and his words echoed in every common room and rectory in the nation. A group of Oxford clergymen, long dissatisfied with the state of religion, heard in his sermon the battle cry of faith. A committee was formed, a declaration of principles drawn up, and the Oxford Movement was launched.

It had been long since England had seen so busy a study of theology, so assiduous an examination of the Church fathers, of Church history, of dogma. Tract followed tract in an attempt to define the nature and rights of the Anglican faith. It was impossible not to take sides and, of the men ranged against Keble, Pusey and Newman, perhaps the most redoubtable was Thomas Arnold. In Keble's eyes he had long been a leader in apostasy.

Of what did the apostasy of the English nation consist? Speaking generally, it was England's conversion to the principle of liberalism avowed by the Reform Bill of 1832. Specifically, it was the exemplification of liberalism in the reformed Parliament's passing of the Irish Church Bill, abolishing ten Irish bishoprics and curtailing some of the financial privileges of the Church in Ireland. The fact that the Irish Church was the church of a small minority, that the mass of the Irish people, bound by the strongest ties to Rome, resented and disliked it and yet were forced, despite dire poverty, to support it, carried no weight with the Tractarians. And the Irish Church Bill was but the momentary culmination of a general movement toward relative religious liberalism which threatened the power of the Church. The dissenting sects, though growing in numbers and economic power, were still kept under galling disabilities, their marriages and burials subject to Church rites, their sons barred from degrees at Cambridge and attendance at Oxford, themselves liable to the payment of Church rates to support a repudiated Church, yet excluded from public office by the Corporation and Test Acts of 1661 and 1673. The repeal of the two Acts in 1828 (they had, to be sure, been annually made inoperative by act of Parliament but the Dissenters felt them to be a statutory monument of distrust) and Catholic Emancipation in the following year seemed, to the Oxford group, a blow at Church supremacy. But the Irish Church Bill was a more serious matter; it struck at the economic foundations of the Church. The sympathetic but very fair historian of the Oxford movement, Dean Church, implies that the Tractarians were at first not so much interested in defending doctrine as in defending ecclesiastical property and the Church's political and economic hegemony. They believed that the abolition of the ten Irish bishoprics heralded the complete disestablishment of the Irish Church and eventually of the Church of England itself.*

No less than the Tractarians, Thomas Arnold saw the danger of disestablishment and dreaded it. But the Oxford group believed that it was coming by the unprovoked and malicious hostility of democratic liberalism, while Arnold put the blame not on democracy but on the dogmatism of the Church which turned it away from the problems with which liberalism was concerned. "My battle was with liberalism," said Newman, in the *Apologia;* "by liberalism I meant the anti-dogmatic principle and its developments." If the Church was right, ran the Tractarian argument, if it was—and it was—the true Church, then no tittle of its powers might be curtailed by dissident, non-conforming men, however large their number. And

---

* They were right: the Irish Church was disestablished in 1869 and Bishop Henson writes (1921), "In the Parochial Church Councils (Powers) Act the disestablishment of the Church in the parishes has been virtually accomplished."—*Anglicanism*, p. x.

Newman, in the first of the Tracts, explained that the clergy was not merely a *ministry* but a *priesthood,* deriving at ordination, from the apostolic hands of the bishop, powers not less than supernal, interference with which was blasphemy.

The Tractarians, moving back to the citadel-rock of dogma, failed to realize that the strength of a fortress is also its weakness: it cannot move to take the offensive. Arnold, temperamentally more the administrator than the theologian, touched with the sociological spirit of his century, believed that the Church was not to be saved by dogma but by social action. It infuriated him that the Tractarians could be mighty warriors for the doctrine of the apostolic succession of the priesthood while they remained decently reticent before the awful spectacle of working class misery. Almost to a man, the Oxford group condemned political, economic and social change: Keble, as we have seen, was the hater of new ideas; W. G. Ward thought social improvement of slight importance to those who looked to heaven; if Newman had a healthy dislike of laissez-faire economics he thoroughly despised popular movements; Hurrell Froude disliked "niggers" for being the symbols of Whiggery, cant and Dissent; and Pusey, personally a charitable man, thought the abolition of slavery absurd because it involved the expenditure of twenty million pounds for "an opinion." As Arnold saw the Church, it was failing of its purpose, for according to what he conceived to be its constitution, one of its immediate aims—Arnold will not say its highest—was the social improvement of man, a work for which no other agency was so well fitted. The task of the Church was to exhort the ruling class to share power with the working class and to refine the working class to wield its new power, and in this the Church had failed—now as in the past it remained socially inactive.

In proof of its failure Arnold pointed to the condition of society—to war, persecution, suffering, low principle and lower practice, and in time made as complete an indictment of the Church's social policy as a Churchman could make. He refused to be softened by the Establishment's appeal to its past of "heroic Martyrs," "pious and learned Reformers," "the mild and tolerant spirit of its Doctrines and Ministers." The Church's connection with the aristocracy, he said, its assumption of the lofty tone of its powerful patrons, its stiffness, its "tastefulness," its condescension to the working classes, its ignorance of their lives were resented by the masses of people. The lower classes knew that the Church wanted its members only when they were good—that is, docile. The factory was forming human groups too large for the Church's outgrown feudal organization to cope with; sprawling cities were replacing the rural parishes, with no one to minister to the swarming thousands. The middle classes, too, suspected the Church's economic power, the great incomes of its prelates, its plural livings, its feudal establishment. And its rigid creed, its "needless multiplication of terms of conformity," kept it from being truly national for a lay population that was increasingly in disagreement with its tenets. Finally, Arnold said, the Church was remiss even to its own communicants; it barely educated its own ministers.

As Arnold watched the spectacle of England's political and social anarchy, his emotions became ever more passionate and his opinions, he said, "became daily more reforming." His earlier Tory creed seemed ridiculous to him; he listened to his neighbors at Laleham, the ultra-reactionary Hartwells who had sheltered Louis XVIII in exile, and they made his "organ of justice stand aghast." He eventually had to disclaim to his conservative friends any revolutionary intention and plead in evidence his seven children, his house and income, all of which he would "be rather puzzled to match in America" were he to become a political outcast.

Actually he hated revolution. Indeed, the end he worked for was the prevention of revolution by an aroused working class. He desired only to purge the *status quo* of its immediate abuses and to prepare for the gradual granting of power to the working class, an event he put well into the future. He was, as he said, instinctively conservative but he saw that to conserve what he loved best he would have to change what he hated. "What I mean then by the original error of the political creed of many good men," he said, "is the principle that in all questions of political alteration the presumption is against change. Now on the contrary the presumption is always in favour of change, because the origin of our existing societies was an unjust and ignorant system." If he feared too great or too sudden a measure of working class power, it was upon the aristocracy that he placed the responsibility for England's anarchy: "The guilt of all aristocracies has consisted not so much in their original acquisition of power, as in their perseverance in retaining it; so that what was innocent or even reasonable at the beginning, has become in later times atrocious injustice; as if a parent in his dotage should claim the same authority over his son in the vigour of manhood, which formerly in the maturity of his own faculties he had exercised naturally and profitably over the infancy of his child."

From the judicious Hooker, perhaps from Milton, surely from Burke who was ever present in his mind, above all from S. T. Coleridge, Arnold derived his ideal of a true and equitable commonwealth. It was not, however, on ideals but on the lesson of history that he based the justification of his conception of the State. For him history was not, as for so many ecclesiastical reformers, the record of a time of primitive righteousness to which men must return, nor was it, as for Burke, the justification of the institutions of the present. Arnold saw the past as the dynamic source of the future and not in linear movement but in cyclical. "Now states, like individuals," he wrote in an appendix to his edition of Thucydides, an essay which he called "The Social Progress of States," "go through certain changes in a certain order, and are subject at different stages of their course to certain peculiar disorders." He saw how "the popular party of an earlier period becomes the antipopular party of a later; because the tendency of society is to become more and more liberal, and as the ascendancy of wealth is a more popular principle than the ascendancy of nobility, so it is less popular than the ascendancy of numbers." It is, indeed, the perfect analysis of English social movement at the time of the Reform Bill and there were few men in England who could have made it with as much insight.

Arnold had chosen good masters. Niebuhr had worked a revolution in historiography not by his prodigious scholarship but by writing the history of a nation as the account of its institutions rather than of its heroes; he had even translated into institutional terms the mythical figures of Roman proto-history. If this seems to us a commonplace of historical method, in its time it was startling enough, especially because of its religious implications. But even more impressive than Niebuhr was the great Italian scholar of the 18th century, Giovanni Battista Vico, who had anticipated Niebuhr in the details of institutional interpretation and Hegel in a general theory of history dazzling in its grandeur and, for some, superior to Hegel's by reason of its lack of teleological optimism. Michelet began in 1827 to make Vico known to the world and Arnold read him with the greatest admiration. Vico's *Scienza Nuova* is the attempt to construct a system to show the operation of the Providential Will, whose plan works out without the assent of man and often in opposition to his desires. Yet, in Vico's view, though man does not *control* his destiny he yet *realizes* it. The study of human history, in short, becomes a means to the understanding of God.*

The historical pattern which Vico demonstrates works out in cycles to be traced, despite minor variations, in the history of all peoples. The first of the three cycles is the age of the gods, in which men, though rude, are endowed with great creative imagination, expressing in their myths a lively if primitive sense of omnipresent deity. Government is patriarchal, the father is king and priest. Sensation, instinct, imagination and poetry rule; rationality and reflection are yet to come. After this infancy of the race comes the

---

* This is, of course, very far from the simple pietism to which Arnold himself subscribed. The defeat of Napoleon, Arnold said, was "effected neither by Russia, nor by Germany, nor by England, but by the hand of God alone." Vico's theological interest was real but it need not be understood in a primitive or pietistic sense. He saw the fruitlessness even for religion of the supernatural explanation of any event.

second stage, the age of heroes whose intellectual character is represented by Homer. Phenomena are conceived in metaphor and symbol. Aristocratic government prevails, marked by an increase of slaves and dependents. But the servile class begins to struggle against the patricians until gradually the *demos* gains the advantage and the age of heroes comes to an end. The age of men follows the age of history; writing passes from ideograph to alphabet, language becomes precise, rationality increases, manners become gentle, civil and political rights are extended and equalized. Religion turns, on the one hand, to philosophical skepticism and, on the other, to the dissemination of practical morality. But the human age, as it advances, degenerates. Despite civil equality, economic inequality increases; the rich become corrupt and effeminate, the poor discontented and aggressive. Discord ripens until there are only three possible futures for a nation: to sink into barbarism from which it must rise again by the three stages of human development; to be saved from barbarism by the conquest of a still strong people (thus Arnold could justify the British conquest of Ireland or India); or, if degeneration has not gone too far, to find salvation at the hands of a Caesar who will reconcile the warring interests which democracy creates but cannot control and thus save society from itself.

For Thomas Arnold, England was in the degenerative part of the third stage. Civil equality was considerable, but the distribution of wealth most unequal, and now numbers were struggling against the wealth that had displaced the class of nobles. "The contending parties of the state," Arnold wrote, "assume the form of rich and poor, the few and the many, instead of the old distinction of nobles and commons, of a conquering race and a conquered." And now England must walk warily and read history aright to learn what she must do to conform with the divine will. The task of far-seeing men, Arnold says, is to compound quarrels. The poor deserve and will get the power they demand; the powerful men of good will must gradually share power with the poor while increasing their intellectual and moral enlightenment. Yet the voluntary efforts of a class are not enough. It is a time of degeneration; is not the Viconian Caesar needed? But to Arnold's credit he does not, like his friend Carlyle, ask for a Caesar or a class of little Caesars. He puts his hope and trust in a strengthened and clarified conception of the *State*.

This exaltation of the State in a time of warring factions is the heart and center of Thomas Arnold's thought, as it is to be of Matthew's. From it radiate his ideas on religion, on social justice, on education. He speaks of it in language as glowing as that of Burke for whom the State was God-ordained, mystical, sacred, in words as passionate as those of Coleridge. He writes to a former pupil that the study of law is "glorious, transcending that of any earthly thing;" it is the articulation of the State's will. The State is a divine and perfect thing and its essence is *power:* the State is "sovereign over human life, controlling every thing, and itself subject to no earthly control."

This State is no mere constable but a creative agency; if its essence is power its aim is human good. It acts positively to bring about the greatest good of the greatest number. "Now it does not seem easy to conceive," Arnold writes, "that a nation can have any other object than that which is the highest object of every individual in it; if it can, then the attribute of sovereignty which is inseparable from nationality becomes the dominion of an evil principle."

Men of the idealistic tendency, like Burke and Coleridge, had been quick to point out that though happiness did largely depend on material well-being, what chiefly mattered was the well-being of the spirit. The heavy-handedness of many early Utilitarians gave some justification for this emphasis, though too often the spiritual insistence had its political outcome in a warped condemnation of physical security, of which Carlyle's denunciation of "pig-philosophy" and his recommendation of proletarian asceticism are examples.* But though Arnold shared the rather academic fear that the lower classes might be debauched by notions of merely material good, he lost neither perspective nor good taste. He merely insisted that the real happiness of most men depended ultimately on enlightenment of the spirit. The State's chief function, then, is education, to be administered by the Church. He denounces a society that calls for "hands" for its factories, forgetting hearts and heads. "The principle of raising the working classes in their bodily, in their intellectual, and in their spiritual condition," he says, should be inculcated in every man of influence, but if individuals do not do the work, the State must.

Against the principle of contemporary Europe, the principle of individualism, Arnold set the collective principle embodied in the State. He hated what he called chivalry because it exemplified an ideal of personal honor and personal glory. He demanded that men think not of themselves but of the whole of which they are a part. Whatever denied his principle of unity Arnold called *Jacobinism*. He took the word from Coleridge (who considered himself the authority on the subject and the word) and used it to mean the demand for "rights without duties." There were two kinds of Jacobinism, Red and White, revolutionary and reactionary. Benthamism was "Red Jacobinism" (though the whole of Benthamism was much more than Arnold conceived); "Priestcraft"—the arrogation of powers by the claim of an apostolic succession to them—was "White Jacobinism." The conservative aristocracy was White-Jacobinical, and really "revolutionary," because "there is nothing so unnatural and so convulsive to society as the strain to keep things fixed, when all the world is by the very law of its creation in eternal progress;"

* "Fascism denies the materialistic conception of happiness as a possibility, and abandons it to its inventors, the economists of the first half of the nineteenth century; that is to say, Fascism denies the validity of the equation, well-being equals happiness, which would reduce men to the level of animals, caring for one thing only—to be fat and well-fed—and would thus degrade humanity to a purely physical existence."— Benito Mussolini in *Enciclopedia Italiana*, vol. 14; translated by Jane Soames and reprinted in *The Living Age*, November, 1933, from *The Political Quarterly*, London. The popularity of Carlyle is now great in Italy and his works are constantly issued: see A. C. Taylor, *Carlyle et la pensée latine* (Paris, 1937), especially Chapter V.

all evils in the world may be traced to the belief that "our business is to preserve and not to improve." If tyranny and democracy were evil they were but sporadic—the "Cholera" of society; but aristocracy "whether of skin, of race, of wealth, of nobility, or of priesthood," was the "Consumption."

Yet Arnold was no less vehement against what he conceived to be the Jacobinism of the working class. His catchword blinded him, he confused the working class demand for rights with a refusal of duties and he tried to distinguish that which was "liberal" from that which was "popular:" "popular principles are opposed simply to restraint—liberal principles to unjust restraint." He hated trade unions with Coleridge's passion and for Coleridge's reason—not so much because they were violent as because he had the Roman fear of any corporation within the State corporation,* and under the shadow of Rome he could suggest flinging a few working class leaders from the Tarpeian rock, a prescription for civil peace which, for a time, and possibly with irony, Matthew thought worth repeating. What Thomas Arnold did not see is that however much the State *should* be the essence of the nation, it was not yet that essence. He knew and yet strangely did not know that there was not even a single nation but two nations—the two nations of which Rousseau spoke, of which Disraeli was to speak, of which, so many centuries before, Aristotle had spoken: the nation of the rich and the nation of the poor. He is passionate on both sides of the question of property. He feared the specter of the French Revolution, the overthrow of the peerage and of the class of gentlemen and the division of great estates and he shared Burke's feeling about property's mystical sanction. "The cry against property," he said, "is just the cry of a slave." Yet he could also say what is often shocking in our time but incredible in his: "I suppose the government may entrench upon individual property for a great national benefit."

* "Roman policy," says Gibbon, "viewed with the utmost jealousy and distrust any association among its subjects, and . . . the privileges of private corporations, though formed for the most harmless or beneficial purposes, were bestowed with a very sparing hand."

The essence of the State is power, but something more than power is needed to make a State. Knowledge is needed too, and an enlightened responsibility and sympathy. And here, Arnold believed, the Church exercised its function: it supplemented power with wisdom and love. It was necessary, then, to discover what the Church really was and what, by its nature, should be its relation to laity and nation. Coleridge distinguished three "Churches:" first, the spiritual and invisible Church, the perfect idea of the Church known only to God; second, the Christian Church, the aggregate of all organized Churches on earth, each one imperfect as compared with the Invisible Church; and last, the particular national body, such as the Church of England, whose "Idea" or "essence" was practical social action. Arnold, following Coleridge's lead, distinguishes between the Christian religion (substantially Coleridge's Invisible Church) and the Christian Church—a distinction which Newman, understanding its real danger to religion, denied with his whole life. The Christian religion, Arnold said, acts upon individuals, the Church upon masses; the former is permanent and incorruptible, the latter capable of disablement and perversion. Of all things known to man, the Christian religion commands the greatest loyalty, but that which has the next claim is not the National Church but the Nation itself, corporeal England, dedicated to the ideal of the Christian religion. *"The Church of Christ* is indeed far beyond all human ties," Arnold said, "but of all human ties, that to our country is the highest and most sacred: and *England,* to a true Englishman, ought to be dearer than the peculiar forms of *the Church of England."* In short, the argument concluded, the Church must secularize itself. Arnold's ecclesiastical theory is the perfect exemplification of that post-Reformation movement which Hegel had described, the "recognition of the Secular as capable of being an embodiment of Truth;" "States and Laws," Hegel declared, "are nothing else than Religion manifesting itself in the relations of the actual world."

To the Tractarians the Church was lovely and forlorn, piteous in oppressed virtue, hurt by dissenting and godless men. To Arnold the Church was lovable indeed but self-indulgent, wilful and un-dutiful; only a career of social usefulness could save it from being deserted. To the liberal, and even to the anti-religious liberal, Arnold's position is the more attractive. But whoever is devoted to traditional religion will see what Newman saw, that once the Church begins to resign its high dogmatic claims there is no place where it can stop; it steps down to the ground of all other social in-stitutions and submits to be judged by their standards. For religion to base its claims to allegiance upon its social usefulness is suicidal. But Arnold did not see the danger and it infuriated him that the Tractarians could be passionate over Councils and rubrics and in-different to the human misery of the great towns. Arnold, indeed, denied the very notion of priesthood in the Anglican Church; the priest's element, he said, "is only what is formal, shadowy, cere-monial; and in order to make himself of importance, he must raise what is shadowy and ceremonial into the place of what is real and moral." The minister was superior to the layman only in his training; his task was practical, not mystical, he was to enlighten rather than bless.*

The conception of priesthood which Newman required was, to Arnold, simply feudalism in religion, implying a class in posses-sion of the truth, and against it he used all the arguments of the old Puritan party. Newman's defense of dogma against the rights of in-dividual reason was essentially an attack upon democracy; but Arnold never abandoned his old Noetic faith in rationality; he de-clared that reason was the very instrument of faith and said bril-liantly, "Faith without reason, is not properly faith, but mere power worship; and power worship may be devil worship." Like Milton, he questioned the whole authority of "primitive antiquity" and much

---

* Coleridge had projected a union of all the intellectual professions, including the clergy, into one great order, to be known as the "clerisy" which was to be devoted to the social and intellectual as well as the spiritual improvement of the nation. Arnold made no positive subscription to this scheme but he wished to see the clergy fulfil all that Coleridge desired of the "clerisy."

as he admired Burke he rejected Burke's belief in the efficacy of articles of conformity. He set the standard of truth in each man's interpretation of Scripture, so long as the reader used his intelligence and the methods he would bring to the interpretation of a text of Thucydides or Aristotle. It was the inevitable attitude of one who was fighting the battle of democracy; "what . . . any Christian . . . believes to be God's revealed will" must be the standard of truth, and we can "only recognise [God's] voice by the words spoken being in agreement with our idea of his moral nature."

Arnold conceived a Church which was at once Protestant and, in the literal sense of the word, catholic—what came to be called a *broad* Church, broad enough to include all shades of Christian opinion and therefore a truly national Church. "I groan," he wrote, "over the divisions of the Church, of all our evils I think the greatest—of Christ's Church I mean—that men should call themselves Roman Catholics, Church of England men, Baptists, Quakers, all sorts of appellations, forgetting that only glorious name of CHRISTIAN, which is common to all, and a true bond of union." It was only by broadening its doctrine to include all Englishmen that the Church could claim the right to administer the economic provision put into its trust and intended for the moral and intellectual improvement of the people. But while Arnold was saying this the Tractarians were demanding both that the Church be further "purified" in point of doctrine and that its right to Establishment be not questioned. Their position seemed to Arnold an arrogant challenge to the nation, tempting men to demand disestablishment and to withdraw the Church's rights to its property.

And such an event, Arnold believed, would be fatal to the true conception of the State, which was simply a religious society armed with power. Under the perfect or perfecting State, the King ("another name for the supreme power of society") is the head of Church and State, and religion must be thought of as coextensive with the State. If the Church should be divorced from the State it would become meaningless, for "what is not more than advice when spoken by philosophy and religion, binding, so far as this world is concerned, only on those who choose to follow it,—that, when adopted by the State, becomes law, and so far as this world is concerned, no man can disobey it with impunity." * Aaron the priest, he said, is the inferior of Moses the leader, and he who "rules God's people . . . is greater than he who ministers at the altar."

Arnold was far from being devoid of mysticism; he had not only the belief in, but the *sense of* divinity which marks the mystic. But this part of him he referred to the Church of Christ, the Invisible Church; in his dealings with the physical Church he was always social and positive. It served, this physical Church, one end only, he believed—the proper administration of Church property, which was wealth "saved out of the scramble of individual selfishness," for the "doing good of every kind to every kind of person." And there was but one way in which this might be done: to "sink into nothing the differences between Christian and Christian," to conceive a Church allowing great varieties of opinion, of ceremonies and forms of worship. It meant the abolition of the notion of priesthood, the revitalizing of the lower clergy by an elective order of deacons, the use of different rituals at different times—in brief, remaking the Church to the demands of the people. For the people were the Church: "What are the laity? The Church minus the clergy." The people of England were trying to break into the government; given a chance, they would come into the Church if the Church were devoted to their welfare, helping, teaching, improving them.

However, even within this scheme of a comprehensive national Church certain sects could not be included—Roman Catholics and Quakers and Unitarians. The first gave allegiance outside the nation, the second held non-cooperative views of civil government and the third Arnold doubted to be Christians. Yet he had hopes of these people; he even believed that the Catholics of Ireland could

* This seems to have its roots in the most enlightened part of the Puritan tradition; Milton said, "For truth is properly no more than contemplation; and her utmost efficiency is but teaching: but justice in her very essence is all strength and activity; and hath a sword put into her hand, to use against all violence and oppression on the earth."

be converted to Protestantism by proper treatment and such was his
concern for all religion that he was anxious to have these people
treated well if only to bring about the purification of the Roman
Catholic faith. But with Jews he was intransigent, believing that
they should be barred from the universities and from citizenship.
He held that citizenship required an almost mystic homogeneity
which was supplied in the ancient world by race (surely a strange
misstatement in the face of the Roman notions of citizenship *) and
in the modern world by religion. He denounced "that low Jacobinical notion of citizenship, that a man acquires a right to it by the
accident of his being littered inter quatuor maria, or because he pays
taxes." England, he said, was the land of Englishmen, not of Jews,
and "lodgers" had no claims to more than an honorary citizenship
which gave them no share in government. The notion of a Jew as
one of the Governors of Christ's Hospital infuriated him and he
dreaded the possibility of examining a Jew in history at the University of London (of which he was a Trustee) and of having to
avoid calling Jesus the Christ. To be sure, his theory of exclusion
differs from that of National Socialism in being based on religion
rather than on "blood," but it is a distinction that scarcely vindicates
his liberalism. And he had his own curious and horrifying genetic
theories; he asserted that the stain of the Australian convict-settlers
"should last, not only for one whole life, but for more than one
generation; that no convict or convict's child should ever be a free
citizen; and that, even in the third generation, the offspring should

---

* "The grandsons of the Gauls, who had besieged Julius Caesar in Alesia, commanded
legions, governed provinces, and were admitted into the senate of Rome. Their ambition, instead of disturbing the tranquillity of the state, was intimately connected with
its safety and greatness." Gibbon, Chapt. II. And certainly Arnold should have remembered the scene from the *Acts of the Apostles:* "And as they bound him with thongs,
Paul said unto the centurion that stood by, 'Is it lawful for you to scourge a man that
is a Roman and uncondemned?' When the centurion heard that he went and told the
chief captain, saying, 'Take heed what thou doest: for this man is a Roman.' Then
the chief captain came, and said unto him, 'Tell me, art thou a Roman?' He said, 'Yea.'
And the chief captain answered, 'With a great sum obtained I this freedom.' And Paul
said, 'But I was born free.' "
Arnold was writing at a time when the Jews were struggling to enter the political
life of England and to acquire the full rights of citizenship.

be excluded from all offices of honour or authority in the colony. This would be complained of as unjust or invidious, but I am sure that distinctions of moral breed are as natural and as just as those of skin or of arbitrary caste are wrong and mischievous."

In 1841 what seemed the first triumphant step toward Arnold's projected comprehensive Church was taken—more, indeed, than Arnold had dared ask for though he had always hoped for it: a comprehensive European Protestant Church. Erasmus and Luther had dreamed of just such a venture, John Drurie, the friend of Milton, had attempted to organize it, Milton himself had advocated and Cromwell approved it. England and Prussia established jointly a bishopric of Jerusalem with the intention of uniting the faiths of the two Protestant countries. Arnold had been close to the scheme, for it had been largely engineered by his friend von Bunsen, Prussian Minister to England. A man supremely fated for the incumbency was selected—Michael Solomon Alexander, of Jewish family, Prussian birth and Anglican faith. But the bishopric was an empty thing: perhaps its only result was to crystallize Newman's position and convince him that Anglicanism was committed to being Protestant; the *via media* no longer existed and Rome more and more seemed the only possibility.

The problems of the Church at home were not, however, to be so easily solved, even in appearance. The Tractarians wanted the State to be an arm of the Church, not the Church an aspect of the State; the Tractarian Faber went so far as to declare that the Church had a right to require the State to put all heretics to death. As for the Dissenters, they were quite as secure in their own particular orthodoxies and purisms as the Church itself and had no desire to be comprehended.

But time, if it has brought a considerable decrease in the economic rights of the Church and some of the loss of its rights of Establishment which Arnold feared, has brought Anglicanism nearer to Arnold's doctrinal plans. The Lambeth Conferences have moved closer and closer to the ideal of comprehension on loose grounds.

The sixth Conference issued an appeal for Christian union which indicates the extent to which the old theory of exclusiveness has broken down. "The sixth Lambeth Conference," writes Bishop Henson, "was dominated by the conviction that the paramount need of the world at the present time is the recovery of the visible unity of the Christian Church." Its plan of unity was exactly Arnold's:

The vision which rises before us is that of a Church, genuinely Catholic, loyal to all Truth, and gathering into its fellowship all "who profess and call themselves Christians," within whose visible unity all the treasures of faith and order, bequeathed as a heritage by the past to the present, shall be possessed in common, and made serviceable to the whole Body of Christ. Within this unity Christian Communions now separated from one another would retain much that has long been distinctive in their methods of worship and service. It is through a rich diversity of life and devotion that the unity of the whole fellowship will be fulfilled.

For most of us, however, Arnold's interest lies not so much in his schemes for ecclesiastical reform as in his insight into the problems of civil government. Eccentricities and extravagances sometimes mar the dignity and even the validity of that insight. Yet he saw the problems truly. To many men of his century there seemed an irreconcilable conflict between democracy and order, between freedom and organization, between populace and State. But Arnold put aside the seeming dilemma and asserted the truth which is at the core of his often confused thought: that there is nothing essentially antagonistic between democracy and State, that, indeed, each demands the other for completeness, that democracy does not imply laissez-faire, that organization does not imply repression. In this synthesis of two dominant and seemingly opposed tendencies of his time and ours lies Thomas Arnold's political achievement. Matthew Arnold's, more complex, is not basically different.

IV

It was only fitting that a man for whom the State was the center of social existence should be an educator: from Plato to Hegel and

Marx the State-idea has had ultimately to rest on education. If Arnold conceived the State as ideally a school teaching the spiritual virtues, he shaped his school to the image of a State functioning by the judicious apportionment of authority. Carlyle, who visited and admired Rugby, might well have written of Thomas Arnold as "The Hero as Schoolmaster," for Arnold ruled like the Carlylean leader, the man in communion with the universal truth. Everyone knows the story of the Rugby victory—how, like the Abbot Samson taking over St. Edmundsbury, Arnold found a scene of material and spiritual desolation, how he faced down the opposition of subordinates and students, gathered power into his hands and molded the school to his will, creating slowly its moral and intellectual tone. "He governed the school," says Arthur Stanley, "precisely on the same principles as he would have governed a great empire." He himself was the hero bringing the law, creating an aristocracy of the most mature students who had power and the duty of bringing the lesser breed into the perfection of Sixth Form aristocracy. It was a fine example of Vico's "second age."

For a long time the public schools had been under severe attack as quasi-national institutions feeling the lash of liberal criticism; and justly, for they were in a deplorable condition. The ground of dissatisfaction was not so much one of pedagogy as of administration and discipline. The schools were the ironically perfect reflection of the laissez-faire theories of the very liberals who attacked them. In even the most richly endowed schools, living quarters were cold, bare and unsanitary and boys were commonly lodged in unsupervised houses. Riots, sometimes severe enough to require military intervention, were not unknown. Fagging was brutal, bullying common and unchecked. Immorality of various kinds was a considerable problem. Games were unsupervised or non-existent. And finally the curriculum was not only absurdly narrow in its classicism but scamped and badly taught.

Arnold came to Rugby sure of his power and surer of his purpose. He announced both by being ordained priest—he had been hitherto but a deacon—and by taking his Baccalaureate and Doctorate of Divinity; when the chaplaincy of the school fell vacant he had the office incorporated with the headmastership. For him secular education was a contradiction in terms; "the idea of a Christian school . . . was to him the natural result . . . of the very idea of a school in itself," wrote Stanley. And as a servant of the Church, as a servant of the State—he wanted his office to be brought directly under the Crown—as a servant of the highest good in the gospel of Christ, he was fiercely jealous of interference with his duties. He felt entirely independent of his trustees, the majority of whom were Tories, and was ready to resign at a moment's notice. When it became suspected that he had written the anonymous article in the *Edinburgh Review,* "The Oxford Malignants," which furiously attacked the Tractarian persecutors of Hampden, the liberal theologian, Earl Howe, a member of the board, wrote to ask if he were indeed the author. Arnold replied in a letter whose Johnsonian tone and excellent principles require its quotation:

My Lord,
  The answer which your lordship has asked for, I have given several times to many of my friends; and I am well known to be very little apt to disavow or conceal my authorship of anything, that I may at any time have written.
  Still, as I conceive your lordship's question to be one which none but a personal friend has the slightest right to put to me or to any man, I feel it due to myself to decline giving any answer to it.

And when Howe pressed for an avowal or a disclaimer on the ground that he might have to take steps in the matter, Arnold replied:

My Lord,
  I am extremely sorry that you should have considered my letter as uncourteous; it was certainly not intended to be so; but I did not feel that I could answer your lordship's letter at greater length without going into greater details by way of explanation than its own shortness appeared to me to warrant. Your lordship addressed me in a tone purely

formal and official, and at the same time asked a question which the common usage of society regards as one of delicacy—justified, I do not say, only by personal friendship, but at least by some familiarity of acquaintance. It was because no such ground could exist in the present case, and because I cannot and do not acknowledge your right officially, as a trustee of Rugby School, to question me on the subject of my real or supposed writings on matters wholly unconnected with the school, that I felt it my duty to decline answering your lordship's question.

It is very painful to be placed in a situation where I must either appear to seek concealment wholly foreign to my wishes, or else must acknowledge a right which I owe it, not only to myself, but to the master of every endowed school in England, absolutely to deny. But in the present case, I think I can hardly be suspected of seeking concealment. I have spoken on the subject of the article in the Edinburgh Review freely in the hearing of many, with no request for secrecy on their part expressed or implied. Officially, however, I cannot return an answer—not from the slightest feeling of disrespect to your lordship, but because my answering would allow a principle which I can on no account admit to be just or reasonable.

Arnold's work at Rugby was not quickly accomplished; at least as late as 1834 drinking and the frequenting of taverns was not uncommon among the boys. He knew that no spiritual reform was possible without a physical reorganization and he set about this at once, transferring the control of residence houses from "dames" to masters, raising the school fees to erect new houses, and increasing the salaries of his teaching staff so that they might give up their pot-boiling curacies and devote all their time to the school, a reform which set a new economic as well as pedagogic standard for the whole teaching profession. Efficiency was demanded in all things; Arnold himself looked into and improved even such details as bedding and laundry. Where his predecessor had, with diffidence, requested parents to withdraw difficult boys, Arnold defined the high authority of the headmaster and stood ready to expel even when the act did violence to the feeling of parents and of himself. The good of the social whole was to be the only consideration.

Arnold's revision of the moral tone of Rugby involved both a system of school government and an influence of personality. Far from being a Benthamite, he yet shared the Benthamite love of efficient social organization. The problems of democracy were being reflected in the schools, and the idea of a self-governing school body, though not yet widespread, was being tried and discussed. Goddard, Arnold's own headmaster at Winchester, had allowed a measure of self-government. The Madras system, responding to the difficulty of controlling large numbers of pupils, had, for utilitarian reasons and with unattractive results, made use of the more advanced to instruct the less. The Quaker school at Bootham and the Hills' elaborate experiment at Hazlewood had used self-government for spiritual ends as well.

Arnold, himself monarch, priest and appellate judge, undertook to rule through the lieutenancy of the Sixth—the highest—Form. Rank as a member of the Sixth automatically gave a boy the responsibility and powers of a "praepostor;" he was both police and magistrate, accountable for the discipline of the whole school; he had the right to flog (up to six strokes) all below the Fifth Form, which alone was answerable directly to the Head. By this arrangement, Arnold sought, successfully, to channel bullying strength into a feudal protective nobility. The members of the Sixth Form, it should be remembered, were not boys but young men, often considerably older than the American college freshman. Nevertheless, investing a whole form with authority involved the daring and perhaps dangerous assumption that the whole school was gradually growing into virtue. Arnold, to be sure, took care to stack his cards of virtue; he saw to it that any boy who might not fulfil his duty satisfactorily never reached the Sixth Form; he was not expelled but quietly dropped.

Arnold's formulated view of the nature of boys does not read pleasantly but its implications have been exaggerated. His famous statement, "My object will be, if possible, to form Christian men, for Christian boys I can scarcely hope to make; I mean that, from the natural imperfect state of boyhood, they are not susceptible of

Christian principles in their full development upon their practice," has been called "Calvinistic" by Professor Whitridge, his great-grandson, and no doubt it is; it is at least Augustinian; and yet it says no more than that boys are not much motivated by moral considerations. When he continues, "And I suspect that a low standard of morality in many respects must be tolerated amongst them," his manner is absurdly portentous but his matter is realistic and sensible. If the Victorians too much disregarded Rousseau and Wordsworth and thought of children as adults *manqués,* we today are perhaps too often tempted to think of adults as children *manqués.* "Frieda says every woman hopes her *Baby* will become the Messiah," said D. H. Lawrence in a letter. "It takes a man, not a baby." And Arnold wanted to make men. If for Wordsworth the influence of society was bound to corrupt the child, for Arnold it was likely to develop him; and his view is the more usable as it is the more logical of the two, if one admits that society has the means to develop without corrupting. For Arnold such a means was the Christian faith truly taught. He wished to speed development, but he was not blind to the dangers of haste: "can the change from childhood to manhood be hastened, without prematurely exhausting the faculties of body or mind?" Arthur Clough's career is the classic negative, but there were other Rugby lives to answer affirmatively.

At least part of his method of hastening change must be admired: he assumed the maturity and dignity of his pupils. Though stern with the older boys, tender with the very little and embarrassed by the intermediate hobbledehoys, he treated them all with unfailing courtesy. He defended flogging, for he believed that objection to it was a remnant of a chivalric code of physical honor which he hated as individualistic and "Jacobinical," * but actually he used it only as the last resort in cases of lying, drinking or habitual idleness and after other punishment had failed. He refused to be a jailer, insisting that discipline be maintained by and not over the boys.

* He liked to tell the story of the Jacobinical French boy who shot the army officer who had presumed to chastise him. This, no doubt, is the same incident that Vigny used in his story "The Malacca Cane."

But the content of Arnold's moral teaching is neither attractive nor judicious. Boyhood may be the time to teach responsibility; it is certainly not the time for imparting the sense of sin. The periods of pubescence and adolescence have their inevitable storms and confusion—they bring only too readily a hypersensitivity to "guilt" which should not be exacerbated by preaching. Arnold certainly induced no religious disorders among his boys; Tom Brown's pious resolutions are priggish but not hysterical. Yet the headmaster's language, if never lurid, was inflated and oppressive. Stanley says of him that he was apt to invent universal rules for particular cases and since he spoke to schoolboys of schoolboy matters his words are often absurd in their disproportion. He found, for example, an increase of childishness in even the best boys, the result of "exciting books of amusement, like Pickwick and Nickleby," and, speaking of domestic influences, he makes an Oxford reading party sound like an orgy because it took students from home.

There can be no doubt that Arnold induced in his pupils a nervous priggishness which, when it failed to jibe with reality, left them high, dry and gasping. Clough, of course, is the notorious example; it is difficult to say how many more like him there were but people spoke of a Rugby temperament and Rugby men were disliked at the universities for their "seriousness." Certainly the avowed effort of Arnold's successor at Rugby to lessen the high moral tension of the school serves to confirm the general impression. Clough's "Uncle" in the Epilogue to *Dipsychus,* that little *Faust* of Victorian religious thought, gives the most notable expression of the common opinion:

"It's all Arnold's doing; he spoilt the public schools. . . . Not that I mean that the old schools were perfect, any more than we old boys that were there. But whatever else they were or did, they certainly were in harmony with the world, and they certainly did not disqualify the country's youth for after-life and the country's service."

"But, my dear sir, this bringing the schools of the country into harmony with public opinion is exactly—"

"Don't interrupt me with public opinion, my dear nephew; you'll quote me a leading article next. 'Young men must be young men,' as the worthy head of your college said to me touching a case of rustication. 'My dear sir,' said I, 'I only wish to heaven they would be; but as for my own nephews, they seem to me a sort of hobbadi-hoy cherub, too big to be innocent, and too simple for anything else. They're full of the notion of the world being so wicked and of their taking a higher line, as they call it. I only fear they'll never take any line at all.' . . . [Take the twelve or fourteen year old boy,] put him through a strong course of confirmation and sacraments, backed up with sermons and private admonitions, and what is much the same as auricular confession, and really, my dear nephew, I can't answer for it but he mayn't turn out as great a goose as you—pardon me—*were* about the age of eighteen or nineteen."

"[But,] my dear sir, you must not refer it to Arnold, at all at all. Anything that Arnold did in this direction—"

"Why, my dear boy, how often have I not heard from you, how he used to attack offences, not as offences—the right view—against discipline, but as sin, heinous guilt, I don't know what beside! Why didn't he flog them and hold his tongue? Flog them he did, but why preach?"

Uncle is right in his unregenerate Tory way. The appeal to abstract virtue in dealing with young people is a kind of bullying only less unfair than that of love, of "If you do that you will hurt me." If it conceivably strengthens the moral sensitivity it is probably a weakening of the moral force.*

Clough defended his old master—but how agonizingly he weighed Arnold's effect on him!—by pleading the religious temper of the time—"the religious movement of the last century, beginning with Wesleyanism, and culminating at last in Puseyism." England, reacting from the religious indifference of the 18th century and from the French Revolution, went into black broadcloth and Rugby cut

* An interesting sidelight on the results of moral self-government in the very young is provided by the Hills' school in which a miniature democratic state was set up with all the appurtenances of governmental business—currency, courts, legislators. The tone was benevolent; honor and responsibility were the virtues cultivated. But a former student, writing of his years at the school, tells us that "the thoughtlessness, the spring, the elation of childhood were taken from us; we were premature men." One of the boys, not naturally morbid, found the responsibility so heavy that he contemplated suicide.

the new fabric. Young Matthew Arnold's physical and spiritual waistcoats were a salutary protest against the prevailing wear.

Yet this much must be said for the priggishness of Rugby men— it was not remote. The young men overestimated their power to change the world, they were vague about what change meant, even about what the world was. But Thomas Arnold was crying his pupils on into life, into aspects of it that, in their natural course, they would not have seen or thought of. He spoke to them of the poor and the oppressed, of social justice and the future of nations. Much in his conception of the social duty of the upper classes is repulsive —the reaching down, the condescension. Yet it was something, it left its mark, it was at least aware.

And toward awareness Arnold pointed his whole curriculum. In respect to subject matter he was not a systematic reformer. The conventional classical education had been attacked on grounds both of narrowness and of uselessness; Arnold admitted the former charge but felt that by doing so he was invalidating the latter: he undertook to make the classics useful by making them broad. He refused the obvious alternative to the classical curriculum—the "useful knowledge" of the Brougham sort, scientific in content only, predigested, marked by the crassest philosophical attitude. He offered instead a reinterpretation, declaring what his son was often to repeat, that the classics were important and useful because *modern*. He replaced the old, polite, Greek-is-a-gentleman's-language conception with philosophical and historical study and the poetic, historical and critical efforts of Germany bore their first pedagogic fruit in England through Arnold. Had he been the missionary for this point of view, his theories might have influenced all of English teaching. But E. F. Benson, who went to Marlborough, one of the new schools that felt the influence of Arnold's other innovations, tells us that he underwent "the methods of tutors . . . who by making their pupils chop up dry faggots of wood, hoped to teach them what was the nature of the trees that once the wind made murmurous on the hillsides of Attica." And Aldous Huxley: "After ten years among the best classical authors, the English schoolboy emerges with a firm conviction of the radical non-humanity of Greeks and Romans." Arnold, in his own school and in his own time, however, made the dry faggots live and the Greeks and Romans human.

Perhaps the fundamental untruth of Lytton Strachey's portrait of Thomas Arnold is that he translates Arnold's seriousness into sedentariness; actually the man was electric with energy; his conversation was mercurial. He was in love with the world and its history; he held it the duty of the schoolmaster to know the world. He would not lecture, holding that it was for the student to talk. The subjects he set for themes are interesting; rejecting "Virtus est bona res" and all its kind, he gave "Conversation between Thomas Aquinas, James Watt, and Sir Walter Scott;" "How far the dramatic faculty is compatible with the love of truth;" "Define 'revolution,' 'philosophy,' 'art,' 'religion,' 'duty,' 'romantic,' 'sublime,' 'pretty.'" He introduced the study of modern history in the upper forms, using contemporary texts, and he required collateral reading. He put mathematics on a firmer basis. With no faith in the school's ability to give a speaking command of French and German, he believed that a reading knowledge of them was indispensable for a modern man.

His educational goal was, in a wide sense, always political, and for this reason he was cool to the teaching of science,* holding that it had "nothing to do with the knowledge which the Reform Bill calls for." The manufacturing class, desiring a reduction of the classical subjects, was likely to quote Milton:

> That not to know at large of things remote
> From use, obscure and subtle, but to know
> That which before us lies in daily life,
> Is the prime Wisdom . . .

Arnold would have concurred in honoring Milton and practicality, but his question would have been, What is practical? For him it was

---

* He had no theological fear of it, however, and encouraged its private study, especially geology, then the most theologically dangerous of the sciences.

always the problems of social life and it seemed quite clear to him that "a man may be ever so good a chemist, or ever so good a mechanic, or ever so good an engineer, and yet not at all the fitter to enjoy the elective franchise."

Where did the Rugby spirit most truly express itself? In Arthur Stanley, pious by temperament and training, secure in his Church, liberal, humane, effecting that synthesis of piety and intelligence that Arnold so desired? Or in Arthur Hugh Clough, set on paths so alien to his temperament and talent, his wings clipped, living out his short life in a misery about integrity and honesty? Or in the honest and simple Thomas Hughes, who wrote the Rugby Iliad, and who, starting in Christian Socialism, carried on Arnold's conception of the inclusive and effective Church and then moved forward to a more ardent socialism and a more militant democratic theory? Or was it William Hodson, of Hodson's Horse, whom Arnold so esteemed, and who, as praepostor, disciplined a riotous house, who in India became the perfect exponent of Stalky and Co. imperialism? Hodson was earnest and hard-working; he was principled: he refused to admit into an asylum for the children of English soldiers "the slightest dash of color;" he rose to prominence but became involved in a matter of peculation of regimental funds and then in a matter of illegally imprisoning a border chief (one can imagine Carlyle for the defense); he organized an irregular troop during the Mutiny, Hodson's Horse, and served with magnificent courage; he was accused of looting but actually he had only bought at a very low price from his commanding officer a herd of cattle he had captured; and when, at Delhi, the three sons of the king surrendered to him, he snatched up a carbine from a trooper and shot them dead; he felt it right and expedient.*

---

* Fitzjames Stephen, who had no love for Dr. Arnold or Rugby but a great respect for the qualities of the administrator, writes of Hodson's "combination of moral and physical force on which Dr. Arnold placed so much value, and which his system undoubtedly tended to develop in some cases." He goes on: "We will venture to say that scores of Major Hodson's contemporaries at Rugby and Trinity were thoroughly equal to him both in mental and physical capacity. Where are they now? They are the leaders of every day English life,—what we may call the non-commissioned officers

Or is the Rugby spirit perhaps to be seen in young William Delafield Arnold, after Matthew the most talented of the Arnold sons? At twenty he went to India as an ensign, lost his health, returned to England and went out again as Director of Public Instruction in the Punjab where he performed notable service. His wife died of the country, and, a broken man, William set out for England, himself to die at Gibraltar. Matthew commemorates him in "A Southern Night" and "Stanzas from Carnac." He wrote an autobiographical novel, *Oakfield,* full of a real sadness that personal virtue cannot prevent a man from being a part of the cruelty of British imperialism, that the "magnificent work of civilizing Asia" cannot be done until the English civilize themselves—even that "the grand work" is all humbug and India only a "rupee mine." Perhaps some form of socialism, he thinks, but more likely the purification of the Anglican Church, will work a change. Not a single native appears in his novel, except as a servant; he feels it "grievous to live among men and feel the idea of fraternity thwarted by facts"—yet "we must not resign ourselves, without a struggle, to calling them brutes."

But the Rugby spirit was the spirit of upper middle class England at its best, supplying its formulae of virtue, its symbols, its attitudes. Under Arnold it was conscious of its aim and reached it.

v

The crown and the end of Thomas Arnold's life came close together. In August, 1841, Lord Melbourne offered him the Regius Professorship of Modern History at Oxford. There was, he said, "no privilege which I more value, no public reward or honour which could be to me so welcome." A week later the Tories came into power and Arnold's delight was spiced with the realization

---

of English society,—the clergy, the lawyers, the doctors, the country squires, the junior partners in banks and merchants' offices, men who are in every sense of the word gentlemen though no one would class them with the aristocracy. Take a man of this order at random, throw him into strange circumstances, repose confidence in him, subject him to responsibility, and Major Hodson is the result."—*The Edinburgh Review*, April, 1859, p. 547 and p. 557.

of how nearly his prize had been snatched from him. He would, he said, have taken the post without salary, so overjoyed was he at the prospect of being in touch with Oxford again, not only because of his love of the place but because of the possibility of forming university opinion. A new activity was open to him, and characteristically he saw activity as combat. The influence of Newman was strong and must be diminished—graciously, courteously, but rigorously, for the Newmanites were not only enemies of the Church of England but traitors to it, and Newman, he believed, had gone so far as to have lost the spiritual right to teach at Oxford. To add to the Oxford triumph, the first Protestant Bishop of Jerusalem was consecrated at Lambeth in September—and Newman was that much closer to making up his mind about Rome.

Arnold believed that in History truth was attainable and that all was not "mere opinion;" under his hand, he hoped, History would clear the way to faith. He would expound the "great principles of Government and Politics" to the end that men would see the true and religious way and, so long as he should still remain at Rugby, he pledged his professorial salary for scholarships to make converts to the historical faith. He gave his inaugural lecture on the 2nd of December. The university was tense at the arrival of Newman's antagonist and the customary lecture room had to be abandoned for the "Theatre" to seat the hundreds who came to hear him.

The new appointment permitted Arnold to think of giving up his Rugby post, but he put off the decision, partly because he wanted to oversee the education of his two younger sons, partly because he loved the Rugby work. Yet, though he still gloried in his vigor, he began to have an increasingly real sense of his own death. "Boast not thyself of tomorrow" had been the last text his own father had used before his death from heart-failure, and Arnold had reason to feel more than the perfunctory morbidities of contemporary piety. He had recently begun to keep a diary and a warning of death runs through it, together with a simple mysticism, a sense of communion with God and Christ.

Sunday, June 5.—I have been just looking over a newspaper, one of the most painful and solemn studies in the world, if it be read thoughtfully. So much of sin and so much of suffering in the world, as are there displayed, and no one seems able to remedy either. And then the thought of my own private life, so full of comforts, is very startling; when I contrast it with the lot of millions, whose portion is so full of distress or of trouble. May I be kept humble and zealous, and may God give me grace to labour in my generation for the good of my brethren, and for His glory! May He keep me His by night and by day, and strengthen me to bear and to do His will, through Jesus Christ.

On Saturday, June 11, 1842, he gave a supper to the boys of the Sixth Form, the tradition of the last evening of the summer half-year. Arnold was lively and cheerful, but in his diary he wrote of his forty-seventh birthday, two days off. "In one sense, how nearly can I now say, 'Vixi.'" Early Sunday morning he awoke with a pain in his chest which grew worse; it was the terrible agony of angina pectoris. "If the pain is again as severe as it was before you came," he said to the doctor later, "I do not know how I can bear it." He had suffered little pain in his life; he thought it good for him to suffer it now. After the physician had questioned him about his family medical history, Arnold asked if disease of the heart was common. "Not very common." "Where do we find it most?" "In large towns, I think." "Why?" The doctor gave reasons. "Is it generally fatal?" "Yes, I am afraid it is." At eight o'clock in the morning Arnold died.

It was surely the death of a Christian, but quite as surely it was the death of a Roman of the great mold, republican, stoic, administrative. For the aim of Arnold's lifelong thought and action was an idealized and Christianized Roman empire, its cornerstone responsibility, its pinnacle unity. It was the perfect ideal of imperialism, irradiated with pity and piety, yet with all imperialism's ineluctable contradictions. At home it was the ruling classes' duty; abroad it was the white man's Christian burden. Hearing of the annihilation of 15,000 British troops by the Afghans in a popular rising under the

Amir, Arnold had said, "It gives me a pain I cannot describe to hear of all this misery, which I have no power to alleviate. Yet it will be as it was with the Romans in Spain; we hear often of 'caesus consul cum legionibus,' but then the next year another consul and new legions go out just as before." If he was disturbed by the basic difference between the truth of Europe and the truth of India he put the doubt aside as resolvable in an ideal of love and self-denial. And certainly the races of mankind, he said, are divided into those improvable by themselves and those only improvable by others. Arnold's feeling for the Hindu was substantially the same as his feeling for the factory operative and this is the best side of the imperialist mind coming into contact with alien people or class. Its worse side is represented by Arnold's friend, Carlyle, who believed that "Niggers" were natural slaves and that the granting of the suffrage to the English masses was the beginning of social anarchy. The side of the coin that bears the motto "Right" is certainly more attractive than that which says "Might;" but the coin is one.

Under the shadow of a man so notable, so strong, so decided, so confused, so representative as Thomas Arnold, the youth of Matthew Arnold was spent. With precocious eyes Matthew Arnold watched his father's battles and triumphs; and all who saw the boy and the youth, even his intimate friends, perhaps even himself, thought the son was the very antithesis of the father. But all who observed or judged him so were wrong, perhaps Matthew himself the wrongest of them all.

Chapter Three

THE MAKING OF MYTHS

There was an awful rainbow once in heaven:
We know her woof, her texture; she is given
In the dull catalogue of common things.
Philosophy will clip an Angel's wings,
Conquer all mysteries by rule and line,
Empty the haunted air. . . .

—KEATS.

MATTHEW ARNOLD'S poetry was on the whole not cordially received. A few people, chiefly young men, understood *The Strayed Reveller, and Other Poems* and the volume which followed, *Empedocles on Etna, and Other Poems,* to be the fine expression of emotions that until now in England had been unexpressed or inadequately expressed. William Rossetti, who reviewed the first volume in *The Germ,* was articulate for the tiny minority; he saw the work as it really was, saw its clarity, simplicity and serious intelligence as well as the intense self-consciousness the poetry displayed. And young Swinburne, who was to skim off many of Arnold's ideas and some of his versification, memorized the "Reveller," the "Merman" and the "Sirens" and at Eton rushed to buy one of the fifty circulated copies of *Empedocles on Etna.* Nor was he alone in his admiration; he tells us that many of his schoolfellows knew and loved "Sohrab" and "Tristram."

But official critical opinion was hostile. Arnold said of his own poetry that it expressed the main movement of mind of his time, and so it did if we mean (as Arnold meant) the thought of a small body of intellectuals. Arnold knew, however, that his work could make its way but slowly, for he knew that it was subversive of the official beliefs of his age and nation. The reviewers, though they could not quite agree on what the poetry was or what it was about, had the blind perspicacity of official thought to recognize what controverts it. With high good humor, with magisterial condescension or with holy horror, they undertook to dispose of the new poet. While the *Times* was grieved that Arnold dealt too much with modern themes, the *North British Review* was sad because, dealing with modern themes, Arnold showed himself unsympathetic with the modern age. The *Times,* again, felt some of the verse forms were too antique—and un-English.* The *English Review* regretted that "A" was a "helpless, cheerless doubter" and, having information of the identity of the author, practiced a fine restraint in not revealing it: "for the sake of his father's memory, we forbear to name him more particularly."

Fraser's, apparently seeing a very different object than the *Times,* displayed its liberal modernism by scolding Arnold for *not* dealing with modern themes. "The man who cannot . . . sing the present age, and transfigure it into melody," said *Fraser's* critic, "or who cannot, in writing of past ages, draw from them some eternal lesson about this one, has no right to be versifying at all. Let him read, think, and keep to prose, till he has mastered the secret of the nineteenth century." The writer (who presumably has himself played Oedipus to the century's sphinx) handsomely acknowledges that the author of *The Strayed Reveller* is a scholar, a gentleman and, indeed, a true poet, but he wants to know what good it does, all this "pure and brilliant imagination;" it teaches nothing, it fiddles while Rome burns; he advises the poet to devote his great talent to energy and God, not to laziness and dreams.

And *Blackwood's* reviewer, after a long, facetious speculation on whether *The Strayed Reveller* is a book of convivial verse or a tract from a pious aunt—it was certainly he who later referred to Sohrab as "known far and wide as a handy lad with the scimitar"—finally reads the volume and discovers its true nature. He too is ready with

* The *Times* reviewer was Goldwin Smith.

advice; it would seem the science of mental hygiene has not yet split
off from literary criticism:

What would our friend be at? If he is a Tory, can't he find work
enough in denouncing and exposing the lies of the League, and in taking up the cudgels for native industry? If he is a Whig, can't he be
great upon sewerage, and the scheme of planting colonies in Connaught,
to grow corn and rear pigs at prices which will not pay for the manure
and the hogs'-wash? If he is a Chartist, can't he say so, and stand up
manfully with Julian Harney for 'the points,' whatever may be their
latest number? But we think that, all things considered, he had better
avoid politics. Let him do his duty to God and man, work six hours
a-day, whether he requires to do so for a livelihood or not, marry and
get children, and, in his moments of leisure, let him still study Sophocles
and amend his verses.

In short, the world of bourgeois enterprise which arranged its
own self-glorification in the Great Exhibition of 1851 could find little
charm in Arnold. Inevitably—for Arnold could find little charm
in the bourgeois world. Like Wordsworth before him, like T. S.
Eliot after, he wrote primarily for a small group of saddened intellectuals for whom the dominant world was a wasteland, men who
felt heartsick and deprived of some part of their energy by their
civilization. To speak of this loss of energy while the rest of England flaunted its own ever-growing strength was to invite contempt and disregard. At a time when official thought was announc-
ing the Englishman's ascent to the heights of human possibility,
Arnold declared that the modern man was crippled and incomplete. His poetry, on the one hand, is a plangent threnody for a lost
wholeness and peace; on the other hand, it is the exploration of two
modern intellectual traditions which have failed him and his peers,
the traditions of romanticism and rationalism, and, moving back
and forth between these two strands, it is an attempt to weave them
together into a synthesis. Each alone, he feels, is insufficient, but
together they promise much. The effort of reconciliation produces a
body of poetry which is philosophical but not systematic; what is

declared at one point is contradicted at another. He wrote to his sister, Mrs. Forster: "Fret not yourself to make my poems square in all their parts, but like what you can my darling. The true reason why parts suit you while others do not is that my poems are fragments—*i.e.* that I am fragments, while you are a whole; the whole effect of my poems is quite vague & indeterminate—this is their weakness; a person therefore who endeavored to make them accord would only lose his labor; and a person who has any inward completeness can at best only like parts of them. . . . I shall do better some day I hope—meanwhile change nothing, resign nothing that you have in deference to me or my oracles; & do not plague yourself to find a consistent meaning for these last, which in fact they do not possess through my weakness." The only certainty is the certainty of weariness and effort, and of the need for peace.

Behind the struggle of romanticism and rationalism lies, of course, the diminution of the power of Christianity. Under the shadow of religion and with many gestures of submission to it, rationalism had tried to construct a new picture of the cosmos. By the 19th century that picture was sufficiently complete to show many men that Christianity, even broadly interpreted, could not explain it wholly. The new cosmos suggested an idea which became paramount in men's minds: the disparity between the course of nature and the values of man. Old as Job, the problem was beginning to press anew upon the modern consciousness, and with terrifying force. Spinoza in his *Ethics* stated it for modern times in its most complete and classic form; every man of the 19th century who speculated at all had to face it—whether to rationalize it away, like Carlyle, or to be obsessed and paralyzed by it, like Vigny, or like Tennyson, to "crush it like a vice of blood." How explain the presence of evil in a world made by a just and benevolent God? Hitherto, religion may have been ineffectual as a compelling ethic (we recall the indictment of Thomas Arnold) but at least it had been pervasive as a cosmology; it had served to answer this terrible question. Evil, said religion, is a punishment for wrongdoing, or evil is a test of moral strength, or evil, in some hidden way, is evidence of God's power. Now, seemingly, religion had lost the ability to make such replies convincing.

There were, to be sure, substitute answers to be made. One might say with Goethe—or with Shaftesbury, Pope and Mandeville—that evil really works good; one might say with Carlyle that in the long run evil is defeated; one might reason with James Mill that evil disproves the existence of a just or benevolent God or, with Spinoza, that the concept of evil is strictly of human invention, not an absolute, that nothing is good or bad in itself, that there is indeed a God but neither just nor benevolent nor yet cruel because not personal, that the moral content of the universe outside the human realm is exactly zero. None of these answers was comforting.

Arnold's "Mycerinus" is a sharp, succinct expression of the religious problem as it struck the men of his time. Death is the natural precipitant of the question of the meaning of life: the young king of the poem (he was Menkaure of the 4th dynasty, called Mycerinus by Herodotus, who first told the story) learns from an oracle that he is to die within six years; and he wants to know why. He has lived a life preeminently marked by justice and virtue. His father, on the other hand, was unjust and wicked; yet his father lived to a ripe old age and he himself is to be cut off in the flower of his youth.* This is the reward of probity? Then it can only follow that there is a fundamental divorce between the divine power and human values. Once he had believed that "man's justice from the all-just Gods was given;" now that faith has proved a cheat. In their apathy to man's life these are not Gods but ghosts. Perhaps they do not even act of their own free will but are themselves, like men, "slaves of a tyrannous Necessity?" Or perhaps in their own happiness they are simply deaf to human misery.

---

* As Herodotus tells the story, the virtue of Mycerinus was a sin, for the oracle explains that Egypt was fated to suffer affliction for one hundred and fifty years and his virtue stood in the way of the prophecy's fulfilment.

The response of the young Mycerinus to this new cosmic conception is immediate, crude, natural. He turns at once to sensual anarchy—

> O, wherefore cheat our youth, if thus it be,
> Of one short joy, one lust, one pleasant dream?
> Stringing vain words of powers we cannot see,
> Blind divinations of a will supreme;
> Lost labour: when the circumambient gloom
> But hides, if Gods, Gods careless of our doom.

Leaving his throne, the young king retires to finish his few remaining years among the cool groves of the Nile, bitterly giving his days to revel and fleshly delight. But the poet conjectures that the Lucretian universe lent a Lucretian calm:

> It may be on that joyless feast his eye
> Dwelt with mere outward seeming; he, within,
> Took measure of his soul, and knew its strength,
> And by that silent knowledge, day by day,
> Was calm'd, ennobled, comforted, sustain'd.

The poem ends, like so many of Arnold's poems, on the sad resolution of clear water, the murmur of the moving Nile.

The religious explanation of evil invalidated, men face a universe of frozen apathy, a world without goal or meaning. The way of Spinoza, of acceptance and understanding, is not enough for most men, as Spinoza himself knew. The frozen apathy of the universe chills them into an apathy of their own. "No longer, [Arnold] seems to say," writes John Dewey, "may man believe in his oneness with the dear nature about him: the sense of a common spirit binding them together has vanished; the sense of a common purpose outworking in both has fled. Nature, in ceasing to be divine, has ceased to be human."

"Empedocles on Etna" is a philosophical poem and very explicit; but it is also a dramatic poem and its drama lies not so much in the internal struggle of its hero or in its resolution as in its juxtaposition of two kinds of poetry. Interspersed among the harsh and crabbed verses by which Empedocles reasons his way from despair to suicide are the restrained but sensuous songs of the faithful harp-player, Callicles, and while the philosopher chants the rational and scientific facts of painful, unharmonious life, the poet continues to sing in rich and fluent verse of the ancient world of myth. But the ancient world, sunlit and warm and mysterious, is a world the weary Empedocles cannot believe in; imagination is quite dead for him, killed by his knowledge. Rationalism and materialism have destroyed mystery "by rule and line," have clipped the angel's wing and emptied the once-haunted air and Empedocles feels that life is no longer to be supported. Leopardi said of his own melancholy and that of his contemporaries that it was the result of the shrivelling of the imagination which resulted from the loss of a world explainable by myth; Nature is no longer animate and sentient but mechanical and necessary.

The 18th century would have called Empedocles' complaint the spleen—a complaint of Yahoos, Swift tells us, and with a prophetic touch of the 19th century Swift assures us that its only cure is hard work. The Middle Ages called the same malady *acedia* and the 19th century spoke of it as the *anhedonia* which William James analyzed, the *ennui* which Tolstoy called a desire for desires, the *noia* in which Leopardi lived. But although the complaint is not wholly generated by philosophy—for the psychiatrist has recognized it as a classic symptom of neurosis—yet, whatever its psycho-biological basis, it is certainly fostered, encouraged and given content by the sufferer's intellectual milieu. Basic to all its expressions is the sense of failure, of helplessness, friendlessness, pointlessness. T. S. Eliot, writing of Baudelaire's *ennui,* says of it that it "may of course be explained, as everything can be explained in psychological or pathological terms; but it is also, from the opposite point of view, a true form of *acedia,* arising from the unsuccessful struggle towards the spiritual life:" two ways of saying the same thing. John Stuart Mill describes his state of mind at the crisis in his own mental history as similar to that of Methodists when they are smitten with the "conviction of sin;" but the question which Mill asked himself and the answer he made, which precipitated and fixed the psychological mood, were philosophical. "Suppose that all your objects in life were realized," Mill said; "that all the changes in institutions and opinions which you are looking forward to, could be completely affected at this very instant: would this be a great joy and happiness to you?" To the question "an irrepressible self-consciousness distinctly answered, 'No!' " and months of despair followed.

Significantly enough, Mill can best communicate the nature of his misery by quoting from Coleridge's "Dejection: An Ode;" the "pain without a pang, void, dark and drear" which Coleridge speaks of had followed upon the loss of his own power of imagination. "I seemed to have nothing left to live for," Mill said. He was rescued from despair by what we must call a psychological process: life simply reasserted itself; he learned again how to feel and drew the conclusion that the emotions are as profoundly important as the intellect. And in most men who, like Mill, go through a period of emotional devitalization, the emotional life does somehow manage to reassert itself—not by any logic but by the simple assertion of the will to live or by some internal adjustment. But usually the sufferer is inclined to give a philosophical or religious reason for his pain and his release; the question "Is life worth living?" must be answered by the long meditations of *In Memoriam* or the many words of *Sartor Resartus*.

The moods of dejection, of emotional stoppage, which in a simpler religious age would have been taken to mean an abandonment by God, in this age of conflict between religion and science are found to stem from the misery of living in a pointless universe which makes pointless everything in it. "The ox is strong and powerful," writes Senancour, "but he does not know it. He absorbs a vast multitude of vegetation; he devours a meadow. What important advantage does he derive from it? He ruminates, he vegetates sluggishly in the stable where he is immured by a man heavy, melancholy, useless as himself. The man will slay the ox, will eat it and will not be the better off, and after the ox is dead the man himself will die. What will then remain of both? A handful of fertilizing matter which will produce new grass to nourish other flesh? What a vain and uneloquent alternation of life and death! How cold an universe! *What can be the advantage of existing rather than of existing not?"*

"O unstrung will!"—thus Arnold apostrophizes the man who, almost more than any other, he acknowledges to be his master. Senancour was undoubtedly a man of high gifts and of ready, if limited, insight; Arnold saw him as the very type of the modern soul, more relevant than either Wordsworth or Goethe, for his icy clarity of despair is of more use, says Arnold, than either "Words-worth's sweet calm" or Goethe's "wide and luminous view." His attitude is more complete than Wordsworth's; for most men it is easier of attainment than Goethe's. With worldly and spiritual hopes destroyed by the French Revolution—this is important—with teleology and goal stricken from his universe by the philosophy that had helped make the Revolution, Senancour came to deny the very roots of life and to exist in a *malaise* which negates every joy save that of nullity. "It is a mournful necessity," he said, "as it is also an unbearable anxiety, this compulsory possession of a will, when we do not know on what to direct it."

It is in a universe such as Senancour describes that Arnold believes he must live. Universal nature has nothing to do with man —this is the theme of "Empedocles on Etna." The idea is one that every man with any philosophical bent must face and accommodate. Goethe was, he tells us, but six years old when the problem occurred to him upon the terrible occasion of the Lisbon earthquake, a catastrophe which had started the same idea in the mind of the sixty-one-year-old Voltaire. "God, the Creator and Preserver of Heaven and Earth," Goethe wrote in his manhood, recalling the horror of this event, "whom the explanation of the first article of the creed represented as so wise and benignant, had, by giving both the just and the unjust a prey to the same destruction, not manifested Himself, by any means, in a fatherly character." Once it has been discovered that both the just and the unjust are "prey to the same destruction," is it not the first impulse to discount the idea of a benevolent God entirely and to find in Nature, which is all that remains, a cruel animus?

> On me dit une mère et je suis une tombe;
> Mon hiver prend vos morts comme son hécatombe;
> Mon printemps ne sent pas vos adorations.

So, in Vigny's poem, Nature can speak of herself.

But a little reflection must soon bring the man who takes this line of reasoning to the point where he finds that the attribution of cruelty to Nature is as futile an anthropomorphism as is the attribution of paternal benevolence to a deity. Arnold is aware of this and his Nature is Spinozistically neutral; any animus it seems to have is but the product of human fancy.

> Scratch'd by a fall, with moans
> As children of weak age
> Lend life to the dumb stones
> Whereon to vent their rage,
> And bend their little fists, and rate the senseless ground;
>
> So, loath to suffer mute,
> We, peopling the void air,
> Make Gods to whom to impute
> The ills we ought to bear;
> With God and Fate to rail at, suffering easily.

Spinoza had written that because men "find in themselves and without themselves many things which aid them not a little in their quest of things useful to themselves, as, for example, eyes for seeing, teeth for mastication, vegetables and animals for food, the sun for giving light, the sea for breeding fish, they consider these things like all natural things to be made for their use." By analogy from this seeming design arises the ideal of a universal justice. "For example, if a stone falls from a roof on the head of a passer-by and kills him, [most men] will show by their method of argument that the stone was sent to fall and kill the man"—and so with all phenomena that affect human welfare. Man, forming notions of the fit, the good and the beautiful from his own experience in the struggle for existence, comes to believe that these are ordained by God and does not understand that they are the results of judgments made by man's own mind, having relation only to and validity only in himself. "The will of God" becomes "the asylum of ignorance."

Nature is neutral, man is part of Nature and there is no morality, in the human sense, to be found in her: for Arnold, at this time, this much is clear.

> Nature, with equal mind,
> Sees all her sons at play;
> Sees man control the wind,
> The wind sweep man away;
> Allows the proudly-riding and the founder'd bark.

The only cosmic morality is that all things fulfil the law of their own being. No special promise has been made to man: he too must fulfil the law of his own physical being. The greater part of the speeches of Empedocles is taken up with the directions for following this law. "Born into life we are, and life must be our mould"—this is Arnold's theme, a doctrine of acquiescence.

> The world's course proves the terms
> On which man wins content;
> Reason the proof confirms;
> We spurn it, and invent
> A false course for the world, and for ourselves, false powers.

"False powers:" for however much man may reason with himself, there is always the sense of something beyond the powers he can actually prove. However logically he may maintain that he is but part of the natural order, a drive within him makes a dichotomy between him and the order. He rebels at the natural order, is insulted by it; as Empedocles bitterly says, "To tunes we did not call our being must keep chime." The world is formed so that our will is not free to function as it would: we can always conceive and desire more than we can do or have. Carlyle yearned for what was beyond human possibility, for a place in the universe no man could achieve; at last, to save himself from the nullity which realization of his relative impotence produced, he elected of his own will to take the humble place; he cried to himself and to all men, "Lessen your Denominator!" Arnold (though now his relations with Carlyle are not cordial) gives the same advice. His Empedocles, mocked by man's puniness and evanescence, realizes that his hopes are frustrated, both in social life and in relation to the vast course of the universe, that there is no hope for a greater or happier fate and so —"make us, not fly to dreams, but moderate desire:" for there is joy to be had if we are quite simple about it. It is no small thing to feel the blood in our veins and to be warmed by the sun. Common human life, neither ascetic nor hedonistic nor given to too much thought, may bring a measure of contentment.

But it is to his friend, the simple-minded physician Pausanias, that Empedocles gives his advice; he himself cannot take it. He himself cannot support a life limited to reconciliation and compromise; he yearns for the absolute, and his own resolution is to flee from choked and circumscribed existence by flinging himself into the crater of Etna. It is not entirely a suicide of escape. The act is done in ecstasy and is, as it were, the affirmation of human desires by merging with the All and mingling with the elements, much as the devotee of the Bhagavad Gita desired absorption in the All. As Empedocles commits his last act the song of Callicles rises again up the slope of Etna: he sings of Apollo and the Muses.

Men needed the air to be haunted again. The whole effort of romantic poetry and philosophy had been toward re-peopling it with new and benevolent spirits. The Art of Goethe, the Beauty of Keats,

Love, History, Mind, Self, Society—all had been used to reanimate
the world, and of all the new myths perhaps the most successful had
been the myth of animate Nature, of which Wordsworth had been
the chief exponent. However frequently Arnold may recur to the
Spinozistic simplicity that Nature is without mind or personality, he
is ever trying some new subtlety to deny what he has affirmed. He
has not yet come to his mature sense of "what pitfalls there are in
that word Nature!"

Indeed, in his poetical youth the variety of meaning Arnold gives
to the treacherous word is in itself sufficient justification for Mill's
famous essay. If, in one sonnet, he cries "one lesson, Nature, let me
learn of thee"—the lesson of quiet work—in another, "To an Independent Preacher Who Preached That We Should Be 'In Harmony
With Nature,' " he furiously attacks the shallowness of the preacher's
sentiment:

> Nature is cruel; man is sick of blood:
> Nature is stubborn; man would fain adore:
> Nature is fickle; man hath need of rest:
> Nature forgives no debt, and fears no grave;
> Man would be mild, and with safe conscience blest.
> Man must begin, know this, where Nature ends;
> Nature and man can never be fast friends.
> Fool, if thou canst not pass her, rest her slave!

The syntax of the sestet of "Religious Isolation" is too confused to
allow us to know its exact meaning, but we can know (from the
octave) that Arnold is scolding Clough—to whom the sonnet is addressed—for despondency at the division between man and Nature.

> What though the holy secret which moulds thee
> Moulds not the solid Earth? though never Winds
> Have whisper'd it to the complaining Sea,
> Nature's great law, and law of all men's minds?
>   To its own impulse every creature stirs:
>   Live by thy light, and Earth will live by hers.

Piercing the veil of syntactical obscurity as best we can, we discover that Arnold, though denying human attributes to Nature, maintains that Nature is not blind matter merely: we note that Nature is not "it" but "she" and she has a "great law" which seems as divine as man's "holy secret." It is possible that the confusion of "Religious Isolation" is dispelled by "Morality," for in this poem, though Nature is said to have a "free, light, cheerful air" which sinks man further into his own gloom, she has, nevertheless, a kind of yearning envy of man's moral earnestness: "I saw, I felt it once," she says, "—but where?" and she answers:

> "I knew not yet the gauge of Time,
> Nor wore the manacles of Space.
> I felt it in some other clime—
> I saw it in some other place.
> —'Twas when the heavenly house I trod,
> And lay upon the breast of God." *

Whether Nature is animate or soulless remains an open philosophical question; Arnold will be "in utrumque paratus," prepared for either alternative, and in the poem which he calls by the Latin tag, he states the two possibilities. Perhaps the world first lay in the mind of God and then the "long mus'd thought" gradually became what it now is—our bright and feeling world. If this hypothesis is true, says Arnold, then consider how little the world needs man, how easily the human vanishes before the universal. But perhaps, on the other hand, the world is not of divine origin but is a "wild, unfathered mass," struggling to form "what she forms, alone." Here too the difficulties of the idea seem to have overwhelmed the clarity of expression, but we may assume that Arnold means us to understand (from the symbol of "the solemn cloud" which circles the "still dreaming . . . world") that the world has not yet come to realize itself in consciousness but is still struggling

---

* A. W. Benn says of this poem that "nowhere in literature is so much of Hegelianism summed up so briefly, or so beautifully." Benn notes that Arnold generally passed for a disciple of Hegel, "probably without ever having read him."

toward the self-knowledge which man believes he has won but which may be part of his self-delusion. Whichever hypothesis he accepts, man is not established in his pride.

And these meditations have dealt only with the Nature of Matter and Law; there is, for Arnold, another Nature—the Nature of sensuous and aesthetic perception, what Wordsworth called the "mighty world of eye and ear." The two Natures are, of course, bound up with each other, but the first is essentially the Nature of the scientist or cosmologist and the second the Nature of the artist. When Arnold speaks of the former, he is largely concerned with man's spiritual connection with it or separation from it; this Nature of Law has its moral implications of permanence and industriousness but to derive them one must be willing to commit the pathetic fallacy and suppose an *anima* in Nature which science does not indicate. The mighty world of eye and ear also yields moral meaning, it also demands the pathetic fallacy, though more legitimately, for in this connection the eye and ear are dominant, the critical mind is in abeyance and whatever morality is found is based avowedly on the subjective insight of the moment's mood. We travel out of the city, come to the isolated house or the sudden hill or the rolling field or the silent river. At once we are calmed and composed: the mind, till this moment absorbed by a thousand nagging necessities and forced to respond to a myriad diverse stimuli, is freed; the sense of self, so long drowned, is restored, the awareness of the body quickened. We feel stronger and calmer and strangely wiser; we believe, indeed, that we "see into the heart of things," and so perhaps we do. Released from the demands of affairs and people, we are more dignified, consequently more magnanimous, consequently more virtuous. What more natural than to ascribe—in a poetical and then in a literal sense—this access of calm dignity and potential virtue to the virtue which lies in Nature?

As often as he speaks of the cosmological aspect of Nature, Arnold speaks of this therapeutic aspect of the countryside and the firmament, the mighty natural world of eye and ear. Nature can calm and soothe him when he is shaken by passion; in "Parting" it is the cold solitude of the mountains that is to cure him of his confusion. "I carry my aching head to the mountains and to my cousin the Blümlisalp!" he writes to Clough when he is in the miserable crisis of his love affair. The Alps can heal a philosophical despair as well as a personal sorrow—as in "Obermann." Nature can restore the calm which allows man to possess his soul ("A Summer Night") and even the mere ghost of the countryside, a city park, can, as in "Kensington Gardens," allow the renewed perception of universal values.

But Arnold writes of Nature not only in a cosmological and in an aesthetic sense, but in another, a metaphysical, sense. In "The Youth of Nature" the personified Nature who speaks to the poet is the Nature which Wordsworth had celebrated—that is, the Nature of "eye and ear" and also of cosmological speculation and belief; it is also a metaphysical concept—it is Externality, the World, the Object—as against the Ego, the Individual, the Subject. Arnold asks a question in epistemology: When we read of Nature as sung by the poet (he is speaking of Wordsworth) are we moved by the fact to which the poet refers or by what he says of it? That is, is there an object which inevitably calls forth our emotion, or does the emotion of the subjective observer give significance to, create, the object? Is the world self-sustaining or is it sustained by the experience of man?

It is the Berkeleyan problem which, from Kant on, had been challenging the romantic philosophers. Fichte and Schelling had both carried forward the Kantian idea of the world-creating self, Fichte seeing the process of creation as a moral one, Schelling as an artistic one. Coleridge's "Dejection," to which so frequent reference has been made, is typical of the romantic philosophy:

> O Lady! we receive but what we give,
> And in our life alone does Nature live:
> Ours is her wedding garment, ours her shroud!
> And would we aught behold, of higher worth,

Than that inanimate cold world allowed
To the poor loveless ever-anxious crowd,
    Ah! from the soul itself must issue forth
A light, a glory, a fair luminous cloud
    Enveloping the Earth—
And from the soul itself must there be sent
    A sweet and potent voice, of its own birth,
Of all sweet sounds the life and element!

Arnold rejects this view categorically in "The Youth of Nature." It is *not* the birth of the soul that brings the world alive; it is not "in our life alone" that Nature lives; the world is not "inanimate" and "cold" without the light and glory that issues from the soul. He asks of Nature

> For oh, is it you, is it you,
> Moonlight, and shadow, and lake,
> And mountains, that fill us with joy,
> Or the Poet who sings you so well?
> Is it you, O Beauty, O Grace,
> O Charm, O Romance, that we feel,
> Or the voice which reveals what you are?
> Are ye, like daylight and sun,
> Shar'd and rejoic'd in by all?
> Or are ye immers'd in the mass
> Of matter, and hard to extract,
> Or sunk at the core of the world
> Too deep for the most to discern?

And Nature replies that its qualities are present, real, and do not depend on the observer:

> "Loveliness, Magic, and Grace,
> They are here—they are set in the world—
> They abide—and the finest of souls
> Has not been thrill'd by them all,
> Nor the dullest been dead to them quite.
> The poet who sings them may die,
> But they are immortal, and live,
> For they are the life of the world."

The poem is philosophically confusing, for Nature concludes her answer in the manner of Spinoza by speaking of race after race of men who "have thought that I liv'd but for them" and "that they were my glory and joy." But the passage quoted above is incompatible with Spinozism, and its theme is taken up again with an even more explicit anti-Spinozism in the companion-piece, "The Youth of Man," in which an aging married couple come to the understanding of the actuality of Nature, repudiating the view which they had held in the arrogance of their youth:

> Fools that these mystics are
> Who prate of Nature! but she
> Has neither beauty, nor warmth,
> Nor life, nor emotion, nor power.
> But Man has a thousand gifts,
> And the generous dreamer invests
> The senseless world with them all.
> Nature is nothing! her charm
> Lives in our eyes which can paint,
> Lives in our hearts which can feel.

Contritely, the couple abandon this concept of Nature which had pervaded "Empedocles."

Whether the composition of "The Youth of Man" preceded or followed that of "Empedocles" and was intended as an advance from it cannot at present be determined. We have said that Arnold never set great store by philosophic consistency in his poetry; conflicting views of Nature appear in each of the two early volumes and seem to have been held simultaneously. The stringent materialistic naturalism of "Empedocles" does, indeed, diminish as Arnold gets older, but it never disappears: it is the inevitable result of his allegiance, tempered though it was, to contemporary science. On the other hand, the Platonic—or "realist"—position of "The Youth of Man" seems to have grown: Arnold's theory of the State, his theory of religion, demanded and expressed it. He did not struggle between the two views and in a sense they did not produce any fundamental contradiction, as they would have had he attempted a systematic philosophy. He allowed them to exist side by side; each was used to mitigate what Arnold thought were the excesses of the other in modern life. The scientific materialistic view he employed to combat theology; with his "realist" position he checked what he believed was the intellectual anarchy of the democratic dispensation: he wished to establish a Truth, a Goodness, a Beauty beyond the uncertain realm which is voted into existence by the counting of opinionated heads.

II

But the myths of Nature are not the only ones with which Arnold sought to reanimate and withstand the mechanical universe. One of the subsidiary myths in the Wordsworth canon was that man's joy, present in youth and fading as maturity and daily life erode it, is the memory of his heavenly origin. Arnold, keeping the form of the myth, changes its content for a less sanguine generation: it is not man's joy but his misery that is the mark of his dignity and divinity; man may live by the myth of his own tragedy. "The greatness of man is great in that he knows himself to be miserable," said Pascal. "A tree does not know itself to be miserable. It is then being miserable to know oneself to be miserable; but it is also being great to know that one is miserable." In "To a Gipsy Child by the Sea-Shore" Arnold finds in an infant's face the very essence of human gloom—the gloom of foreknown sorrow and of a lost heritage.

> Thou hast foreknown the vanity of hope,
> Foreseen thy harvest—yet proceed'st to live.

It is the glorious gloom of the exiled angel, the deposed king: "all these same miseries prove man's greatness," said Pascal. "They are the miseries of a great lord, of a deposed king."

> Ah! not the nectarous poppy lovers use,
> Not daily labour's dull, Lethaean spring,

Oblivion in lost angels can infuse
Of the soil'd glory, and the trailing wing;

.   .   .   .   .

Once, ere the day decline, thou shalt discern,
Oh once, ere night, in thy success, thy chain.
Ere the long evening close, thou shalt return,
And wear this majesty of grief again.

And the same theme of conscious tragedy appears in "The Quietist" where Arnold compares the sorrowing poet to the slave who whispers the *memento mori* to the king at the height of the feast so that the king's sense of momentary power may be the more poignantly experienced.

Yet, as the wheel flies round,
With no ungrateful sound
Do adverse voices fall on the World's ear.
Dearen'd by his own stir
The rugged Labourer
Caught not till then a sense
So glowing and so near
Of his omnipotence.

Arnold, looking into the chasm which had once been filled by the poetry of a belief in the divine origin of man and the world, feels, no less than the romantics, the difficulty of a life in which man has no point beyond himself to which he may refer his action, thought and aspiration. The Fichtean and the Kantian philosophies—and in England the thought of Coleridge—had advanced the self as a spirit which, in a metaphysical sense, creates the world. But even in a non-metaphysical connection, the new conception of the self seems the inevitable result of a world in which the existence of a divine creator is no longer sure. When the new "frozen" universe was thrust upon Mycerinus, Arnold tells us, he responded to it by an assertion of the self—in sensual anarchy, the gratification of desires formerly checked by a divine morality, and in an arrogant strength of soul. The gods dead, the self must fill the world; the goal of the spiritual life removed, the furious search for strength and experience begins. Arnold himself indulged, as we have seen, in a kind of mild Byronism of conduct to preserve imagination and self from the corroding effects of his society in order that he might still be a poet. The sensual anarchy and the arrogance of Mycerinus are the essence of the romanticism of (at least the legendary) Byron—save that, unlike Mycerinus, Byron was not "calmed"—and for the same philosophic reasons.

Selfhood forms the theme of "The Strayed Reveller." But it is the selfhood of Keats, rather than of Byron, the celebration of the self-conscious creation of which Keats tells us, an almost barbaric paean to the whole of life, even to pain. A young shepherd-poet, come down from his mountain pastures to attend the rites of Iacchus, wanders into the courtyard of Circe, finds a winebowl and drains it. This is not the Circe of Homer, for the wine effects no swinish transmogrification; it is the wine of vision and ecstatic madness, bringing dreams in which the youth sees the various spectacle of life as the gods see it: for the human bard may see what the gods see, but with this difference, that almost always he must suffer the pain that the spectacle contains; human insight must be paid with human suffering.

> —Such a price
> The Gods exact for song;
> To become what we sing.

To see the glory of human experience the human bard must know the anguish of Tiresias as well as his wisdom, the wounds of the Lapith spears as well as the Centaurs' joy, the travail of the Heroes as well as their triumph. Yet the youthful singer himself, because he is still young, has had, even without the visionary wine, moments of vision without pain; he has even had a glimpse of Iacchus, the sad, ambiguous god in whom the Greeks symbolized the mystery of life and its relation with death.

But I, Ulysses,
Sitting on the warm steps,
Looking over the valley,
All day long, have seen,
Without pain, without labour,
Sometimes a wild-hair'd Maenad;
Sometimes a Faun with torches;
And sometimes, for a moment,
Passing through the dark stems
Flowing-rob'd—the belov'd,
The desir'd, the divine,
Belov'd Iacchus.

And in ecstasy at his own poetic gift he cries

Ah cool night-wind, tremulous stars!
Ah glimmering water—
Fitful earth-murmur—
Dreaming woods!
Ah golden-hair'd, strangely-smiling Goddess,
And thou, prov'd, much enduring,
Wave-toss'd Wanderer!
Who can stand still?
Ye fade, ye swim, ye waver before me.
The cup again!
Faster, faster,
O Circe, Goddess,
Let the wild thronging train,
The bright procession
Of eddying forms,
Sweep through my soul!

The poet reveller *is* all the human life he sings; all suffering, all action, all existence is referred to himself. His pride is that *he* has seen, *he* has felt all that there is to see and feel. He bodies it forth by identifying himself with it and it with himself. And if he submerges his personality in the pain or joy of another he does so to win the dignity of the other's existence and action. An acute analyst of the 19th century, George Mead, says, "As a characteristic of the romantic attitude we find [the] assumption of rôles," the action by which the discovery of the self is made possible. "The self belongs to the reflexive mode. One senses the self only in so far as the self assumes the rôle of another so that it becomes both subject and object in the same experience." But this assumption of the rôle of another may produce not merely self-consciousness but unhappy self-consciousness as well. "[Man] has got the point of view," Mead continues, "from which he can see himself as others see him. And he has got it because he has put himself in the place of the others." Now, in the romantic period, men "could contrast themselves with [an] earlier period and the selves which it brought forth. . . . Not only does one go out into adventure taking now this, that, or another part, living this exciting poignant experience and that, but one is constantly coming back upon himself, perhaps reflecting upon the dulness of his own existence as compared with the adventure at an earlier time which he is living over in his imagination."

"Fausta," to whom Arnold addresses his poem "Resignation" (she is his favorite sister Jane, whom he calls "K," later Mrs. William Forster), is the type of romantic who desires poignant experience to relieve the dulness of her life. The female Faust frets at her inaction; she wants a life of accomplishment and adventure and to check her fruitless yearning her brother contrasts the romantic adventurers who lust for power and action with the more admirable life of the Poet. Now his Poet, however, is not the Poet of "The Strayed Reveller;" if, like the latter, he identifies himself with the life of others, it is not to increase his sense of selfhood but rather to lose it. Unlike Keats and certainly unlike Byron, like the later Goethe or Wordsworth, the chief characteristic of the Poet of "Resignation" is that he lives without *personal* feeling or desire: he is sensitive to the world's charms but he "bears to admire uncravingly." "The man whose spirit is controlled," says the Bhagavad Gita, "who looks on all impartially, sees Self abiding in all beings, and all beings in Self." This self is the Higher Self, beyond all mere personality.

                                Tears
                Are in his eyes, and in his ears
                The murmur of a thousand years:
                Before him he sees Life unroll,
                A placid and continuous whole;
                That general Life, which does not cease,
                Whose secret is not joy, but peace;
                That Life, whose dumb wish is not miss'd
                If birth proceeds, if things subsist:
                The Life of plants, and stones, and rain:
                The Life he craves; if not in vain
                Fate gave, what Chance shall not control,
                His sad lucidity of soul.

The penultimate part of Spinoza's *Ethics* is called "Of Human Bondage, or The Strength of the Emotions;" it is followed by "Concerning the Power of the Intellect, or Human Freedom." "The Strayed Reveller" is Arnold's celebration of the painful glories of man's bondage to the strength of the emotions but "Resignation" is the assertion of the way to human freedom in the abandonment of the romantic temperament and in the search for a kind of *amor intellectualis Dei,* the poet's loving, non-personal vision of the world, or what Arnold calls, with a suggestion of Emerson, a drawing closer to "the general Life."

   The general life, then, is the life of the whole universe, both human and natural; to approach it means to abandon the romantic striving self. There is pain in that life; something "infects" the world. But activity and experience, as the romantic preaches them, are only opiates. And though most sects in England may agree that activity can accomplish all things as well as answer all questions, Arnold is certain they are mistaken. Action is the creed of the commercial and industrial classes and of dissenting religion; it bolsters the more elegant poise of established religion (Keble recommended "holy living" as the best cure for Thomas Arnold's theological doubts); it is no less the creed of the advanced intellectuals who see the world as the field upon which they may religiously exercise their souls. Yet not the romantic activists and certainly not the utilitarian activists, but those spirits are happiest who have something of the Poet's "sad lucidity of soul."

> Yet they, believe me, who await
> No gifts from Chance, have conquer'd Fate.
> They, winning room to see and hear,
> And to men's business not too near,
> Through clouds of individual strife
> Draw homewards to the general Life.

This, not activity, not the assumption of attractive rôles, is the best way of personal living.

> Not milder is the general lot
> Because our spirits have forgot,
> In action's dizzying eddy whirl'd,
> The something that infects the world.

Arnold is explicit that the poet must give up all action if he is to live his true life, no matter how socially useful the action may be. And as for the philosophical man, if he is to approach the lucidity of the poet, he, too, must be "to men's business not too near:" he must not expect action to answer doubts, though it may quiet them.

And not only does Arnold reject the romantic nostalgia for activity, but also another aspect of the romantic self whose goodness most poets had agreed upon—romantic love, which, like the self, is another benevolent myth that can give warmth and meaning to the world. In the key to "The New Sirens" which Arnold supplied to Clough—for the poem is obscure: a "mumble," Arnold called it— he explains that these sirens are "new" because they are "romantic." They are not the fierce sensual lovers of antiquity; they are gentler and more lawful, if actually no less dangerous and with charms that are no less ephemeral. They can give no peace; the passion they excite vanishes in boredom and satiety, and even though it revive, "yet were this *alternation* of ennui and excitement the best discoverable existence, yet it cannot last: time will destroy it: the time will come, when the elasticity of the spirits will be worn out, and nothing left but weariness." The romantic way must fail even here. Even when (as in "The Voice") romantic love speaks with all the pathos of spiritual beauty, Arnold still turns from it.

> In vain, all, all in vain,
> They beat upon mine ear again,
> Those melancholy tones so sweet and still;
> Those lute-like tones which in long distant years
>   Did steal into mine ears:
> Blew such a thrilling summons to my will
>   Yet could not shake it:
> Drain'd all the life my full heart had to spill;
>   Yet could not break it.

The problem is not yet settled, as it could not be in a young man; but the whole conception of romantic love is seen as false. Like action, romantic love is an anodyne; it seems a way to assert the self, but actually it is a way of dulling the *true* self. And though the romanticists may exaggerate and even misconceive it, the *true* self is of the profoundest importance and must be preserved.

It is in defense of the true self, too, that Arnold makes his youthful first attack upon the rationalistic psychology. In the sonnet "Written in Butler's Sermons" he speaks of the blueprint conception of the mind which splits the self into

> Affections, Instincts, Principles, and Powers,
> Impulse and Reason, Freedom and Control

and which cannot take into account the chaotic flux of thought, the multifariousness of impression, the unceasing creative combinations unconsciously made—and, above all, the sense of wholeness of the human personality. It is precisely the ground on which William James will attack the psychologists for creating a mental "atomism, a brickbat plan of construction" which denies the "continuous flow of the mental stream." In 1876, Arnold returns to Butler and in "Bishop Butler and the Zeitgeist" again criticizes the rationalistic psychology which leads Butler to go "clean counter to the most intimate, the most sure, the most irresistible instinct of human nature"—which is not the mere negative instinct to avoid pain, uneasiness and sorrow but the positive one to seek happiness. He finds the genesis of this instinct in "the simple primary instinct, . . . or effort *to live*" and, he implies, this desire for joy involves the *whole* human organism. He quotes Senancour: "The aim for man is to augment the feeling of joy, to make our expansive energy bear fruit, and to combat, in all thinking beings, the principle of degradation and misery." Arnold finds the proto-utilitarianism of Butler going counter to the very voice of religion, to the "Rejoice and give thanks!" of the Old Testament, to the "Rejoice evermore!" of the New.

The declaration of the unity and integration of man's being—

> Deep and broad, where none may see,
> Spring the foundations of the shadowy throne
> Where man's one Nature, queen-like, sits alone,
> Centred in a majestic unity—

is Arnold's refutation of the limitations of rationalism. When the Reason aspires beyond its just place and sets itself up, Godwin-fashion, as the monarch of the self, it is to the Reason alone that all things must be referred. Instead of the Soul of religion, we have the Reason of science. But though the Reason may pretend to certainty in the realm of science (for here it may claim identity with the order of the universe) in the realm of morals it has no such validity. It avows its pragmatic method: such action is good which brings about the greatest happiness of the greatest number. It is the rational humanitarianism of the French Revolution and of all democracy thereafter—a sufficient cause in itself for its rejection by men of other political creed. Nor can the method of rationalism be acceptable to men trained in the certainties of religious faith. In a world in which science narrows the frontiers of mystery, one realm at least defies its advances, or seems to—the realm of mind itself. If the foundations of "the shadowy throne" upon which man's mysterious Nature is placed are so deep and mysterious, perhaps they are founded in an Order no less mysterious, possibly divine. If the self —or the soul—is truly non-rational and intuitive, then one impulse from a vernal wood may tell it more of moral nature and of good than all the rationalistic sages can. A universe which can thus breathe its eternal truths to the receptive spirit of man is nearly as good as God and a great deal better than Godwin.

And so, in a world of uncertainty, Arnold toys with the possibility of an eternal law. The first of the gnomic choruses of his "Fragment of an 'Antigone'" praises a kind of individualistic Benthamite hedonism, an enlightened self-interest which suggests that each man, without infringing justice, shall make "his own welfare his unswerv'd-from law;" but we are quickly told that there is a better way than this: the "austere Birth-Goddess" has given us a "clue"— the primal law which "consecrates the ties of blood." Obedience to the law of the family and the group is better than the life of self-elected good in a world where death is constantly breaking and disordering, where loneliness brings bewilderment.

> In little companies,
> And, our own place once left,
> Ignorant where to stand, or whom to avoid,
> By city and household group'd, we live: and many shocks
> Our order heaven-ordain'd
> Must every day endure.

The man who is linked to family or group stands not only with other men but with divine forces. This is indeed the negation of the liberal-rationalistic society; it is the assertion of the feudal code of the family; it is the voice of Greek tribal ethics, of the Bhagavad Gita on caste and family. It is the echo of Burke and Wordsworth commenting on democratic rationalism.

It is hard to doubt that we hear the mystic voice of Wordsworth again in "The Sick King in Bokhara," more especially the voice of the author of the "Sonnets on the Punishment of Death." It is difficult to know how serious Arnold is in this poem but he is at least not relating a mere psychological oddity when he tells us of the man who insists that he be punished by death; he is at least experimenting with a philosophical position. The poem has a certain relevance to the "Antigone" fragment, for it concerns a man, a Mohammedan, who has acted according to self-elected good. In a time of drought he has found water which he does not share with his family; indeed, when they discover his hidden supply and drain it, he curses his brothers and his mother, thus committing the terrible breach of the blood-bond. And again and again he appears before the king, demanding that he be killed as the Mohammedan law dictates. At first the king thinks him mad; then, when he believes the story, he seeks to extenuate it to the criminal himself and refuses to order his death. But the criminal persists, scornful of such liberal humanitarianism, and dies in joy when at last the king gives way and grants him punishment.

The doctrine of the criminal's search for his own punishment is perhaps an idea characteristic of philosophies that are at once idealistic and reactionary. It is certainly the very converse of the rationalistic or utilitarian concept of crime as a failure not so much of the individual as of society, and of punishment as an education to virtue. Wordsworth, in Sonnets III and XII of the "Death" series, pictures the criminal embracing his death. The modern reader will recall how the heroes of Dostoievsky insist on retribution. Hegel maintained that the criminal sought his punishment in a certain philosophic sense and F. H. Bradley, following Hegel (and, to a lesser degree, Kant), insisted that punishment could not be properly understood either as a deterrent from further crime or as an example to other criminals—but only as punishment, *tout simple,* the affirmation of the divinity of the order of justice. This, Bradley believed, was the sentiment of the mass of people as against the liberal, rationalistic reformers: "Our people believe to this day that *punishment is inflicted for the sake of punishment.*" It is the other side of responsibility; it is the affirmation of the will and personality.

Such an idea must presuppose a law based on something more
general than rationalistic expediency. Inevitably it must refer to a
transcendental order on which society is established. Wordsworth,
though he is willing to admit in one sonnet that punishment has a
deterrent purpose, yet finds its real justification in the metaphysical
nature of the State which it affirms. "What is a State?" the sonnet
asks:

> The wise behold in her
> A creature born of time, that keeps one eye
> Fixed on the statutes of Eternity,
> To which her judgments reverently defer.
> Speaking through Law's dispassionate voice the State
> Endues her conscience with external life
> And being, to preclude or quell the strife
> Of individual will, to elevate
> The grovelling mind, the erring to recall,
> And fortify the moral sense of all.

The statutes of Eternity: are we to infer that Arnold, despite his
rejection of orthodox religion, admitted their existence? Wordsworth, when he wrote the Sonnets, was a strong churchman. Believing the law of nature and of man to be divergent, can Arnold believe in a supernal law? He does not know, he cannot be sure. On
hearing the Duke of Wellington mispraised he defends him, in a
sonnet, as one who saw "one clue" to life—again the "clue"—and
followed it. Wellington had the "vision of the general law"—which
was that the wheels of history go round not urged by human hands
only, but also by powers more efficacious, powers not human. Arnold
had in mind a particular historical complex, the condition of Europe after the French Revolution, against which the Duke had taken
his stand: he had helped brace England against the "chafing tor-
rents after thaw" and had supervised the defense of London against
the Chartists. Yet it was Wellington who had made the phrase that
Arnold was later to use—England, he said, was going through a
revolution by due process of law. And Arnold is concerned with

revolution, trying to see how far it is consistent with the order of the universe. In the first of two sonnets to Clough—"Citizen" Clough, Arnold called him for his sympathies with the French Revolution, which he had witnessed in Paris with Emerson—Arnold admits his own sympathies with revolutionary ideals; but in the second he withdraws from sanguine and precipitant action because the slow processes of the universe forbid it:

> . . . This Vale, this Earth, whereon we dream,
> Is on all sides o'ershadow'd by the high
> Uno'erleap'd Mountains of Necessity,
> Sparing us narrower margin than we deem.

He is not at all sure that the great day of human regeneration will "dawn at a human nod," though he will not say it will never dawn.

He had tried many resolutions of the weariness that comes with an acceptance of the Empedoclean universe and with the frustrations of the promise of Christianity. None had really succeeded. In "Stanzas from the Grande Chartreuse," published in 1855, Arnold stands in the ancient monastery, surrounded by the remembrance of the disproved promises, seeming to hear the surprised voices of the teachers who had "seized" his youth

> And purged its faith, and trimm'd its fire,
> Show'd me the high white star of Truth,
> There bade me gaze, and there aspire.

These teachers are the men of the Enlightenment and their heirs who had destroyed in him the faith among whose monuments he meditates. They are asking, "What dost thou in this living tomb?" He answers that he knows their world to be true, knows the past world to be past—yet cannot quite reconcile himself to the new, nor quite forget the yearning for the old. And somehow among the sepulchres of the dead Carthusians he finds an apter place for his melancholy than in modern life.

> Wandering between two worlds, one dead,
> The other powerless to be born,
> With nowhere yet to rest my head,
> Like these,* on earth I wait forlorn.
> Their faith, my tears, the world deride;
> I come to shed them at their side.

If not an answer, here is at least a refuge for one who does not yet possess his soul. His melancholy is but a fashion, he is told by those who, shallow and pretentious, cry up the new age. But the new age does not impress him; it has not solved the fundamental problems of life for all that it is fulfilling the Baconian dream of man's dominion over matter. Nor have the agonies of the romantics—Byron bearing through Europe the pageant of his bleeding heart, Shelley's lovely wail, Obermann's stern page—lessened the pain of the men who come after: "the pangs which tortured them remain."

> For what avail'd it, all the noise
> And outcry of the former men?
> Say, have their sons obtain'd more joys?
> Say, is life lighter now than then?

In the face of the "exulting thunder" of the forward-rushing world, there are those who must feel that the call to action has come too late for them.

> "Long since we pace this shadow'd nave;
> We watch those yellow tapers shine,
> Emblems of hope over the grave,
> In the high altar's depth divine;
> The organ carries to our ear
> Its accents of another sphere.

> "Fenced early in this cloistral round
> Of reverie, of shade, of prayer,
> How should we grow in other ground?
> How should we flower in foreign air?

* i. e., the dead monks.

Pass, banners, pass, and bugles, cease!
And leave our desert to its peace!"

Between the two worlds lies a wasteland indeed—the wasteland of a Nature that is blind, dying, phantom, empty, a Nature un-
divine that can no longer give laws or direction. There remains
only a world in which man's senseless uproar drowns his pain and
confusion. Balder dead, the *Götterdämmerung* of the Great Exhibition of 1851 casts its shadow upon men. Idealists, like Carlyle, may
juggle Nature as they will, make it the garment of God, full of
meaning and purpose—but even Carlyle despairs. There is a world
of longing in the italics when Arnold, in "Self-Deception," asks,
"Some end is there, we indeed may gain?" Without a God, fundamentally separated from Nature, there is nothing to bind man to
the universe, scarcely anything to bind him to life, strangely enough,
little even to bind him to his fellow-man.

Chapter Four

※ ❊

THE DARKLING PLAIN

A God, a God their severance rul'd;
And bade betwixt their shores to be
The unplumb'd, salt, estranging sea.
— ARNOLD

Necquiquam deus abscidit
Prudens oceano dissociabili
Terras . . .
— HORACE

THOUGH the misery of Empedocles is chiefly the misery of a man facing a cosmic fact he cannot endure, there is another cause for his despair: he cannot endure the social world; not only has he lost community with Nature, he has lost community with his fellow-men. Arnold chose his hero aptly to embody his own social feelings, for according to the legendary accounts of his life, Empedocles became the leader of the democracy in his native Agrigentum and sought to stem the encroaching aristocracy to which he himself had been born. For some time the adored hero of the populace, he refused its offer of the crown; then the tide of favor turned and he became a political outcast. As we see him on the mountain he is full of social bitterness; hearing the sound of the volcano, he remembers the myth which ascribed it to the roars of Typho, the Titan whom Jove had deposed and chained beneath Etna; and Jove's unjust triumph typifies for him the ethical failure of society and what happens when the "plain" man and the crafty man meet:

The brave impetuous heart yields everywhere
To the subtle, contriving head.

But more: the very social organism seems to be fatal to the best of human values.

Great qualities are trodden down,
And littleness united
Is become invincible.

The author of "Empedocles" had read Tocqueville on democracy.

The loneliness which Arnold represents in the person of Empedocles is no small part of the burden of his own age. "We mortal millions live *alone*"—the italics are Arnold's and the theme is constant with him. Liberty and Equality seem to negate Fraternity; the sons of democracy and of the industrial revolution are isolated men. Science pictures a cosmos without soul, and science creates the machines that shape the new society. Loss of belief in a cosmic order requires men to retreat to their individual selves, and the result of this philosophic act is confirmed by the individualism of a manufacturing society. "In our modern capitalistic age . . ." says Franz Oppenheimer, in *The State*, "there occurred a breach in all those naturally developed relations in which the individual has found protection. . . . The 'community bonds' were loosened. The individual found himself unprotected, compelled to rely on his own efforts and on his own reason in the seething sea of competition which followed. The collective reason, the product of the wisdom of thousands of years of experience, could no longer guide or safeguard him. It had become scattered."

The individual has to rely upon himself and his own intellect and he is told that this is the mark of his pride and glory, whether or not the result is a happy and fertile one. W. K. Clifford was to lay down the ethics of belief, the irrefrangible commandments of scientific method which make a perpetual analytic laboratory of the mind. Such austere rigor was surely admirable, yet the men who carried the scientific analysis into all departments of life often found the results unfortunate. To face everything with the intellect is to create a world where everything is double, where everything floats in a thaumaturgic atmosphere, waiting to be anchored to the solid earth, since before we may ascertain a truth we must doubt it. And worse yet: the intellect, pushed into this new dominance, may displace emotion and check the warm and simple flow of natural life. Not the emotional response, conforming to a traditional social pattern, something simple and straightforward, now determines moral conduct; a new conception of duty arises, based on the intellect. The ideals of the Puritan divine and the romantic philosopher, marching the same road of individualism, must save their faces before their respective adherents by affecting to ignore each other, yet under cover of the thicket of philosophy they join hands. Kant puts the terrible burden of the categorical imperative upon the individual and tells him that his every act must be examined to provide a universal moral principle and he, like Fichte after him, finds the test of true morality in the very difficulty of the moral act—so that by his rule, as Schiller wittily said, one first must hate one's friends before one can act morally toward them.

Perhaps more than any poet of his time, Arnold saw what was happening; "The Scholar Gipsy" is a passionate indictment of the new dictatorship of the never-resting intellect over the soul of modern man. It is a threnody for the lives of men smirched by modernity, of men who have become, in the words of Empedocles, living men no more, nothing but "naked, eternally restless mind." And Arnold warns the Scholar Gipsy back to the age when this anomaly had not yet appeared:

> But fly our paths, our feverish contact fly!
> For strong the infection of our mental strife,
> Which, though it gives no bliss, yet spoils for rest.

Empedocles had suggested that one might evade the unhappiness of life by escaping into the self. But in the end this does not serve, for man no longer has a single mind; he is two-minded, the Dipsychus of Clough's poem. The mind is always in dialogue with itself, a slave, not of sense, but of thought, wearing itself down to dryness; one is likely to become, like Empedocles, "a living man no more."

> And we should win thee from thy own fair life,
>   Like us distracted, and like us unblest.
>   Soon, soon thy cheer would die,
> Thy hopes grow timorous, and unfix'd thy powers,
>   And thy clear aims be cross and shifting made:
>   And then thy glad perennial youth would fade,
>   Fade, and grow old at last, and die like ours.

The great truth that Arnold is now to keep ever before him and to develop with increasing explicitness is that all human values, all human emotions, are of social growth if not of social origin. His poems do not rest in the statement of his individual emotion; they are always hinting a cause. Understanding what the human individual must do for himself, Arnold knows how much of what man does for himself depends upon what society allows him to do. He is clear—and grows clearer—about the cause of human isolation and the sterilization of the emotions. He knows it is not merely a religious problem—though that too—but a social problem. He finds its historical analogue in the decline of the Greek State; in the Preface to the 1853 edition of his poems he points out that the cosmological despair of Empedocles was not eccentric but part of a general cultural condition, similar to the contemporary one, and in his inaugural address as Professor of Poetry at Oxford (1858) he insists on the intimate relation between this condition in its aggravated form and the economic and political decline of Athens after the Peloponnesian War. What the individual was likely to feel toward modern society he had felt in Greece as she neared the end of her autonomy. "The individual, absorbed in separate interests, withdrew from the service of the commonwealth," says Professor Butcher. "The Greek State in its distinctive form and true idea was then approaching its end. . . . The unity of Greek life could not survive the growth of a conscious individualism." And in Arnold's time England was falling into the hands of the manufacturing Whigs, men who could declare with Macaulay that "No ordinary misfortune, no ordinary misgovernment, will do so much to make a nation wretched, as the constant progress of physical knowledge and the constant effort of every man to better himself will do to make a nation prosperous." * For Macaulay, society did not exist; there was only an aggregate of individuals. But for Arnold this is not enough for human life. "It is not enough," said Balzac, "to be a man. One must be a system. It is not enough to observe and think: one must observe and think with a definite object." And, in the end, this "system" which one must be, this "object" toward which one must think, are supplied by society. Only the greatest minds can even seem to be free of this dependence—and they but seem to be.

One looks to Victorian London for the image of the society of this industrial time—London with its ungainly spread and sprawl, its lack of organization, political or architectural, its undirected expansion, its noise, its "mud salad" streets, its terrible contrasts of wealth and poverty. The city is not merely a symbol, it is the actual product of the 19th century economic life, of the uncontrolled development of manufacture. And just as the latter-day Greeks and the imperial Romans felt deracinated in their great cities, so the modern men feel that their roots lie elsewhere and, like the ancients, yearn back to nature in idyl and pastoral. Arnold's great lament for the present, "The Scholar Gipsy," and "Thyrsis," his elegy for Clough, which pursues the same theme, use the idyllic form consciously and completely. The city is confusion and despair; for Thomson it is the City of Dreadful Night and for T. S. Eliot, in a later day, the "unreal City," symbol of all meanness and boredom. When Arnold, in "A Dream," is carried away from love on the river of life, it is to the "burning Plains" which "bristled with cities" that he must come. The city, too, is the scene of uncongenial labor, and Arnold, one of the first modern literary men and one of the few eminent Victorians

---

* Macaulay, of course, is echoing Adam Smith.

forced to support himself by hard, non-literary work, speaks, in "A Summer Night," of a world where

> . . . most men in a brazen prison live,
> Where in the sun's hot eye,
> With heads bent o'er their toil, they languidly
> Their lives to some unmeaning taskwork give,
> Dreaming of naught beyond their prison wall.
> And as, year after year,
> Fresh products of their barren labour fall
> From their tired hands, and rest
> Never yet comes more near,
> Gloom settles slowly down over their breast.

The city is the recipient of men whose old ties—to estate, parish or town—have been broken by the new order. It has no real relation with the mass of its citizens; it is merely the container of unassorted atoms—and for this reason Wordsworth condemned it and Shelley demanded municipalities with populations no larger than that of Athens. Men lose their sense of communion with the social environment. "The local powers [of government]," as Oppenheimer tells us, "are reduced to complete impotence." Power shifts to the centralized government which seems a thing far removed and separate, without connection with the individual. If the melancholy and divided spirit of the later Greeks could be ascribed to the separation of state and society, on the whole the same explanation can be made of the spirit of Europe in the 19th century.

Nothing in the literature of the time—especially in France—is more striking than the sense of frustrated energy and talent which haunts its pages. The heroes of Stendhal and Gobineau feel that Europe is in the grip of a dull, malignant power—which they strongly suspect to be the bourgeoisie. They cannot be used by a society which hates their high spirit; they are wasted men. Stendhal's heroes give up in despair, allow themselves to be executed, retire to a charterhouse: "Great qualities are trodden down." *Energy*, Stendhal's magic word, is frustrated by modern society and that is what he means by tragedy. For Balzac, on the other hand, energy itself is the evil; for it is perverted to bad ends by "the decay of religion and the preeminence of finance, which is simply solidified selfishness."

Money used not to be everything [says the physician, Bianchon, in *Cousine Bette*]; there were some kinds of superiority that ranked above it—nobility, genius, service done to the State. But nowadays the law takes wealth as the universal standard and regards it as the measure of public capacity. The perpetual subdivision of estates compels every man to take care of himself from the age of twenty. Well, then, between the necessity for making a fortune and the depravity of speculation there is no check or hindrance; for the religious sense is wholly lacking in France, in spite of the laudable endeavors of those who are working for a Catholic revival.

Sensitive young men must fly from such a world to distant lands or to the past. Or they must revolutionize their souls in isolation from the life around them, engage in an energetic self-cultivation without reference to actualities, like the hero of Gobineau's novel, *The Pleiads*:

My opinion is that the honest man, the man who feels himself possessed of a soul, is more than ever imperiously bound to concentrate upon himself and, being powerless to save others, to strive for his own improvement. It is the only thing to do in such a time as ours. All that society loses does not disappear, but takes refuge in the lives of individuals. The whole surroundings are petty, wretched, shameful, and distasteful. The isolated individual remains, and as amongst the rubbish and mutilated fragments of Egyptian ruins, hard to recognize, with walls broken down, fallen in, there survive, towering to the heavens, colossal statues or obelisks testifying to noble ideals, perhaps transcending even the town or temple razed to the ground, so isolated human beings, finer or nobler than ever their ancestors were, testify to the sublimity of God's creatures. To work upon oneself, to cultivate whatever good qualities one possesses, to suppress one's bad qualities, stifle one's worst ones, or, at the very least, discipline them—that henceforth is one's duty and the only form of duty that is also of any use. In a word, so to contrive as to count among the Pleiads.

For Alfred de Vigny, ᴖ ᴖᴖ abstract idea of Duty, all else failing, remains to give him certitu ᴖᴖ and hope. He desires for himself and for his class a morality independent of social function or sanction, dispensing with both hope and fear, a morality of unreasoning and unquestioning obedience to some inner voice. And in his great story, "The Malacca Cane," the generous soldier who has learned self-abnegation from an English admiral has utterly given up the desire for recognition and reward at the hands of Napoleon whom he knows to be corrupt and wicked; he enters battle, armed only with a walking-stick, refusing to kill, but bent on taking all possible risks. This is his creed and Vigny's:

What idea will support him [the soldier] if not that of Duty, and the word of honour given; and amid the uncertainties of his road, and his scruples, and his heavy remorse, what sentiment is there that can buoy him up and exalt him in the days of discouragement? What is there that yet remains sacred? In the universal shipwreck of beliefs, to what debris can generous hands still cling? Outside of the love of daily comfort and luxury, nothing seems to swim on the surface of the abyss. One would almost believe that egoism had submerged all. [Yet] I believe I can see a solid point on this sombre sea. I looked under and over it; I put my hands on it and I found it strong enough to lean on in times of trouble, and I was reassured. This is not a new faith, a freshly invented cult, a confused thought; it is a sentiment born with us, independent of time, place and even religion; a proud and inflexible sentiment, an instinct of incomparable beauty, which only in modern times has found a worthy name, but which already had produced sublime grandeurs in ancient days and fertilized them as did those wonderful rivers which at their source and first detours have not as yet an appellation. This faith which it seems to me still remains and reigns supreme in the army is called Honour. While all the virtues seem to descend from heaven to take us by the hand and lift us up, this one alone appears to spring from our inner selves and tends to mount heavenward. It is a splendid human virtue born of earth, without the celestial palm that comes after death; it is the virtue of life.

One is honorable and loyal. To what object one directs one's honor, what it is that makes action a duty, to what one gives loyalty except to loyalty itself—to these questions Vigny has no possible answer.

Self-sufficiency has always been the classic advice of philosophy in a disorganized society. "Live in yourself," wrote Senancour, and added: "and seek that only which does not perish." Self-cultivation in loneliness, in the face of the degeneracy of the world, with reference to some eternal but ill-defined idea—it is a familiar burden of Matthew Arnold's communion with himself. In the midst of a jangled and uncertain world he tells himself to learn

> That an impulse, from the distance
> Of his deepest, best existence,
> To the words "Hope, Light, Persistence,"
> Strongly stirs and truly burns.

But the poem is entitled "The Second Best."

Self-discipline, however, is only one way of responding to an unsatisfactory society. Another way is action. The miasmic Senancour cried out, "Take back your gifts and your chains; let [man] act, let him suffer even; let him act, for this is to enjoy and to live." Action—fierce, individualistic, anti-social, half ironic—becomes admirable in itself and without reference to its end. A society which forces upon men the consciousness of their selves and makes it difficult for them to act happily in the simple routine of life fosters the doctrine of "experience," a doctrine of strange implications and one whose most significant exponent was Goethe. Experience, for Goethe, is a moral duty as a way of developing the personality. Faust cries:

> I tell you pleasure's not in question:
> I am the reeling votary of strife,
> Of joy's most savage pang, hate sick with love,
> And sullen anger that can stab to life.
> The knowledge-fit has left me. There is no
> Ache I will bar my door to: all that's dealt
> The heart of man, all, all that men have felt,
> Shall throb through my heart with an equal throe.
> I'll grapple the great deeps, the heights above;
> Upon my head be all men's joys and griefs;

So to their stature my sole self shall grow
And splinter with them on the roaring reefs.

But to set out to *look* for "life"—as, say, Tennyson's Ulysses did
—what could that have meant to a Greek or a Jew of the great
periods? To feel that the spirit of man must be carefully exercised
by extraordinary activity, that there is not enough of life at hand,
not even enough of the right kind of suffering: how strange a complaint and what a comment upon society! The moral implications
are momentous. "Experience" means a passing-through events for
the sake of knowledge, hence there is always a core of insincerity;
the romantic assumption of "rôles" may eventually discover the true
self but there is perhaps always present an unreality of intention.
"Experience" means, too, that one incurs only temporary moral consequences, not final ones—that Faust suffers misery and remorse
but not, in the end, damnation. It is with a touch of Calvinism that
the God of the Prologue in Heaven points out that the good man
can do no wrong in his search for self-development. Carlyle, leaping beyond the Goethe of experience to the Goethe of resolutions,
said, "Close thy *Byron,*"—meaning the Byron who sought to taste
all of life and who (in Arnold's phrase) fought the sun itself—and
commanded, "Open thy *Goethe*"—meaning the Goethe of Faust's
dyke, of the man who resolves his discords in *work*. But it did not
occur to Carlyle that Goethe would have desired no one to close
his Byron, that his doctrine of work was but an appendage to the
ideal of emotional experience.

Yet "experience," after all, is something which only the members
of certain classes can afford. "Experience" takes life as a game,
though a serious one, and most men cannot afford to play games.
They have their way to make in the new kind of world, a world
like that which Balzac's Rastignac saw when he came from the
provinces to Paris, which forces them to make the choice between
being a sheep or a wolf, devoured or devouring. The artists who,
like Balzac, can make such a world their own are few enough. Balzac himself is inoculated with a saving touch of the new world's

money-lust and charlatanry. More delicate souls find the atomistic society beyond their control and utterly arid; they must look to another age and place for the warmth and comfort their own will not give. Even the direct relation which the poet might once have had with the ruling group in the status of a protégé is no longer possible; he must seek his dubious support in a disorganized society, by which he is either repulsed or disgusted. A few of the more realistic may refuse to put the blame wholly on society: "Why is poetry dead in France?" asks Musset, and he answers: "Because the poet stands aloof from everything." But something sick either in society or in the poet makes Greece or Carthage or Touraine call temptingly. As Georg Brandes says, "Lacking any social field in which to work, all activity necessarily takes the form either of war with reality or flight from it." Men dream of a past that has never been and treasure the sweet feeling that the present does not exist, that all is yet to come and yet to be shaped. In Thomas Mann's *Death in Venice,* the vigorous man of the North cannot make the effort to leave the lovely Hellenic boy with the bad teeth who signifies to him all the sad quiet beauty of an earlier day, even though he knows that to indulge the dream means death.

Nor is the flight to the past the gesture of the individual artist only; it is also the gesture of a society itself which has not yet found the forms in which to crystallize its own new life. The 19th century, trying to hide its ugliness, raises the Gothic façade to mask the machine, and calls upon the artist to assist its dull masquerade. But the critical artist, abashed by this clumsy imitation of his own gesture, begins to use the word *vulgar* and means it not in the old sense of something pertaining to the mass of people and therefore common and coarse but in the peculiarly modern sense of something pretentious and false. Coarseness reveals something, as E. M. Forster says, vulgarity conceals something. And the search for satisfactory life in the forms of the past produces a mad mélange of insincere styles. "Our age has no form of its own," said Musset. "We have impressed the seal of our time on neither our houses nor our gardens nor on anything that is ours. . . . We have every century except our own—a thing which has never been seen at any other epoch: eclecticism is our taste; we take everything we find, this for beauty, that for utility, this other for ugliness even, so that we live surrounded by debris as though the end of the world were at hand."

As though the end of the world were at hand: so many men felt that it was, in some subtle and pervasive way. "Youth gone, life is only a deadly defeat, our career is like that of a star which is being slowly chilled into extinction." It is Sainte-Beuve speaking and he is voicing the thought of many of his contemporaries—of Arnold for one, who could never relinquish the memory of his youth and its hope, and who, while youth lasted, was ever conscious of the pathos of its evanescence. It is a world of sterile life, the young are dying, and it appears to many that Art is dying too; for the epigraph to the 1853 edition of his poems Arnold takes the lines from Chœrilus of Samos, "Yea, blessed is the servant of the Muses, who in the days of old ere the meadow was mown, was skilled in song. But, now, when all is apportioned and a bound is placed to the arts, we are left behind like stragglers who drop in at the tail-end of the race."

II

When Octave, the hero of Musset's *Confessions of a Child of the Century,* wishes to explain how he "was first taken with the malady of the age," he interrupts an acute analysis of philosophic despair to tell a love story. This is disappointing, but as he continues we see that his philosophico-historical insight has not failed him. His life, he tells us, has been made miserable by his torturing distrust of his quite faithful mistress; at last, maniacally jealous, he is about to stab her as she sleeps but is prevented by the sight of the crucifix on her breast. He drops his dagger: now everything is clear to him: it is all the fault of Voltaire! "Poisoned, from youth," he cries, "by all the writings of the last century, I had sucked at an early hour the sterile milk of impiety." Behind his inability to love his mistress trustfully is the Encyclopedia. No amount of intellectual analysis could tell us as much as this. And not all of Arnold's more explicitly philosophical poetry can give us so clear an insight into his feelings about the cosmos and society as can his poems of sexual love.

It used to be frequently said—in fact, it is the tradition of Arnold's own family—that the two series of love poems which Arnold called "Switzerland" and "Faded Leaves" were not inspired by an actual love affair. However, the evidence of several sentences in the letters of Arnold to Clough seems to refute this belief that the Marguerite of the poems was only a poetical figment. Yet even without the refutation of external evidence, it is almost impossible to read the poems themselves without being convinced that here is the attempt of a man to tell the truth about an important experience. Arnold is a very intimate poet; he is an occasional poet who writes of the hour as it passes; he is a literal poet who tries to say what he means at the moment even if what he says contradicts what he said the moment before. It is quite true that if we accept the evidence of the poems completely and literally, we accept what seems a tangle of contradictions: the girl rejects the lover, he rejects her; she is unworthy of him, he is unworthy of her; her love is his dearest need, or again, it is a deviation from his true path. It is very confusing but so much the better: these very contradictions attest to the actuality of the affair and certainly the whole point of the story lies in them.*

* Professor Garrod, always a discerning critic and distinguished for the care with which he uses biography to illuminate poetical meaning, accepts the reality of Marguerite on the evidence of the poems alone: "I used at one time to pooh-pooh Marguerite. In part, I was fearful of vulgarising a great poet. In part, I did not sufficiently believe that poets mean what they say; but they do—even when they do not say what they mean; from our failure to recognise that proceed nearly all the faults of our criticism. Moreover, I had not learned to read Matthew Arnold's poems in their proper connexions:—I had a robust distaste for bibliography. I say it with hesitation, but I think now that it is a mistake to disparage Marguerite. The volume of 1852 has a somewhat surprising unity, the unity, I feel, of a single and intense experience. When you have added to it the poems which should never have been taken away [Mr. Garrod means "The Forsaken Merman" and "The Voice;" with these he might have included "To My Friends, Who Ridiculed a Tender Leave-Taking"—with its interesting change of the phrase of the first edition, "ere the parting kiss be dry," to "ere the parting hour

The story of ambivalent love is a characteristic one of the 19th century. Rousseau's *Confessions* had laid the ground for the understanding of emotional ambivalence and, from Pushkin to Clough, poets tell of lovers separated not by difficult circumstances but by

---

go by"—and also "The New Sirens"], it is difficult not to assign to Marguerite an important place in that experience."

But the evidence of the poems holds good only for emotional truth and not for matters of biographic detail. The exuberant imaginations of Mr. Kingsmill (touched with cheerful malice) and of Mrs. Sells (touched with a sentimentality as pertinacious as her scholarship) can give us only "actualities" which amusingly contradict each other. Mr. Kingsmill is certain that Marguerite was a governess, or a teacher of French, or a paid companion and he bases his certainty upon the belief that Arnold left her because she was of inferior social station; and since she was of inferior social station how could she have summered at Thun save she made her living there? The evidence that Marguerite was a paid *companion* Mr. Kingsmill finds in the fact that in Arnold's poem, "The Dream," she *accompanies* another girl; Mr. Kingsmill ignores, however, the evidence that Arnold caught Marguerite at the housework (a chambermaid?) for in "The Terrace at Berne" he speaks of "the kerchief that enwound thy hair." Mrs. Sells is quite certain that Marguerite was a young French aristocrat who summered with her parents at Thun, that she was not very tall, that she wore a certain kind of bonnet and assumed certain attitudes when she walked with Arnold, that she had a very French nose and chin.

I have treated the love poems as though all of them—except "Calais Sands"—refer to Marguerite. But I ought to mention the theory, held by several writers, that they refer to *two* women. Mr. Andrew S. Cairncross in a communication to the *Times Literary Supplement* (March 28, 1935) offers the opinion that "Urania" must be distinguished from "Marguerite" and that the poems must be divided between the two. Mr. Kingsmill had previously put forward a similar idea and his attribution of the poems is much the same (though not entirely) as Mr. Cairncross's; he gives "Calais Sands" to Frances Lucy Wightman, whom Arnold married, and also the five poems which, in the *Poems, Second Series* of 1855, Arnold grouped under the title "Faded Leaves;" four of these poems had appeared in the *Empedocles* volume of 1852 ("The River," "Too Late," "On the Rhine," and "Longing") and one ("Separation") appeared first in 1855. Although I do not find conclusive, as Mr. Kingsmill does, the discrepancies between blue and gray eyes and brown and ash-colored hair (nor does Sir Edmund Chambers in his Warton Lecture on Arnold), it is perfectly possible that "Faded Leaves" might have been written to another woman, very conceivably Arnold's wife. They might be excepted from the Marguerite cycle without doing much harm to the emotional pattern I trace. Sir Edmund Chambers excludes "Urania" from the Marguerite group, nor will he admit Professor Garrod's guess that "Lines Written by a Death-Bed" is the "morbid imagination of [Marguerite's] death." No one writing about the poems without further documentary evidence can be quite safe from the temptation to use the method of Serjeant Buzfuz explaining the *true* meaning of Mr. Pickwick's "Chops and Tomata sauce;" nor is the present writer confident that he has escaped temptation. Any actual facts about Marguerite will, apparently, have to wait upon the efforts of the scholar who will analyze the register of the Hotel Bellevue at Thun for 1848 and 1849 and, by gradual steps, track down the names, letters and portraits that will solve the mystery and make his scholarly fortune. All that we have now are the poetical and emotional facts.

the inability of the man to know the true tendency of his heart. If his love story was paradoxical no one was more aware of it than Arnold himself and nothing could be more explicit than his statement of it in "Destiny:"

> Why each is striving, from of old,
> To love more deeply than he can?
> Still would be true, yet still grows cold?
> —Ask of the Powers that sport with man!
>
> They yok'd in him, for endless strife,
> A heart of ice, a soul of fire;
> And hurl'd him on the Field of Life,
> An aimless unallay'd Desire.

He believes that his affair has been an emotional failure and it becomes for him typical of the general inability of human atoms to meet; it bears in upon him the realization that: *"Thou hast been, shalt be, art, alone."*

Certainly one of the lovers made the attempt at union under an almost insuperable handicap. For the affair has another year of life and suffering when Arnold writes to Clough from Thun, where Marguerite is, saying that he is getting bored with his once-favorite Béranger and that he is rather glad to be tired of an author, for it is "one link in the immense series of cognoscenda et indaganda despatched." And then: "more particularly is this my feeling with regard to (I hate the word) women. We know beforehand all they can teach us: yet we are obliged to learn it directly from them." The love affair, it would seem, has its pedagogical side; it is part of Arnold's "experience." And although this does not preclude true passion or real involvement, it is certain to preclude an absolute whole-heartedness, to produce that literary self-consciousness which aroused Baudelaire to write, "Remember this, that one must beware of all the paradoxical in love. It is simplicity which saves, it is simplicity which brings happiness. . . . Love should be love." Arnold's love was perhaps not quite love; it was not what Baudelaire called "ferocious" and "Oriental;" it was "paradoxical." Yet this is not to deny its poignancy and the reality of the suffering it caused.

The girl, it would seem, sensed the reservations and the intellectualistic-emotional dubieties with which the paradox was attended and she was repelled by them. Marguerite was a creature of a single mind and that mind, as Arnold perceived it, was fulfilled by the simple acceptance of life without thought of the possibility of ever being "sick or sorry." She partakes of the spirit of the old pagan world, "clear, positive, happy," to which, years later, Arnold is to pay his respects even while he speaks of its failure as a way of life for the millions of mankind who must forego the "religion of pleasure" for Christianity, "the religion of sorrow." She is the Gorgo or the Praxinoe of the idyl of Theocritus which Arnold translates in his essay, "Pagan and Mediæval Religious Sentiment," to illustrate both the charm and the insufficiency of pagan feeling. She was the Célimène to Arnold's Alceste; he understood something of the profound human value of Célimène's refusal of sorrow and could scorn his own Alcestean dumps. Célimène-Marguerite, paganly unconcerned with pain, stands in perfect contrast to the self-torturing, uncertain young man, half in, half out of his religious shell; Arnold-Alceste is the man with the "teas'd o'erlabour'd heart," yearning to be rid of dubiety and the need for "hourly false control."

Together the pair read Foscolo's *Letters of Ortis,* Italian brother to Werther, René and Obermann (Marguerite has lent him the book), but though Marguerite may understand, she will not respond to his self-torturing doubts; her eyes are "arch," her mouth is "mocking." Arnold cannot blame her for not giving him sympathy and love. Rather he must look upon her as the symbol of a past and desirable way of feeling and blame his failure upon himself and upon the modern race of men:

> I too have suffer'd: yet I know
> She is not cold, though she seems so:
> She is not cold, she is not light;
> But our ignoble souls lack might.

> She smiles and smiles, and will not sigh,
> While we for hopeless passion die;
> Yet she could love, those eyes declare,
> Were but men nobler than they are.

And in accents reminiscent of Coleridge's vision of himself transformed by the music of the Abyssinian maid, he calls for the heroic new man to whom she will respond:

> His eyes be like the starry lights—
> His voice like sounds of summer nights—
> In all his lovely mien let pierce
> The magic of the universe.

He knows that Marguerite is not "true;" she is Euphrosyne, heart-easing, blithe, debonair—and it is by the name of this nymph that he later calls the poem he had first entitled "Indifference;" but fidelity, he says, is a word relevant only to those lovers who see the world as a place of sorrow and in their common suffering require the comfort of constancy; the theme is taken up in "Dover Beach:"

> Ah, love, let us be true
> To one another! for the world, which seems
> To lie before us like a land of dreams,
> So various, so beautiful, so new,
> Hath really neither joy, nor love, nor light,
> Nor certitude, nor peace, nor help for pain;
> And we are here as on a darkling plain
> Swept with confused alarms of struggle and flight,
> Where ignorant armies clash by night.*

Of these sorrowing lovers he himself is one, but Marguerite, for whom the world is "so various, so beautiful, so new," is among

---

* Although "Dover Beach" was not published until 1867, Professor Lowry and Professor Tinker, in a letter to the *Times Literary Supplement* (Oct. 10, 1935), adduce evidence to show that it was written in 1850. "Dover Beach" is perhaps the most admired of Arnold's poems today. Two modern responses to it are worth mentioning. Samuel Barber has composed a musical setting to it which has been recorded (Victor #8998B). A more gratifying comment is the poem by Archibald MacLeish, "Dover Beach: A Note on That Poem," in *Public Speech*.

the souls "charm'd at birth from gloom and care," happy in herself, asking no love and plighting no faith. And her indifference brings home to Arnold, sharply and dramatically, what he believes to be the emotional situation of the modern man—his insufficiency, his uncertainty, his dilution of spirit. At times he feels the indifference as a betrayal and a humiliation and thus he speaks of it in "To Marguerite," comparing his own constancy to her fickleness.* But chiefly he realizes that the warm, tender, pathetic love of "Dover Beach," the utterance of a need arising from despair, can mean nothing to one in whom the outgoing emotion which her lover mistook for love is merely the "bliss within," an exuberance of spiritual poise.

Marguerite, then, is the past as a romantic modern conceives it. She is of the company of the Strayed Reveller and the Scholar Gipsy.

* The mention of Marguerite's fickleness raises the question of her chastity—or lack of it. In two separate poems Arnold speaks very explicitly, it seems, of her "immorality." Remembering his literalness in most matters, we cannot but think that he means what he says:

> In the void air towards thee
> My strain'd arms are cast.
> But a sea rolls between us—
> Our different past.
>
> To the lips, ah! of others,
> Those lips have been prest,
> And others, ere I was,
> Were clasp'd to that breast.

Thus "Parting," written in the midst of the affair; and ten years later Arnold recalls his love affair in "The Terrace at Berne," and because the memory is a charming and still poignant one, he tells himself that he ought not give it a "shadowy durability" and so he calls up the possible transformations that have taken place in the girl he loved. One of them is the following:

> Or hast thou long since wander'd back,
> Daughter of France! to France, thy home;
> And flitted down the flowery track
> Where feet like thine too lightly come?
>
> Doth riotous laughter now replace
> Thy smile, and rouge, with stony glare,
> Thy cheek's soft hue, and fluttering lace
> The kerchief that enwound thy hair?

Mrs. Sells says nothing at all about this aspect of the affair; Mr. Kingsmill would have it that Arnold, having acted like a disgusting prude, turned his anger at himself upon the girl and that, with the prejudice of a respectable Briton, he assumed that because she was of inferior station she was immoral—and concluded that his prudish response to her love was therefore justified.

And Arnold himself is the present, beclouded and diminished in emotion.

Stendhal had thought of calling *Lamiel,* his last novel, by the name of *The French Under King Louis Philippe,* for, through its heroine, it is the exposure and condemnation of modern men—Lamiel, like Marguerite, "look'd, and smiled, and saw them through" and the only man who could arouse love in her was a philosophical burglar, devoted to Corneille and Molière and ennobled by his courage and by his contempt for society. Arnold would have understood the intent of this novel; he knew that women look for more than devotion, that they seek in those they love a strength that need not be always moral.* And he himself desires this erotically attractive strength.

> I too have felt the load I bore
> In a too strong emotion's sway;
> I too have wish'd, no woman more,
> This starting, feverish heart, away:
>
> I too have long'd for trenchant force
> And will like a dividing spear;
> Have prais'd the keen, unscrupulous course,
> Which knows no doubt, which feels no fear.

The rejection of the romantic personality which "Resignation" had made is not too easily completed. The social need is clear: the social

---

* "I love Wordsworth best," writes Lady Blandish to Sir Austin Feverel, "and yet Byron has the greater power over me. How is that?" And Sir Austin pencils his answer to her question in the margin of the letter: "Because women are cowards, and succumb to Irony and Passion, rather than yield their hearts to Excellence and Nature's Inspiration." But other people answered the question differently from Sir Austin, for not only George Sand, in the interests of her sex, but the male novelists, to the despite of theirs, were exhibiting women putting modern men to shame for their lack of passion. The 19th century set Woman up in place of the 18th century's Noble Savage as a criterion of nobility and even of masculine strength. Stendhal's heroines are bright crystals of passion beside the male lumps of money-grubbing France. Gobineau's women lose no feminine charm by being more than the equals of men in spirit and intelligence. In England Meredith took from Molière the idea of the sensible woman's "comic" superiority. Shaw, combining this tradition with that of Ibsen, contraposes the clarity and affirmation of women to the sentimentality and negation of men, and D. H. Lawrence, in a different tone, reiterates the theme of the modern woman betrayed by man's vacillation and confusion.

world requires tenderness and love, however much the individual needs trenchant force and unscrupulousness. But although the moral order is important, the self-regarding, self-prizing soul is important too.

Self-assertion and energy and courage—these, Arnold feels, are valuable in themselves, even without regard to the end to which they are directed. In "Courage," admitting that perhaps men such as the second Cato and Byron did not clearly recognize "the tendence of the whole," he yet finds them impressive for their non-intelligent "strength of soul." Cato is admirable not for the moral choice of his suicide but for the sheer dauntlessness of the deed itself, and Byron, whom Arnold is now inclined to dislike for "vulgarity," is admirable as the very symbol of the romantic personality.

> And, Byron! let us dare admire,
> If not thy fierce and turbid song,
> Yet that, in anguish, doubt, desire,
> Thy fiery courage still was strong.
>
> The sun that on thy tossing pain
> Did with such cold derision shine,
> He crush'd thee not with his disdain—
> He had his glow, and thou hadst thine.

The 19th century—and Arnold himself—taking the lines out of their context, liked to quote for edifying purposes Faust's speech on renunciation:

> Entbehren sollst du! sollst entbehren!
> Das ist der ewige Gesang,
> Den, unser ganzes Leben lang,
> Uns heiser jede Stunde singt.

"Thou must go without, go without! that is the everlasting song which every hour, all our life through, hoarsely sings to us!" But Faust is not accepting the necessity of renunciation; he is rejecting, in a satiric passion, the whole Christian ideal of self-abnegation. Arnold, more mildly, does the same:

> True, we must tame our rebel will:
> True, we must bow to Nature's law:
> Must bear in silence many an ill;
> Must learn to wait, renounce, withdraw.

Yet—and the *yet* looms large—there is something else besides the law. Facing the depressing vastness of the illimitable and indifferent universe, Arnold is wistful for the raw, assertive energy of Byron.

This desire for the Byronic way of headlong, violent and even unintelligent and immoral action for its own sake is but the other side of depression and inaction. The soul swings first to the deepest depression and to the inability to feel, and then to the desire for extreme activity. In *Dichtung und Wahrheit* Goethe speaks of "those whose life is embittered in the most peaceful circumstances by want of action and by the exaggerated demands they make upon themselves." Freud, whom Thomas Mann links with Goethe in a brilliant essay, would no doubt interpret that "needlessly embittered life" and the "want of action" as symptoms of neurotic conflict and the "exaggerated demand" upon the self as the working of the "superego," the repository of all the ideals which family and society erect and which the individual magnifies to such a degree that he can never achieve them. And Clough's "Uncle," in his racy language, had accused Thomas Arnold of ruling Rugby by creating an unusually enlarged superego in his boys, implanting in them a set of more than usually "exaggerated demands upon themselves." Matthew Arnold, like Clough, suffered the consequences. Arnold had charged his friend with always looking for something nearer the truth than his own way of being, and with thus incapacitating himself for positive action; but he himself is prey to the same malady.

The disease is one of the inevitabilities of a social organization in which the wisdom of society can no longer be accepted: put the burden of ethical judgment entirely upon the individual, make him accept the rightness of the Kantian imperative and almost certainly, unless he be insensitively arrogant, he will end in doubt and inaction.

One can, perhaps, escape from the morass which this personal responsibility entails by a flight to the self. John Dewey has put the moral problem in this way:

Which shall he decide for, and why? The appeal is to himself; what does *he* really think the desirable end? What makes the supreme appeal to him? What sort of an agent, of a person, shall he be? This is the question finally at stake in any genuinely moral situation: What shall the agent *be?* What sort of a character shall he assume? On its face, the question is what he shall do, shall he act for this or that end. But the incompatibility of the ends forces the issue back into the question of the kinds of selfhood, of agency, involved in the respective ends. The distinctively moral situation is then one in which elements of value and control are bound up with the processes of deliberation and desire; and are bound up in a peculiar way: *viz.,* they decide what kind of a character shall control further desires and deliberations. When ends are genuinely incompatible, no common denominator can be found except by deciding what sort of character is most highly prized and shall be given supremacy.

Arnold, like Clough, tries out the ways of being in an effort to discover what his true self is; he believes that once he finds it he will be free; a "voice" tells him

> "Resolve to be thyself: and know, that he
> Who finds himself, loses his misery."

But it is not easy to find the true self. Fichte said that we create the self (as we do the world) by moral action. But there is a vicious circle: we must choose the self before we can act, yet we make the self by acting.

Arnold left Marguerite, for to do so was to approach his true self. The separation was, he felt, indicated on the "inly-written chart" which the "heavenly Friend" had given him—by which he means his true but unrealized nature. He counsels himself to a mild *amor fati:* the dalliance with Marguerite is, after all, not blameworthy:

> Ah! let us make no claim
> On life's incognizable sea

> To too exact a steering of our way!
> Let us not fret and fear to miss our aim
> If some fair coast has lured us to make stay,
> Or some friend hail'd us to keep company!

But "man cannot, though he would, live chance's fool;" a line must be taken, limitations put upon the self to define it.

Arnold turns to work and to objectivity. He gives up his doubts, his fears, his melancholy—apparently by an act of will. But between his separation from Marguerite and the full course of his life of action there intervenes a period of profoundest melancholy. It is not the old cosmic and philosophical melancholy: it is personal and intimate. Life presents itself in an aspect more immediately depressing than ever before, and there is no grandeur in the memory of the soiled glory and the trailing wing. Not cosmological tragedy haunts him now but frustration, weariness, boredom. What emerges from "Tristram and Iseult" is not the suffering of any of its three characters but the despair of the poet himself, speaking in his own person of the conditions of human life that erode and deaden the human spirit.

> Dear saints, it is not sorrow, as I hear,
> Not suffering, that shuts up eye and ear
> To all which has delighted them before,
> And lets us be what we were once no more.
> No: we may suffer deeply, yet retain
> Power to be mov'd and sooth'd, for all our pain,
> By what of old pleas'd us, and will again.
> No: 'tis the gradual furnace of the world,
> In whose hot air our spirits are upcurl'd
> Until they crumble, or else grow like steel—
> Which kills in us the bloom, the youth, the spring—
> Which leaves the fierce necessity to feel,
> But takes away the power—this can avail,
> By drying up our joy in everything,
> To make our former pleasures all seem stale.

On all sides the rich, full life is threatened. The end of the love affair, it seems to Arnold, has brought the end of his youth and its passions; it is not peace that follows but a dead unfeelingness. He looks forward "some ten years hence" to the actual end of youth, and knows that he will then praise the heat he now condemns; the "hurrying fever" of youth will be remembered as "generous fire." In "Lines Written by a Death-Bed" (Marguerite's imagined death-bed, as Mr. Garrod believes) he regards the dead girl's calm and asks:

> Yet is a calm like this, in truth,
> The crowning end of life and youth?

And there is a fierce sense of the passing hour and a fierce desire for joy as he answers with bitter certainty:

> Ah no, the bliss youth dreams is one
> For daylight, for the cheerful sun,
> For feeling nerves and living breath—
> Youth dreams a bliss on this side death.

He is not yet the man who is to seem to so many the prophet of the "classic" and mannerly life; "calm's not life's crown, though calm is well" is his judgment now. And his dread of the passing of youth and the drying up of the emotions is no transitory thing. Fifteen years later he feels it strongly enough to republish the Death-Bed poem, revised and called "Youth and Calm." At forty-five the mood of twenty-seven and thirty has been tested and found true. And in his middle years he supplements it with "Growing Old," foretasting with the grim, fascinated realism of the later Greek writers the miseries and diminutions of old age. "What is it to grow old?" he asks—and finds no comfort in the answer, for growing old is not merely to lose power and beauty, certainly it is not to see life mellowed:

> It is to spend long days
> And not once feel that we were ever young.

It is to add, immured
In the hot prison of the present, month
To month with weary pain.

It is to suffer this,
And feel but half, and feebly, what we feel.
Deep in our hidden heart
Festers the dull remembrance of a change,
But no emotion—none.

In "Mycerinus" the theme of youth stricken down had been exploited for its cosmological implications; "Balder Dead" is less philosophical and more poignant. It laments the passing of spring and of
the gods with a more immediate and personal emotion; and "Sohrab
and Rustum" makes the same helpless plaint. The spirit of Homer—
from whom Goethe had learned what a hell this life is—broods over
the latter poem, not the Homeric energy but the pathos of the young
man doomed to an early death which is the *Iliad's* recurrent theme.

Unwillingly the spirit fled away,
Regretting the warm mansion which it left,
And youth and bloom, and this delightful world.

The famous passage follows, of the river Oxus on its course to the
sea. Flowing from its mountain heights through the lone Chorasmian
shore, a wide and melancholy waste of putrid marshes,* forgetting its
bright speed, dammed and prevented, it at last reaches the sea and
the stars, *a riveder le stelle.* The brooding pity of the famous passage
is self-pity; like the despair of "Tristram," it refers not to the lives
of the characters but to the life of the poet; Arnold himself is the
"foil'd circuitous wanderer."

However dangerous may be the practice of unraveling unconscious literary symbolism, it is almost impossible not to find throughout "Sohrab and Rustum" at least a shadowy personal significance.

* Cf. Shelley, "Alastor," l. 272.

The strong son is slain by the mightier father; and in the end Sohrab draws his father's spear from his own side to let out his life and end the anguish. We watch Arnold in his later youth and we must wonder if he is not, in a psychical sense, doing the same thing. The avid lust for life and youth, and the desire for maturity which seems to Arnold to imply giving up all that youth means, live side by side. He has been seeking the poise and equilibrium of his energies; now he begins to look for what he calls "fixity"—not quite the same thing. It is as though, acting as his own surgeon, he has tried to strengthen a weak joint by fusion and has indeed added resistant strength but at the cost of flexibility. He stood ready to sacrifice poetic talent, formed in the solitude of the self, to the creation of a character, formed in the crowding objectivity of the world.

He wants peace and health—what he called *Tüchtigkeit,* which was to be emancipation both from melancholy and from the desire for romantic violence. He wants the activity of what he called quiet work, and by consciously manipulating his personality and career he gets what he wants. The dangers of romantic melancholy had been formulated for him by a master. As far back as the summer of 1848 he had written to Clough, ". . . Do you indeed as you suggested mean to become 'one of those misanthropical hermits who are incapable of seeing that the Muse willingly *accompanies* life but that in no wise does she understand to *guide* it?'" He is translating from Goethe's essay, *"Wohlgemeinte Erwiderung,"* and *"misanthropische Eremiten"* are what the young men become when their serene company of poets is scattered and their youthful spontaneity cut off by romantic subjectivism—by "the sorrow over vanished joys, the languishing over the lost, the longing for the unknown, the unattainable." And after telling the young men of talent *"dass die Muse das Leben zwar gern begleitet, aber es keineswegs zu leiten versteht,"* Goethe goes on to say she will rather take up her abode with those who, upon their entrance into active and effective, if sometimes unhappy life, cheerfully give up their dreams, accept what each hour brings in its sea-

son, learn to assuage their own sorrows and look for opportunities to
lighten the sorrows and foster the joys of others.*

Yet when a man rummages among his various selves and creates
a character for himself by selection, how does he know that he has
made the right choice? † Men feel, as they leave youth, that they have
more or less consciously assumed a rôle by excluding some of the
once-present elements from themselves. But ever after they are
haunted by the fear that they might have selected another, better,
rôle, that perhaps they have made the wrong choice. In his acquired
Tüchtigkeit, Arnold always carried this doubt of fulfilment, this
question of a life that he—or the world—has wrongly buried. Under
the ice that has three parts covered him flows the stream of a hidden
life.

> But hardly have we, for one little hour,
> Been on our own line, have we been ourselves;
> Hardly had skill to utter one of all
> The nameless feelings that course through our breast,
> But they course on for ever unexpress'd.
> And long we try in vain to speak and act
> Our hidden self, and what we say and do
> Is eloquent, is well—but 'tis not true.

No writer of his time—except perhaps Emerson—understood in terms
as clear and straightforward as Arnold's this psychological phenomenon of the distortion of purpose and self and the assumption of a
manner to meet the world. The divorce between the reality of self
and its appearance is something the world demands. Yet still—

---

* In the Weimar edition (vol. 41. 2, pp. 375-8) Goethe's essay is called by the title
given above; in the Stuttgart edition (vol. 32, pp. 377-8) it is called *"Für junge
Dichter."* In his edition of the *Letters to Clough* (p. 84), Professor Lowry does not
identify the author from whom Arnold quotes, but I learn from him that he has since
made the identification. Goethe's essay has the additional interest of having convinced
the young Friedrich Engels that he had better give up poetry as a life work: see Franz
Mehring's *Karl Marx* (English trans., 1935), pp. 116-7.

† At some time in his youth, Arnold tells us in "A Liverpool Address"—the passage will be quoted at length in Chapter XI—he thought that he might take up medi-
cine as a career; we may conjecture that the search for objectivity led him to consider
the idea.

Yet still, from time to time, vague and forlorn,
From the soul's subterranean depth upborne
As from an infinitely distant land,
Come airs, and floating echoes, and convey
A melancholy into all our day.

Arnold left Marguerite. Were we considering the affair in factual and biographical terms, it would be absurd to say that he did himself an injury by the separation. Assuming that it was marriage that was in question, we have no ground for supposing that Marguerite was the right wife for Arnold. But treating the matter in the realm of poetry, we may say that Arnold, unhappily, was giving up an excellent part of himself. Those who believe that Marguerite was but a poetical figment and who yet want to give the figment a reality in Arnold's life might consider that she was the symbol of his youthful self—for what does he say about her that his Oxford friends did not say about him? He too was—in one part of him—a soul charmed at birth from grief and care; he too, it was said, could give light and warmth and joy but not love and tears; he too was moved by the bliss within. And this self he gave up.

Marguerite gone, the tragic world is replaced by a melancholy one. Arnold lives with a terrible sense of the loneliness of man, deepened, no doubt, by his growing estrangement from Clough. A twilight comes upon him; his personal sorrow—it is very real—deepens his sense of the dimness of the twilight of the gods. Leopardi saw melancholy as the "desire for happiness in its purest form"—joy desired so passionately and absolutely that its denial is a positive pain. Melancholy differs from the tragic sense of life in that the former is a symptom, the latter a therapy. Tragedy recognizes the defeat of virtue but the recognition is health-giving, for men have found the philosophic essence of tragedy not in the pain of the individual defeat but in its affirmation of human values. Whereas melancholy is the very opposite; at its root lies the diminution of all belief in human possibility.

Arnold shared the avid historical appetite of the 19th century which his father had helped to increase, and he looked back to find in history prototypes of the spiritual dissolution of modernity. He found them in the pessimism of Theognis, in the threnodies of Mimnermus for lost youth and diminished sense. He found them in the response of Empedocles to the intellectual conditions of his day, and in those periods of antiquity when, in the words of Professor Butcher, "poets became self-scrutinising and self-pitying" and when "the reign of reverie and melancholy" brought the perplexed twilight after "the glad surprise of morning." These meditations were to issue in a critical doctrine, and Arnold's first lecture as the Oxford Professor of Poetry undertook to consider the problem which the ages of dissolution offer to literature. The ages of melancholy, whatever their time, had for Arnold an affinity to the present; the bright morning of glad surprise was always in the past, when wits ran clear beside the sparkling Thames or when

> —some grave Tyrian trader, from the sea,
>   Descried at sunrise an emerging prow
> Lifting the cool-hair'd creepers stealthily,
>   The fringes of a southward-facing brow
>   Among the Aegean isles;
> And saw the merry Grecian coaster come,
>   Freighted with amber grapes, and Chian wine,
>   Green bursting figs, and tunnies steep'd in brine;
>   And knew the intruders on his ancient home,
> The young light-hearted Masters of the waves;
>   And snatch'd his rudder, and shook out more sail,
>   And day and night held on indignantly
> O'er the blue Midland waters with the gale,
>   Betwixt the Syrtes and soft Sicily,
>   To where the Atlantic raves
> Outside the Western Straits, and unbent sails
>   There, where down cloudy cliffs, through sheets of foam,
>   Shy traffickers, the dark Iberians come;
>   And on the beach undid his corded bales.

The charm of "The Scholar Gipsy" exemplifies the almost constant success Arnold has with the theme of controlled self-pity. As a poet,

Arnold cannot escape the impeachment of being "made;" T. S. Eliot calls him academic, which is much the same thing. Those who are moved by his effort to come to grips with important problems, to think as well as feel in verse, to transmute emotion into thought, thought into emotion, are inclined to overlook the frequent failure of the effort, the lapses into prosiness and stiff intellectuality. But there is one mood that assures Arnold the lyric gift—the mood of self-commiseration. Then the stiffness vanishes and he becomes truly a poet. In the face of the frequent strictures on Arnold's cacophony, on his insensitivity to music (attested to by his friends), he is primarily a *musical* poet. Spengler tried to give a pejorative meaning to the phrase "the musical man"—implying a decadence in the yearning, in the infinite aspiration of the music of Beethoven and Wagner. The word *decadence* means little enough, but there is a truth in the assimilation which Spengler makes of the "musical" to the "Faustian" man. The particular kind of pain and pity, the particular kind of aspiration of Arnold's poetry, expressing itself in a lovely legato so unlike the tight, crabbed movement of the bulk of his verse, is best contained in music. Chopin gives us its excess; we find its perfection in certain pieces of Mozart—in the viola quintet in G Minor; and Arnold, like Mozart, though in a less remarkable way, could set off self-pity by the knowledge of the gaiety of health, that gaiety which Stendhal, perhaps Mozart's greatest admirer, found to be one of the first of virtues; in Arnold's mind there is always the vision of the day when wits were clear beside the sparkling Thames and when the merry Grecian coaster breasted the waves.

But the mood of self-pity, set off by the knowledge of gaiety, producing the best of his poetry, is the very mood Arnold undertook to banish from himself. He refused to be of the race of Chateaubriand's René which Sainte-Beuve had scorned because it cherished and proclaimed its unhappiness. He would not be one of those of whom the earlier Samuel Butler said that they

> Find racks for their own minds, and vaunt
> Of their own misery and want.

He knows with Spinoza that melancholy is "always bad." He wants calm, resolution, cheerfulness: *"cheerfulness*—a sort of Tüchtigkeit, or natural soundness and valiancy, which I think the present age is fast losing." He blames René and Werther "and such like:" they surrendered to their melancholy and did not analyze "the modern situation in its true *blankness* and *barrenness,* and *unpoetryless-ness."* * Analysis, the action that Wordsworth and Keats and the tendency of romanticism had condemned, the typical action of the rationalists, peeping and botanizing on their mothers' graves—analysis was now to come to the help of the young man caught in the romantic melancholy. Later he was to say that the romantic poets did not know enough; now he himself turns to knowledge and reason and analysis. He reads Locke on the understanding and writes, "My respect for the reason as the rock of refuge to this poor exaggerated surexcited humanity increases and increases." The analytical reason, in the opinion of the romantics, had destroyed the imagination and the joyous life; it is now called upon to restore it. "Woe was upon me," Arnold writes, "if I analysed not my situation." Melancholy was always bad, and in 1853, the year of crystallization of great intellectual changes in Arnold, the year in which he gave his reasons for the suppression of the melancholy *Empedocles on Etna,* he writes that what the complaining millions of men want

* This perhaps disposes of the interpretation which Professor Irving Babbitt made of Arnold's experience of romantic melancholy. With Arnold's whole life a struggle to conquer melancholy, Professor Babbitt wrote: "The romantic poets enter into a veritable competition with one another as to who shall be accounted the most forlorn. The victor in this competition is awarded the palm not merely for poetry but for wisdom," and based this conclusion on the following misread lines from Arnold's "Scholar Gipsy:"

> . . . amongst us One
> Who most has suffer'd, takes dejectedly
> His seat upon the intellectual throne;
> And all his store of sad experience he
> Lays bare of wretched days.

Dr. Chilson Leonard has shown, in *Modern Language Notes,* Feb. 1931, that Arnold intended this to mean Goethe.

"is something to *animate* and *ennoble* them—not merely to add zest to their melancholy or grace to their dreams." He continues, "I believe a feeling of this kind is the basis of my nature—and of my poetics."

Yet only in a limited sense is Arnold's judgment of his poetry true; the best of his poetry is exactly an abandonment to melancholy. Arnold did indeed go forward to *Tüchtigkeit*. But as he progressed, he left poetry behind.

Chapter Five

※》》 《《※

THE WORLD RESTORED

*. . . paus'd
Betwixt the world destroy'd and world restor'd
. . . .
Then with transition sweet new speech resumes.*
                                        —MILTON

THE rough-and-ready critics of the reviews were irritated by the matter of Arnold's poetry; they were frankly puzzled by its manner. "Tristram," they said, was harder to understand than Kant and "Tristram" is, for us, scarcely a difficult poem. Their confusion should remind us of the fact which time and fashion have obscured: that Arnold was trying to do something new with the technique of poetry. The reviewers saw traces of Elizabeth Barrett Browning in his manner—led to this perception, perhaps, by the Greek subjects, by the strongly marked rhythms of "Stagyrus," or, more likely, by the subject and treatment of the very bad dramatic monologue, "A Modern Sappho;" they also remarked upon the influence of Tennyson, and Arnold admitted a little ruefully that they were right.* But beyond this they saw that Arnold was trying to do something quite his own, although they were not quite

---

* In a letter to John Duke Coleridge, after admitting that "Sohrab and Rustum" contained conscious imitations of Milton's manner, Arnold says: "Tennyson is another thing; but one has him so in one's head, one cannot help imitating him sometimes: but except in the last two lines I thought I had kept him out of 'Sohrab and Rustum.' Mark any other places you notice, for I should wish to alter such." It was *after* receiving this admission from Arnold that Coleridge reviewed Arnold in *The Christian Remembrancer* and took him severely to task for imitations of Tennyson; Stanley said it was rather like seething the kid in its mother's milk.—*Life and Correspondence of J. D. Coleridge,* vol. i, pp. 210–11.

sure what it was except that it seemed rather "Greek" in manner and metric.

Greek Arnold intended it to be, but more than Greek. "Who of us has not dreamed, in moments of ambition," Baudelaire wrote, "of the miracle of a poetic prose, musical without rhythm and without rhymes, subtle and staccato enough to follow the lyric motions of the soul, the wavering outlines of meditation, the sudden starts of the conscience?" It is this—though in verse and without abandoning rhyme, yet with a tendency toward prose—that Arnold's poetry in large part attained.

D. H. Lawrence makes an interesting distinction between what he calls the poetry of the past and future and the poetry of the present. The poetry of the past and future is crystallized, it has the perfection of vanished things or of things to come. The poetry of the present lacks this crystallized perfection and seeks to catch the moment in all its confusion; it is what Lawrence called "plasmic." Arnold could achieve the lovely crystallization; it is what he desired most and when he gets it he is most the poet. When he does not achieve it, however, he has not necessarily failed; he produces another kind of poetry—less ingratiating, perhaps, but having its own standard of failure and success. More than most poets, Arnold had the sense of the present in its passage, of time as it flows away, of "modernity" and the peculiarity of his own age, and his very failures and gaucheries serve to express his sense of speaking to the moment.

R. H. Hutton used an apt phrase of certain of Arnold's poems whose unrhymed, loosely-cadenced verse was modeled after Goethe's *"Grenzen der Menschheit;"* he called them "poems of recitative," and though Hutton meant his phrase to apply only to poems like "Haworth Churchyard," "Memorial Verses" and "Rugby Chapel," it may be extended to much more of Arnold's poetry.* For

* Arnold is sometimes spoken of as one of the harbingers of English free verse— Amy Lowell spoke of him so—but the tradition of freely-cadenced, unrhymed forms is so steady in English poetry that it cannot be right especially to distinguish Arnold in this respect. There is a good account of the tradition in *An Introduction to Poetry* (Revised Edition, 1936) by Jay B. Hubbell and John O. Beaty. Perhaps, even more

Arnold breaks into melody only occasionally, but through all his verse runs the grave cadence of the *speaking* voice. Its halt and stammer may be what make us feel that Arnold is only occasionally a complete poet, or rather, that he is usually a poet not so much by grace as by good works. Yet his very colloquialism (not so much of vocabulary as of tone) is one of Arnold's charms; it is the urbanity of the ancient poets (and of Wordsworth, too, and Coleridge) which assumes the presence of a hearer and addresses him—with a resultant intimacy and simplicity of manner that is often very moving.

But to Arnold's admiration of the Greek poetic language must be charged much of the awkwardness of his verse and much of its coldness. He is too willing to make the naked statement which causes so much classic poetry to read unmagically in translation. The flash of color is largely lacking from the post-Homeric Greeks and almost wholly lacking from Arnold. Lafcadio Hearn speaks of Arnold's poems as "colorless" and, in a literal sense, he is right, especially if one refuses to accept as "color" certain warm and changing grays which the poems suggest. Miss Edith Sitwell dismisses Arnold as "an educated versifier" because he had no sense of touch and Miss Sitwell's observation is accurate, though her epithet implies a somewhat limited notion of poetry. Arnold does indeed avoid all the devices which give color and tactility—the dazzling epithet and the rich metaphor which the Elizabethans and their modern followers loved. Sometimes, though rarely, he achieves a plastic effect without them, as in "The Strayed Reveller," which contains not a single trope and is yet full of delicately-realized objects. All this is simply to say that Arnold's most effective devices are musical; his affinities in English are the sonnets of Milton and Wordsworth whose finest lines so often defy technical analysis, made up as they are of the subtlest vocal pauses, accelerations and crescendoes.

Arnold's reliance on the impact of the word itself (which seemed to mean more to him than to most: hence, perhaps, his later reliance

---

than Goethe, the model Arnold had in mind for his free forms was Milton in the choruses of *Samson Agonistes*.

on the *magical* power of his critical formulas*) too often turns what he intends for cool chasteness into a spinsterish lack of charm. We may take the hint from Edmund Wilson's essay on Pushkin and say that Arnold, in his preoccupation with the classical vocabulary, ignored its relation to the classical syntax: he lacked, on the whole, the epigrammatic juxtaposition which highly inflected languages easily produce and which corresponds in effect to English figures of speech.†

With Arnold's plainness of diction goes a versification which is often uneuphonious. Much has been made of Arnold's lack of a fine ear though not with entire justice. Arnold could, if he would, do the kind of thing which usually gives a poet the cachet of aural sensitivity: "Stagyrus," with its meter of a kind later to be called Swinburnian, may be taken in evidence. His verse does not always "please," but we know that not to "please" is no fault of music, that iron harmonies are no less harmonies and that dissonance has its value. The Victorians, with Keats and Tennyson in mind, liked to watch for the soft intertwining of vowels and liquid consonants. But what slips easily off the tongue may slip easily from the mind, and the soft liquidity could not represent the struggle with the world and the self—as Tennyson himself knew when he invented the clangorous and uningratiating stanza of *In Memoriam,* surely his finest poem. But the point need not be pressed for a literary generation which is inclined to find an affinity to the harsher poets—to Donne, who revolted against the golden singers of his age and who

---

* Professor Lowry says illuminatingly: "Arnold was used to putting quotations in his notebooks and reflecting on them repeatedly. This habit made him attach to certain phrases overtones and connotations that escape his reader, who sees these same phrases time and again in his essays."—*Letters to Clough,* p. 44.

† ". . . The Russian language, which is highly inflected and able to dispense with pronouns and prepositions in many cases where we have to use them and which does without the article altogether, makes it possible for Pushkin to pack his lines (separating modifiers from substantives, if need be) in a way which renders the problem of translating him closer to that of translating a tightly articulated Latin poet like Horace than any modern poet that we know. Such a poet in translation may sound trivial just as many of the translations of Horace sound trivial—because the weight of the words and the force of their relation have been lost with the inflections and the syntax."—Edmund Wilson, *The Triple Thinkers* (1938), pp. 44–45.

"wreathe[d] iron pokers into true-love knots," to Hopkins, to Skelton and the early alliterative poets. Often enough, to be sure, Arnold's lines are intolerable to say by any standard. Yet even such lines as "Germany, France, Christ, Moses, Athens, Rome," or "Who prop, thou ask'st, in these bad days, my mind?" clumsy as they are, are merely the ill-advised exaggeration of his attempts to exploit the clangor of English, just as Tennyson's "mellow ouzel fluting in the elm" is the exaggeration of its murmur.

The periodical critics saw the influence of Tennyson and Mrs. Browning; they did not see the touches of Goethe, of André Chénier, of Dryden, of Milton, perhaps of Herbert. And their confusion about the form intensified their confused irritation at the matter of Arnold's poetry. This is scarcely surprising. What is surprising, however, is the blindness of one critic—Clough.

It is difficult not to feel that the criticism which Clough wrote for the *North American Review* of July, 1853, reflects the friendly but profound quarrel that had long been in progress between him and Arnold. For through Clough's Emersonian-Carlylean prose runs an acidulous current. He is attacking the whole structure of Arnold's mind and his method is to compare his friend's poems with *A Life Drama* by one Alexander Smith. Of Smith, Arnold had written to Clough two months before: "As to Alexander Smith I have not read him. . . . I think the extracts I have seen most remarkable—and I think at the same time that he will not go far. I have not room or time for my reasons—but I think so." To Arnold, Clough's comparison, from which Smith emerged the victor, must have been significant and distressing—even insulting.

Alexander Smith, now unknown * but very popular in his day, received part of his acclaim on the ground of being a poet of the people. He had been a mechanic and this seems to have induced Citizen Clough to read into his pretentious work a democratic sig-

---

* His *Dreamthorp*, however, was republished in 1914 with an introduction by Hugh Walker (*World's Classics*: Oxford University Press).

nificance which was simply not there. Actually, no one could have been of higher degree or greater elegance than the characters of *A Life Drama;* even *The Princess* was no more cozily swaddled in romantic aristocracy. Yet Clough saw in this tale a poetic departure, a realism of everyday life, a "something substantive and lifelike," something which, because it drew its imagery from the "busy seats of industry," coped with the new and ugly civilization in a way that no poem could do which sprang from "Pindus or Parnassus, or by the side of any Castaly."

For Clough, Smith's poetry and Arnold's represent opposed responses to life and he must choose between them. Arnold's poems are in the tendency of intellection and doubt. Smith's story, with its theme of the poet's fierce desire for fame, and its febrile (and, though Clough did not see it, puerile) energy, represents the tendency of courage and accomplishment. Clough chooses Smith because not only Smith's philosophy but his expression of it make him a better guide than Arnold:

Individuals differ in character, capacity, and positions; and, according to their circumstances, will combine, in every possible variety of degree, the two elements of thoughtful discriminating selection and rejection, and frank and bold acceptance of what lies around them. Between the extremes of ascetic and timid self-culture and of unquestioning, unhesitating confidence, we may consent to see and tolerate every kind and gradation of intermixture. Nevertheless, upon the whole, for the present age, the lessons of reflectiveness and the maxims of caution do not appear to be more needful or more appropriate than exhortations to steady courage and calls to action. There is something certainly of an overeducated weakness of purpose in Western Europe—not in Germany only, or France, but also in more busy England. There is a disposition to press too far the finer and subtler intellectual and moral susceptibilities; to insist upon following out, as they say, to their logical consequences, the notices of some organ of the spiritual nature; a proceeding which perhaps is hardly more sensible in the grown man than it would be in the infant to refuse to correct the sensations of sight by those of touch. Upon the whole, we are disposed to follow out, if we must follow out at all, the analogy of the bodily senses; we are inclined to accept rather than investigate; and to put our confidence less in arithmetic and antinomies than in

"A few strong instincts and a few plain rules."

Clough, it would seem, has indeed taken his "assiette." He has turned the tables on his friend: now *he* is the solid, *tüchtig* soul and Arnold the shifting and doubtful. But for us Clough cannot have the better of it: Arnold is groping in the dark of modern Europe and the admired Smith is being courageous in a trivial world of his own contriving. We may guess that Clough's personal weariness and frustration at this time, his desire for success and recognition, led him to interpret Smith's own lust for fame and self-assertion as the energy for social reform and blinded him to the fact of Smith's affinity with the brash assurance of commercial and industrial expansion.

Arnold's letter had not said why he dismissed Smith but his reasons became apparent some months later—in the Preface to the 1853 edition of his poems, which explains the withdrawal of the 1852 volume and the omission of "Empedocles on Etna" from the new publication. The Preface of October is, in effect, an answer to Clough's review of July. But if it dismisses the kind of poetry that Clough had praised, it does not offer a defense of Arnold's own. Indeed, Arnold's first public critical act is the rejection of his most ambitious single work; few critics have given such earnest of their disinterestedness or acquired a better right to be absolute with their contemporaries.

"A true allegory of the state of one's own mind in a representative history is perhaps the highest thing that one can attempt in the way of poetry"—it is in this sentence from a contemporary critic that Arnold finds the whole tendency of modern poetry against which he is taking his stand. Keats had helped to establish this poetic credo; Browning was exemplifying it; it was the very essence of Alexander Smith and of his confrères of the Spasmodic school.

It is not very clear just what the Spasmodic school was; in fact, it may be doubted if there was rightly such a "school" at all. But since W. E. Aytoun is commonly said to have killed it with his parody, *Firmilian: A "Spasmodic" Tragedy,* we must grant its former existence. It seems to have consisted almost entirely of Smith, Sidney Dobell and John Stanyan Bigg though Philip James Bailey, of the famous *Festus,* is often counted in the group despite the fact that his characteristic work came much earlier. As laid down by "T. Percy Jones," the putative author of *Firmilian,* the Spasmodic principle was a simple one: "The office of poetry is to exhibit the passions in that state of excitement which distinguishes one from the other." "Passion," indeed, was all; bombast, formlessness, the straining of metaphorical language to its limit were the result of this preoccupation.

The very great popularity of the Spasmodics may be accounted for easily enough: they were intense yet pious; they made a fine show of rushing out to meet the problems of modern life but their endowment was limited enough to keep them safe and platitudinous. Their "modern" qualities may be observed in Browning—in his free, even slovenly, treatment, his intimate manner, his psychologizing, his realism and—above all—his multitudinousness; indeed, Browning might not unjustly be called a Spasmodic poet who managed to be good. The smaller men, without Browning's genius or intellect, evolved a kind of respectable Satanism, a romanticism of the chapel. Members of the dissenting lower or middle classes, they combined what Newman called "a sort of methodistic self-contemplation" with the dregs of romantic passion and produced something which passed for a reflection of the confused, Faustian mind of contemporary Europe. Their chief literary device was an Elizabethan violence of imagery; even Clough must temper his praise of Smith by trying to correct the young man's belief that "the one business of the poet is to coin metaphors and similes." The Spasmodics saw something of the complexity of modern life, but saw it without a coherent idea and responded to multitudinousness with the multitudinousness of a literary method which paid more attention to parts than to their integration.

Arnold felt that, in a very real sense, his "Empedocles" had shared this confusion of the Spasmodics. His own response to modernity had been as unsatisfactory as theirs. He had expressed the modern dubiety and discomfort and perhaps by the expression of these emotions had done something to relieve them. But perhaps, too, he had merely confirmed them; perhaps he had only reiterated the confusion of the methodistic self-contemplation.

The Preface, then, is a renunciation of subjectivity. It brings us back yet again to the theme of Joy. "All Art," Arnold quotes from Schiller, "is dedicated to Joy;" "Empedocles" had been unable to give Joy, hence its suppression. The poem may have been timely, for the age of Empedocles, bringing, as it did, the breakdown of an ancient synthesis and the "dialogue of the mind with itself," is in many ways the prototype of the 19th century. Too, the poem, as representation of a modern state of mind, may be accurate. Neither its timeliness nor its accuracy answers the question, Is the subject a good one?

To that question Arnold's own answer is absolute: his story of Empedocles is not a good subject because it cannot give Joy. Not because it is sad, for it is the strange power of art that it can give Joy through sadness—indeed, "the more tragic the situation, the deeper becomes the enjoyment; and the situation is more tragic in proportion as it becomes more terrible." But there is a kind of situation which, though terrible, cannot give Joy—the situation in which "a continuous state of mental distress is prolonged, unrelieved by incident, hope, or resistance; in which there is everything to be endured, nothing to be done." A situation such as this is inevitably morbid, finding no vent in *action*. Human action is and always has been the material of true poetry; in Empedocles there is suffering but no relief in doing.

Relevance and accuracy, in short, are not enough to justify a work; it must be judged by its psychological and moral effect on the whole personality of the reader. Looking for a psychological therapeutic, Arnold finds it in the stability or poise of the faculties which follows upon the *catharsis* Aristotle had described, the quieting of the mind in equilibrium, not the bald presentation of confusion itself. Nothing can assure that eventual equilibrium save action, for by action all the confusions of the emotions are cleared. Goethe spoke of the splenetic nature of men whose lives are embittered by "want of action;" Arnold understood the malady. His theory of poetry is a theory for mental health. And concern with the psychotherapy of action in poetry must lead inevitably to a new consideration of style and form. In order to present the necessary action, a work must be subordinated to the mechanics of making clear the events in the most efficient way. No incident or detail may lure the poet from his chief concern, nor may rhetoric and brilliancy charm him to forget his single intention. The kind of play which Shakespeare wrote is admirable not because, but in spite of, its confusion and curiosity of expression. It is only the Aristotelean psychology, if not the Aristotelean poetic principles, which will, Arnold feels, produce an art of the highest usefulness.

That literature must be *useful* is, of course, the constant demand of the periodical critics: "What does it *do,* all this pure and brilliant imagination?" as *Fraser's* reviewer had asked about Arnold himself. The demand for usefulness, properly stated, is one no sensible man may refuse. Arnold thinks it is being most improperly stated in England at a time when criticism is at a low ebb and the anti-artistic philosophy of dissenting religion and of a less sensitized utilitarianism than John Stuart Mill's is having its way with the intellect. Ironically enough, could the magazine reviewers have but seen it, "Empedocles" fulfilled their own requirements for a significant poem; aside from the negativism which brought their censure, it was perfectly "modern" and it was "an allegory of the true state of one's mind in a representative history." But Arnold, agreeing that poetry must be useful, has a very different conception of usefulness and is quite certain his own poem does not satisfy its requirements.

What exactly must a poem do to be truly useful? Arnold's answer is unequivocal; he speaks of the effect that the ancient writers have upon their readers:

—a steadying and composing effect upon their judgment, not of literary works only, but of men and events in general. [Readers of ancient literature] are like persons who have had a very weighty and impressive experience: they are more truly than others under the empire of facts, and more independent of the language current among those with whom they live. They wish neither to applaud nor to revile their age: they wish to know what it is, what it can give them, and whether this is what they want. What they want, they know very well; they want to educe and cultivate what is best and noblest in themselves: they know, too, that this is no easy task . . . and they ask themselves sincerely whether their age and its literature can assist them in the attempt. . . . They do not talk of their mission, nor of interpreting their age, nor of the coming Poet; all this, they know, is the mere delirium of vanity; [as writers] their business is not to praise their age, but to afford to the men who live in it the highest pleasure which they are capable of feeling. If asked to afford this by means of subjects drawn from the age itself, they ask what special fitness the present age has for supplying them: they are told that it is an era of progress, an age commissioned to carry out the great ideas of industrial development and social amelioration. They reply that with all this they can do nothing; that the elements they need for the exercise of their art are great actions, calculated powerfully and delightfully to affect what is permanent in the human soul; that so far as the present age can supply such actions, they will gladly make use of them; but that an age wanting in moral grandeur can with difficulty supply such, and an age of spiritual discomfort with difficulty be powerfully and delightfully affected by them.

With our own modern feelings about literature, we might conclude that Arnold's Preface proceeds from the ivory tower; quite the contrary, it is a theory which recognizes the conditions of modern life and is directed toward them. It is not to the purpose to call it an "aristocratic" theory because it seeks self-cultivation—though it is perhaps "aristocratic" in contrast with the bourgeois demand that art be immediately "useful" in settling problems. It implies that true art can settle no questions, give no directives; that it can do no more than cultivate what is best in the reader—his moral poise. If a name must be attached to it, we may call it a religious theory of art, for like certain aspects of religion, it offers to help meet current life by giving man a refuge in the contemplation of nobility; it undertakes to provide a mood which does not pretend to spring from the ruck of living. It is not, however, an "escape" from life; it seeks to send men back into daily living with spirits restored.

Arnold's basic insight is a sound one—that the most invigorating literature is that which *resolves* itself, and that action is the best means of resolution.* Only so is Aristotle's tragic *catharsis* secured and the tragic *catharsis* is still the fullest literary emotion. The tragic *catharsis*, however, even if it be the richest, is not the only literary emotion, nor the only one that gives Joy. Arnold, reiterating the Aristotelean poetic, betrays the Aristotelean method, for where Aristotle is inductive, discovering psychological principles in the study of literature, Arnold argues *a priori*, discovering principles of literature in his conceptions of psychology. When the reader himself turns to experience he is very likely to refute Arnold's conclusions. Perhaps "Empedocles" itself gave him Joy. The suffering of its hero may conceivably have brought relief to the reader's own moments of philosophic despair, naming and ordering his own incoherent emotions, taking them beyond the special misery of privacy. "Nothing has comforted and helped me more," said Gamaliel Bradford, not a great critic but a man who was forced to rely, more than most of us, on the consolations of literature, "than the most pessimistic of writers, Senancour and Leopardi and the poetry of Arnold." For there is a *catharsis* of expression, formulation and understanding as well as of action. Too, if the suicide of Empedocles does not constitute

---

* It should be remembered that Arnold was not talking about lyric poetry, as he pointed out in the Advertisement to the Second Edition of the poems (1854). His Preface, he says, leaves "untouched the question, how far, and in what manner, the opinions there expressed respecting the choice of subjects apply to lyric poetry; that region of the poetical field which is chiefly cultivated at present." This invalidates the implied charge of E. E. Sikes, in his *Greek View of Poetry* (1931), that Arnold said that human action was the proper subject for *all* poetry (p. 100).

the resolution of action itself—and it might be argued against Arnold that it does—it at least constitutes the resolution of *logic*.

In short, the human mind is far more complex than Arnold allows in his Preface, and finds its literary therapy in more ways than Arnold admits. From *Faust* through *In Memoriam* to *The Wasteland* and *Remembrance of Things Past* a multitude of modern European books, based on the dialogue of the mind with itself, repudiating deeds, have been illuminating and health-giving. We read to live but we do not live only by the literature of resolution. The many ways in which literature can help us to live and the many ways it can clarify us are brilliantly suggested by E. M. Forster, who tells how, during the madness of the War, he found sanity in—of all books—Huysmans' *A Rebours*!

Oh, the relief of a world which lived for its sensations and ignored the will—the world of des Esseintes! Was it decadent? Yes, and thank God. Yes; here again was a human being who had time to feel and experiment with his feelings, to taste and smell and arrange books and fabricate flowers, and be selfish and himself. The waves of edifying bilge rolled off me, the newspapers ebbed. . . .

But Arnold saw "Empedocles" as a traitor to the position Arnold himself had taken in the cultural battle between the ideal of methodistic self-contemplation and the ideal which lay in "a lofty sense of the mastery of the human spirit over its own stormiest agitations," in the *"sentiment of sublime acquiescence in the course of fate,"* which it is the highest aim of tragedy to produce. The romantic ideal had become so dominant—and debased—in English culture that Arnold could complain that "the Athenians fined Phrynichus for representing to them their own sufferings: there are critics who would fine us for representing to them anything else." The traitorous "Empedocles" withdrawn, the high command of Arnold's criticism sent *Merope* (1858) as replacement at the breach. Its classical form and non-personal subject were intended to remind the readers of England that there is a dignity of emotion beyond that of self-pity.

Had Arnold been content with a purely critical maneuver he would have done far worse execution upon the excesses of the romantic ideal, for the preface to *Merope* is most persuasive as it considers the advantages of the classical dramatic form; *Merope* itself is not a compelling example. The preface, beginning with the physical arrangement of the earliest Greek stage, shows how, as the Greek theater developed, it dictated the style of its drama, demanding broad and simple effects, a minimum of shades of tone or gesture, unity, and the balanced symmetry of poetic masses—in short, "distinctness and depth of impression." This technical method produced a mold in which the most violent emotions were firmly contained and the great aesthetic and philosophical achievement of Greek drama is the tension of perfect equivalence between the force of the emotion and the strictness of the restraint. "Sophocles does not produce the sentiment of repose, of acquiescence, by inculcating it, by avoiding agitating circumstances: he produces it by exhibiting to us the most agitating matter under conditions of the severest form."

But it is exactly here that *Merope's* utter failure lies. Its matter is not "the most agitating." It has neither philosophical nor emotional weight. Indeed, so largely does the fable hang upon a mother's failure to recognize a long-absent son that it is almost trivial, and so largely does its climax depend on the mother's just-prevented murder of the youth that it approaches the melodrama of the buzz-saw. Despite the sanction of Euripides, Maffei, Voltaire and Alfieri, despite Aristotle and Lessing, the story of *Merope* is one of incident merely, and of rather pointless incident at that. From so inferior a fable no profound emotion can issue; inevitably, after admiring Arnold's exposition of severest form, one recalls Roy Campbell's couplet:

> They use the bridle and the bit, all right,
> But where's the bloody horse?

One cannot make a school-horse into a stallion by bridle and bit; the attempt is bound to be ridiculous, as *Merope* is ridiculous with its paraphernalia of classical tragedy—the long and complicated genealogical history of which the audience presumably only needs to be reminded by carefully casual references, but which, in this case, it could know only by memorizing the author's long synopsis; the plunge *in medias res;* the disguised returning hero; the recognition after the usual difficulty; the gnomic chorus; the tirade, canonically relieved by stychomythia. All this is contained in verse which is the least attractive Arnold ever wrote, wooden in the dialogue, harsh in the choruses and—paradoxically in this setting of "sanity"—for the first time eccentric. Nor are the characters more distinguished than their speech. The villain, Polyphontes (whom Arnold rather cherished), is drawn with a mechanical "understanding," a little of light and a little of dark, and all the people act with the chaste decorum which, it is commonly believed, marks the characters of Greek tragedy. Indeed, the decorum proved a little too much for one decorous reviewer: he is summarizing the plot and he comes to the incident of Merope about to murder a young man with an axe; she is stopped by the sudden cry, "Thy son!" and she drops her weapon and cries "Ah!" Worlds of inarticulate horror are intended by the cry, but the reviewer cannot forbear explaining in a footnote, "She was an Oxford woman."

The cause of the *Merope* fiasco does not lie in its philosophic intention, which is sound; nor does it lie wholly in its execution, unsuccessful as that is. It lies rather in Arnold's failure to see that the subjectivism in romantic poetry had its roots in historical reality, that it could not be dismissed by turning away from it to its seeming opposite, "classical" objectivity. What was logically indicated to Arnold by his desire to minimize the romantic mood was the comprehension of that mood itself in a severe form and in action. The synthesis of romanticism with the objective drama of action cried out to be made and was not made until Ibsen. Arnold does little more than direct our *taste* from the romantic to the classic; the problem goes beyond mere taste.

Ion of Chios said that virtue, like a poet's group of plays, should have one part of the satyric element to three of the tragic. It is the satyric element which is perhaps lacking in Arnold's life now; perhaps the man who cannot plan to conclude his dramatic group with a satyr play cannot write tragedy. Now Arnold sees only the advantages of order, not the volcanic disruptive forces in life to which order refers. "I think and hope," he wrote of *Merope,* "it will have what Buddha called the 'character of *Fixity,* that true sign of the Law.' " Perhaps no poet ever hoped a more inauspicious thing for his work. *Merope* has Fixity; it is as firm-fixed as a letter-box and as firmly rooted in the Law: it is but little more interesting. In 1857 Arnold, assisted by the vote of his godfather Keble, was elected Professor of Poetry at Oxford. "[*Merope*] is calculated . . . to inaugurate my Professorship with dignity," he wrote, apparently intent on blighting his own child in every possible way.

"It means shipwreck for a poet to turn critic," said Sainte-Beuve. Yet most poets, if they are critics, do not *turn* critics; they are critics and the best of critics; Sainte-Beuve was rationalizing his own failure as a poet by means of his critical success. But Sainte-Beuve has a truer description of the relation of the poetic and critical talents in those in whom the poetic seed is but lightly rooted:

In youth [criticism] hides under art, under poetry, or, if masquerading by itself, poetry and exaltation are intermingled with it and trouble it. It is only when poetry gets a little dissipated and enlightened that the second phase is truly disclosed and that criticism slips in and infiltrates itself from all sides into the talent. Sometimes it is limited to tempering the talent, oftener it transforms it and makes it different. . . . At the bottom of most talents lurks a makeshift which is honorable enough, if not despised and if regarded as a sort of progress. To this evolution we must, sooner or later, submit, whether we will or no; and criticism in the long run falls heir to our other more stately or more naïve qualities, to our errors, our fondled successes, our reverses rightly interpreted.

Arnold's criticism fell heir to his poetry's more stately qualities. Between 1858, the year of *Merope,* and 1867, the year of the publication of his last volume of verse, *New Poems,* Arnold published but three pieces, of which the only remarkable one is the great

"Thyrsis." This last volume contains the whole poetic production of the decade; some of it is admirable, all of it is interesting. But the smallness of the volume is significant, its content is chiefly critical, not lyrical, and the poet, knowing that the Muse has gone away, knows too that he is harping on what he had heard years before.

Was the change of Arnold's direction his own choice? Aldous Huxley believes that Arnold accepted the post of inspector of schools, which Lord Lansdowne had procured for him in 1852, as a kind of philosophical action. He knew the work would be a burden, dull, irksome, time-consuming; and for some time after he undertook it he disclaimed all active interest in it. He wanted to marry now and he needed an income. He did his job and did it well, but it hastened his poetic end for, as he said, to "attain or approach perfection in the region of thought and feeling, and to unite this with perfection of form, demands not merely an effort and a labour, but an actual tearing of oneself to pieces, which one does not readily consent to (although one is sometimes forced to it) unless one can devote one's whole life to poetry." To be a poet in the intervals of a routine job is well-nigh impossible. Yet work—routine work—is one of the "ways" of the Bhagavad Gita, an alternative to contemplation and an escape from despair.

II

In the autumn of 1857, Arnold, at his inaugural as Professor of Poetry at Oxford, spoke to a full hall of the "modern" element in literature and undertook to account for the fact that, though Aristophanes and Menander had been equally esteemed by antiquity, the works of Aristophanes had been preserved, while those of Menander had been allowed to disappear. He explained this by saying that humanity, with its inevitable desire to live and develop itself, clings to a literature which exhibits it in vigor but abandons a literature which exhibits it in decline. Aristophanes treated Greek society in its prime but Menander wrote after the failure of Athens in the Peloponnesian War; "the free expansion of her growth was checked," Arnold said; "one of the noblest channels of Athenian life, that of political activity, had begun to narrow and to dry up. . . . From that date the intellectual and spiritual life of Greece was left without an adequate material basis of political and practical life."

However questionable this may be as an explanation of the disappearance of Menander's comedies, it indicates perfectly the method of literary criticism which Arnold will employ throughout his career. The search for affirmation has brought him to the definite and the actual—to society in its ever-changing forms. He begins at once to think of the social and political determination of literature and the need for social and political reorganization. Behind every critical judgment of literature that Arnold will henceforth make lies a social and political judgment. His theory of style, we have already seen, was actually a theory of morality; this is to become increasingly explicit. His poetry had probed the spiritual lacks of modern life; his critical effort undertakes to help the growth of a life molded to a nobler style.

The author of the poems had almost always been passive; his utmost activity had been the erection of defensive attitudes against the slings and arrows of the new era which History had brought. Now the passivity vanishes. History still brings change—how or why Arnold does not attempt to say. All he is sure of is that the spirit of man, unknown to himself, is shifted and veered, that old forms of society vanish and that new ones arise, that the cadence of living changes, that fresh needs of the mind develop and must be satisfied. But he now sees, apart from this unconscious movement, the possibility of a conscious activity on the part of people to control the almost blind tendency of History. If an historical tendency be really the dominant one of an age, social groups that oppose it will be swept away; those that go along with it may modify and aid it and themselves eventually become ascendant.

To discover and define, then, the dominant tendency of his age, to analyze the good from the bad, foster the good, diminish the bad—this will be Arnold's program of criticism. Its keynote is activism and affirmation: objectivity, in short. The Preface of 1853 stated in literary terms the psychological and personal need for objectivity; that is not sufficient. Arnold sees now that he must move beyond individual psychology to what so largely determines the quality of the mind itself—to society. He sees that if the individual is to rescue himself from the toils of *ennui* he must indeed make the personal effort to grasp *Tüchtigkeit* but he also sees that society aids the individual with an opportunity for affirmation, just as the individual, if he is to live harmoniously, must advance society toward the condition in which it will give him health and sustenance. We have said that Arnold's acceptance from Lord Lansdowne of the school inspectorship was not wholly dictated by financial necessity but was, in part, a philosophic gesture; he was taking the advice of the *Blackwood* reviewer: to find the peace he needed he had to make a *practical* effort to substitute objectivity for subjectivity.

Through nearly a decade almost all of Arnold's critical work came from Oxford, in the brief intervals of escape from his Education Office routine. He could have no more gratifying pulpit, he felt, for Oxford was grown from the national organism. If many liberals might see the university as merely vestigial, Arnold saw it as vital and important. To speak as an Oxford professor gave him a special right to speak of the nation's mind and soul. And when he spoke of poetry he spoke of the nation that makes poetry, of the poetry that makes a nation.

Arnold's incumbency of the chair of poetry was revolutionary. Not, to be sure, that innovations as great as his were needed to constitute a revolution at Oxford. He might have been a radical merely by lecturing frequently, for nothing could have been more otiose than the poetry professorship through its history of a century and a half; Arnold's predecessor, Claughton, had been entirely inactive and, with the exception of Keble's lectures, the professorship had pro-

duced scarcely a single work of importance.* But even Keble, like all
the other incumbents when they lectured and published at all, had
lectured and published in Latin, and certainly none of the chair-
pieces (to use Saintsbury's phrase) had ever acknowledged modernity. Arnold destroyed this deadly tradition. He requested and received permission to lecture in English; he spoke not of rhetoric,
imagination, taste, but of a modern age "copious and complex," of
the "vast multitude of facts awaiting and inviting . . . comprehension," and of the task that faced poetry to comprehend this complexity. He spoke of the demand which humanity makes for a
poetry *adequate* to the time in which it is written.

Perhaps never before had *adequacy* been demanded so explicitly
of literature. Adequacy was asked of philosophy; if literature had
given it, criticism had seldom demanded or defined it. Aristotle, it is
true, spoke of a kind of psychological adequacy; the German romantics with Carlyle in their train raised art to new heights of philosophic
and religious importance. No one had said as sharply as Arnold
what literature must be and do.

Arnold spoke of a world confused and hostile and demanded that
poetry give men an "intellectual deliverance" from its oppressiveness.
That deliverance, he says, is perfect, "when we have acquired that
harmonious acquiescence of mind which we feel in contemplating a
grand spectacle that is intelligible to us; when we have lost that impatient irritation of mind which we feel in presence of an immense,
moving, confused spectacle which, while it perpetually excites our
curiosity, perpetually baffles our comprehension." Only literature
which orders the world for us in this way is *adequate*. There is, says
Arnold, a particular factor in the modern world which makes an
intellectual deliverance of first importance and that factor is democracy. For the first premise of democracy, as of Puritanism, is that
each individual has the capability—actual or potential—of inter-

---

* Copleston is perhaps notable for his satire, *Advice to a Young Reviewer,* but this,
of course, had not been delivered from the chair. Conybeare is distinguished for
having given impetus to Anglo-Saxon scholarship.

preting the world for himself and of choosing his own course. Democracy is based on the intellect; it can progress only by the intellect, by the circulation of sound ideas so clear and distinct as to win general agreement.

In 1859 Arnold was to enter directly into a discussion of politics in a pamphlet, *England and the Italian Question*. The "Italian question" had temporarily been settled by the hostile indifference of the Derby ministry toward Louis Napoleon's plan to drive the Austrians from Italy and to establish throughout the whole peninsula a federation of free states, governed by a liberal Pope and dependent on France for protection. It was a purely political scheme to establish the power of France on the Continent, but Louis Napoleon, with his talent for allowing liberalism to take him where he wanted to go, had rallied the liberal forces of France by representing his plan as an issue of nationalism and democracy against clericalism and tyranny. Napoleon's scheme failed; he was forced to conclude the not very advantageous peace of Villafranca which, though it freed Milan, left the rest of Italy under the old Austrian rule. No small factor in his frustration was the aloofness of England. Arnold's pamphlet was a rebuke to the opinion that had determined English policy.

Not quarreling with the policy itself—for he feels that Italian freedom should be a prize of Italian effort, not a gift from the French, and he agrees that Louis Napoleon must not be too strong on the Continent—Arnold nevertheless believes that the philosophy behind the Derby policy produced the right result for the wrong reasons. Essentially, he feels, it is the philosophy of an aristocratic administrative class unable to understand that Louis Napoleon is the exponent of rising democratic opinion in France. Louis Napoleon's attempted liberation of Italy is not to be interpreted as a war of conquest: to believe that is to misunderstand modern France which is distinguished from all other nations by the fact that "the mass of her population is so accessible to considerations of an elevated order. It is the bright feature of her civilisation that her common people can understand and appreciate a language which elsewhere

meets with response only from the educated and refined classes."
The desire to liberate Italy springs not from the interests but from
the principles of this people.

But though the French masses may be preeminent for the high
quality of the ideas by which they are moved, it is, says Arnold, the
characteristic of masses everywhere to be moved by ideas. And the
English aristocracy cannot understand this motivation for, of course,
aristocracy itself is immaculate of such impulse.

Members of an aristocracy, forming more or less a caste, and living in
a society of their own, have little personal experience of the effect of
ideas upon the masses of the people. . . . An aristocracy has naturally a
great respect for the established order of things, for the *fait accompli*. It
is in itself a *fait accompli*, it is satisfied with things as they are, it is
above everything, prudent. Exactly the reverse of the masses, who regard themselves as in a state of transition, who are by no means satisfied with things as they are, who are, above everything, adventurous.

The history of the last half-century, Arnold points out, is a history
of advancing ideas against which the aristocracy of England with its
powers of "endurance and resistance" has stood as a barrier. Sometimes the resistance was useful, as when it checked the French masses
who had sought "with Mohammedan fury" to impose on the rest of
Europe the essentially sound but crudely organized ideas of the
Revolution. Now it is no longer a time for resistance but for "intelligence and ideas." The aristocracies settled the destiny of Europe for
many years by their treaty of Vienna, using the instrument peculiar
to them, *force,* and bringing peace not by rational settlement but by
physical exhaustion. Now the time for such methods has passed.
Force, the political instrument of aristocracies, must give way to
reason, the instrument of the democratic masses. Gently and sweetly,
Arnold sweeps away the old order, while he holds out a gracious
hand to detain it:

When I consider the governing skill which the English aristocracy
have displayed since 1688, and the extraordinary height of grandeur to

which they have conducted their country, I almost doubt whether the law of nature, which seems to have given aristocracies the rule of the old order of things, and to have denied them that of the new, may not be destined to be reversed in their favour. May it be so! May their inimitable prudence and firmness have this signal reward! May they have the crowning good fortune, as in the ancient world of force, so in the modern world of ideas, to command the respect and even the enthusiasm of their countrymen.

Arnold's father had made the same prophecy of the disappearance of the aristocracy. Arnold stands where his father had stood nearly three decades before, when the democratic flood was not quite in full spate after the first rush of the Revolution.

It becomes apparent now why literature must occupy a new place —as the inaugural lecture implied it must—and be judged by the new criterion of *adequacy*. In a world dominated by aristocracy, literature was the ornament of a political and social *fait accompli;* now it must be more. It must guide the idea-moved masses; it must clarify their ideas. Further, it must quiet and compose them—for Arnold, circumspectly hailing the new day, believes that something good has passed with the old, the very power of endurance and resistance which characterized the aristocracy. To the criterion of adequacy, therefore, he adds the qualities of dignity, nobility and objectivity. The literature of Athens in the 5th century is the peak of adequate literature as Homer is the peak of ennobling literature. Arnold presents both to his time as the means of intellectual deliverance.

In effect, Arnold's inaugural lecture is a belated answer to the critics of his poetry who bedeviled him for not being modern enough. For, as he defines it, the modern element in literature is not the product of mere contemporaneity but of attitude, the attitude of a "significant, a highly-developed, a culminating epoch." A society is a *modern* society when it maintains a condition of civil peace allowing repose, confidence, free activity of the mind and the tolerance of divergent views; when it affords sufficient material well-being for the conveniences of life and for the development of taste; when, finally, its members are intellectually mature—when they are willing to judge by reason, to observe facts with a critical spirit and to search for the law of things.

Comparing the Athens of Pericles with the England of Elizabeth, Arnold finds the two societies equally vigorous in their genius. But the society that produced Aeschylus, Sophocles, Aristophanes, Pindar and Thucydides was the truly "modern" one—not only in the material basis of its life and in condition of civil peace but in intellectual maturity. Besides Raleigh's *History of the World,* splendid in prose, merely quaint in content, Arnold sets Thucydides with his willingness to judge by reason, his critical observation of facts, and—above all—his search for the law behind facts. And in every department of literature, he finds, Athens is not only *modern* but preeminently *adequate,* able to induce "that harmonious acquiescence of mind which we feel in contemplating a grand spectacle that is intelligible to us."

The literature of Rome, on the other hand, though modern, is not adequate: it does not make us lose our impatient irritation of mind; it leaves us excited but baffled by the immense spectacle of life. Lucretius, for example, with his skepticism, his scientific bent, the amazing picture he gives, in the third book of his poem, of *ennui* in Roman society, is obviously modern; yet, living in a brilliantly vigorous society, the poet retreats from the life around him; he is negative; he is morbid—and "he who is morbid is no adequate interpreter of his age." Vergil, too, great and touching as he is, is not adequate. The very epic form is a confession of inadequacy, for not the epic but the drama can possibly render the ethical conflicts of a complex and ever-changing society (surely a perverse notion when we consider the futility of Seneca and the success of that descendant of the epic form, the novel, in treating the ethical conflicts of a changing society); Vergil, like Lucretius, was escaping and knew it: hence the sadness of his poem, the shrinking melancholy and self-deprecation which are traditionally ascribed to his personality. Or Horace, yet another example of inadequacy: Horace refused to meet his civilization; he fled from seriousness to a light cynicism which has always prevented his best readers from being satisfied with his poetry.

Arnold insists that an adequate literature must be what he calls *fortifying*. This is, of course, the doctrine of his Preface of 1853; it is the theme of so many of his letters. Paraphrasing a line of Horace, "For Nature there is renovation, but for man there is none!" he comments, "It is exquisite, but it is not interpretative"—not fortifying. What now of Senancour—who surpassed Wordsworth and Goethe, though they sought consciously to bring health and he lived only in icy morbidity?

Arnold, seeking to check the tendency of romantic self-contemplation, goes so far, it would seem, as to confuse melancholy subjectivism with the recognition of life's tragic circumstance. As poet he had a better understanding; Arnold the poet knew that the tragic fact could be both interpretative and fortifying for the societies and the individuals which have stamina and integration. The prose Arnold would seem to have lost something of this insight. *Die Stille* in which the poet creates *ein Talent* makes no conflicting demands, insists upon no reconciliation of irreconcilables, but *der Strom der Welt* in which an effective and influential *Charakter* is formed is likely to blunt and pervert the exquisiteness of a man's perceptions.

Arnold falls, indeed, into "rationalizations" and contradictions in his attempt to forge an affirmative attitude to modern life. But his frequent failure in realism does not diminish the truth of the basic insights which his inaugural lecture contains and which his critical work was to develop—the nature of the full and healthy life of the spirit, the conception of literature as no mere ornament of life but one of its prime instruments, the recognition that literature depends not upon the effort of the individual but upon the effort of a whole society.

Chapter Six

-»» «««-

THE GRAND STYLE

He said that when modes of music change, the fundamental laws of the State always change with them.—PLATO

AFTER his inaugural address, Arnold's first venture into criticism was the series of lectures *On Translating Homer*. It is one of his finest performances, with an athletic quality in which austerity and elegance combine. The sunlight of commonsense plays over the sentences and the cool breeze of irony sweeps through them. The lectures undertake to provide a guide to the future translator of Homer by means of a discussion of the Homeric qualities and by an investigation of the insufficiencies of existing English translations. They range over the translations from the 16th to the 19th centuries, over the styles of the ballad, the metrical romance, over the verse of Chaucer, Spenser, Wordsworth and Tennyson: they are, in effect, a sweeping survey of English versification and diction.

Arnold isolates four Homeric qualities which must be rendered by the English translator—Homer's *rapidity*, his *plainness and directness of diction and syntax*, his *plainness in thought*, and, last, his *nobility*. Of the translators he discusses, none has been able to render all four qualities, though many have rendered some. Cowper (and Wright, who followed him in the Miltonic form) failed to reproduce Homer's rapidity, for Miltonic blank verse is slow and self-retarding. Pope (and Sotheby) failed to render his plainness of syntax and diction, for the heroic couplet is inescapably complex and rhetorical. Chapman failed to reflect his plainness of thought because Chapman loved the Elizabethan complexity and fancifulness. And Francis Newman, a recent translator, failed to evoke Homer's nobility.

To lack in nobility is, of course, to fail utterly; it is the peculiarly modern failure; we begin to see that Arnold's lectures are not merely technical discussions—that, beginning with technique, he is moving by devious ways to a comment on modern life. He is talking about style, and whenever Arnold talks about style he is talking about society. The condemnation of Francis Newman bulks large in the lectures not only because Newman replied to the second lecture and forced Arnold to a defense but because Newman is really the game he is stalking throughout the series. Homer, says Arnold, is in the "grand style" and this is the sum of his qualities of rapidity, plainness and nobility; Francis Newman's translation has none of these qualities, least of all the last. Arnold knew a good deal about Francis Newman's personality and he might well have suspected that the translation failed of nobility because Newman himself failed of nobility. He suspects, too, that Newman's failure goes beyond mere personal inadequacy and represents a national characteristic.

Francis Newman not noble? It must have been a shocking pronouncement to some very eminent and intelligent people. To George Eliot, for example, who had called him "our blessed St. Francis;" his soul, she said, "was a blessed *yea.*" To the good John Sterling—who made Professor Newman the guardian of his eldest son. To Carlyle —though perhaps not so much to him as to the others: there may be a certain embarrassment in Carlyle's tone when he talks of Newman as "an ardently inquiring soul, . . . of sharp-cutting, restlessly advancing intellect, and the mildest pious enthusiasm."

Francis Newman has managed to achieve an eminent place in the history of 19th century thought because at first glance he seems the perfect foil to his brother, the Cardinal. Thus Professor Hugh Walker represents him as living in the dry, clear air of reason while John Henry walks in the warm but dubious glow of mystical orthodoxy:

"The one brother hears and obeys the call of reason," Professor Walker writes, "the other takes shelter under authority." But Matthew Arnold, who knew Francis Newman through their common friends the Martineaus, and who knew other of Newman's writings than the translation of Homer, would have understood that such a comparison was scarcely fair to the Cardinal. For though John Henry Newman might be the beloved child of the authoritarian tradition, Francis was scarcely the Benjamin of the tradition of reason: "F. Newman's book I saw yestern at our ouse," Arnold writes to Clough. "He seems to have written himself down an hass. It is a display of the theological mind, which I am accustomed to regard as a suffetation, existing in a man from the beginning, colouring his whole being, and being him in short. One would think to read him that enquiries into articles, biblical inspiration, etc. etc. were as much the natural functions of a man as to eat and copulate . . ."

Francis Newman, after a brilliant career at Oxford—he was a Double First—and after some time spent helping John Henry at Littlemore, found himself troubled by doctrinal doubts and gave up his fellowship at Balliol. In 1830, the year of his resignation, he joined a religious mission which the eccentric devotee, Lord Congleton, was organizing for Syria. The expedition, which included wives, a baby in arms and an old lady, was a mad jaunt whose real tragedy—two of the wives died and the men of the party were many times near death—is blurred by the silly incompetence and downright nonsense of most of its members. Newman returned to England and married an old love, a pretty Plymouth Sister who did not understand the later development of his intellect. In 1840 he was appointed Professor of Latin at the Unitarian Manchester New College and, six years later, at University College, London.

Henceforth Newman gave himself with pertinacious enthusiasm to a variety of studies and causes. His philological pursuits were unremitting; besides Hebrew, Greek, Latin, Sanscrit, French, Spanish, Italian and Danish, he learned Berber, Libyan, Arabic, Abyssinian, Gothic, Chaldean, Syriac and Numidian; he translated Horace into

English, *Hiawatha* into Latin and *Robinson Crusoe* into Latin and Arabic. In Syria he had taken up tobacco, believing that smoking enlarged the lungs; now he believed it harmful and sought to have its use checked. He became a militant vegetarian, an intransigent anti-vivisectionist, an enthusiastic anti-vaccinationist. "I am anti-everything," he said in one of his rare moments of self-consciousness. He was much concerned with politics; he believed firmly in democracy but desired to "ward it off" for England. He loved "the people" but thought them lazy and shiftless, too highly paid and too much addicted to beefsteak. He was a partisan of Hungarian independence and believed that Hungary would benefit considerably from the introduction of the Bactrian camel. He thought the English rule in India was reprehensible and desired native independence. He denounced the "four Barbarisms of civilization"—cruelty to animals, the degradation of man (by which he meant the use of alcohol), war and the methods of English punishment. The perfection of the soul, he said, lay in its becoming *woman*. He believed in woman's right to vote, to educate herself and to ride astride.

He was rational in all things. In the summer he wore a tail-coat of alpaca. In the winter he wore three coats, the outer one green. In bad weather his ulster was a rug with a hole for his head, and for sloppy days he wore trousers edged with six inches of leather. He had no sense of humor whatever, and when little boys, fascinated by his great felt hat, ran after him yelling, "Who's your hatter?" his chief concern was that he had forgotten the hatter's name which he would sincerely have liked to tell them.

For forty-five years he preached a kind of rational-mystical agnosticism which informed several poems. An extract from one of the better-known of these, *Hebrew Theism: The Common Basis of Judaism, Christianity and Mohammedism,* will indicate the general tenor of the volumes:

> When Woman is duly honoured and homes are purified,
> And Fiery Drink is withheld from the weak in mind,
> And the traffickers in Sin are pursued as Felons,

And Truth is open-mouthed, and Thought is Free;
God shall soon bless the land with blessings undreamed of.
Labour shall be honoured and enmity of classes cease,
Poverty shall be light-hearted, Pauperism shall wane,
Beggary and Roguery shall be trades extinct,
The jails and the houses of the Insane shall be idle,
Health shall be robuster and Orphanhood rare,
Orphans shall meet new love in families,
Youth shall be reared to pure thought, pure fancy,
High hope, high desire and tender piety.
Religion shall grow wise and Knowledge religious,
Atheism shall waste away, and Selfishness learn to blush,
And God shall be our God and we will be his people.

However, despite nearly half a century of this belief, he turned in his old age to his old faith; the short period in which he was in communion with the Church of England was sufficient, his biographer tells us, to wipe out his mistaken past; for, as she says, "Time, as sex, is purely temporary."

A straight chin-beard, long straight hair and a tight but kindly mouth gave Newman exactly the appearance of the cartoonists' Uncle Sam or Brother Jonathan. For Arnold this Americanism of countenance must have given final point to the man's whole character, for it was a time when, under the influence of Alexis de Tocqueville's *Democracy in America* (1835-39), critics were muttering "Americanism" whenever Europe displayed cultural manifestations which they disliked. Tocqueville's book made John Stuart Mill modify his faith in democracy, and Sainte-Beuve, Renan, Scherer, and Arnold himself, foresaw for Europe a wave of Americanism— by which they meant vulgarity, loss of distinction, and, above all, that eccentricity of thought which arises when each man, no matter what his training or gifts, may feel that the democratic doctrine of equality allows him to consider his ideas of equal worth with those of his neighbor.

The faddist Newman represented for Arnold the English approximation to the decentralized and faddist thought of America, with its

multitudinous diversification of religious sects, its "causes," its lack
of any intellectual authority—exactly as Tocqueville had described it.
Within the limits of his class and place, Francis Newman was a
democrat; "The People! The People!" his biographer says, was his
constant thought. "What are 'the People' suffering; what are *their*
needs, their wrongs which call for justice? The People is the living
nation; the Court and the Army may be inevitable adjuncts of a
nation's being, as things at present are constituted; but they are
artificial adjuncts; the People are the very life essence of the Nation,
its real motive power. Let their voice be heard and the soul of empire
at once springs into being."

Arnold, welcoming the modern dispensation of democracy, but
seeking to channel and refine it, could surely find no more convenient
symbol of its dangers than the mind of Francis Newman. Short of
re-writing Tocqueville's work to make it apply to England, nothing
could be more revealing than to examine Francis Newman. Here
was a man of intellectual position, of learning and pretension, living
in a topsy-turvy world in which tobacco and religion, the Bactrian
camel and democracy received an almost equal emphasis. He turned
his energies against much that needed to be attacked but weakened
the attack of others by the absurdity of his own; he was a man who
might indeed seek to advance the modern spirit, but who utterly
lacked the method—a man, in short, wasted by personal wilfulness,
giving a liberal's faith to the liberal catchwords of freedom, but
unable to consider in how far they were only catchwords. The British
mind, in its depths where it was aflame with spiritism, mesmerism,
hydropathy and the innumerable sects of Protestantism, and on its
heights where it was hot after all the modernisms of the intellect,
was summed up for Arnold in Francis Newman. Faddist, populist,
liberal, agnostic, eccentric, this man puts his hand to Homer. The
juxtaposition is almost too pat; the opportunity cannot be missed:
"The eccentricity . . . the arbitrariness, of which Mr. Newman's
conception of Homer offers so signal an example, are not a peculiar
failing of Mr. Newman's own; in varying degrees they are the great

defect of English intellect, the great blemish of English literature."
Homer is in the grand style and Professor Newman, it would
seem, is not. What, exactly, is the grand style? Arnold refuses to say
—exactly. With facetious haughtiness he tells us that one must feel it
to know it—and "woe to those who know it not." Like the "Sublime"
of Longinus, it must be understood, not defined; indeed, in many
respects, the grand style *is* the "Sublime" and Arnold's method of
criticism close to Longinus's. Apparently the grand style can best be
understood by its opposite, the style of Professor Newman. The most
that Arnold will—or can—tell us is that the grand style is the style
that arises in poetry *"when a noble nature, poetically gifted, treats
with simplicity or with severity a serious subject."*

This, perhaps, is not sufficiently clarifying. But Arnold had read
and admired Sir Joshua Reynolds: "As for Sir Joshua," he wrote to
his friend Coleridge, "your mention of his lectures recalls to my
mind the admiration with which I read them and the debt I owe
them." Reynolds can give us a fuller explanation of what lies behind
Arnold's phrase, for in his *Discourses* the President of the Academy
is very explicit about the grand style in painting. Despite the woeful
effect of the *Discourses* upon English art in the 19th century, making
painting the distressed cousin of literature by promulgating the notion that "genius" must be subordinated to "thought" and technique
to meaning, they still retain a considerable critical value. By the
grand style Reynolds meant a certain kind of historical painting in
which generalization and idealization are dominant; he meant "leaving out particularities, and retaining only general ideas." This style
is "metaphysically just," he says, because the *whole* is the important
thing in a work of art. But the whole must be concerned only with
certain subjects "with some eminent instance of heroic action, or
heroic suffering." The events of Greek and Roman literature are the
best source of these subjects. But not only must the grand style be
whole and heroic, it must also be ideal, and though St. Paul was
notoriously a man of mean stature he must be represented as of
dignified physique, and Alexander must not be represented as short

nor Agesilaus lame. It is a theory that sired innumerable bad pictures but we must do Reynolds the justice of remembering that he was not handing down mere academic rules. He was trying to rationalize in words, as he tried to represent on canvas, a *Weltanschauung* which he deeply felt. He revered Michelangelo and if he missed much of the fire and daemonism in Michelangelo's work (and drew down Blake's everlasting curse) he saw something else: "The effect of the capital works of Michael Angelo," he said, "perfectly corresponds to what Bouchardon said he felt from reading Homer; his whole frame appeared to himself to be enlarged, and all nature which surrounded him, diminished to atoms." This is what he wants from painting, and what Arnold wants from poetry. This is the grand style.

When Arnold, like the great critics of the Continent, talks with fear and disgust about Americanism, he means, among other things, the diminution of the stature of man's spirit. Arnold's whole feeling about democracy is, perhaps, summed up in this passage from a letter to Clough in which the romantic nostalgia does not dim the social insight: "Au reste, a great career is hardly possible any longer—can hardly now be purchased even by the sacrifice of repose dignity and inward clearness—so I call no man unfortunate. I am more and more convinced that the world tends to become more comfortable for the mass, and more uncomfortable for those of any natural gift or distinction—and it is as well perhaps that it should be so—for hitherto the gifted have astonished and delighted the world, but not trained or inspired or in any real way changed it—and the world might do worse than to dismiss too high pretensions, and settle down on what it can see and handle and appreciate." Democracy has its revenge on genius, Arnold feels, by diminishing the chances of great stature. Tocqueville had gone so far as to say that democracy encouraged the scientific and philosophic attacks on the old anthropocentric cosmology which had allowed man to bulk so large in the universe, because only by reducing the stature of all men could democracy succeed:

In aristocratic societies, the class which gives the tone to opinion, and has the guidance of affairs, being permanently and hereditarily placed above the multitude, naturally conceives a lofty idea of itself and of man. It loves to invent for him noble pleasures, to carve out splendid objects for his ambition. Aristocracies often commit very tyrannical and inhuman actions, but they rarely entertain grovelling thoughts; and they show a kind of haughty contempt of little pleasures, even whilst they indulge in them. The effect is greatly to raise the general pitch of society. In aristocratic ages, vast ideas are commonly entertained of the dignity, the power, and the greatness of man. These opinions exert their influence on those who cultivate the sciences, as well as on the rest of the community. They facilitate the natural impulse of the mind to the highest regions of thought; and they naturally prepare it to conceive a sublime, almost a divine, love of truth.

Just as today the movement toward a co-operative state is combated by calling it a struggle between "enterprise" and "mediocrity" so, by many writers in the 19th century, the struggle between aristocracy and democracy was represented as the struggle between spiritual nobility and spiritual pettiness. Joubert, that gentle reactionary, defended the heightened style of Corneille because "to lift ourselves up and avoid being soiled by earthly meanness we need all the stilts we can find." Arnold, who has much sympathy with Joubert and who, with Goethe, fears *das Gemeine,* would agree.

With the passing of aristocracy the model of nobility has passed. Something is needed to take its place, and literature has to supply it: had, indeed, supplied it in the Homeric poems. Homer, perhaps, was not the Tory that Keble believed him, but the qualities which Arnold finds in Homer—rapidity, directness of manner, plainness of thought, nobility—are the virtues of the warrior and ideally the virtues of aristocracy. Arnold retells the story of Lord Granville, dying, but occupying himself with the details of the treaty that ended the Seven Years' War, who, when Wood (who first told the story) sought to postpone the business in consideration of his weakness, replied that he could not prolong his life by neglecting his duty and quoted Sarpedon's speech from Book XII of the *Iliad:*

> O my friend, if we,
> Leaving this war, could flee from age and death,

I should not here be fighting in the van,
Nor would I send thee to the glorious war,
But now, since many are the modes of death
Impending o'er us, which no man can hope
To shun, let us press on and give renown
To other men, or win it for ourselves! *

"I quote this story," Arnold says, "first, because it is interesting as exhibiting the English aristocracy at its very height of culture, lofty spirit, and greatness, towards the middle of the last century." Of course, the character of the English aristocracy might have been exemplified with equal accuracy by the story of Lord George Germain (Sir George Sackville) who, in haste to get to his country house, did not complete the orders to General Howe in America, thus preventing the juncture of Howe and Burgoyne and ensuring the loss of the American colonies by Britain.

Francis Newman set his hand to Homer to make him available to the modern man and produced a work that was little short of travesty. There was no doubt that Newman's classical learning was great—too great, Arnold implies, declaring his gratitude for the limitations of his own scholarship, for

to handle these matters [of poetical criticism] properly there is needed a poise so perfect that the least overweight in any direction tends to destroy the balance. Temper destroys it, a crotchet destroys it, even erudition may destroy it. To press to the sense of the thing itself with which one is dealing, not to go off on some collateral issue about the thing, is the hardest matter in the world. The "thing itself" with which one is here dealing,—the critical perception of poetic truth,—is of all things the most volatile, elusive, and evanescent; by even pressing too impetuously after it, one runs the risk of losing it. The critic of poetry should have the finest tact, the nicest moderation, the most free, flexible, and elastic spirit imaginable; he should be indeed the "ondoyant et divers," the *undulating and diverse* being of Montaigne. The less he can deal with his object simply and freely, the more things he has to take into account

* Arnold quotes the Greek. The translation is from William Cullen Bryant's version of the *Iliad* which he began in 1865, four years after Arnold's lectures. Bryant's translation, it should be said, is an excellent one, conforming to Arnold's requirements to a considerable degree.

in dealing with it,—the more, in short, he has to encumber himself,—so much the greater force of spirit he needs to retain his elasticity. But one cannot exactly have this greater force by wishing for it . . .*

Newman had approached the *Iliad* with the theories of his learning but with no poetical comprehension of the subject he was treating. His declared intention was to present to the English public a work which should have the same effect that the *Iliad* had had upon the citizens of Athens; to the Athenian, Homer was both archaic and difficult and therefore he should be archaic and difficult for the English reader. Following out his own logic, Newman uses words that even an amateur of early English literature would not be likely to know. Arnold cites some of the incredible jargon—*plump* for *mass, bulkin* for *calf, bragley* for *proudly fine*—but he charitably omits such horrors as *beknow* for *recognize, bestray* for *torment, gride* for *cut gratingly, hurly* for *hubbub, gramsome* for *direful, pight* for *built, wight* for *vigorous.*† He dismisses Newman's whole estimate of Homer's diction by pointing out that though indeed the language of Homer was very different from that used in the Athenian market-place, it was taught to the cultivated Athenian and presented as little

---

* A. E. Housman, in his *Introductory Lecture,* deprecates the exactness of Arnold's scholarship, citing a pair of errors, but then goes on: "But when it comes to literary criticism, heap up in one scale all the literary criticism that the whole nation of professed scholars ever wrote, and drop into the other the thin green volume of Matthew Arnold's Lectures on Translating Homer . . . and the first scale, as Milton says, will straight fly up and kick the beam."

† We may get some notion of Newman's feeling for language and of his reliability from the following anecdote told by his biographer: "He was very much interested in language, and it was characteristic of him never to pass a word that he did not know. He had a great dislike and contempt for *slang,* and he deplored the growing use of it, and the impoverishment of the language that resulted. But dialect words, or old words that lingered in some parts of the country, while they had dropped out of common speech, interested him greatly. One day a younger sister of mine brought him a footstool as he sat reading, and in offering it to him called it a 'buffet.' It is not a word in common use, but I think we had adopted it from the nursery rhyme about 'Miss Muffet, who sat on a buffet.' The Professor was on the alert at once.

" 'That word is quite new to me,' he said. 'Did you say "bussock?" I wonder is that a Lancashire word, or does it come from Ireland? "Bussock!" Will you spell it for me, please?'

"My sister was far too young and too shy to correct him, and after faintly murmuring 'buffet' again, she ran away in extreme confusion. I am afraid 'bussock' went down in the Professor's notebook as an interesting variant of 'hassock.' "—Sieveking: *The Life of Francis Newman,* pp. 118–119. Newman had that special love of language which made him call his vegetarian society "Anti-creophagite."

difficulty to him as the language of the Bible presents to a modern Englishman. The important point for Arnold is that Newman's grotesque vocabulary is the result of his erroneous perception of Homer's style, and his meter (a typographical rearrangement of the ballad measure) the result of the same misapprehension. Homer, for Newman, is "direct, popular, forcible, quaint, flowing, garrulous . . . rises and sinks with his subject, is prosaic when it is tame, is low when it is mean." But nobility is in the eye of the beholder; Newman's eye lacks nobility; he makes a translation which veils all of Homer's stature and delicacy and brings him into incongruous approximation to the worst tastes and tendencies of the age.

Arnold never claims for Homer the unquestionable relevance of the Periclean writers, for Homer was not *modern* and he lacked the peculiar interest of matter which they had. Style nevertheless can be matter: the style of Homer, simple, noble, centric and sane, stands as condemnation of the eccentric, verbose, petty mind of Newman, a liberal catchall for the catchwords of his day, the very type of the vices of contemporary thought.

II

When a man sees life under the aspect of a distinct and illuminating idea, all things become interrelated and it is no step at all from the investigation of Homer to the investigation of elementary schools. Before the lectures on Homer, Arnold had been sent on a pedagogical tour of France to observe the methods of French education; *Popular Education in France* (1861) is the parliamentary report he prepared and its preface, the essay later published as "Democracy," contained his conclusions not only about education, but about English society in general. Arnold carried with him on his rounds of school-inspection the idea of the grand style and it made distressingly clear the ignobility of what he saw. That the schools themselves were not in the grand style went without saying; more important and what needed to be pointed out was the lack of the grand style in the national consciousness which permitted them to be what they were.

France's education, said Arnold, was conceived in the grand style and England's was not, for France possessed and England lacked the conception of the one agency in modern society capable of giving a high and noble tone to the national life. Once the aristocracy had been that agency, infusing the grand style into a nation's spirit; now aristocracy was gone, or its function curtailed, and democracy must find a new model of grandeur. French democracy had already found it; English democracy seemed not to desire it at all; the modern source of the grand style, says Arnold, is the *State*.

Today, the contemporary American, much more than the Englishman, can appreciate the full and shocking force of this idea, for in England the idea of centrality of government has to a large degree been accepted and the old catchwords are not used with quite the same assurance, while in America the idea of the central State is still in dramatic dispute. However, in Arnold's time he might as well have told the English middle class that only Popery or Mohammedanism could save the national life from meanness as that in the State lay spiritual salvation. Liberalism means many things, but to a member of the British middle class of Arnold's time liberalism meant one thing primarily: a State that could not control him except when he indulged in common law crime, an activity which did not attract him. The 19th century Englishman still saw feudalism as the *status quo* and his own industrialism as a much put-upon agency of progress forced to struggle against unfair odds. The State was the very institution which his class forbears had combated. The State had sought to limit his industrial expansion and keep him from political power; it had given monopolies to the aristocracy and at one time even attempted—fortunately without success—to set up standards of quality for his merchandise; it had gone so far as to try to regulate the wages and hours of his workmen; finally, the State had tried to coerce him into a way of worship which he despised. From this leviathan the middle class Englishman had won a freedom which he intended to keep; if certain of its dismembered parts were still strongly instinct with life, he must be wary of their movements.

But there was one critical lesson that Arnold never ceased to teach and that was that history must be considered neutrally—and dialectically.* The ambivalence of opinion which the dialectical method produces is an impossible burden to some people but to others it is a positive pleasure; Arnold was one of the latter. He knew that a thing that is good at one point in the historical process may lose its virtue at another and that an idea or an institution, harmful now, may once have been necessary and good. Feudalism had once been a political necessity, but history had replaced it with the centralized State of monarchy and this with the various stages of liberal democracy. If the movements of bourgeois political liberalism were seen as *tendencies* they were progressive; they had produced or had associated themselves with admirable ideas. But if they were seen as stopping-places they were not progressive; they were even retrograde. Industrialism and bourgeois democracy had become themselves the *status quo*. The middle class did not want to realize this but there were individuals who saw it in one way or another and their ranks were strangely assorted: Chartists, Owenite Socialists, Dr. Arnold, Carlyle,

---

* "The great basic thought that the world is not to be comprehended as a complex of ready-made *things,* but as a complex of *processes,* in which the things apparently stable no less than their mind-images in our heads, the concepts, go through an uninterrupted change of coming into being and passing away, in which, in spite of all seeming accidents and of all temporary retrogression, a progressive development asserts itself in the end—this great fundamental thought has, especially since the time of Hegel, so thoroughly permeated ordinary consciousness that in this generality it is scarcely ever contradicted. If . . . investigation always proceeds from this standpoint, the demand for final solutions and eternal truths ceases once for all; one is always conscious of the necessary limitation of all acquired knowledge, of the fact that it is conditioned by the circumstances in which it was acquired. On the other hand, one no longer permits oneself to be imposed upon by the antitheses, insuperable for the still common old metaphysics, between true and false, good and bad, identical and different, necessary and accidental. One knows that these antitheses have only a relative validity; *that that which is recognised now as true has also its latent false side which will later manifest itself, just as that which is now regarded as false has also its true side by virtue of which it could previously have been regarded as true."* (Italics mine.)—Friedrich Engels: *Ludwig Feuerbach.* At the risk of seeming to call Arnold a Marxist, I use this well-known statement of the method of dialectical materialism to underscore and illuminate Arnold's characteristic method of judgment. The method is especially marked in Arnold's treatment of religion.

the Saint-Simonians, not a few enlightened Tories, the revolutionists of the Continent, among them Marx and Engels.

These men saw that industrialism and democracy had given little or no power to the working class, apparent power to the small bourgeoisie, and actual power to the group of large industrialists who shared it with the landowners. But while the critics pointed out this failure of democratic hopes, the "liberal" industrialists themselves kept pointing to the still-existent, if diminished, power of the aristocracy and its attendant Church and shouted that *here* lay the threat to the liberties of all, that control was always a danger and that the hope of civil welfare lay in "the uniform, constant, and uninterrupted effort of every man to better his condition," no matter what that effort involved. The doctrine of individual freedom which Milton had so superbly stated in the *Areopagitica* and which John Stuart Mill made so attractive in the essay, *On Liberty,* was also the doctrine of the selfishness, the blindness and the cruelty of the factory owners which was to be formulated in the "scientific" terms of Herbert Spencer's *The Man Versus the State.* The principle of the political equality of man, the justification of free activity, the doctrine of self-development through effort and struggle—these fair doctrines were used by a class which called itself a "rising" middle class but which was already entrenched. Individualism meant ruthless self-seeking; laissez-faire was the letting-alone not of useful personal energies but of a man's illegitimate power over his fellow-men, the letting-alone of "the iron law of wages." A trade union was an attempt to interfere with this iron law, which was in reality iron only at one end and quite golden at the other. A State which took cognizance of the relation of employer and employee was really nothing more than an extension of a trade union, a big combination in restraint of trade.

Insistence on freedom of worship accompanied the insistence on freedom of business enterprise and served as its rationale. The Church still existed as an establishment, which is to say a monopoly with huge landholdings; and it had an organic and legal part in government. True, there seemed little likelihood of the kind of religious reaction which France had suffered, though the Anglican revival of 1833 hinted of its possibility. But the Church was claiming power in a new sphere—that of popular education. As the problem of popular education became more obvious and pressing, the fear of the dissenting middle class grew, lest its rights be compromised by the old order.

Theoretically at least, the tradition of the Puritan middle class in respect to education was a good one. Puritanism rested on the ability of every man to read the Bible and to interpret it for himself; it rested on the relative freedom of the inquiring mind. At the height of the Puritan power Milton had advocated free education and Cromwell had attempted to establish it. The astonishing urge for schooling in Scotland, the even more commanding place which education held in New England life, producing that well-nigh incredible desire for learning that Van Wyck Brooks has described in *The Flowering of New England,* the natural assumption in earliest America that free education was a right to receive and a duty to give, are all of Puritan origin. The best of the middle class prophets —Adam Smith and Bentham among them—were agreed that education was the State's duty, and even Macaulay desired State control in this realm.

The new desire to provide popular education was in part disinterested, but in large part it was motivated by the desire of religious and political groups to extend their power. In the old days of the *Anti-Jacobin* the government met unrest by appropriating money to build new churches. Now the Church sought to advance itself by building new schools and thus attracting adherents by the offer of the schooling the populace was beginning to need and want. In 1811 the Church founded the National Society for Promoting Education of the Poor in the Principles of the Established Church Throughout England and Wales. In 1814 the dissenting sects, not to be outdone, established the British and Foreign School Society, supported by the philosophical radicals, Bentham, James Mill and Francis Place, and by Brougham.

Both organizations were maintained by voluntary contributions and in part by small fees, but in 1833 the State appropriated 20,000 pounds to aid the Societies and from that date until 1902 English education was torn by an endless internecine struggle. The government desired to advance popular education and was content to use the existing agencies; it made increasingly large grants-in-aid to the National and British Schools. But the existing agencies watched each other with jealous eyes. Disinterested students of the history of education agree in condemning equally the action of both Church and Dissent. The Church, desiring to advance religion through its schools, and even dreaming of the old days of complete ascendancy, declared that its function was to instruct the whole nation and did not want the State to contribute to the spread of Dissent by grants to the British Society schools. The sects, on the other hand, fearing the ambitions of the Church, insisted that the government refrain from aiding the program of the National Society, and formed the Voluntaryist Society (led by the Edward Baines and the Edward Miall of whom Arnold has so much to say in *Culture and Anarchy*) which sought to bar all government aid whatever. Each party felt that the State was in the control of the other and each feared interference; nor was the idea of a neutral State an attractive compromise, for that would mean the refusal to recognize the sectarianism of either group.

On the whole, the government occupied the only respectable position, though a weak one. Its Committee in Council on Education knew what was needed. It knew that something had to be done to raise both the standard of instruction and the standard of living of the teachers. But when it appropriated 100,000 pounds for normal schools, for grants and for pensions, its offer was rejected by the two societies lest the opposing party should gain by it—and this at a time when the École Normale Supérieure was becoming so impor-

tant a force in the national life of France. The Committee's inspectors
—inspection was one of the government's requirements for grants
and the Societies fought it in every way—knew that the curriculum
was inadequate and that the instruction by undertrained and under-
paid teachers who were usually compelled to use the mass-production
methods of Bell and Lancaster * were of little use. They knew that
the cause of even sectarian religion was not served when little boys
answered the catechism questions, "What is thy duty towards God?"
and "What is thy duty towards thy neighbor?" with "My duty toads
God is to bleed in Him, to fering and to loaf withold your arts,
withold my mine, withold my sold, and with my sernth, to whirchp
and give thanks, to put my old trash [whole trust!] in Him, to call
upon Him, to onner His old name and His world, and to save Him
truly all the days of my life's end," and with "My dooty toads my
nabers, to love him as thyself, and to do to all men as I wed thou shall
and to me; to love, onner, and suke my farther and mother; to onner
and to bay the Queen and all that are pet in a forty under her; to smit
myself to all my gooness, teaches, sportial pastures, and marsters." †

The State encroached on what seemed so clearly a sectarian liberty; inevitably finance lost the day for the religious Societies because they could not maintain the ever-increasing cost of instruction.
But they continued to fight on for decades, seeking to dictate the
terms of governmental aid, confirming their young charges in their
religious antagonisms.

Weary and disillusioned with this situation, Arnold went to

---

* The National Schools used the method of Bell, the British Schools used that of
Lancaster; both systems were designed for cheapness—they were a kind of development of Bentham's "panopticon" jail by which a single teacher, with the help of
student monitors, could control, if not teach, hundreds of pupils. Both Lancaster and
Bell were proud that their systems were "mechanical;" the manufacturing class was
charmed that a school could actually be run like a factory! A good notion of the
quality of a relatively well-run school may be had from the opening chapter of *Hard
Times* (1854). The improvement in the system is reflected in *Our Mutual Friend*,
written ten years later; but even in 1864 a large part of the story can turn on the
struggle of the schoolmaster, Mr. Headstone, for self-respect in the face of social
contempt of his profession; and the priggish formalism of the method and content
of popular education is still the object of Dickens' brilliant satire.

† Quoted in Henry Craik's *The State and Education* (1884) pp. 55–56. The answers
were submitted by children of average intelligence in an inspected school in 1855.

France and found something very different. He found that France recognized three religions, Catholic, Protestant and Jewish, whose ministers were salaried by the State. He found that liberty of instruction—Voluntaryism—had never been a dominant idea—except once, as he pointed out with malice, "in 1793, under the Reign of Terror;" at all other times, there had existed the knowledge that education must be held responsible to some corporation, clerical or lay. He found in operation there the "high Roman and Imperial theory as to the duties and powers of the State." He found a complex system of financial support, dividing control among parish, department and State (substantially the same as that evolved in England in 1902) but a very simple control of the method and matter of education by the State. He found that the State allowed the three religious groups their separate schools but itself remained neutral. He found no touch of sectarian pettiness in their inspection. In short, he found that the French State had refused to "shackle its own reason and its own equity" by submitting to all the anomalies of sectarian religion. And he insisted, though he knew English opinion would not believe him, that the French State, in refusing to shackle its own reason, was not therefore shackling the reason of its citizens, and cited the authority of Napoleon Bonaparte: "it is impossible for the State, in modern France, to go counter to a great current of national sentiment."

But for Arnold the State was more than an efficient organ of administration. It had a spiritual value beyond this. Once the priesthood and the aristocracy, he says, had been the schoolmasters of the nation:

The great ecclesiastical institutions of Europe, with their stately cathedrals, their imposing ceremonial, their affecting services; the great aristocracies of Europe, with their lustre of descent, their splendour of wealth, their reputation for grace and refinement—have undoubtedly for centuries served as ideals to ennoble and elevate the sentiment of the European masses. Assuredly, churches and aristocracies often lacked the sanctity or the refinement ascribed to them; but their effect as distant ideals was still the same: they remained above the individual, a beacon to the imagination of thousands; they stood, vast and grand objects, ever present before the eyes of masses of men in whose daily avocations there was little which was vast, little which was grand; and they preserved these masses from any danger of overrating with vulgar self-satisfaction an inferior culture, however broadly sown, by the exhibition of a standard of dignity and refinement still far above them.

Democracy had destroyed the power and example of the priesthood and aristocracy and it had not yet acquired a new model and ideal. In modern life there was only one agency which could resolve the crotchets of sect, unify the diversity of individual aims, improve the insufficiency of individual effort—that was the State. What is the State? Arnold asks, and he replies with Burke's answer: It is the nation in its collective and corporate character. Arnold has picked up his father's great theme.

It is at this point that Arnold formulates his conception of a State which shall be above all classes, above all sects, synthesizing their diversities, resolving their conflicts. Democracy, which had advanced at the expense of the Tudor and Stuart State (which themselves had risen, though Arnold does not say so, to take over some of the regulative functions of the Church) must now, if it is to fulfil itself, understand the necessity of State power. The day has passed when it is progressive and revolutionary to cry for freedom from the State. The breaking-up process has done its work; democracy has been achieved; now the time has come for synthesis. For in itself, Arnold says, democracy is neither good nor bad; it is the neutral result of an historic process. Democracy may be *made* either good or bad by the conscious acts of its supporters. It is not an end in itself, none of its component ideas is an end in itself (equality, for example, even though it is preferable to the depressing effects of inequality, is not an end in itself)—but only a means to an end: the end of true liberty and true humanity. Democracy can realize its essence only by understanding such truths as these, and to understand them it must establish a measure beyond itself by which it may judge ideas. It is the characteristic of all democracies to be moved by ideas. If English democracy is to come to full growth it must make sure that it is not tossed in a chaos of pointless ideas in the American way—in the way of Professor Newman—and to this end it must ally itself with strong and central State action.

Nations are not truly great solely because the individuals composing them are numerous, free, and active; but they are great when these numbers, this freedom, and this activity are employed in the service of an ideal higher than that of an ordinary man, taken by himself. Our society is probably destined to become much more democratic; who or what will give a high tone to the nation then?

Arnold is speaking to the middle class and he knows that there are very obvious barriers in the middle class mind to the adoption of a strong State. For one thing, though the State may be ideally the nation in its corporate character, actually, in the words of Mirabeau, he who administers, governs—and undoubtedly the aristocracy still administers England. The middle classes, Arnold admits, will give their support only to a strong State which "shall be one of their adoption, one that they can trust." But first the middle class must lose its fear of the State in the abstract, a fear which its history had instilled. For, as he said in *A French Eton*, "in the youth and early manhood of the English middle class, the action of the State was at the service of an ecclesiastical party. . . . [The middle class] has never forgotten that the hand which smote it—the hand which did the bidding of its High Church and prelatical enemies—was the hand of the State." With an unfortunate lack of realism, Arnold says nothing of the earlier State's discriminations in favor of the landholding interests and certain mercantile groups, or of its repression of free enterprise and large-scale manufacture, or of its fiscal policy—matters which were quite as influential in the shaping of the attitude of the middle class as the religious repression which the State had carried out for the Church.

As Arnold talks to the middle class, his conception of the State as "the nation in its corporate character" begins to go by the board, for the State he projects is one that the middle class can indeed trust: it is to be one of their own adoption. He speaks of *middle class democracy*—of a transformed middle class, "raised to a higher and more genial culture," a class "strong by its numbers, its energy, its industry, strong by its freedom from frivolity;" he foresees it "liberalised by an ampler culture, admitted to a wider sphere of thought, living by larger ideas, with its provincialism dissipated, its intolerance cured, its pettiness purged away." And when this consummation has been reached: "Then let the middle class rule, then let it affirm its own spirit, when it has thus perfected itself." Of the relations of the middle class with the other classes of the nation he says nothing.

Yet Arnold must not be taken too literally or even too seriously here. True, even when he evolves a more elaborate theory of the State he does not solve his contradictions of omission. At this time, however, he is not entirely without a touch of banter; the conditions he sets for middle class rule are so clearly impossible—the middle class raising itself by its own moral and intellectual bootstraps, renovating itself by an act of the profoundest self-criticism and humility! This, we must suppose, is that "play of the mind" of which Arnold is to speak, that non-practicality he is later to exalt. He is addressing himself to the middle classes and were they to attempt to come to power by an act of aggression merely against their own vices, merely by a seizure of power over their own souls, or by a conspiracy to perfect themselves, there is no one who would oppose their attempt. Arnold can scarcely believe that this is in the realm of likelihood but, using a language not unlike that of middle class religion, with its habit of soul-searching, he establishes the notion of the State in the abstract, speaks for the need of right ideas, of reason and culture to supplement the rigid morality of the bourgeoisie. He speaks of the movement of history and of the need of fresh attitudes to conform to new conditions. The words with which he concludes, assimilated as they are to middle class notions of progress and to a Biblical culture, may have moved some to reconsider an old position:

Openness and flexibility of mind are at such a time the first of virtues. *Be ye perfect,* said the Founder of Christianity; *I count not myself to have apprehended,* said its greatest Apostle. Perfection will never be reached; but to recognise a period of transformation when it comes, and to adapt themselves honestly and rationally to its laws, is perhaps the nearest approach to perfection of which men and nations are capable. No habits or attachments should prevent their trying to do this; nor indeed, in the long run, can they. Human thought, which made all institutions, inevitably saps them, resting only in that which is absolute and eternal.

Chapter Seven

✤✤✤

THE SPIRIT OF CRITICISM

*For to be possessed of a vigorous mind is not
enough; the prime requisite is rightly to apply it.
The greatest minds, as they are capable of the
highest excellences, are open likewise to the greatest aberrations; and those who travel very slowly
may yet make far greater progress, provided they
keep always in the straight road, than those who,
while they run, forsake it.*—DESCARTES

ARNOLD was the most influential critic of his age: the estimate must be as unequivocal as this. Other critics may have
been momentarily more exciting; none was eventually more
convincing. T. S. Eliot has said that the academic literary opinions
of our time were formed by Arnold; F. O. Matthiessen, recalling
this comment, specifies George Saintsbury, Charles Whibley, A. C.
Bradley, W. P. Ker and Irving Babbitt as the continuators of the
Arnold tradition; and in another essay Eliot finds that the assumptions of Arnold's criticism were adopted by Walter Pater, Arthur
Symons, J. A. Symonds, Leslie Stephen and F. W. H. Myers. "For
half-a-century," says R. A. Scott-James, "Arnold's position in [Eng-
land] was comparable with that of [Aristotle] in respect of the
wide influence he exercised, the mark he impressed upon criticism,
and the blind faith with which he was trusted by his votaries."

What were the causes of Arnold's success? First of all, Arnold
had a manner and a style rather new to England and perfectly
adapted to the art of criticism—elegant yet sinewy, colloquial yet
reserved, cool yet able to glow into warmth, careful never to flare
into heat. It was a style which kept writer and reader at a sufficient

distance from each other to allow room between them for the object of their consideration. The opposite of Macaulay's, of which it has been said that no one could tell the truth in it, Arnold's prose was sinuous and modulated, permitting every nuance and modification that exactness required. A prose of "line" rather than of "color," it avoided the Wagnerian giantism of Carlyle and found its musical affinity, perhaps, in Gluck; it was the so-called Oxford prose which Newman also wrote, touched with Latinity and Addison, in which urbanity did not preclude vigor.

Moreover, with this style went a biographical talent nicely suited to the critical purpose, not so brilliant and dramatic as to overshadow the literary evaluation but alert to the tone and inflection of personality, able, by reference to these, to illustrate the spiritual meaning of style. In part learned from Johnson and Cotton, in larger part from Sainte-Beuve, it was a biographical method whose results, for all their frequent wrong-headedness, were perhaps more reassuring than Sainte-Beuve's because they sprang from a more firmly based temperament.

Sainte-Beuve had called himself a naturalist of souls and from Sainte-Beuve, his acknowledged master, Arnold learned the attitude of the "scientist" in literature. The "science" to which Sainte-Beuve subscribed was not Taine's; it had no system, no categories; it was an attitude merely—an insatiable curiosity and, so far as possible, the abrogation of passion and partisanship. But, as Arnold was later to say, Sainte-Beuve had stopped with curiosity; skepticism, the result of frustrated hope for himself and for society, had kept him from going further. Arnold went further; the tradition of his father, of moral strenuousness, was strong in him. He might use Sainte-Beuve's grave, imperturbable amenity, but beneath it was the intense desire to correct the world and to make right prevail.*

* If Arnold helped establish Sainte-Beuve's reputation in England, Sainte-Beuve, by his translation of "Obermann" in his *Chateaubriand et sa groupe littéraire,* by quotation of the Homer lectures and by other references, helped to make Arnold's name known to France. The two men met on Arnold's educational tour of 1858 and dined together. Their literary relations have been studied in A. Fryer Powell's essay, "Sainte-Beuve and Matthew Arnold," in the *French Quarterly,* vol. iii, September 1921 and in great detail

Style, biographical talent, the "scientific" attitude, were only the servants of Arnold's literary point of view; it was his point of view which made the success of the first series of *Essays in Criticism*. It had been variously expressed in Arnold's earliest critical writing; now it was summed up in the phrase which has been a gage thrown to all critics since: *Literature is a criticism of life.*

For Arnold's contemporaries, living closer than we do to the tradition of the French Revolution, the phrase was an indication of the age's true tendency. For the Revolution of 1789, said Renan, had been wrought by philosophers; it was the first time that humanity undertook to reflect upon itself: "Condorcet, Mirabeau, Robespierre are the first instances of theorists meddling with the direction of affairs and endeavouring to govern humanity in a reasonable and scientific manner." It was "the advent of the power of reflection in the government of humanity," and Hegel used even more dramatic language about the same phenomenon:

Never since the sun had stood in the firmament and the planets revolved around him had it been perceived that man's existence centers in his head, *i.e.* in Thought, inspired by which he builds up the world of reality. Anaxagoras had been the first to say that [Thought] governs the World; but not until now had man advanced to the recognition of the principle that Thought ought to govern spiritual reality.

Arnold's distinction in criticism lay in his comprehension of this very fact. He had said that democracy is characterized by its response to ideas and can advance only by the discovery and maintenance of the best of them. Criticism, he announced, was the instrument for their discovery and evaluation; the close relationship between literature and life which Arnold perceived and explained gave him his first hold upon his readers.

Yet of the principal essays between 1863 and 1865 only four deal

---

by Paul Furrer in *Der Einfluss Sainte-Beuves auf die Kritik Matthew Arnolds*. Arnold's essay on the occasion of Sainte-Beuve's death has been reprinted in the Oxford edition of his essays; his article on Sainte-Beuve in the ninth edition of the *Encyclopedia Britannica* (1886) is excellent.

primarily with the literary life, with poetry and criticism: "The Function of Criticism at the Present Time," "The Literary Influence of Academies," "Maurice de Guérin" and "Heinrich Heine." But six deal, directly or indirectly, with religion: the nub of the essay on Eugénie de Guérin is the comparison of her life of Catholic piety with a Protestant lady's life of good works; the essay on Joubert reflects the Platonic religiosity of the "French Coleridge's" mind; "Pagan and Mediæval Religious Sentiment" gives the palm to the medieval while pleading for an understanding of any religion, even the decadent pagan; and the essays, "Spinoza and the Bible" (or its earlier and more topical version, "The Bishop and the Philosopher"), "Dr. Stanley's Lectures on the Jewish Church," and "Marcus Aurelius," are all concerned with distinguishing between the life of religion and the life of the intellect. For one of the discoveries of Arnold's criticism was that intellect was not enough, that it could not be the guide to a multitude of matters for the multitude of mankind—that religion still had its important place. It was this discovery that constituted a final assurance of Arnold's charm for a large class of cultivated but sorely-tried people.

Here, at a time when the modern spirit was questioning both the validity of religion and the intelligence of those who desired still to accept it, an avowed proponent of the modern spirit came forward and not in his own name only but in the name of *criticism,* which was the modern spirit itself, said that religion was good and necessary and must not be touched by the intellect:—and this was Professor Arnold, whose own religious doubts and denials were well known from his poems. True, he was not at all willing to admit that there was any reason to believe religion could be *proved*—that was perhaps disquieting; but it was something to have him say that, human nature being what it is, religion is necessary to it. Nor did he say that men should worship the All or the Absolute; although he did not regard all aspects of Christianity with equal pleasure, it was Christianity and no new philosophic religion that he recommended.

If we are to understand Arnold's appeal to his contemporaries, we must understand this dual intention of his criticism. If we are to follow the fluctuations of his opinion, his often confusing modulations, we must see that his criticism is the reconciliation of the two traditions whose warfare had so disturbed his youth—rationalism and faith. It is an attempt to bring this synthesis to bear on all the aspects of modern life. He steers a course both by compass and by stars: reason, but not the cold and formal reason that makes the mind a machine; faith, but not the escape from earth-binding facts. "The main element of the modern spirit's life," he says, "is neither the senses and understanding, nor the heart and imagination; it is the imaginative reason."

The imaginative reason: with this phrase Arnold feels he has closed the gap between head and heart, between feelings and intellect, a schism, as it had appeared in his poetry, of which John Dewey has said:

We must bridge this gap of poetry from science. We must heal this unnatural wound. We must, in the cold, reflective way of critical system, justify and organize the truth which poetry, with its quick, naive contacts, has already felt and reported. The same movement of the spirit, bringing man and man, man and nature, into wider and closer unity, which has found expression by anticipation in poetry, must find expression by retrospection in philosophy. Thus will be hastened the day in which our sons and our daughters shall prophesy, our young men shall see visions, and our old men dream dreams.

If not exactly in the way Dewey suggests, if not quite "in the cold, reflective way of critical system," Arnold's criticism makes the instauration Dewey asks for. And only when we understand this synthesis can we understand the phrase which has bothered so many of Arnold's modern readers: "Poetry [or "literature:" Arnold interchanges] is a criticism of life;" for Arnold, poetry is the highest expression of the imaginative reason.

There is scarcely a true poet, whatever the philosophical or political intention of his work, who would accept literally Arnold's famous phrase as an adequate definition of poetry. Consequently, many interpretations of it have been offered by poets and critics. Professor Garrod, for example, interprets it to mean merely that insofar as a work possesses organic unity it is a criticism of the chaos of life; he quotes Edward Caird who said that "literature is a criticism of life exactly in the sense that a good man is a criticism of a bad one." This would bring Arnold's phrase close to Sir Philip Sidney's "golden world" of art which is a model and corrective for the "brazen world;" and in this sense music presents us with a golden world; so does dancing; so does a consummate athletic achievement or a circus feat—for in each we have a perfection of organization and execution which, by suggesting that we can overcome the limitations of the usual way of feeling or of moving, is (even though it has no explicit content) a *criticism* of the usual way.* Arnold, it is apparent, meant something more literal by his words than this, something which seems to justify T. S. Eliot's protest that his definition of poetry is "frigid to anyone who has felt the full surprise and elevation of a new experience of poetry." He is writing of Joubert when he first uses the phrase (here it is "literature" not "poetry") and Joubert was no architect of a golden world but a critic, in a very literal sense, of this brazen world; Arnold simply meant that Joubert put his finger on aspects of life and judged "Good" or "Bad." So poetry (or literature generally), Arnold feels, sometimes by accident and implication but sometimes by intent, says "Good" or "Bad." And if Mr. Eliot's objection is valid, that poetry does much more than make such ethical and spiritual judgments, we must remember that Arnold is not offering a *definition* of poetry comparable to "The best words in the best order," or any other of the scores of classic at-

---

* An important and illuminating corollary to this is given by Professor I. A. Richards: "The artist is an expert in the 'minute particulars' and *qua* artist pays little or no attention to generalizations which he finds in actual practice are too crude to discriminate between what is valuable and the reverse. For this reason the moralist has always tended to distrust or to ignore him. Yet since the fine conduct of life springs only from fine ordering of responses far too subtle to be touched by any general ethical maxims, this neglect of art by the moralist has been tantamount to a disqualification. The basis of morality, as Shelley insisted, is laid not by preachers but by poets. Bad taste and crude responses are not mere flaws in an otherwise admirable person. They are actually a root evil from which other defects follow. No life can be excellent in which the elementary responses are disorganized and confused."

tempts at definition. He is stating the *function* of poetry, at least what he considers to be its chief function. Criticism is not what poetry *is;* it is what poetry *does.* How it does it is another matter. Insofar as poetry helps us to live, not merely by occupying us or by delighting us but by clarifying us with delight, it is a criticism of life.

"The grand work of literary genius," says Arnold, "is a work of synthesis and exposition, not of analysis and discovery; its gift lies in the faculty of being happily inspired by a certain intellectual and spiritual atmosphere, by a certain order of ideas, when it finds itself in them; of dealing divinely with these ideas, presenting them in the most effective and attractive combinations,—making beautiful works with them, in short." If literature is a criticism of life, it is of a very special kind. The synthetic and expository character of literature, as against the analytical and exploratory character of philosophy or science, keeps them each in their different spheres. "Poetry is the interpretress of the natural world" as well as of the moral world, and as the interpretress of the natural world it is linked with science yet does what science cannot do, for "the interpretations of science do not give us this intimate sense of objects as the interpretations of poetry give it; they appeal to a limited faculty, and not to the whole man."

Natural magic and *moral profundity*—these are the two attributes of great poetry. But the pressure of moral ideas is more constant and immediate than the stimulus of natural magic. We can observe in the greatest poets—in Shakespeare and Lucretius, preeminently in Wordsworth—that the sensuous element diminishes as the moral increases and that, though the task of making "magically near and real the life of Nature, and man's life . . . so far as it is a part of that Nature" is a fair half of the function of poetry, there is a tendency for philosophy and moral profundity to dominate and destroy natural magic. The grand power of poetry is not, as with philosophy and science, "a power of drawing out in black and white an explanation of the mystery of the universe, but the power of so dealing with things as to awaken in us a wonderfully full, new, and intimate sense of them, and of our relations with them."

But poetry nevertheless lives by ideas and if the poet is to deal with them only in a synthetic way, he cannot be expected to create them: that is the task of philosophy and science. The poet must live in an atmosphere of the best ideas; how determine the best? It is here that criticism proffers its good offices as a kind of broker between abstract thought and poetry. "Life and the world being in modern times very complex things, the creation of a modern poet, to be worth much, implies a great critical effort behind it; else it must be a comparatively poor, barren, and short-lived affair."

Goethe had asked, "What are the conditions that produce a great classical national author?" His answer was substantially the one which Arnold makes to the same question. Goethe said:

He must, in the first place, be born in a great commonwealth, which after a series of great and historic events has become a happy and unified nation. He must find in his countrymen loftiness of disposition, depth of feeling, and vigor and consistency of action. He must be thoroughly pervaded with the national spirit, and through his innate genius feel capable of sympathizing with the past as well as the present. He must find his nation in a high state of civilization, so that he will have no difficulty in obtaining for himself a high degree of culture. He must find much material already collected and ready for his use, and a large number of more or less perfect attempts made by his predecessors. And finally, there must be such a happy conjuncture of outer and inner circumstances that he will not have to pay dearly for his mistakes, but that in the prime of his life he may be able to see the possibilities of a great theme and to develop it according to some uniform plan into a well-arranged and well-constructed literary work.

In short, the poet needs civil and intellectual order.

Of course, in England a kind of civil order prevailed, but were England's peace and her liberalistic economic system a true order or of a very fertile kind? Many men of divergent political views were united in believing they were not. They perceived energy and enterprise, but also waste and essential chaos. And Arnold saw this condition reflected in the intellectual life of the nation. Romanticism had abandoned the anti-individualistic poetic theories of the 18th century and the new reading public enshrined the mere energy of genius, just as liberal economic ethics had enshrined the mere energy of enterprise. The British public admired genius—and rather preferred it raw, like Alexander Smith's. The genius was the Bounderby of the arts, the man who could boast that he had started with nothing and had achieved everything—by himself alone, in the face of opposition. One might draw one's figure from industry and believe that genius was 10 % inspiration and 90 % perspiration: that was a comfortable notion, it gave every honest man a chance for genius. Or one could reverse the proportion and thus draw the figure from the dissenting chapel—make it 90 % inspiration, and then the genius was very much like the religious man seized with the spirit. In either case the idea of genius was attractive to the middle class: a genius was an absolute success and he had won his way *all by himself.* The notion that society contributes to the making of genius was as antipathetic as the notion that society contributes to the making of a wealthy brewer. But one of the great comic moments of the 19th century is Dickens' unmasking of Bounderby: so far from having started life in a gutter with only a shirt, the enterprising manufacturer had had a comfortable home, a devoted mother and a nice little capital. Arnold undertook to unmask the Bounderby conception of genius and poetic success.

The reality or validity of "genius" is unquestionable, obviously, and Arnold did not question it. Genius is *energy,* he said, and the first necessity of poetry. But genius is not all of poetry, for poetry is "simply the most beautiful, impressive, and widely effective mode of saying things" and if the things that are said are not the right things, no amount of energy—of genius—can excuse them.

Arnold, in his essay, "The Literary Influence of Academies," pointed to the body of literature of England's latest burst of poetical energy, the Romantic Movement, and found it deficient. For one thing, it had produced no single work comparable in execution to the perfection of form of the Greek best, or equal in profundity of insight. For another, it had sired no line of poetical descendants of an interest equal to its own. It had been dominated by energy but had lacked order and this was typical of the British spirit.* England's geniuses had been solitary, individualistic—and discontinuous. Shakespeare may have far surpassed Corneille, Newton had excelled Leibnitz: the Continental instinct for order, however, had compensated for the inferiority in endowed energy. The English literature that followed Shakespeare and his group was provincial and parochial while the literature that followed Corneille was the world-shaking literature of the 18th century. And Newton, an isolated genius, had fathered disciples who were comparatively powerless whereas the less-gifted Leibnitz had generated on the Continent a great tradition of research.

The French people, indeed, were preeminent in their understanding of the virtue of submitting the individual genius to law, of subordinating energy to intelligence. The English lacked this perception and in the Romantic period they had been unable to advance beyond a wonderful outburst of energy. "According to the Romantic doctrine," says Georg Brandes, "the artistic omnipotence of the Ego and the arbitrariness of the poet can submit to no law." In this direction, says Arnold, lies brilliance—but also failure and sterility. Samuel Rogers records a remark of Burke's that "England is a moon shone upon by France. France has all the things within herself; and she possesses the power of recovering from the severest blows. England is an artificial country: take away her commerce, and what has

---

* In fairness to the British spirit, we ought perhaps to remember Dr. Johnson's comparison of it with the French: "The English are the only nation who ride hard a-hunting. A Frenchman goes out upon a managed horse, and capers in the field, and no more thinks of leaping a hedge than of mounting a breach. Lord Powerscourt laid a wager, in France, that he would ride a great many miles in a certain short time. The French academicians set to work, and calculated that, from the resistance of the air, it was impossible. His lordship, however, performed it."—Boswell's *Journal of a Tour to the Hebrides* (1936) p. 217. Voltaire's description of the English genius is interesting: "The poetic genius of the English resembles, at this day, a spreading tree planted by nature, shooting forth at random a thousand branches, and growing with unequal strength: it dies if you force its nature or shape into a regular tree fit for the gardens of Marly."—*Short Studies in English and American Subjects.*

she?" Arnold agrees, in effect. He finds the strength of France in her ability to establish an interrelation of parts, to create centrality and order.*

Arnold had called to the attention of the British public the effect upon education of the French feeling for centrality and order embodied in the strong State. This same feeling created a State in the French Republic of Letters—the Academy—and Arnold is willing to consider the benefit that would accrue to English letters by the establishment of an English Academy. Swift had once proposed to Lord Oxford that the government undertake the erection of "a society or academy for correcting and settling our language, that we may not perpetually be changing as we do" and Southey, conceiving that men would quickly abandon their principles and the charms of popular adulation for the distinction of an R.A., had outlined a Royal Academy whose purpose was to draw off men of letters from subversive activity. Arnold's plan has nothing in common with Swift's rather trifling scheme or with Southey's amusingly base one. Indeed, he always insisted that he had no scheme at all, but was merely exemplifying that enlightening play of purely theoretical fancy which criticism must be. He wanted to explore English intellectual life by showing what an Academy might accomplish in every field from journalism to poetry and to discover what English energy might gain from French order. An Academy, he indicated, would control the helter-skelter laissez-faire of English thought. Criticism's function was to determine the best thought of an age and to disseminate it and the Academy might well be the critic enlarged and endowed with the prestige of establishment. It might serve as a cen-

---

* In his book, *The Civilization of France* (1932), one of the mementoes of an extinct German culture, Ernst Robert Curtius speaks of the profound French feeling for centrality: "So far as I know, France alone, of all modern countries, has a myth of centrality. At Bruère in Département Cher a Roman milestone is described as the 'Centre Géographique de la France.' . . . [The French pupil] learns from the explanations in his atlas that the outline of France can be defined as a hexagon, divided into two equal parts by the meridian of Paris. Thus his fatherland has a harmonious, almost geometrical shape. . . . It is at an equal distance from the North Pole and from the Equator. . . . The different 'regions' are nowhere separated by physical obstacles, and they form an organic unity." This is, for Curtius, the symbol of the French method of organizing social, political and intellectual life.

ter for the best opinion of the time, checking the whim of the individual, advancing his talent. Where there was power, it could help to prevent its dissipation in personal crotchets and eccentricities—such as those of Ruskin. Where there was genius it might warn of *too much* genius: genius has been too busy there, Arnold says of a brilliant sentence of Jeremy Taylor's—too much force without justification. Where there were ideas it could insist upon the ethical value of style, where there was style it could point out the provincialism of the commonplace and the necessity for maturity.

Arnold, in questioning the value of untrammeled genius, never makes the mistake of Joubert, who felt that energy itself was evil, nor has he the daintiness of Sainte-Beuve, for whom Balzac's vitality was suspect. Yet sometimes we feel that certain characteristics of manner which Arnold praises in the Academy and the "center"—the qualities of "amenity," "urbanity," and "unction"—are also too much the characteristics of the courtier and the abbé. And sometimes they are present in Arnold's own style at the cost, we feel, of the true virile metal, and we are inclined to cherish our sub-Olympian humanity and cry, "Less light, more heat!" For Arnold's prepossession with discipline leads him to forget that the romantic poets, if they did not have order themselves, were struggling toward it and that our perception of the struggle is itself a vivifying experience. He does not see that order is not only a Greek temple at the end of a clear path, but also finding one's path in the wilderness, or clearing the wilderness away. The aesthetic theory and practice of the romantic poets was just such a struggle:—Wordsworth's development is almost too obvious and extreme an example; Coleridge became almost Aristotelean in his poetics; Keats was constantly moving toward chastity of expression and objectivity of content; and Byron, whose admiration of Pope was constant and significant, turned in the end to the Greek dramatic form. What is even clearer is the effort of all of these men to achieve not only formal but *philosophic* order.

Yet Arnold's exaggeration of urbanity, amenity and order was not without justification in his time. The tone of the intellectual life of

his day was fairly raw; it was much invaded by the acerbities of party
politics, the critic choosing the knout or the butter-spreader according to the politics of the author he was reviewing; and political life
was too little touched by the intellect. Carlyle was threatening all
classes with his mighty but often irresponsible voice: "part man of
genius," as Arnold called him in a letter to his brother, "part fanatic
—and part tom-fool." Macaulay had only recently stopped parading
his apodictic-seeming priggishness as objectivity. Ruskin was exercising the incomparable orchestra of his prose, often to good ends but
often to confusion. And these were the best, the men who were dark-
ening counsel with great talents. The lesser men were yet more cul-
pable and increasingly influential: Arnold watched the growth of
journalese, saw the soulless flashiness of James Gordon Bennett's
editorials appearing in Kinglake's historical prose and insisted that
language like this was inevitably a falsification of fact. Consciously,
he sought to move to a way of thought which would allow the sight
to be undimmed by factional or personal interests or by foibles of
personality, to a new manner of speech which should be the outward
and visible sign of this new manner of thinking—new, that is, to
English intellectual life. Thought and speech of this kind he called
criticism.

Often Arnold's *criticism* has little enough to do with literary criticism; its meaning is often so loose and general as to make it seem a
kind of magical incantation, but it is enough for its purpose. Criticism's first function is to "see the object as it really is"—to see behind
the fine word and the inflated rhetoric to the actuality. Hegel had
exemplified the critical attitude in Arnold's sense when he said:
"When liberty is mentioned, we must always be careful to observe
whether it is not really the assertion of private interests which is
thereby designated."

It is the age of science and it is the age of party—on the one hand
there is the effort for clarity and the passionless definition of meaning, on the other, calculated obfuscation and the appeal to passion
and interest. The statistical societies, already flourishing in the 1830's,

could amass the facts; the party presses could display them to partisan ends. While the honest if fumbling effort of thinkers was trying to formulate the law behind society and to erect new sciences, the servants of interest were bending social concepts to their own social purposes. In such an age it was the duty of criticism to take the part of science and advance its unclouded disinterestedness. And this was especially necessary in England, for nothing was harder for the English, Arnold felt, than to see the object as it really was. Marked as they were by "energy" and "honesty," they lacked the virtues of the quick and lively intelligence which implements true honesty. They saw what they wished to see and ignored what diminished their peace of mind. They could talk easily of the splendors of their civilization because they never allowed themselves to realize anything that would gainsay their belief. They needed criticism because criticism confronts the ideal with the fact. Sir Charles Adderley and Mr. Roebuck congratulate the nation on its achievement in population, coal and liberty? Criticism quietly asks, What of the case of Wragg, the girl discharged from the Nottingham workhouse, who murdered her child in a ditch?

In short, at a time when class set itself against class and interest against interest, Arnold, in his great essay, "The Function of Criticism at the Present Time," speaks of criticism, whose peculiar quality it is to be disinterested. Criticism, like science, espouses no party, no cause, however good, except the cause of truth and the general welfare of man. In practical life, party and the taking of sides may perhaps be a necessity; even this necessity does not inevitably preclude disinterestedness. At a later time Arnold is to speak of Falkland, his father's hero, who, forced to choose sides in the civil war, criticized the party he chose and was so torn by shame at its deficiencies that he seems to have courted his own death. Now Arnold gives the example of Burke, who, after years of attack on the French Revolution, was still able to write:

If a great change is to be made in human affairs, the minds of men will be fitted to it; the general opinions and feelings will draw that way.

Every fear, every hope will forward it; and then they who persist in opposing this mighty current in human affairs, will appear rather to resist the decrees of Providence itself, than the mere designs of men. They will not be resolute and firm, but perverse and obstinate.

And Arnold comments, "That return of Burke upon himself has always seemed to me one of the finest things in English literature, or indeed in any literature."

But Falkland, after all, was rendered ineffectual by his disinterestedness. And Burke's disinterestedness did not prevent his long attack upon the French Revolution or keep the attack from being scurrilous and often unfair. Practical activity is either checked by disinterestedness or, if not, allows it but a moment in a lifetime. No doubt, Arnold would reply; and therefore if criticism is to assure its own disinterestedness it must remove itself from practical life.

It is of the last importance that English criticism should clearly discern what rule for its course, in order to avail itself of the field now opening to it, and to produce fruit for the future, it ought to take. The rule may be summed up in one word,—*disinterestedness*. And how is criticism to show disinterestedness? By keeping aloof from what is called "the practical view of things;" by resolutely following the law of its own nature, which is to be a free play of the mind on all subjects which it touches. By steadily refusing to lend itself to any of those ulterior, political, practical considerations about ideas, which plenty of people will be sure to attach to them, which perhaps ought often to be attached to them, which in this country at any rate are certain to be attached to them quite sufficiently, but which criticism has really nothing to do with. Its business is, as I have said, simply to know the best that is known and thought in the world, and by in its turn making this known, to create a current of true and fresh ideas. Its business is to do this with inflexible honesty, with due ability; but its business is to do no more, and to leave alone all questions of practical consequences and applications, questions which will never fail to have due prominence given to them.

If the English mind, with its love of action, finds advice such as this difficult to grasp, without its comprehension, the intellectual—and, indeed, the practical—effort of the century must become sterile.

For the French Revolution was not so much the fulfilment, Arnold believes, as the betrayal of the great ideas of France in the 18th century and failed because of the desire of men to give "an immediate and practical application to all these fine ideas of the reason."

Criticism must maintain its independence of the practical spirit and its aims. Even with well-meant efforts of the practical spirit it must express dissatisfaction, if in the sphere of the ideal they seem impoverishing and limiting. It must not hurry on to the goal because of its practical importance. It must be patient, and know how to wait; and flexible, and know how to attach itself to things and how to withdraw from them.

The spirit of criticism, then, is that which measures the actual and the practical by the ideal. It never relinquishes its vision of what *might be* and never says that what *can be* is perfect merely because it is better than what *is*. Criticism does an even more difficult thing than this:

It must be apt to study and praise elements that for the fulness of spiritual perfection are wanted, even though they belong to a power which in the practical sphere may be maleficent. It must be apt to discern the spiritual shortcomings or illusions of powers that in the practical sphere may be beneficent.

Perhaps no man has ever formulated—though some have practised —so difficult an intellectual course. "To study and praise elements that for the fulness of spiritual perfection are wanted, even though they belong to a power which in the practical sphere may be maleficent!" It is dangerous but it is a necessary study for cultural completeness; only the man of perfect equipoise and great spiritual strength may undertake it, the man utterly sure of the beneficent goal toward which he is striving. Here, if anywhere, we have the key to Arnold's importance and to his method. Here, too, we have the key to the reason why he is the common butt of people of such diverse views, and why he is admired by people who harm him with their admiration.

Yet behind Arnold's generalizations lie specific facts which we must examine if we ourselves are to use upon him the critical method he himself taught. Arnold, like his father, lived in the shadow of the French Revolution and of the Reign of Terror. He welcomed the new democracy but he suspected it. He welcomed rationalism but feared its effects. He was far from being at one with established religion yet he feared the void which its disappearance would leave. He saw old institutions crumbling and was glad, but he was uneasy lest their fall bring down more than themselves. He wanted progress but he feared the "acridity" which would characterize the forward movement. Consequently he found it necessary to formulate a point of view which, while it affirmed the modern spirit with its positive goal and scientific method, would still allow him to defend the passing order. Arnold's criticism was, in effect, his refusal to move forward until Burke and Voltaire compounded their quarrel, bowed to each other and, taking him by either hand, agreed on the path to follow.

In his essay on Heine, Arnold defines the modern spirit. "Modern times," he says, "find themselves with an immense system of institutions, established facts, accredited dogmas, customs, rules, which have come to them from times not modern. In this system their life has to be carried forward; yet they have a sense that this system is not of their own creation, that it by no means corresponds exactly with the wants of their actual life, that, for them, it is customary, not rational. The awakening of this sense is the awakening of the modern spirit." In effect it is the "sense of want of correspondence between the forms of modern Europe and its spirit, between the new wine of the eighteenth and nineteenth centuries, and the old bottles of the eleventh and twelfth centuries, or even of the sixteenth and seventeenth." Arnold is very clear that to "remove this want of correspondence is beginning to be the settled endeavour of most persons of good sense." He concludes that "dissolvents of the old European system . . . we must all be, all of us who have any power of working." But this is not all: "What we have to study is that we may not be acrid dissolvents of it."

Not acrid dissolvents: to only one dissolving agent of the old European system does Arnold give his full approval—to Goethe, who never fell into acridity and whose "profound, imperturbable naturalism is absolutely fatal to all routine thinking." Goethe "puts the standard, once for all, inside every man instead of outside him; when he is told, such a thing must be so, there is immense authority and custom in favour of its being so, it has been held to be so for a thousand years, he answers with Olympian politeness, 'But *is* it so? Is it so to *me?*' Nothing could be more really subversive of the foundations on which the old European order rested; and it may be remarked that no persons are so radically detached from this order, no persons so thoroughly modern, as those who have felt Goethe's influence most deeply."

But this way of working, Arnold knows, is slow; it must be supplemented with the headlong force of Heine, the true follower of Goethe, for Heine too, as he said of himself, is a soldier in the Liberation War of humanity. Arnold had begun by despising Heine; the letter to his mother in which he describes his disgust at the false "Byronism" of this "Voltaire au clair de lune" is a masterpiece of misunderstanding. We comprehend something of the nature of Arnold's critical mind when we see how the years brought the tempered but profound appreciation manifested in the essays, "Heinrich Heine" and "Pagan and Mediæval Religious Sentiment," and in the sonnets, "Heine's Grave." For Arnold, Heine becomes important not only because he is a soldier of liberation, but because his manner of fighting conforms to the demands of criticism. Heine understood the reality of ideas and knew that they were not marbles or counters but the basis of right conduct. Though he attacked reaction, he attacked it in his own way, with his eye on the realm of ideas and therefore his hatred of reaction was no greater than his hatred of the Philistine liberals who, though they too attacked the old order, betrayed the ideals of true liberalism.

Arnold nevertheless refuses to grant that Heine is a completely adequate interpreter of the modern spirit. True that he conforms to all the requirements that criticism might make of the intellect; he is the very embodiment of intelligence. But criticism demands more than intelligence; criticism demands that intelligence be not acrid, that it go hand in hand with "moral balance" and "nobleness of soul and character." Heine lacks these; he has everything save love.*

In other words, the social and intellectual ideas of the French Revolution—or most of them—must be made to prevail but the moral tone of the French Revolution must be replaced with something different and better, with what Arnold calls "unction."

Bishop Colenso wrote a book, no ordinary book but the center of a long and acrimonious battle in which the forces of progress were aligned against the old institutions; it was, clearly, a book that sought to remove the "want of correspondence between the forms of modern Europe and its spirit." Arnold condemned the book. Was he, as his liberal colleagues insisted, allying himself with the forces of reaction? He replied that he was not. Colenso had brought acridity to a situation which required unction and Arnold explains that when he denounces the mistake of a fellow-fighter in the liberal camp, he is not betraying liberalism but following the dictates of true criticism.

John William Colenso, bishop of the obscure African see of Natal, had set out to convert the heathen and found to his dismay that the heathen had converted him. It is rather like an 18th century tale of mythical exploration in which the simple rationalism of the savage triumphs over the dialectic of the priest; Voltaire would have enjoyed it. Colenso had made himself proficient in the Zulu tongue and had engaged the help of some intelligent natives to translate the Bible into their difficult language. But the intelligent natives began to ask questions. With their natural interest in wild life, they wanted to know how Noah had managed to get all the animals and all the necessary fodder into the ark with him. It was a simple question but

---

* Arnold quotes Goethe to this effect, but he was mistaken; Goethe did not say this of Heine but of Platen. See *Conversations with Eckermann*, the last conversation of 1825.

it checked Colenso, and he tells us his heart answered, "Shall a man speak lies in the name of the LORD? Zech. xiii. 3." He was the more embarrassed because he had lately been reading geology. He equivocated with his Zulu friends, sent for books, found that the apologists for the ordinary view were unsatisfactory but that the liberals, Ewald and Keunen, confirmed many of his own ideas.

Colenso saw at once the consequences of his position. He believed now that the so-called Mosaic narrative of the Pentateuch, "whatever value it may have, *is not historically true.*" There was no book in English which stated this simply and unequivocally and after some doubts Colenso published the work he had been preparing. He knew that he stood a good chance of being expelled from the Church but it was a "matter of life and death" and he decided to take the chance.

So far was Colenso from attacking the Church and religion that he believed he was contributing to their intellectual support. For it was no longer possible to keep things quiet: the simple fact that the biblical narrative was non-historical by modern standards of history was rapidly weakening faith in religion—exactly as Voltaire knew it would. It was significant that the brilliant university men were not going into the Church; the creed demanded a credulity which their intelligence could not allow. Colenso saw a general drift toward irreligion among thinking people; "The Church of England," he said, "must fall to the ground by its own internal weakness,—by losing its hold upon the growing intelligence of all classes,—unless some remedy be very soon applied to this state of things." And this state of things, he believed, was all the more dangerous because the skepticism of the intellectual middle classes was being shared by the multitudes of more intelligent factory operatives.

Colenso, in short, wanted religion to live on a somewhat reduced budget and to maintain its solvency by giving up the literal (or the slightly concessionary "apologetic") interpretation of the Bible. It was an obviously necessary move. It was, however, not so obvious to Colenso and his liberal partisans what dangers lay in this reduction of religion's budget; for though the modern highly-instructed man may accept religious supernaturalism without the evidence of miracle, simpler people cannot. Without supernaturalism religion is in danger of becoming little more than ethical culture, and often less. By reducing its budget in this one item religion may become undercapitalized. Yet there seemed nothing else to do.

Colenso was right to fear ecclesiastical punishment. England had not yet quieted down from the storm in 1860 over *Essays and Reviews,* a plea by several Churchmen for a more liberalized religion. The anger of the conservative Church had been enormous; the matter had come to legal prosecution and Dr. Pusey had so far forgotten himself as to write private letters to one of the judges to influence his decision in the interests of eternal damnation. The case had been brought before the House of Lords and the essayists and reviewers had been vindicated. But the forces which had been defeated in 1860 rallied now against Colenso in 1863, captained by the same Bishop Samuel Wilberforce who had led them in the earlier struggle. Soapy Sam—for such, because of his slippery arts in Church politics, was this prelate's unfortunate nickname—won a condemnation of Colenso from Convocation. A colonial bishop excommunicated his episcopal colleague, barred him from his own cathedral as a heathen man and a publican, and there were more lawsuits. Colenso's clerical supporters were persecuted; the press groaned with attack and defense. In court, despite the talents of Mr. Gladstone who was of counsel for the conservative faction, Colenso, to the misery of John Keble, was eventually sustained, his salary continued and his excommunication voided. But though Colenso had triumphed and his victory indicated an important change in English religious thought, he lived a miserable life; he was cut by his old friends and even his servants feared to stay with him.

Almost to a man, the liberals, in Church and out, defended Colenso. Arnold, however, though deprecating the belief that he was flinging a brother liberal to the High Church "hyenas," aggressively dissociated himself from the defense. He consulted the spirit of criticism and announced that Colenso's treatise had failed of the two requirements of a religious book, which are that it either inform the "much-instructed" or edify "the little-instructed." So far from instructing the much-instructed, the book had raised "a titter from educated Europe." It was, he said, useless to slay the slain and to tell portentously what everybody knew.

But Arnold's estimate on this point is not accurate. If indeed a titter had been raised from educated Europe it was probably at the spectacle of the English bishops gravely defending the propriety of the Leviticus hare that chewed its cud.* The commotion that was created among the English scarcely testified to the ease with which their much-instruction sat upon them. Colenso, it is true, was the equal neither in learning nor in analytical subtlety of the great biblical scholars of the Continent; his foreign colleagues were nevertheless ready to admit the importance of his work and to confess his influence upon them. If his mathematical demonstrations of discrepancies were perhaps too detailed for a reader impatient of naive literalness, he could yet scarcely be condemned apart from the whole movement of biblical criticism.

But Arnold's chief objection to Colenso was not his relative failure to inform the much-instructed, but rather his absolute failure to edify the little-instructed. Arnold insists that the factory operatives whom Colenso had had in mind could not possibly be edified—that is, their spirits could not be raised, their moral sense heightened nor their religious faith strengthened—by this work. But perhaps, Arnold suggests, Colenso had not sought to edify but to enlighten them? And perhaps

a religious book which attempts to enlighten the little-instructed by sweeping away their prejudices, attempts a good work and is justifiable before criticism, exactly as much as a book which attempts to en-

* "Prof. Hitzig, of Leipsic, one of the best Hebrew scholars of his time, remarked: 'Your bishops are making themselves the laughing-stock of Europe. Every Hebraist knows that the animal mentioned in Leviticus is really the hare; . . . every zoölogist knows that it does not chew the cud.' "—A. D. White: *History of The Warfare of Science with Theology in Christendom,* v. ii, p. 351.

lighten on these matters the much-instructed. No doubt, to say this is to say what seems quite in accordance with modern notions. . . . [But] the highly-instructed few, and not the scantily-instructed many, will ever be the organ to the human race of knowledge and truth. Knowledge and truth, in the full sense of the words, are not attainable by the great mass of the human race at all. The great mass of the human race have to be softened and humanised through their heart and imagination, before any soil can be found in them where knowledge may strike living roots. Until the softening and humanising process is very far advanced, intellectual demonstrations are uninforming for them; and, if they impede the working of influences which advance this softening and humanising process, they are even noxious; they retard their development, they impair the culture of the world. All the great teachers, divine and human, who have ever appeared, have united in proclaiming this.

And he continues:

Old moral ideas leaven and humanise the multitude: new intellectual ideas filter slowly down to them from the thinking few; and only when they reach them in this manner do they adjust themselves to their practice without convulsing it.

Many readers found this disturbing and Arnold had to explain that he was not throwing the multitude the sop of any convenient religious fiction. He had also to defend himself against the charge that he was making religion the prop of the political *status quo:*—he sought to correct this impression by shifting the argument from the factory operatives to men of all classes. Yet his position was an awkward one. He had said that democracy is moved by ideas, now he says that the vast majority of the members of a democracy must be protected from a certain set of ideas, those about religion. Obviously he cannot have it both ways. If democracy is to subsist by the current of ideas, it is inevitable that questions of religion will rise in that current.

It is a dilemma, certainly—but as much the dilemma of democracy as of Arnold. If Arnold's language is not of the clearest, at least he is trying to face an inescapable problem. If democracy assumes the ability of all men to live by the intellect, it argues that every man's faculty to know his own best interests indicates his ability to reason on all the problems of existence. But looking at the difficulties of the intellectual life and the enormous effort required of even our greatest philosophical minds, the mental rigors truth demands, we surely must question with Arnold the number of those who can support the intellectual life, even in a secondary way as pupils of the great. Especially today a survey of the condition of things cannot confirm our faith in the intellect either of masses or leaders and our optimism must be strong indeed if we are to believe in the dominion of reason in the future.

Arnold, having raised the question, answered inevitably that the number of those who can live in the rarefied air of the intellect must be small. He might have used the words of Rousseau: "Although it might belong to Socrates and other minds of the like craft to acquire virtue by reason, the human race would long have ceased to be, had its preservation depended only on the reasonings of the individuals composing it." How, then, do the great multitude live? If not by philosophy, then by religion, Arnold answers, and is sure there is no other way. For those who cannot reason out what is right, religion lays down the path; for those who cannot find an abstract ethical basis for their action, religion provides the code.

Arnold, now as later, believes that religion is morality's best stay and he rejects Colenso's book because it unsettled faith among the factory operatives and offered nothing new to stabilize it. Yet if Colenso was not especially notable for his subtlety of insight, at least in this instance he was more realistic than Arnold because he knew that the secret was out, that no amount of "edification" could offset the influence of Tom Paine—long a favorite among the better-instructed factory workers—and of the hundreds of pamphlets that Paine's followers were supplying them. These men, suspicious of miracle with all the natural skepticism of men who spend their lives with machinery, had little interest in the Bible of miracle and they were increasingly indifferent to a Church which sought to supply them with a way of life based upon supernaturalism. As well ask them to believe that their looms could go without the power-belt as that Jericho's walls fell at a trumpet. The Church's only hope lay in renouncing or making secondary its claims to miracle. But Arnold is not sure. He even goes so far as to question the loyalty to the Church of the liberals who hold this view and to doubt whether they are in the right or in good taste to convulse the Church with questions: "The clergy of a Church with formularies like those of the Church of England, exist in virtue of their relinquishing in religious matters full liberty of speculation." It is a position that would much have surprised his father.

The certainty that the choice lies between religion and the rigors of philosophy leads Arnold back to Spinoza's *Political-Theological Tractate*. Spinoza's theory of biblical criticism, which was epoch-making, undertook to establish religion of a kind acceptable to men of good will who stood on a middle ground between the vulgar, superstitious masses and those very few who were capable of understanding and supporting the strenuous conclusions of the author's naturalistic philosophy as set forth in the *Ethics*.* It had, too, a political purpose, for it sought to prove what its title declared, "that freedom of thought and speech not only may, without prejudice to piety and the public peace, be granted; but also may not, without danger to piety and the public peace, be withheld."

Spinoza's conception of religion is simple but daring. He set religion apart from philosophy and science and forbade either to interfere with the other. For one is the product of the imagination, the other of the intellect, and the two are not interdependent. Religion deals with morality, which can never be proved true but only good; philosophy deals with what can be demonstrated by mathematics. Religion is a matter of revelation, though by revelation we must understand the imagination and intuition of man apprehending the

---

* Arnold recalls that Spinoza refused to allow the Tractate to be translated out of its original Latin for fear lest it upset the faith of the "crowd." Spinoza had, perhaps, a justified fear of the "crowd;" his friends, the brothers de Witt, had been murdered in a political riot and Spinoza would have courted the same fate by denouncing the rioters to their faces, had he not been prevented by solicitous friends.

order of the universe, so far as that is moral; through human agency, not by miracle, the simple idea of the "Divine Mind" is given to man —and that idea is only "obedience to God in singleness of heart, and in the practice of justice and charity." And justice and charity are not things that require speculation; everyone knows them.

Spinoza is very clear, and rather depressing, on the limits of religion as well as on its practical advantages.

Therefore this whole basis of theology and Scripture, though it does not admit of mathematical proof, may yet be accepted with the approval of our judgment. It would be folly to refuse to accept what is confirmed by such ample prophetic testimony, and what has proved such a comfort to those whose reason is comparatively weak, and such a benefit to the state; a doctrine, moreover, which we may believe in without the slightest peril or hurt, and should reject simply because it cannot be mathematically proved: it is as though we should admit nothing as true, or as a wise rule of life, which could ever, in any possible way, be called into question; or as though most of our actions were not full of uncertainty and hazard.

Arnold seizes on this ticket of leave which Spinoza gives religion. Philosophy and science and biblical criticism may assert anything they like; they are censurable only if they offer their ideas in contradiction to the ideas of the religious life—then they are censurable indeed. For then they disturb men of comparatively weak reason (the mass of mankind) without providing a new source of peace.

Arnold, in defending religion, was chiefly concerned with the advantages to the individual life which religion offered. He was convinced that a rational ethic was inevitably depressing and he desired the joy and affirmation which religion afforded, even if the expansion of the human spirit was the response to a poetic and not to a scientific truth. But beyond the motive of defending the poetic truth of religion, Arnold saw in it a fundamental instrument of civil order— not only in its tenets but in its method of approach. There were in France many men who had brought the method of a sophisticated religion into conjunction with politics, but Arnold avoided the diversely extreme examples of Bonald, Maistre and Lamennais and chose Joubert. In "The Function of Criticism at the Present Time," Arnold had quoted one of Joubert's maxims: "C'est la force et le droit qui règlent toutes choses dans le monde; la force en attendant le droit. (Force and right are the governors of this world; force till right is ready.)" In essence, this idea and the system of thought it implies hark back to Pascal who had sought to erect an intelligent and realistic anti-rationalism to combat the growing rationalistic analysis of the injustice of government.* Arnold aligns himself with the Pascalian position and amplifies the maxim of Joubert: "And till right is ready, force, the existing order of things, is justified, is the legitimate ruler."

Divide life into two realms, one of speculation and the other of practice or obedience, and this is perhaps bound to be the outcome. The idea of right exists for Arnold—now at least—only in the world of ideas; force exists in the world of practice. To the comment made to him that a thing's being an anomaly is no objection, Arnold replies with a *distinguo*: "I venture to think . . . that a thing is an anomaly *is* an objection to it, but absolutely and in the sphere of ideas: it is not necessarily, under such and such circumstances, or at such and such a moment, an objection to it in the sphere of politics

---

* Pascal says: "Nothing, according to reason alone, is just in itself; all changes with time. Custom creates the whole of equity, for the simple reason that it is accepted. It is the mystical foundation of its (equity's) authority; who ever carries it back to first principles destroys it. Nothing is so faulty as those laws which correct faults. He who obeys them because they are just, obeys a justice which is imaginary, and not the essence of law; it is quite self-contained, it is law and nothing more. He who will examine its motive will find it so feeble and so trifling that if he be not accustomed to contemplate the wonders of human imagination, he will marvel that one century has gained for it so much pomp and reverence. The art of opposition and of revolution is to unsettle established customs, sounding them even to their source, to point out their want of authority and justice. We must, it is said, get back to the natural and fundamental laws of the State, which an unjust custom has abolished. It is a game certain to result in the loss of all; nothing will be just on the balance. . . . We must not see the fact of usurpation; law was once introduced without reason, and has become reasonable. We must make it regarded as authoritative, eternal, and conceal its origin, if we do not wish that it should soon come to an end." In the following, we may almost see the direct inspiration of Joubert's own *pensée:* "Justice is subject to dispute; might is easily recognized and is not disputed. So we cannot give might to justice, because might has gainsaid justice, and has declared that it is she herself who is just. And thus being unable to make what is just strong, we have made what is strong just."

and practice." It might be Burke speaking of the irrational wisdom of States. For he is saying something more than that right ideas cannot be immediately put into practice; the language is almost that of Pascal himself, as Arnold says:

But right is something moral, and implies inward recognition, free assent of the will; we are not ready for right,—*right,* so far as we are concerned, *is not ready,*—until we have attained this sense of seeing it and willing it. The way in which for us it may change and transform force, the existing order of things, and become, in its turn, the legitimate ruler of the world, should depend on the way in which, when our time comes, we see it and will it. Therefore for other people enamoured of their own newly discerned right, to attempt to impose it upon us as ours, and violently to substitute their right for our force, is an act of tyranny, and to be resisted.

We must admire the realism with which Arnold sees the nature of government, for by "force" he means only that—government as we know it. But, as Arnold himself implies, his "force," his government, is founded not on reason and justice but on irrational things, on property and the ascendancy of some classes over others. The critic who follows Arnold's own method of criticism must immediately ask when he reads the passage just quoted who are "we" and who are "they," we with "our force," they with "their right"? Are "we" the ruling classes? Then Arnold has himself chosen a party. Are "we," by some chance, the followers of criticism? Then Arnold has lost his precious disinterestedness and entered serenely into the world of practice. Finally, should not "we," who are so quick to brand "their" attempt to impose "their" right upon us as tyranny, be equally quick to accuse "our" force of being tyrannical to "them"?

Hegel's theory of history had found the justification for force in the success of force, and Hegel denounced the school-masterish moralism which would vainly introduce the concept of right and bootlessly mumble such words as justice. Arnold is ready to accept, in some measure, the Hegelian justification of force, but he shrinks from making the consequent dismissal of a liberal morality. He will have both "force" and "right;" confusion results—and Arnold's *criticism* retires before the brutal questions of power.

Arnold, we must perceive, labors always under the fear of revolution. He desires progress and he sees in the peace of Europe the promise of "an epoch of expansion" in which the old institutions may be "dissolved" by the current of modern ideas. But the acrid yeast of rationalism is still working strongly; the later revolutions in France are fresh in memory and likely to recur; agitation in England among the working class is growing again after the Chartist defeat. The pressure of democracy he believes must again be channeled. The spirit of criticism with its separation of theory from practice, and the spirit of religion with its assurance of permanent values supply ways to check the tide or to lay out its direction. Arnold turns to Joubert and finds in him the virtues of criticism and religion brought directly to bear upon politics and social life.

Arnold does not present the whole of Joubert's philosophy. Had he done so we might understand more immediately the fears behind Arnold's effort to advance the cause of modern thought, for Joubert in his entirety is the very essence of refined reaction. Even Arnold, who did not quite see that Joubert's "light" is the phosphorescence of decay, is constrained to reject some of Joubert's most typical thoughts and when he cries "Liberty! Liberty! in all things let us have *justice,* and then we shall have enough liberty," Arnold replies, "The wise man will never refuse to echo these words; but then, such is the imperfection of human governments, that almost always, in order to get justice, one has first to secure liberty." On the whole, however, Arnold finds Joubert an admirable antidote to "acridity." Neo-Platonism had assured Joubert the belief in the "reality of ideas;" Schleiermachian pietism had lifted his eyes above sordid realities; his adoration of literary classicism made him stand in opposition to all that did not conform to the ancient pattern; his aristocratic background and his horror of the French Revolution made him live in a kind of sweet and passive resistance to modernity and to the notions of the *philosophes.* But Arnold misses the essential vulgarity of Joubert's refinement. Joubert sought timeless wisdom and produced an exquisite Bourbonism; he sought perfection but meant a denial of the body; he fostered the spirit, which only meant that he hated vigor. Someone said of him that he was "like a spirit which has found a body by accident, and manages with it as best it may" and Joubert was very pleased:

My wish, I tell you, is to be perfect. That alone suits me and can give me satisfaction. So I am going to make for myself a region more or less heavenly and very peaceful, where everything will please me and call me again. . . . Here, I hope that my thoughts will take on more purity than glitter, yet not lose all colour, for colours appeal to my mind. As for what they call strength, vigour, nerve, energy, "life," I hope I have no more use for it than just to climb up to my star.

Even Arnold feels this kind of thing is a bit too thick—or thin: of another similar self-glorification he says, "No doubt there is something a little too ethereal in all this."

But Joubert's ethereality did not keep him from laying down rules for the bodies and vitality of other men. With the provoking, unexplaining calm of the *pensée*-writer * he declares, "We must be pleased with our state, that is, the meanness or superiority of our condition. The king should enjoy his sceptre; the flunkey his livery." A staunch anti-libertarian in the philosophic interest of monarchy, Joubert admired the Chinese fixity of government, order and the abandonment of passion, and for the establishment of these qualities felt that the belief in a heaven was necessary. He hated Rousseau because Rousseau represented morality as positive and not merely negative. "Morality," he said, "is formed only to repress and constrain; it is a criterion, a criterion immovable and unchangeable, and for that very reason is a barrier: morality is a bridle and not a spur." For to give morality a positive function was to rob religion of some

---

* Which Aldous Huxley has so well hit off in the words of Sidney Quarles, the ridiculous scholar of *Point Counter Point:* "Dragged from the ivorah pinnacles of thought into the common dust comma I am exasperated comma I lose my peace of mind and am unable to climb again into my tower." "True greatness is invarsely proportional to myah immediate success."

of its province. He felt the loss of the Catholic synthesis keenly and we understand what endeared him to Arnold—who did not always approve of the Goethean method of self-reference—when he exclaims, "What lamentable ages these are, in which each of us measures everything by his own standards, and goes, in the Biblical phrase, by the light of his own lamp!" The new welter of facts which were presenting themselves to literature enraged him. " 'I'm hungry, I'm cold, help me!' There is material for a good deed, but not for a good work [of art]." And again: "From the fever of the senses, the frenzies of the heart, and the afflictions of the mind; from the disasters of the times and the great scourges of life—hunger, thirst, shame, sickness, and death—they can make many tales to draw many tears; but the soul whispers: 'You are hurting me.' " And yet again: "To be a good man and a poet, it is necessary first to drape the objects of one's contemplation, and to look upon nothing in its nakedness. At least, to interpose goodwill and a certain amenity."

Joubert epitomizes the cardinal vice of the intellectual: the substitution of words for things, of tropes for ideas. The only remedy for the deficiencies of such a mind, one feels, would be the hunger, thirst, cold which he excluded from art, or whatever else might give it the sense of the presence of the world of matter and the resistance it offers to the spirit of man. But though Arnold suspected something of Joubert's vice, he himself shared it in some measure and he had use for Joubert's unctuous religiosity to confront acrid rationalism and utilitarianism. Joubert's mind might be vague but it saw life under the glowing aspect of myth, evanescent and illusory perhaps, but more enchanting than utilitarianism and the compromise of practice.

"In your metaphysics," said Emerson, "you have denied personality to the Deity: yet when the devout motions of the soul come, yield to them heart and life, though they should clothe God with shape and color." Shape and color were necessary to the moral life, Arnold believed: the "sage" can perhaps take his morality without them, the "rest of mankind" cannot. The "mass of mankind have neither force of intellect enough to apprehend them clearly as ideas," says Arnold, "nor force of character enough to follow them strictly as laws." The philosophical way of life cannot give *joy:* "It is impossible to rise from reading Epictetus or Marcus Aurelius without a sense of constraint and melancholy, without feeling that the burden laid upon man is well-nigh greater than he can bear." He rejects Mill's accusation that the ideal of Christian morality is negative rather than positive, passive rather than active. For what Christianity can give is "the emotion and inspiration needful for carrying the sage along the narrow way perfectly, for carrying the ordinary man along it at all." The essay on Marcus Aurelius insists on the advantages of religion over philosophy; the essay "Pagan and Mediæval Religious Sentiment" shows the advantage of the religion of sorrow over the religion of pleasure despite all the charm of the latter. If negativism lies anywhere, Arnold insists, it does not lie in Christianity but in the intellectual and philosophic systems of morality which guide life but cannot affirm it. The old theme of joy has recurred once more, the theme of *positive* happiness to which the intellect cannot minister and which paganism cannot serve, exactly because it sees only happiness and does not recognize the possibility of being sick or sorry. It is, again, the theme of the "whole man" who needs religion for his completeness.

Chapter Eight

➤➤➤ ◄◄◄

THE FAILURE OF THE MIDDLE CLASS

*". . . There is in the Englishman a combination
of qualities, a modesty, an independence, a responsibility, a repose, combined with an absence
of everything calculated to call a blush into the
cheek of a young person, which one would seek
in vain among the Nations of the Earth."*

—MR. PODSNAP

PALMERSTON died in 1865, at the height of six decades of
political power. England rang with his loving praise: eighty
years of life had made the Prime Minister an institution and
a monument. He linked the Britain of the present to the Britain of
Nelson and Pitt, to a time not safer but simpler and more confident, when England, having defeated Napoleon and checked the
Revolution, had put her welfare into the hands of a strong aristocracy and had dominated Europe.

An aristocrat and by heritage a Tory, Palmerston had turned
Whig in the struggle over the Reform Bill of 1832, supporting it
to prevent a more drastic reform. Finance capital had merged the
interests of aristocracy and middle class and Palmerston had become the very symbol of the new union. Here was the True-Born
Englishman, by no means brilliant but by all means effective, without pretensions to intellect but with a remarkable ability to muddle
through to success. He had no special sensitivities and no special
scruples. He was erratic and even eccentric, but strictly within the
bluff national pattern, and he was superbly fitted by a love of bravura
to dramatize England's power.

222

Arnold watched the newsprint laurels being heaped upon the crafty old head and wondered whether this was the True Englishman or the True Philistine. Another, even more stringent, critic of Philistinism has said that Palmerston's chief ability was to substitute "phrases for facts, phantasies for realities, and high-sounding pretexts for shabby motives;" Arnold did not read Karl Marx but what else had he himself been saying about all of Whiggery?

With boisterous liberalism, Palmerston's foreign diplomacy had undertaken the defense of oppressed nations while at home his policies hewed close to the conservative Whig line. But actually even Palmerston's policy abroad was a tangle of what Marx calls the "shams and contradictions that form the essence of Whiggism." "If the oppressors were always sure of [Palmerston's] active support," Marx wrote, "the oppressed never wanted a great ostentation of his rhetorical generosity;" his whole art lay in knowing how to "conciliate a democratic phraseology with oligarchic views, how to cover the peace-mongering policy of the middle classes with the haughty language of England's aristocratic past—how to appear as the aggressor where he connives, and as the defender where he betrays—how to manage an apparent enemy, and how to exasperate a pretended ally—how to find himself, at the opportune moment of the dispute, on the side of the stronger against the weak, and how to utter brave words in the act of running away." What better servant of its anomalies could Whiggism desire? Finding no virtue in consistency of words with actions, he could fly the liberal banner abroad while at home he reinforced the stand of the older industrialists against the renewed pressure of change.

Palmerston's death, however, seemed to signalize an era when change was inevitable; 1866 was an agitated year of great mass meetings, of the Hyde Park railings and flowerbeds, of class feeling grown explicit and bitter, exacerbating the nervousness resulting from financial panic and from a series of disastrous agricultural failures. A wide extension of the suffrage was unavoidable and the middle class stood on the verge of a new phase of its existence. Up to 1866 Arnold had been trying to mitigate the "acridity" and the "eccentricity" of liberalism—to check, that is, the intellectual excesses of the French Revolution in both its rationalistic and its romantic aspects. But in 1866 he turned sharply upon himself to say that middle class liberalism had not gone too far but actually not far enough in the revolutionary tradition. The work of that year—it comprised the essay "My Countrymen," many of the letters to the *Pall Mall Gazette* which were later made into *Friendship's Garland,* and the Oxford lectures on the study of Celtic literature—had a single theme: the calloused betrayal by middle class liberalism of the best of modern Europe, the betrayal of the French revolutionary tradition, both in its rationalism and in its romanticism, in its social good sense and in its spiritual aspiration.

II

The grounds of Arnold's indictment of the middle class have been confirmed by more recent and more systematic historical scholarship; Weber and Tawney have amplified but scarcely modified his basic idea of the organic connection between the religious doctrine of the middle class and its social and political philosophy. Indeed, the modern problem of the State was formulated in the religious quarrels of the 16th and 17th century and not until the end of the 19th do its terms become wholly secular.* The French writers who had forged the revolutionary philosophy turned constantly for inspiration to an English liberalism which had fought many of its battles on the high ground of religious freedom. The English Reformation, in settling the chief political problem of the Middle Ages, the relations of the Catholic Church and the national State, had but disclosed a new problem, the relation of the individual or of the dissident group to the national Church and (since Church and

---

* Gladstone's career exemplified the change. The young politician thought that the Reform Act of 1832 had "a certain element of Antichrist" in it; his *The State in its Relations with the Church* declared that the State was properly the Church's servant. But the old minister, without decreasing his allegiance to the Church, became increasingly willing to divorce religion from government.

State were one) to the national State. The man who in religion refused to be answerable to any Church, in politics was likely to refuse to be answerable to any State; the theories of religious freedom
and of economic freedom were assimilated to each other and the
rights of the spirit became the rights of business enterprise.

The essence of feudalism had been a centralization which limited
the privilege of the predatory rôle to a relatively few members of
society. This order of things, however, depended upon a social organization based on land, whereas the new society was increasingly
based on money. Money was a middle class medium which had
always been scorned by an aristocratic ethic and literature; it had
been high tragedy to lose broad acres, but low farce to cry; "My
ducats! My ducats!" But now, with an expanding capitalism of trade
and manufacture, aggression could no longer be the prerogative of
the high-born alone; all men who could scrape together the minimal
grace of cash might claim the right to be predatory. And while, in
the ordinary nature of things, the possession of land is in itself no
assurance of the eventual possession of more land, a sensible man's
possession of a sum of money over and above the necessities of life
becomes the handsel of greater glories: the anatomist of capital
speaks of money as "a monster quick with life, which begins to
'work' as if love were breeding in its body." A class whose economic
life was based on money was inevitably expanding and a rising class.

Even in its infancy the money class was in conflict with the central government. The concept of the *nation* was largely the property
of the aristocracy if only because the aristocracy controlled what
was most typically national, the policy in foreign affairs. As early
as the 14th century the middle class, excluded from participation in
diplomacy, withdrew from the court and formed its own circles;
sullen at being forced to finance what it could not direct, it left the
State to the aristocracy and entrenched its power in the city: "citizen"
became a contemptuous word in the mouth of the aristocrat. Individualism, provincialism, indifference to the concept of a whole nation—these were the inevitable products of exclusion and coercion;

the medieval Jew was not alone in his secretiveness about money; the Christian merchant, too, learned to hide his cash and send his silver out the back door when the tax-collector entered the front.

A class which, for whatever reasons, lives in conflict with national institutions is likely, when it comes to economic power, to repudiate the responsibilities of power. The modern apologist for feudalism may make too much of the feudal sense of responsibility but even Marx, who had no love for the "idiocy of rural life," could find advantages in the feudal as against the bourgeois social relationship: "The contrast between the power that is based on personal relations of dominion and servitude, the power that is conferred by landed property, on the one hand, and, on the other, the impersonal power conferred by the ownership of money, is well expressed by two French proverbs, which may be translated as follows: 'There is no land without a seigneur,' and 'Money has no master.'" And Tawney comments: "An interesting illustration of [Karl Marx's] thesis [that capitalism brutalizes the relationship between master and man] might be found in the discussions of the economics of employment by English writers of the period between 1660 and 1760. Their characteristic was an attitude towards the new industrial proletariat noticeably harsher than that general in the first half of the seventeenth century, and which has no modern parallel except in the behavior of the less reputable of white colonists towards colored labor." The cash nexus had replaced any other.

And there was a force which strengthened and rationalized for the middle class employer his repudiation of any connection between master and man—his Calvinist creed. A famous Calvinist divine of the 19th century described the system of Elizabethan poor laws as based on "the principle that each man, simply because he exists, holds a right on other men or on society for existence;" and when Dr. Chalmers characterized the principle in this way, it was not to praise but to denounce it; he was thinking in the true tradition of Puritan social morality. It was Calvinism that spoke through Nassau Senior's report on poor-law administration; when it was adopted and the so-called "Bastilles" were established, being in the public charge in England became the one condition of life more miserable than working for wages. Nor was it an accident that Calvinism abrogated the old Church law (long inactive, to be sure) against taking interest. Calvinism and the business activities of the middle class complement each other with a gratifying neatness; the Economic Man and the Calvinist Christian sing to each other like voices in a fugue. The Calvinist stands alone before an almost merciless God; no human agency can help him; his church is a means of political and social organization rather than a bridge to deity, for no priest can have greater knowledge of the divine way than he himself; no friend can console him—in fact, he should distrust all men; in the same fashion, the Economic Man faces a merciless world alone and unaided, his hand against every other's.

Calvinism hated the questioning mind after it had done questioning the value of other creeds. Part of its doctrine of faith was that no man can know his own condition of grace, whether saved or damned, yet if one has no confidence in one's grace, by that very fact one is weak in faith and hence probably damned. Calvinism therefore recommends the therapy of intense worldly activity and it is perfectly consistent with his Calvinist training that Carlyle should tell the young men of England that only in work—almost any work—lies their hope of salvation from the transcendentalized fear of damnation; after his own period of *Weltschmerz* Carlyle always felt that consciousness was a weakness, that the failure of the French Revolution lay in its having become aware of itself. So when Arnold speaks of a middle class "drugged with business" he speaks not merely of an accident of Puritan culture but of one of its requirements: the profound unintellectuality of the middle class surely had its roots deep in religious doctrine.

Industriousness leads to the sinless life and industriousness leads to the acquisition of capital. But to Calvinism work has still another virtue. A man's work is his vocation, his "calling," in exactly the same sense that a man is "called" to a priesthood. Work is a holy thing, a spiritual effort in itself; if a man is successful in his calling it is because of his virtue and as a sign of his grace; his failure hints damnation. Financial success is a mark of spiritual election and, by implication, the poor man (to whom the Church once attached at least a formal virtue) is a sinful man.* Riches, the pursuit of riches, once regarded as the enemy of the religious life, now becomes its instrument and not to be thrifty or shrewd is no longer an impracticality, it is a disregard of duty!

In short, the doctrines of Calvinism involved a reversal of values with which Arnold became increasingly concerned. Work had always been a curse and a *means,* but it had now turned into a blessing and an *end.* The production of goods had become an end in itself and the consumption of goods only the means to further production. The factory was not made for man but man for the factory. It was a revaluation of things which extended to the whole of England's thinking as the middle class came to dominate the national life: last things had become first and first things last. A society based on such a paradox surely makes rational thought an impossibility. It can speak of liberty but it must despise equality. It can speak of freedom, but it must never inquire into freedom's meaning or uses. It is a society increasingly ruled by the class that lives by irrationality, the class that Palmerston represented—a class, as Arnold said, "testy, absolute, ill-acquainted with foreign matters, a little ignoble, very dull to perceive when it is making itself ridiculous."

But it is such a class that Arnold undertakes to lead to the light of a new era, not now by an appeal to a higher notion of reason but by a simple appeal to utility and the state of the Empire. "Unless you change," he warns England, "unless your middle class grows

---

* Herbert Spencer made this attitude boldly explicit: "The feeling which vents itself in 'poor fellow!' on seeing one in agony, excludes the thought of 'bad fellow,' which might at another time arise. Naturally, then, if the wretched are unknown or but vaguely known, all the demerits they may have are ignored; and thus it happens that when the miseries of the poor are dilated upon, they are thought of as the miseries of the deserving poor, instead of being thought of as the miseries of the undeserving poor, which in large measure they should be."—*The Man vs. The State,* p. 36.

more intelligent, you will tell upon the world less and less, and end by being a second Holland." For by the contradictions of Palmerston's policy, essence of the middle class's anomalies and of its divorce of word from deed, England has already been reduced to a third place among the nations after France and America.

Once, says Arnold, England had the "secret" of the world, the secret of 1815, the secret of force, of a powerful aristocracy and of Pitt. With this "secret" England defeated France's intention of a European confederacy of states under French domination and the Continent followed England in spirit, emulating both her culture and her politics. But now a new time has come whose secret England does not know, the secret of *intelligence*. It is a secret that will do the work of the French Revolution—"the work of making human life, hampered by a past which it has outgrown, natural and rational." But England, Palmerston-led, using the haughty language of an aristocratic past to cover the policies of its middle class, is anything but intelligent and consequently the Continent can say to her: "You are losing the instinct which tells people how the world is going; you are beginning to make mistakes; you are falling out of the front rank. The era of aristocracies is over; nations must now stand or fall by the intelligence of their middle class and their people."

The *people* of England, says Arnold, is still in embryo. The whole weight of the country rests upon the middle class, and the intelligence of the middle class is virtually non-existent. It is the middle class which has betrayed the work of the Revolution. There is no equivocation in Arnold's statement of what constitutes the intention of the French Revolution. It is the intention of making life natural and rational by the criteria of the utilitarian hedonism of that very Bentham, at whom, but two years before, he had sneered rather vulgarly in the Preface to the *Essays in Criticism;* the measure of its success is the greatest happiness of the greatest number.

What, Arnold wants to know, could be less enviable than the lot of the English masses, the greatest number? Indeed, what—he points to the House of Commons, representative of the great English middle class, the pride of the English political system, and asks—what could be less enviable than the lot of the middle class itself with all its legislative power? "What," he asks, "brings about, or rather tends to bring about, a natural, rational life, satisfying the modern spirit?" "This:" he answers, "the growth of a love of industry, trade, and wealth; the growth of a love of the things of the mind; and the growth of a love of beautiful things. There are body, intelligence, and soul all taken care of." But of these three things the middle class is concerned only with the body:

> The fineness and capacity of a man's spirit is shown by his enjoyments; your middle class has an enjoyment in its business, we admit, and gets on well in business, and makes money; but beyond that? Drugged with business, your middle class seems to have its sense blunted for any stimulus besides, except religion; it has a religion, narrow, unintelligent, repulsive. All sincere religion does something for the spirit, raises a man out of the bondage of his merely bestial part, and saves him; but the religion of your middle class is the very lowest form of intelligential life which one can imagine as saving. What other enjoyments have they? The newspapers, a sort of eating and drinking . . . a literature of books almost entirely religious or semi-religious, books utterly unreadable by an educated class anywhere, but which your middle class consumes, they say, by the hundred thousand; and in their evenings, for a great treat, a lecture on teetotalism or nunneries. Can any life be imagined more hideous, more dismal, more unenviable?

All that the legislation of the middle class has accomplished has been the increase of trade, but in "all that goes to give human life more intelligence and beauty, [it] is no better than was to be expected from its own want of both."

Here, then, is the result of the Puritan ideology: the middle class man thinks he has reached "the highest pitch of development and civilisation when his letters are carried twelve times a day from Islington to Camberwell, and from Camberwell to Islington, and if railway-trains run to and fro between them every quarter of an hour. He thinks it is nothing that the trains only carry him from an illiberal, dismal life at Islington to an illiberal, dismal life at Cam-

berwell; and the letters only tell him that such is the life there."
And this same transvaluation of means to ends blinds the middle
class man to the truth that "Freedom, like Industry, is a very good
horse to ride;—but to ride somewhere. You seem to think that you
have only to get on the back of your horse Freedom, or your horse
Industry, and to ride away as hard as you can, to be sure of coming
to the right destination."

"My Countrymen," as Arnold called his indictment, appeared in
February of 1866 and caused a stir; Arnold followed and defended
it with a series of letters to the *Pall Mall Gazette* (later published
as *Friendship's Garland*) in which he fathers his ideas upon a certain young Prussian of his invention, Arminius von Thunder-ten-
Tronckh, lineal descendant of the house which had reared and
expelled Candide; Arminius is the embodiment of German intelligence and he has only contempt for the English system.* "Liberalism and despotism," he roars at his creator, "let us get beyond these
forms and words. What unites and separates people now is *Geist.*
. . . You will find that in Berlin we oppose 'Geist,'—*intelligence,* as
you or the French might say,—to 'Ungeist.' The victory of 'Geist'
over 'Ungeist' we think the great matter in the world. The same
idea is at the bottom of democracy; the victory of reason and intelligence over blind custom and prejudice." And so, Arminius
points out, the German liberals have sympathy with France and its
governors so far as they believe in democracy, but they have no sympathy with English liberalism because its center is the "Ungeist" of
the manufacturing middle class.

The English liberal's betrayal of the basic ideas of democracy, his
prevention of the victory of reason and intelligence over blind cus-

---

* Henry Adams reminds us: "The literary world then agreed that truth survived
in Germany alone, and Carlyle, Matthew Arnold, Renan, Emerson, with scores of
popular followers, taught the German faith. . . . The middle class had the power,
and held its coal and iron well in hand, but the satirists and idealists seized the press,
and as they were agreed that the Second Empire was a disgrace to France and a
danger to England, they turned to Germany because at that moment Germany was
neither economical nor military, and a hundred years behind western Europe in the
simplicity of its standard."—*The Education of Henry Adams,* Chapter IV.

tom and prejudice—these are the objects of Arminius's ill temper. A perfect Bentham in Prussian clothes, he attacks the irrationality of English education, English law, English land systems, English legal administration; he rages against a middle class which maintains the irrationality of feudalism; with red-revolutionary passion he points out that the strength of France is in the French working class, baptized in the fire and ideas of the Revolution, possessed of *Geist* and kept vital by it, though the classes above it rot. But the English have no *demos* with which to make a democracy—only masses with vulgar tastes, corrupted by the Philistines, the more substantial half of them in training to be Philistines themselves, the rest a mere rabble.

The spectacle is not merely distasteful; it is dangerous. Unless, Arnold warns, the middle class learns to think a little more and bustle a little less, and changes this condition of things, England will not be at the top of the next historical wave.

III

But thinking is not, for Arnold, the whole of the secret: there are also practical and political advantages in right *feeling,* and it is with these that the lectures *On the Study of Celtic Literature* are concerned. If Arnold's essay on the Greek dramatic form and his lectures on Homer had, in their discussion of an ordered style, pointed toward an ordered society, the lectures on Celtic literature point now toward an expansive social feeling. They are concerned not with the chaste but with a warm style, not with the sharply defined but with the illimitable, and by implication with the generosities of desire and the ideal.

The subject of these lectures afforded Arnold a peculiar pleasure. It allowed him to bring together, in what he conceived to be the modern way, the literary and scientific methods. Science, the anthropology of his day, told him that the spirit of a nation—what we might call its national *style*—is determined by "blood" or "race" and that these are constants, asserting themselves against all other determinants such as class, existing social forms, and geographical and economic environment. The idea was a pervasive one and ten years later the English public had a conclusive demonstration of how race might work when Daniel Deronda, reared as an English aristocrat and believing himself to be of Spanish "blood," began in maturity to exhibit specific Jewish qualities—chiefly a Prophetic morality—and found himself, despite his complete ignorance of a common ancestry, irresistibly drawn to other Jews.

Arnold embraced the whole of the racial assumption and was at pains to show that the English are an amalgam of several "bloods" —German, Norman, Celtic. Each blood, he believed, carried specific constant qualities, each quality preserved in the mixture of all. It was his task to make the English understand the existence and nature of the mixture that they might give proportionate play to each distinct component.

Today, when the anthropological doctrines which Arnold found so stirringly fruitful are supported only by political partisans or by writers whose scientific method Arnold himself, were he now living, would not accept, we must take his elaborate theory only as a kind of parable. Tested by truly scientific criticism, there is probably not a single generalization about race that will stand, and all careful and disinterested specialists agree with Franz Boas that "it does not matter from which point of view we consider culture, its forms are not dependent upon race." Indeed, as Julian Huxley and A. C. Haddon say, "the term 'race' is freely employed in many kinds of literature, but investigation of the use of the word soon reveals that no exact meaning is, or perhaps can be, attached to it, as far as modern human aggregates are concerned." The geneticist will not allow that specific moral and cultural qualities are carried in the genes or in the (physiological) blood. Without a genetic proof and without the possibility of specific moral and cultural qualities being isolated and exactly defined, the word "race" can have no meaning. As Jacques Barzun says in *Race: A Study in Modern Superstition,* race-thinking is but a "tangle of quarrels, a confusion of assertions, knot of facts and fictions that revolt the intellect and daunt the cour age of the most persistent. In its mazes, race-thinking is its own bes refutation. If sense and logic can lead to truth, not a single system of race-classification can be true." It is, to quote Barzun again, ": vulgar error because it denies individual diversity, scouts the com plexity of cause and effect, scorns the intellect, and ultimately bar Mind from the universe of created things."

But in Arnold's day the racial theory, stimulated by a rising nationalism and a spreading imperialism, supported by an incom plete and mal-assumed science, was almost undisputed. The concep tion of race served to sustain oppressed nationalities in their strug gle for freedom (Italy, Poland), to unify diversified states in thei attempt at integration and power (Germany), and to justify power ful imperialistic nations in their right to rule others. The theory sprung from the desk of the philosopher and the philologist, had at unfailing attraction for the literary and quasi-religious mind; the conception of a mystic and constant "blood" was a handy substitute for the *soul*. There were few men of literature and science—Buckle was one—to agree with John Stuart Mill that "of all vulgar modes of escaping from the consideration of the effect of social and moral influences on the human mind, the most vulgar is that of attributing the diversities of conduct and character to inherent natural differ ences." * But there were many to foster and elaborate the notion of a racial constant—Gobineau, who gave it its greatest impetus, who explained the enormous superiority of the blond northerners over the other Whites and of the Whites over the Blacks and Yellows; Moses Hess, who contrasted the eternal differences of Rome and Jerusalem; Heine who followed Hess and Ludwig Börne in making firm the distinctions between Hellenism and Hebraism; Disraeli who set Saxon industry against Norman manners and Jewish cul ture against Baltic piracy; Stendhal, Meredith, Mme. de Staël, Car-

---

* Mill is attacking the theory that ascribed the economic condition of Ireland to a "peculiar indolence and *insouciance* in the Celtic race."

yle, J. A. Froude, Kingsley, J. R. Green, Taine, Renan (from whom Arnold got much of his interest in the Celts), Sainte-Beuve—all built the racial hypothesis into their work. Indeed, the list could be made to include nearly every writer of the time who generalized about human affairs. And if some used it for liberalizing purposes, as Arnold himself did, still, by their very assent to an unfounded assumption, they cannot wholly be dissociated from the quaint, curious and dangerous lucubrations of Houston Stewart Chamberlain, Richard Wagner, Woltmann, Treitschke, Rosenberg and the whole of official German thought in the present day. It is not, after all, a very great step from Arnold's telling us that the Celt is by "blood" gay, sensual, anarchic, to Treitschke's telling us that Germans excel Latins in artistic appreciation because when a Latin reposes in the woods he crassly lies on his stomach whereas "blood" dictates to the German that he lie, aesthetically, on his back.

Arnold dismissed all doubts of the theory with a single sentence which seems to have direct reference to Buckle's insistence on the non-racial determinants of culture: "Modes of life, institutions, government, climate, and so forth,—let me say it once for all,—will further or hinder the development of an aptitude, but they will not by themselves create the aptitude or explain it. On the other hand, a people's habit and complexion of nature go far to determine its modes of life, institutions and government, and even to prescribe the limits within which the influences of climate shall tell upon it." On its face this seems like a telling retort, but it really says little more than that scientists have found no single way to account for cultural differences between various groups. This inability does not, however, as by a kind of scientific despair, admit the acceptability of the explanation of "blood." For one thing, the categories of what H. G. Wells calls the "governess theory" and what Huxley and Haddon call the "systematized anecdotal" method of classification, which give us such concepts as "the phlegmatic Dutch," "the volatile French" or "the morbid Spanish"—none of which can be observed, measured or proved constant but all of which are "intuited" by persons whose prejudgments and assumptions are certain to be many—can scarcely be "explained" because they have not been established.

Arnold's untenable theory of race, however, differs in one important respect from many others—in that it was not intended to separate peoples but to draw them together. Indeed, his own use of the theory contradicts the theory itself. For, having defined the constant qualities of Celtic blood, and having pointed out that the present English are an admixture which includes the Celt, he proceeds to urge his countrymen to give a greater prominence to their Celtic part. But the very characteristic of blood-determination seems to be that it is not intellectual; it cannot *decide:* just as it determines, so it is determined and as soon as a people admits an imperative higher than that of its blood—the imperative of reason, for example—the imperative of blood itself is totally negated; we all have the human qualities in some degree and once we *choose* to increase one quality over another something other than "blood" is at work.*

Just how to define a Celt, modern anthropology does not know— or knows too variously. Indeed, according to Hankins, "nothing illustrates better the tangled skein of anthropological and historical data than [the] so-called Celtic question." But in anthropology's less critical day Arnold knew that a Celt was a man who lived in certain parts of the British Isles (Scotland, Wales, Ireland) or in Brittany, or perhaps in Spain. Once the Celt had inhabited England itself but had been driven out by the invaders from Germany. As a visitor or immigrant to contemporary England the Celt is known by Englishmen as a great borrower of money and a teller of tall stories (see *The Tremendous Adventures of Major Gahagan* and Thack-

---

* Perhaps Wyndham Lewis has this fallacy of Arnold's in mind when, after a furious and characteristically brilliant and incoherent attack on Arnold as a "race-snob" (in the appendix to *The Lion and the Fox*), he says: "Arnold is not himself at all the dupe of the 'celtic' notion: his whole essay is written to expose it."

It is amusing to notice that after repudiating the theory of race, Mr. Lewis goes on to use it—"correctly." This is a not uncommon occurrence. H. G. Wells after his denunciation, in *Experiment in Autobiography,* of the "governess theory" of diplomacy which has corrupted the political thought of the British aristocracy, a theory based on the "virtues" and "vices" of nations, himself goes on, in effect, to employ it.

eray *passim*); in Ireland he is very noisy at Donnybrook Fair over the matter of a pig. Yet, according to Arnold, if we see the Celt in his literature * we find characteristics which the common English conception is likely to overlook. We perceive then that the Celt has "an organisation quick to feel impressions," that he has a "lively personality," that he is "keenly sensitive to joy and to sorrow." He is "soon up and soon down . . . the more down because it is so his nature to be up." He is "sociable, hospitable, eloquent." He is sentimental, and the nervous exaltation of his sensibility is essentially feminine; from him come the extravagances of chivalry. Nature draws him to her, seeming to speak her secret to him, and natural beauty and natural magic pervade all his literature.

The Celt, in short, may be summed up for good or ill in his readiness *"to react against the despotism of fact."* To this he owes his charm, his delicacy, his spirituality, but to this also he owes his lack of practical accomplishment. He cannot use his sensibility and perception with the sense of measure which marked the Greeks nor with the prosaic honesty of the Germanic races; he cannot, according to Arnold, continue the prolonged wrestling with matter or with form that makes great art out of talent, style and even genius. He lacks utterly in architectonics; he can make lovely melodies, but no cantatas or symphonies; his love of color, sensuality † and luxury does not lead him to create a great civilization; his infinite perception and lyric feeling have not led him to produce great poetical works but only "poetry with an air of greatness investing it all." And so, "for ages and ages the world has been constantly slipping, ever more and more out of the Celt's grasp."

In 1866 Ireland, under Sinn Fein leadership, was becoming violent, and England, with her old official self-righteousness and bridling aggrievement in Irish matters, was replying with coercion and

---

* Arnold made no pretense to a scholarly or "scientific" knowledge of Celtic literature; he relied upon the work of specialists for all matters of fact and he himself was "the mere literary critic."

† Arnold's idea of the sensuality of the Celt is ironically controverted by the aggressive Puritanism of the new Irish Republic.

anger. Arnold's picture of the Celt was in some part calculated to
allay the English fears and to represent Ireland in the rôle of, as it
were, court-Druid of the Union, mumbling lovely and ineffectual
words of a vanished glory. ("From the day I first set foot on this
foreign soil," says Bernard Shaw in the Preface to *Man and Superman,* "I knew the value of the prosaic qualities of which Irishmen
teach Englishmen to be ashamed as well as I knew the vanity of the
poetic qualities of which Englishmen teach Irishmen to be proud.
For the Irishman instinctively disparages the quality which makes
the Englishman dangerous to him; and the Englishman instinctively
flatters the fault that makes the Irishman harmless and amusing to
him.") But had Arnold's description been motivated simply by this
intention of conciliation it would have shared the vulgarity of race-
thinking in general; actually, he saw the Celt as something more
than a remnant of the past to be sentimentally cherished by a dominant people with its face to the future. For Arnold the Celt is the
perfectly contrived corrective to the Saxon, which is to say, to the
Philistine, the Philistine whose face was, after all, not so truly set
to the future as he himself thought.

Speaking for the Celt, Arnold speaks for romanticism's revolt
against Philistinism. By the Celtic sense of style Arnold does not
mean style in general, nor elegance, nor order; Pope, for example, has
style above almost everything else, but in this connection style, for
Arnold, means exactly what Pope did not have and what Gray so
preeminently did have—the delicate melancholy, the tone of old, unhappy, far-off things, of the light that never was on land or sea, of
magic casements, of lost causes and impossible loyalties. It is, in
short, the style of the dream and the ideal, all that is the opposite of
getting and spending, the Philistine activities which have laid waste
the powers of England. The feminine sensibility of Shelley and
Keats; Byron's "chord of penetrating passion and melancholy," his
Titanic Ossianism challenging the sun itself; the prophetic Druid-
ism of Wordsworth in his mystic communion with Nature; the natural animism of Coleridge;—and back beyond these to Shakespeare

and the dying fall of "On such a night as this"—the Celtic is synonymous with the romantic. Celtic style has for Arnold a moral content —the refusal to accept the despotism of fact and of the merely practical world. Its virtues are its vices, to be sure; it lacks architectonics and the practical world slips out of its grasp; but its vices are its virtues and it offers a continual refreshment from a world that is too much with us.

And how did the Celtic strain come into the English mind to give it its romantic poets? Thomas Arnold had once declared, in vehement language, the essential divorce between the Celtic and the English nature; his son contradicts him by conceiving the English nature as "a vast obscure Cymric [i.e., Celtic] basis with a vast visible Teutonic superstructure." He is perfectly literal in understanding this as a fact of genetics; when the Germanic conquerors took England, he says, the Celtic Britons did not all die or flee to Ireland, Scotland and Wales; some of them stayed behind and these, by miscegenation, mingled their blood with that of their conquerors and infused into the German prosaic nature their own love of the impalpable and the ideal.

The connection of the Celtic emotions with the Revolution is clear. The Revolutionary tradition was not of reason only but of the heart and the intuition. To the people who have betrayed the Revolution—the Puritan and Philistine middle class of England—Arnold is recalling their true heritage.

But Arnold had no intention of urging upon the English a nature of unalloyed idealism and poetry. There is, after all, the strong German element in the English admixture and now he discloses yet another—the Norman.* The Celts may have lacked a love of fact but this deficiency the Normans supplied in a high degree, and with it a "love of strenuousness, clearness, and rapidity, the high Latin

---

* Arnold's racial theory turns on him here but he blandly ignores its treachery. "No doubt," he says, "the basis of the Norman race is Teutonic; but the governing point in the history of the Norman race,—so far, at least, as we English have to do with it, —is not its Teutonic origin, but i.s Latin civilisation." But this is surely tantamount to saying that not blood but civilization determines "racial" traits.

spirit," missing in the Saxons. The excess of the Norman spirit was hardness and insolence, but it always had the Roman talent for affairs; neither prosaic nor poetic, the Normans were essentially rhetorical.

This mixture of bloods—Arnold's sermon goes on—is England's great good fortune, for it makes her people in so many ways superior to the single-blooded Germans. Though the agglomeration may confuse the English, making them awkward, embarrassed and hampered, yet it saves them from being dull in the German way. Thus the French speak of the "Allemand *balourd*" but of the "Anglais *empêtré*," making the distinction between heaviness on the one hand and awkwardness on the other. Where the German spirit may be defined as steadiness with honesty, the English spirit is energy with honesty. (Bernard Shaw was but ten years old and not yet able to speak his mind about English honesty, and Arnold, though he thinks that the truth about one's own country can best be learned from foreigners, forgets *perfide Albion*.) The Germans, purely Teutonic, tend to degenerate into *Gemeinheit;* but the English are saved from their Germanism by the Norman clarity and the Celtic gift for style—by the classic order of Greece and Rome and by the magic of the vanished Druids:

. . . Just what constitutes special power and genius in a man seems often to be his blending with the basis of his national temperament, some additional gift or grace not proper to that temperament; Shakespeare's greatness is thus in his blending an openness and flexibility of spirit, not English, with the English basis; Addison's, in his blending a moderation and delicacy, not English, with the English basis; Burke's, in his blending a largeness of view and richness of thought, not English, with the English basis.

The absurdity of this line is obvious. What Arnold is really saying is that Shakespeare has a greater openness and flexibility than most men have, English or other, and so with Addison and Burke. Who, after all, was the typical Englishman to whom openness and flexibility of spirit was not "proper"? Why should we not, with as much reason, take Shakespeare as the standard of Englishmen and say that all Englishmen who have not flexibility and openness of spirit are not Englishmen? Nothing, of course, could be more irrational than to set up arbitrary standards of national quality and then say that an unusual amount of that quality indicates another national "strain." Were we to adopt Arnold's method we might analyze the popular American conception of Abraham Lincoln in this way: "To the Saxon basis of honesty and energy is added the Norman talent for affairs, the Greek clarity of style as well as the Celtic magic; he had, too, the Celtic melancholy with its obverse of gaiety; yet this latter was infused with the degeneration of the French mind into lubricity [a later concern of Arnold's], for his jokes were often Rabelaisian. Add to all this the cool French skepticism of Montaigne in matters of formal faith as well as the fundamental piety of the French as seen in Pascal and strengthened with the moral sense of the Jewish Prophets, qualified and enlarged by the Hebraic Pantheism which Spinoza exemplifies; perceive the touch of German *Gemeinheit* in his manners, a Chinese patience and a Japanese ingenuity; impose the whole upon the love of independence of the Redskin—and we begin to understand the genius of Lincoln." * It is such juggling of "strains" which leads Arnold to pervert his own critical logic and his own notion of the personality. We find him, for instance, saying that the turn for style, derived from the Celtic strain, in English poets, "sometimes . . . doubles the force of a poet not by nature of the very highest order . . . and raises him to a rank beyond what his natural richness and power seem to promise." Arnold is talking of Gray and what he says is meaningless; it separates the poet's tal-

---

* The anthropological method of Arnold is carried to its extreme by so eminent a scientist as Havelock Ellis who professes in his *Study of British Genius* to be able to mark out the mental and emotional qualities of the British *counties*. There are, he says, three "great foci of intellectual ability in England: the East Anglian focus, the south-western focus, and the focus of the Welsh Border." The Arnolds are the product of the East Anglian focus, but Matthew Arnold belongs in part (through his mother) to the Goidelic-Iberian southwestern focus. The whole book is an amazing tissue of unfounded assumptions. Part of Ellis's description of the East Anglian temperament fits Arnold with such amusing neatness—the love of compromise, the tendency to scholarship and ecclesiasticism, the flexibility, the inaptitude for abstract thinking and metaphysics (of which Arnold was so proud)—that we almost forget Ellis's statement that a very large number of the villains of English history come from the same section.

ent from his sense of style, attributing the first to the man, the second to his race.

But we need not follow Arnold through all the vagaries which his anthropology thrusts on him—his acceptance of the "pregnant and striking ideas of the ethnologists" which inform us of the true natural groupings of the human race into the great "Indo-European unity comprising Hindoos, Persians, Greeks, Latins, Celts, Teutons, Slavonians, on the one hand, and, on the other hand, of a Semitic unity and of a Mongolian unity, separated by profound distinguishing marks," and attested to by such proofs as the violence with which the depths of von Humboldt's nature rejected Semitic religion. The point he wants to make—a point which becomes at once clearer and less "racial" in *Culture and Anarchy*—is that England is following a mistaken course in abandoning herself to the middle class creed of Calvinism. For Calvinism is what Arnold calls Hebraistic, which is to say that it is concerned with morality to the exclusion of all the other human faculties. And though the German honesty has a natural affinity to the Hebraic, in its best form it is concerned not with a narrow moralism but rather with science which, by being complete as well as dependable, serves the modern spirit.

Using the terms of "race," Arnold is, actually, speaking of reason and the complete man. He does so by "scientifically" offering England a far wider range of temperament than she had conceived. Whether he is literally committed to his concepts or is using them only anagogically, he insists that what is necessary for the English to understand is the nature of their temperamental composition. Only so will the German part be kept from the Semitic fidelity to a mechanical moral law, and made to produce a science by which England will be preserved from insolence and pride. The Norman-Latin decisiveness and sense of order will give a clear and strenuous method in the management of affairs and free England from fumbling in the Palmerston manner. The Celtic quickness of perception may bring delicacy of feeling and release England from the hardness and practicality of Philistinism. "But now we have Germanism enough to make us Philistines, and Normanism enough to make us imperious, and Celtism enough to make us self-conscious and awkward; but German fidelity to Nature, and Latin precision and clear reason, and Celtic quick-wittedness and spirituality, we fall short of. Nay, perhaps, if we are doomed to perish . . . we shall perish by our Celtism, by our self-will and want of patience with ideas, our inability to see the way the world is going."

He was not talking in an academic vacuum. In 1866 the case of Governor Eyre was splitting the intellectual world, conservatives defending the decisive stringency and liberals attacking the stupid brutality with which Eyre had put down a Negro uprising in the West Indies. Carlyle's philosophy had been exemplified and Mill's outraged. Clearly, it would seem, England needed a new method of governing others as well as herself, a new principle based on a new kind of temperament. The problem which was being so dramatically stated by the trial of Eyre for murder was underscored by the Fenian disturbances of early 1867. Arnold's readers * knew what he was talking about when he said:

At this moment, when the narrow Philistinism, which has long had things its own way in England, is showing its natural fruits, and we are beginning to feel ashamed, and uneasy, and alarmed at it; now, when we are becoming aware that we have sacrificed to Philistinism culture, and insight, and dignity, and acceptance, and weight among the nations, and hold on events that deeply concern us, and control of the future, and yet that it cannot even give us the fool's paradise it promised us, but is apt to break down . . . at such a moment it needs some moderation not to be attacking Philistinism by storm.

Even as he spoke the reasons for alarm were increasing apace.

IV

Arnold delivered the last of his Celtic lectures on May 26, 1866. On May 10, the great and historical London discount firm of Over-

---

* The lectures, delivered in the spring of 1866, were printed in the *Cornhill* in the spring and summer of that year and in a volume in 1867.

end, Gurney and Company had failed, the result of an ominous series of stock exchange failures and the cause of many more. On "Black Friday" crowds filled the City to besiege even the solidest banking houses, some of which gave way and all of which shook under the pressure. Financial panic spread and England's credit soured on the foreign market. At home the discount rate had been pushed to ten percent; * the resultant tightness of capital caused many enterprises to be abandoned; unemployment took on alarming proportions. Upon the heels of the financially disastrous May followed an agriculturally disastrous August, wet and stormy; the English harvest failed. The next year's crop was no luckier and wheat prices rose in 1867 to half as much again as those of 1864. The rinderpest which had stricken cattle in 1865 raged all the next year; the price of milk and meat rose a full quarter.

By January of 1867 the *Times* was reporting that the situation in the London slums was critical. During the summer months cholera had brought severe distress; it was then that Arnold had walked through Spitalfields and Bethnal Green and had the conversation with the Nonconformist Mr. Tyler which he commemorated in the sonnet, "East London." The present winter was inflicting its hardships upon people who had no means to withstand it. The parish workhouse was full; not a space but was occupied by a bed. Those workers who had not yet sought the scant relief of the workhouse lived within bare walls, having pledged all their possessions at pawnshops which could loan but trifling sums. Provident workmen whose providence had availed them little fought for the three hours' work on the workhouse stone-pile that would give them threepence and a loaf of bread. This was the condition in London and the provincial districts were nearly as bad.

By the beginning of 1866 the old agitation for a wide extension of suffrage had taken on new and greater vigor; in the spring and summer it increased enormously. The technique of huge mass meetings was being widely used; on the 5th of July the Reform

---

* In the version of the lectures in the *Cornhill*, Arnold refers to this discount rate.

League assembled a great crowd in Trafalgar Square—a crowd that was orderly and well-behaved in its demands for Liberty and Reform; at this meeting plans were announced for another to be held in Hyde Park on the 22nd of July. Although Hyde Park was normally an upper class preserve, it had been used by the working class for meetings since 1855. Now the Home Secretary, Spencer Walpole, whether upon his own decision or upon representations by his parliamentary colleagues, forbade the demonstration. The Reform League, which had been organized not only to press for manhood suffrage, but also to protest just such prohibitions as this, decided to make a test case of Walpole's order. Accordingly, a great crowd met in Trafalgar Square on the appointed day and marched to Hyde Park in two detachments; they arrived to find the park gates closed and 1800 metropolitan police inside the railings. The crowd was calm, even good-natured; there were many women with children in arms. Edward Beales, leader of one of the detachments, a barrister, president of the League and a man of high character and genuine devotion to the working class cause, formally demanded of the police that the crowd be admitted. Refused, he turned and led part of his contingent back to Trafalgar Square. The other half of the crowd, however, remained and was soon swelled on both sides of the park by home-going workers. There was a good deal of genial chaffing and hooting of the police. Then, whether by accident or design (Trevelyan believes by accident), the park railings fell and the crowd surged down the neat walks, trampling the lawns and flowerbeds. The police used their truncheons freely; several demonstrants were seriously hurt. Two troops of Horse Guards and two companies of foot were called into readiness.

The people, up to this time tractable enough, were now aroused and angry. For three days they trooped through the park, seemingly fascinated by the damage they had done. The working class members of the Reform League wished to continue defiance of the government by holding another meeting in the park; the government kept its troops in wait for their move. As a result of the roughness of the police, "the exasperation of the working men was extreme," wrote John Stuart Mill; "they showed a determination to make another attempt at a meeting in the Park, to which many of them would probably have come armed." The League council was split and its middle class members, Beales and Dickson, who were against another meeting, called upon Mill (who was not a member of the League but at the time a proponent of Reform in Parliament) to dissuade their more militant colleagues. Mill succeeded by having "recourse to *les grands moyens.*" He told them "that a proceeding which would certainly produce a collision with the military, could only be justifiable on two conditions: if the position of affairs had become such that a revolution was desirable, and if they thought themselves able to accomplish one."

With the intransigents of the League under control, Beales could call upon the Home Secretary with the situation well in hand. Plans for the meeting had already been abandoned but this Walpole did not know and it is said that the Secretary wept as he begged that the meeting should not take place. The story is probably not true (a member of Beales' committee denied it) but Arnold accepted it and its circulation indicates the disgust which the upper classes felt at what seemed the weak-kneed action of Government. Then the Reform League took—perhaps unfair—advantage of its position; after agreeing with Walpole that it would keep the masses from the park upon the understanding that the legal right of meeting therein should be tested, it issued a placard stating that there would be no attempt to hold "a meeting in Hyde Park, except only by arrangement with the Government, on Monday afternoon July 30." This seemed to imply that the Government had conceded the principle as the price of the League's assistance. Among the respectable classes indignation with Walpole was so great he almost lost office.

The Reform League, as a result of the Hyde Park incident, grew enormously in influence over the working class. It began the organization of monster meetings in the great industrial centers and though the demonstrations were always peaceful, the implied threat of their size began to be effective; the whole working population of a factory city would march to the outlying fields, perhaps a hundred thousand men in orderly ranks; a meeting at Leeds numbered nearly 200,000. The Hyde Park affair of July was a matter of joking pride; one of the speakers would announce with solemn irreverence, "And now, dearly beloved, the Gospel of the day is the Hyde Park railings and the cause of their destruction," and the crowd would roar with laughter and cheers. But the great feature of the meetings was John Bright; indeed, it was his tour and it was for him that the working populations turned out, carrying their slogan, "Honour Bright." Bright was himself a factory owner and he had once been a leading opponent of factory reform.* How did he come to be the leader of the working class?

The fact is that the middle class was divided. The old-established manufacturing families had in almost all respects assimilated themselves to the Tories; † the suffrage reform of 1832 had given them all the power they wished. "The Reform Act of 1832," says Trevelyan, "had left half the middle class unenfranchised and the rest insufficiently represented under the arbitrary system by which the seats were distributed in favor of the landed interest. The Whigs and Conservatives should, long before 1866, have given votes to all the middle classes if they wished to separate their interest in the matter from that of the working men. It was now too late to make such offers." And Bright said at Manchester, "There is no greater fallacy

---

* To be sure, Bright's notable opposition to factory legislation lay twenty years behind him. It was based on his fear of interference by the State; he never denied that factory workers were overworked, nor that this was an unjust condition, but he believed that the principle of freedom of contract demanded that the State refuse to legislate. However, he was perfectly willing to face the logic of his position—he encouraged the growth of trade unions so that the workers themselves might be able to win from the employer the concessions that Bright admitted were necessary. He never questioned the right of the State to legislate for working children, who, as minors, had no freedom of contract anyway. Another reason for his opposition was his justified belief that the Tories, in exposing the conditions of the factories, were hiding the conditions in the fields; Bright insisted that the agricultural workers were as much exploited as the operatives, and so they were. It should be said that Bright's own cotton-spinning plant was considered a model for its time.

† Trevelyan in his *British History in the Nineteenth Century* suggests a reading of Meredith's *Beauchamp's Career* for an understanding of this evolution.

than this—that the middle classes are in possession of power. The real state of the case, if it were put in simple language, would be this —that the working men are almost universally excluded, roughly and insolently, from political power, and that the middle class, whilst they have the semblance of it, are defrauded of the reality." The reality of power lay with the great Whigs of whom Robert Lowe was the representative and nothing Bright himself could say was of greater effect than a passage from the speech Lowe had made to the House, which Bright quoted and which appeared on the placards of his meetings:

If you want venality, if you want ignorance, if you want drunkenness and facility for being intimidated; or if, on the other hand, you want impulsive, unreflecting, and violent people, where do you look for them in the constituencies? Do you go to the top or to the bottom? . . . We know what those persons are who live in small houses—we have had experience of them under the name of "freemen"—and no better law, I think, could have been passed than that which disfranchised them altogether.

And Bright made sure to point out with what thunderous applause Lowe's remarks had been greeted.

Bright's appeal to the country was finally intimidating to the conservatives of both parties. The radical wing of the middle class triumphed, and the Tories, under Disraeli in the House and under Lord Derby in the Lords, saw that there was nothing for it but to save what prestige they could from Reform. On August 15, 1867, the Tories took what Derby called "a leap in the dark" and "dished the Whigs" by proposing and passing the bill that Bright had proposed fifteen years earlier.

A large measure of political democracy had at last come to England, subject, of course, to all the restrictions which the politically astute upper classes could fasten upon it. "[The upper class] policy after 1867 was to minimize the effects of the success of workingmen having won such a position," writes F. E. Gillespie in *Labor and Politics in England, 1850–1867.* "The method adopted was to strive to attach the labor vote to one or the other of the old parties." But the participation of the working class even in a formal suffrage filled the upper classes of the nation with fear. Arnold, in his essay on Eugénie de Guérin, speaks of the fear of the Chateau which haunted the imagination of the French peasant well into the 19th century. The dark, unknown force of the lower classes was a no less chilling terror to the upper classes of England. The fear was unwarranted, for not only was the power of the working class soon minimized, but the old spiritual ascendancy of the upper classes remained strong. And, apparently, it still does; it is difficult to judge these things, but according to the observations of one thorough investigator (E. W. Bakke in his *The Unemployed Man*) the average English worker still regards—with resentment, to be sure—the old ruling classes as his natural governors—and this despite Labor Governments, the general strike and the inroads of socialist doctrine. But in 1867 it seemed to many people of good intelligence that a political cataclysm had occurred, that the working classes would now, at once, throw down all before them. Respectable England was very much like Lady Bastable in the story by Saki who, "obsessed with a favourite foreboding that one of these days there would be a great social upheaval, in which everybody would be killed by everybody else," was sent flying by the sight of her gardener with his sickle.

The great cry of "leveling down" was heard through the land; at the gate were the Goth and the Vandal. George Eliot, in the person of her Felix Holt, the Radical, wrote an address to the newly liberated workers (in the middle class *Westminster Review*) begging them not to be hasty, telling them that what they needed was culture, asking them where they would be if, in their new-found liberty, they took it upon themselves to destroy the middle class which had been culture's custodian. A year after the Reform Bill she pointed out that if they were as good as their leaders had said, bribery, corruption and injustice would not infest the state as they apparently still did. The feeling was abroad that now the workers would inevitably cease working and George Eliot made clear to them what the function of their class must be. For in addition to working, she said, they must also guard law and order; they must not let the many "bad poor" take control of the nation. "That these degraded fellow-men could really get the mastery in a persistent disobedience to the laws and in a struggle to subvert order, I do not believe; but wretched calamities would come from the very beginning of such a struggle, and the continuance of it would be a civil war. . . . We have all to see to it that we do not help to rouse what I may call the savage beast in the breasts of our generation."

But for Carlyle, fresh from his defense of Governor Eyre, enfranchisement of the working class was the end of the world. The Reform Bill was England shooting Niagara and what was to come was only a frightening question mark. Here was the natural end of Swarmery, the "Gathering of Men in Swarms." It was part and parcel of the democratic process which had liberated the American "Niggers," "absurd blacks," so clearly marked for servitude, which had prosecuted Governor Eyre for the slaughter of the English "Niggers" and had denied the validity of Martial Law "as if it were not anterior to all written laws . . . and coeval with Human Society." The aristocracy which is still granted a vulgarly human admiration by the masses constitutes England's most useful class, and the bravery of its men and the beauty of its women must still be of use in even a vulgar and chaotic world. But inevitably, says Carlyle, that class will withdraw from politics, disgusted by democracy, until things will get so very bad that, in a last desperate Ragnarok, it will seize slavish England by the beard, saying, "Behold, we will all die rather than that this last." Perhaps the feudal aristocracy will then provide the great speculative heroes to formulate new definitions of liberty; the new industrial aristocracy, still a little rough, will provide the practical heroes. England will then have a drilled population, the Drill-Sergeant will be great (partaking as he does of the nature of the Great Frederick) and a disciplined nation will be the final foe of Anarchy.

Out of a political situation sufficiently disturbing to call forth such pronouncements as George Eliot's and Carlyle's sprang Arnold's

Culture and Anarchy. Here, in universal franchise, was a long step, Arnold thought, toward revolution by due process of law; he was apprehensive but he did not let fear make him silly or brutal. Now more than ever, he felt, it was necessary to understand the principle of the State and of authority. Viewing the affair of the riots he says: "Even W[alpole]'s absurd behaviour and talking and shilly-shallying and crying have been of use in bringing about a state of good feeling in which the disturbance may gradually die away without either side getting a victory." But he feels that all this blundering cannot continue: "In itself [it is] a bad thing that the principle of authority should be so weak here; but whereas in France since the Revolution, a man feels that the power which represses him is the *State,* is *himself,* here a man feels that the power which represses him is the Tories, the upper class, the aristocracy, and so on; and with this feeling he can, of course, never without loss of self-respect accept a formal beating, and so the thing goes on smouldering." It was necessary, therefore, to crystallize the notion of the State, to show it in its true and proper relationship to the individual and his class and Arnold wrote the book that was to be the keystone of his intellectual life. Significantly, the first chapter of *Culture and Anarchy* was Arnold's farewell lecture as Professor of Poetry at Oxford.

Chapter Nine

➳➳➳ ⤛⤛⤛

CULTURE OR ANARCHY

Later on, Liberty will not be . . . enough: men will die for human perfection, to which they will sacrifice all their liberty gladly.—BERNARD SHAW

TIME and familiarity have faded the drama which lies in the title of Arnold's book and have obscured the tragedy it implies. *Culture and Anarchy*—culture *or* anarchy: it is a grim alternative, for Arnold's culture, as he was careful to point out, does not signify what the word commonly does, a vague, belletristic gentility; it means many things but nothing less than reason experienced as a kind of grace by each citizen, the conscious effort of each man to come to the realization of his complete humanity. And upon this urge to perfection, upon this "possible Socrates" in each man's breast, Arnold bases the sanction which alone can prevent anarchy—the authority of the State. It is so much a counsel of perfection that it becomes a counsel of despair.

The problem of the State, as, in a class society, it is generally considered, is simply this: given divergent interests and conflicting parties, how create a perfectly fair umpire, endowed with sufficient power to deal reasonably and for the good of all with individuals and classes not themselves reasonable and not concerned with the good of all? In actuality we observe that not theory but the ratio of class power determines the fairness of this umpire: the appearance of impartiality is less when the relative powers of the classes are unequal and greater when the relative powers of the classes approach an equality. But Arnold, facing a time of strong class feeling, wished to avoid just this notion of a State based upon class power or even upon the compromise of class power. Class struggle, even to the outcome of a neat balance of power in the State, was precisely what he feared. He wished to base the State on something less pragmatic and found what he called the "best self" of each class—that is, the reason of each class voided of its interest.

But he was building with a fallacy. "Class" is a category whose very essence is interest; take away the idea of special interest and, in its usage in modern society, "class" ceases to have meaning. Or, to put it differently, the reason of a class is its interest. This, it need scarcely be said, is not extensible to the individual who may follow the dictates of reason or affection at the cost of his own immediate benefit. But it is a fallacy of definition to speak of a class without interest, just as it would be to speak of an object without extension.* In effect, to speak of a State based on classes voided of interest is to assume a classless society and this, though Arnold truly desired it, he was not now contemplating.

Deprived of the logical possibility of a class State based on the voidance of class interest, Arnold's whole problem is thrown into the field of epistemology. The everlasting question of philosophical politics is how to place power and reason in the same agent, or how to make power reasonable, or how to endow reason with power. Clearly a State—which implies power—is required because some classes or individuals refuse to conform to reason and must be coerced for the good of the rest. But the recalcitrants, while forced to admit the power of the coercing agent, will naturally deny its reason. Therefore, if Arnold is to make his State both logically and practically valid, he must say that some people may have reason and others not and that the possession of reason by some people gives them the right to coerce others. He must, therefore, declare that reason is ascertainable and show what it is. Not the least important part of *Culture and Anarchy* is the attempt to do just this.

* Speaking broadly, of course. It is certainly possible for a class to act against its own interest and it is possible, too, for many members of a class to act in the interest of another class either out of social habit or reasoned conviction.

Yet no sooner has Arnold established a rationale of authority, a reason which implies power, than he becomes acutely uncomfortable. Although he scotches the superstitious Liberal fear of authority, he is, after all, himself a Liberal—of the Future, to be sure, but still a Liberal. The reason upon which the power of the State is to be founded is not quite warrant enough, for the State must be embodied in government—that is, in people. The State is to be made up of classes; not, to be sure, the classes in their imperfections but in their best aspects; but classes are people, not moral essences. Who among these people are to judge reason? We remember: "Right is something moral, and implies inward recognition, free assent of the will; we are not ready for right,—*right, so far as we are concerned, is not ready,*—until we have attained this sense of seeing it and willing it." In the end Arnold must turn to the individual, to that possible Socrates in each man's breast, and make reason wait upon the assent he gives.

Growth, development and the knowledge that he is needed will create this Socrates and bring this assent; the question, however, is still begged, for the possibility of growth and of the increasing dominion of the individual best self upon which the State is to be built, itself depends, as Arnold tells us, on the State. "How may we constitute the State?" "Be ye perfect. Love one another." "How shall we be perfect and love one another?" "Constitute your State." Here is confusion in a circle. Yet it is the confusion which lies not only in Arnold's thought but in the nature of the problem. The way in which society is ordered determines the moral life of individuals and classes, but the moral life of individuals and classes determines the way in which society is ordered. One may escape from the circle, but not if one thinks in terms of both personal morality and social instrumentality; one may escape by an Hegelian renunciation of pious liberalism and by admitting some process of history in which morality is a goal of the long range but not a means, in which the evil of the moment may work the good of the developmental process, and in which power is its own temporary justification. And Arnold, as we have seen, does indeed advance, though tentatively, along this way out of the dilemma.*

Arnold's theory of the State does not hold up as a logical structure, nor does it hold up as a practical structure. Its failure is the typical liberal failure, for it evades—it was intended to evade—the problems of what H. N. Brailsford calls "the crude issue of power . . . always the last of the realities that sensitive and reasonable men can bring themselves to face." Yet in the enterprise of theoretical politics failure is of the essence. We may best think of Arnold's effort as an *experimentum luciferum,* an experiment of light, rather than as an *experimentum fructiferum,* an experiment of fruit. It is that play of the mind over the subject, of which criticism consists: immediate practicality is not its point any more than it is the point of *The Republic* and we ought not, perhaps, to behave like Adeimantus, suggesting that we "try now to convince ourselves of this, that the thing *is* practicable, and *how* it is practicable, leaving all other questions to themselves."

Arnold, however, would not himself relish our leniency; he protested the practicability of his theory. His essentially mystic conception of the State reads almost like a Platonic myth, but, for good or ill, the research of theoretical politics seems to proceed on myths. Divine law, natural right, the state of nature, the social contract, the general will, "national blood"—all of them, the liberating and the debasing, are myths, partial and undemonstrable, constructs embodying complex assumptions and desires, and Arnold's State is but such another. The value of any myth cannot depend on its demonstrability as a fact, but only on the value of the attitudes it embodies, the further attitudes it engenders and the actions it motivates. In these respects Arnold's myth is still fertile and valuable—and morally inescapable.

* Aldous Huxley has refused either to go around the circle or to escape from it; he insists on breaking it by affirming the need for a personal and largely Socratic morality. With Huxley's *Ends and Means* (1937) two other considerations of what Sidney Hook calls "the basic moral problem of our time" may be mentioned: Reinhold Niebuhr's *Moral Man and Immoral Society* (1932) and E. F. Carritt's *Morals and Politics* (1935).

II

All men, Heine said, are either Jews or Greeks—either men who ascetically question life and nourish their apocalyptic visions, or men who love life with a realism generated by their personal integration.* It is a neat pair of categories and inevitably attractive to Arnold, for, like the categories of Celt and German, those of Hebrew and Hellene offer him a splendid means of analyzing English society by quantity rather than quality; he can say, "Here is too much of a good thing," or too little, and spare the offense of saying, "Here is a bad thing." He unravels the Hebraic and the Hellenic concepts to their last strands of implication and with them weaves a philosophy of history.

Like buckets in a well, Arnold found, Hebraism and Hellenism have been passing each other through the ages, the decline of one bringing the rise of the other; neither constitutes the whole law of human development and apparently mankind has not yet learned to possess itself of either without submerging its antithesis and complement. Thus the Hellenism of the pagan world gave way to the Hebraism of early Christianity, only to be revived in the Renaissance and then again discarded for the Hebraism of the Reformation. On the Continent this last reaction against Hellenism had been comparatively mild, but in England it was virulent, rooting itself deep in the tradition of the people—a fact which Arnold believed to be

---

* Heine derived the antithesis from Ludwig Börne. It was a not uncommon comparison, especially among Jewish writers. Professor Hans Kohn says of Moses Hess, one of the ideological founders of modern Jewish nationalism: "The contrast between Judaism and Hellenism, the relation between these two forces concerns Hess as it concerned Heine and Tschernichovski; as, indeed, it came to concern all analytical and self-conscious Jews upon their entrance into European life at the close of the eighteenth century and their renewal of contact with the influence of Hellas. For Hess, the Greeks stand for multiplicity and variety, while the Hebrews represent unity. The former think of life as eternal *being;* the latter as eternal *becoming.* The Greeks seek to penetrate through the space dimension; they are the people of the eye, of nature and of plastic beauty. The Jews, on the contrary, are preoccupied with the *time* dimension. They are the people of the time sense, of the ear, of lyricism, of historical outlook and social ethics. The task of all cultural history is to effect a reconciliation between these opposing principles."—"The Teachings of Moses Hess," *The Menorah Journal,* May, 1930, p. 403. See also the Epilogue of Hess's *Rome and Jerusalem.*

as anomalous as it was unfortunate, for the Indo-European, non-Semitic blood of the English should have made them tend toward Hellenism. However, if Hellenism was checked in England by the triumph of Puritanism, it continued to be cherished on the Continent and in the 18th century became the dominant tendency of the western world, for the Enlightenment and the Revolution were triumphs of Hellenism.

Because she stepped aside from this tendency of the modern age and because she held with a racially anomalous tenacity to the Hebraic tradition, England has endangered herself in the modern world. The demands of this increasingly complex world are for Hellenism rather than for Hebraism. Though both seek the same end—the perfection of man—and at times even use the same language, Hebraism is concerned primarily with conduct and with obedience to a law of conduct—with strictness of conscience—whereas Hellenism is concerned primarily with seeing things as they are—with spontaneity of consciousness. Where Hellenism is chiefly occupied with the beauty and rationality of the ideal and tends to keep difficulties out of view, Hebraism lacks this sunny optimism and, marked by the sense of sin, pessimistic of perfection, asks whether man is indeed "a gentle and simple being, showing the traces of a noble and divine nature; or an unhappy chained captive, labouring with groanings that cannot be uttered to free himself from the body of this death:" it is the difference between the basic assumptions of rationalism and Christianity—or between Square and Thwackum.

The great value which Arnold sees in Hellenism's response to the modern world lies in its sense of the wholeness of the human personality; it does not, perhaps, give quite sufficient weight to morality, but whatever consideration of morality it does make is always in relation to the rest of the human faculties. Aware of the world without, Hellenism knows that the externality of living is a true index of the inner life and it knows that the quality of externality is as much determined by intelligence, imagination and the sense of beauty as by morality. Hebraism, however, lacks exactly this insight. Indifferent to the external world, Hebraism claims "that within which passeth show;" concerned with obedience to a law, it is ever inclined to suspect whatever complicates its obedience and tends to seek for "the one thing needful"—the *porro unum est necessarium* of St. Peter. It wants the formula, the spiritual talisman which will make it conform to this law, and in this desire cuts off morality from all the other human faculties. Its great error, the error of the Pharisees,* is to make conduct an end in itself rather than the means to the end of the whole, good life. "Nothing is more common," says Arnold with a touch of mystical authority, "than for people to confound the inward peace and satisfaction which follows the subduing of the obvious faults of our animality with what I may call absolute inward peace and satisfaction,—the peace and satisfaction which are reached as we draw near to complete spiritual perfection, and not merely to moral perfection, or rather to relative moral perfection." To stop short of complete moral perfection, to stop at relative moral perfection, is to make of morality an end in itself, to make the instrument of the good life the good life utterly.

This inversion of values is, in Arnold's opinion, the source of England's confusion: Hebraism is the root of anarchy. The result of the extension of the Hebraic principle into public life is obvious; if conduct itself has been made an end, then so have things much more obviously instrumental—coal, manufacture, population-increase, religious organizations. Aristotle began his *Ethics* with these words: "Every art and every scientific inquiry, and similarly every action and purpose, may be said to aim at some good. Hence the good has been well defined as that at which all things aim. But it is clear that there is a difference in the ends; for the ends are sometimes activities, and sometimes results beyond the mere activities. Also, where there are certain ends beyond the actions, the results are naturally superior to the activities." *Culture and Anarchy* reflects Aristotle in many

---

* Arnold, of course, is using the common conception of the Pharisees which two modern scholars—George Foot Moore in *Judaism* (1927-1930) and R. Travers Herford in *The Pharisees* (1924)—have rejected.

ways but chiefly in this, that its chief undertaking is to distinguish "results" from "activities."

For Arnold the immediate result of the doctrine of the one thing needful—of the error of considering an instrument as an end—is the value given to personal liberty by contemporary England. The destruction of the Hyde Park railings; the Home Secretary in tears before the deputation; the Aldermanic Colonel Wilson refraining from the use of the city militia upon a mob of "roughs;" the labor disturbances in Manchester; the vituperative Mr. Murphy, anti-Catholic lecturer, who had the power and the willingness to move his Nonconformist audiences to bloody riot and whom the police would not stop—all the noisy but, to us, scarcely serious disorders and confusions of a nation in transition Arnold sees as the signs of anarchy, springing from the mechanical treatment of the idea of personal liberty. There is no principle of authority in England sufficiently strong to judge and control the excesses of doing as one likes; there is only the mechanical principle that doing as one likes is a "result" and a good. It is obvious, then, that the establishment of a principle of authority is the clearest need. But before Arnold will attempt the formulation he must analyze the philosophy which rationalizes the anarchic tradition.

Although John Stuart Mill's essay, *On Liberty,* is not mentioned in *Culture and Anarchy,* Arnold could scarcely have found a better philosophic defense of liberalism, and he is patently aware of Mill throughout the book.* Mill, to be sure, was not the philosopher of Puritanism—on the contrary—nor even of liberalism of the vulgar, industrial sort. A fine and sensitive spirit, Mill wrote in defense of fineness and sensitivity, and Arnold knew it. "Have you seen Mill's book on Liberty?" he wrote in 1859. "It is worth reading attentively, being one of the few books that inculcate tolerance in an unalarming and inoffensive way." But the defense of fineness and sensitivity might involve, as Mill himself was aware, the defense of

* For example, the title of his second chapter, "Doing As One Likes," was probably suggested by Mill's "liberty of . . . doing as we like, subject to such consequences as may follow," in the Introduction to *On Liberty.*

crudeness and stupidity. The defender of the "anarchy" which sprang from Hebraism was, paradoxically, too Hellenic to do more than mark crudeness and stupidity for what they were; Mill would not go to the moral length of trying to suppress them, lest crudeness and stupidity themselves be thus given a sanction to attack fineness and sensitivity. Yet if *Culture and Anarchy* may be understood as in large part an indirect answer to *On Liberty,* the difference between the two books must be seen through their many similarities. They shared an assumption of human progress: to both Arnold and Mill it seemed clear that the destiny and duty of man was to improve morally and spiritually; for both men the idea of development of the full personality was precious * and both looked to Periclean Athens as the ideal condition for it; both had read Tocqueville and caught his fear that personal development would be prevented by democracy's dull sameness; and finally, both shared a profound reliance upon reason. Here, however, Arnold and Mill part, for Mill so firmly believed in reason that he thought that nothing, apart from its exercise and free utterance, might be done to establish it. Arnold, on the other hand, believed so firmly in reason that he was certain it justified the use of its antithesis, force, without which it was powerless.

Upon this difference in their estimates of reason Arnold and Mill founded their opposing theories of authority and the State. Or perhaps an approximate converse would be more precise: upon his estimate of the nature of society each of the two men founded his theory of truth. Mill's social theory is essentially an atomic one; the shades of a rather primitive contract-conception hover unexpressed

---

* "The true end of Man," said Wilhelm von Humboldt, "or that which is prescribed by the eternal and immutable dictates of reason, and not suggested by vague and transient desires, is the highest and most harmonious development of his powers to a complete and consistent whole." Von Humboldt's treatment of the idea of the development of the whole personality in his *Sphere and Duties of Government* had considerable influence upon both Arnold and Mill. Their treatment of his book marks the difference in their critical method. Von Humboldt is making an impassioned and poetic plea for a bare minimum of government and Mill quotes him to support his own feelings on that subject; Arnold, on the opposite side, praises the book but questions whether Von Humboldt, had he not been writing in a still feudal state, would have taken the position he did.

over his thought. He is inclined to see the individual, full-grown, fully endowed, *joining* an aggregation of other individuals for mutual protection, surrendering certain rights, but not others, in order to make the contract effectual. In Arnold's more organic conception of society, the individual is scarcely a member of an aggregate, but, as it were, a particular aspect of an integral whole. His individual does not *join* society, but springs from it, is endowed by it; therefore it is difficult, if not impossible, to conceive of his rights as against or apart from the rights of society as a whole.

If there seems to be a certain failure of insight in Mill's position, he nevertheless drew from it a lively and salutary sense of the opinionative nature of truth and of the dependence of opinion on class, on national culture and on time. If Arnold's position, on the other hand, is the more valid, because it forbids the sterile, atomic view of the individual, it nevertheless carried him to a conception of truth which looks to an ultimately mystical sanction.

Arnold felt that the theory of truth which Mill defended was nothing less than "atheism," for it seemed to deny any standard of excellence. And he saw in England's judgment of the things of the mind a growing inclination to consider all things as of equal value —the natural outcome of the Nonconformist belief that each man's religious insight and interpretation of the Bible is the equal of any other man's:

Each section of the public has its own literary organ, and the mass of the public is without any suspicion that the value of these organs is relative to their being nearer a certain ideal centre of correct information, taste, and intelligence, or farther away from it. I have said that within certain limits, which any one who is likely to read this will have no difficulty in drawing for himself, my old adversary, the *Saturday Review,* may, on matters of literature and taste, be fairly enough regarded, relatively to the mass of newspapers which treat these matters, as a kind of organ of reason. But I remember once conversing with a company of Nonconformist admirers of some lecturer who had let off a great firework, which the *Saturday Review* said was all noise and false lights, and feeling my way as tenderly as I could about the effect of this unfavourable judgment upon those with whom I was conversing. "Oh," said one who was their spokesman, with the most tranquil air of conviction, "it is true that the *Saturday Review* abuses the lecture, but the *British Banner* . . . says that the *Saturday Review* is quite wrong." The speaker had evidently no notion that there was a scale of value for judgments on these topics, and that the judgments of the *Saturday Review* ranked high on this scale, and those of the *British Banner* low.

In religion the *size* of the fact takes precedence over the *value* of the fact—Mormonism and Shakerism are accepted as important phenomena simply because they are the creeds of multitudes of men and their apostles are spoken of as seriously as Plato or St. Paul; the intellectual and spiritual contents of their doctrines receive no serious criticism. And it is exactly this condition of affairs that Mill has justified. Not that Mill has the slightest desire to see Mormonism or Shakerism or the Oneida Colony advanced or that he would want mitigated the criticism they deserve. But where Arnold finds a kind of disease in such enterprises, Mill is inclined to see a kind of health.

We must admit a sensible realism in Mill's view and a certain over-refined finickiness in Arnold's; the blind groping of unhappy people determined to find a reasoned if not wholly reasonable way out of their unhappiness was something more than blindness, and the multitude seeking dignity and safety in phalansteries was a symptom of the very disorder Arnold was dealing with—social anarchy. A follower of Mill would surely be quicker to see the symptomatic nature of social movement if only because he would be less able to condemn it by an assured standard. For Mill himself, any diversity of ideas was to be cherished as another guarantee against the growth of monolithic opinion and, indeed, where Arnold believed that the task of the enlightened was to bring opinion to a conformity with right reason, Mill went so far as to blame "those who have been in advance of society in thought and feeling . . . [for having] occupied themselves rather in inquiring what things society ought to like or dislike, than in questioning whether its likings or dislikings should be a law to individuals." The search for universal standards, even supposing it to be successful, was, in Mill's opinion, an actual danger, and the fact that Marcus Aurelius, with all his enlightened saintliness, should have persecuted Christianity was enough, Mill thought, to give pause to any man who believes he has the whole truth. But for Arnold, touched as he was with what, for convenience, we may call the Hegelian tradition, the deed is forgivable.*

Mill could conclude that the organization of opinion must be utterly fluid, certainly never institutionalized, that truth emerges from the clash of opinion in the marketplace. When truth has emerged, he said, let it continue to struggle against untruth: its "clearer perception and livelier impression" is "produced by its collision with error." But to this Arnold countered by the response he made to the Nonconformist manufacturer who was delighted by the sharp religious conflicts that were taking place in the midland counties because of the invasion of Dissent into Church territory: "I said that this seemed a pity. 'A pity?' cried he; 'not at all! Only think of all the zeal and activity which the collision calls forth!' 'Ah, but, my dear friend,' I answered, 'only think of all the nonsense which you now hold quite firmly, which you would never have held if you

* For Fitzjames Stephen it was more than forgivable: it was justified. Like *Culture and Anarchy*, Stephen's *Liberty, Equality, Fraternity* (1873) is a critical examination of Mill's *On Liberty*. It is a brilliant and delightful book—one of the few defenses of the *status quo* that undertake to demonstrate the evils of what they defend; its hard-headedness makes it an interesting complement to *Culture and Anarchy*; its prose is admirable. Arnold knew Fitzjames Stephen who, an inveterate commissioner, was a member of the Education Commission which sent Arnold on his first European inspection tour in 1858. Stephen wrote a reply to *England and the Italian Question* in the *Saturday Review* of August 13, 1859.

In passing, it may be mentioned that Stephen's "ill-treatment" (as Matthew called it) of Thomas Arnold in his review of *Tom Brown's School-days* (*Edinburgh Review*, cvii, 1858) was the occasion which called forth Matthew Arnold's "Rugby Chapel." Stephen had disparaged the elder Arnold for his humorless evangelicism which resulted in the Rugby schoolboy being unable to tie his shoes without asserting a principle. In *The Letters of Matthew Arnold to Arthur Hugh Clough*, Professor Lowry prints a letter which Matthew Arnold wrote to his mother in 1867 telling her that Stephen's representation of Dr. Arnold as a "narrow bustling fanatic" had stirred him to the composition of the poem. However, it should be noted that the poem is dated "November 1857." There was no quarrel between Matthew Arnold and Stephen; Arnold's later letters indicate a friendly relation.

had not been contradicting your adversary in it all these years!' "

Mill saw life as a series of "experiments" of which some succeed and some fail—the freedom to fail is the guarantee that the successful experiment may be made.* Truth is the product of error just as success is the product of failure; in much the same way genius is the product of energetic eccentricity. Only by free departure in any direction do we get that departure in the right direction which we call genius: it is a conception perfectly antithetical to Arnold's.

It follows from Mill's belief in the evasiveness of truth that "the sole end for which mankind are warranted, individually or collectively, in interfering with the liberty of action of any of their number, is self-protection. That the only purpose for which power can be rightfully exercised over any member of a civilised community, against his will, is to prevent harm to others. His own good, either physical or moral, is not a sufficient warrant." In short, the strong State is inevitably a tyranny. But Mill's position may be held only if one dismisses the organic view of society, for as soon as one accepts it, the whole notion of "self-protection" and of "harm" becomes infinitely complex; then the relation of the members of society is integral, of the essence, irrefrangible, and the perfection of

---

* Perhaps the greatest and most effective exponent of Mill's philosophy of opinion in our time was Mr. Justice Holmes. The following is from his dissenting opinion in the case *Abrams* v. *United States* (250 U.S. 616, 1919):

"Persecution for the expression of opinions seems to me perfectly logical. If you have no doubt of your premises or your power and want a certain result with all your heart you naturally express your wishes in law and sweep away all opposition. To allow opposition by speech seems to indicate that you think the speech impotent, as when a man says that he has squared the circle, or that you do not care wholeheartedly for the result, or that you doubt either your power or your premises. But when men have realized that time has upset many fighting faiths, they may come to believe even more than they believe the very foundations of their own conduct that the ultimate good desired is better reached by free trade in ideas—that the best test of truth is the power of the thought to get itself accepted in the competition of the market, and that truth is the only ground upon which their wishes safely can be carried out. That at any rate is the theory of our Constitution. It is an experiment, as all life is an experiment. Every year if not every day we have to wager our salvation upon some prophecy based upon imperfect knowledge. While that experiment is part of our system I think that we should be eternally vigilant against attempts to check the expression of opinions that we loathe and believe to be fraught with death, unless they so imminently threaten immediate interference with the lawful and pressing purposes of the law that an immediate check is required to save the country."

any man's life is prevented by his neighbor's error and unhappiness.
The organic society, the interrelation of man with man, seems of
itself to imply a principle and a standard of reason. Yet—what is
perfection and what is error? Can they be known?

It is this epistemological problem that Arnold has to face. He
believes that the nature of perfection and error can be determined
and he utterly rejects the negativism of Mill's kind of epistemology:

> . . . A kind of philosophical theory is widely spread among us to the
> effect that there is no such thing at all as . . . a right reason having claim
> to paramount authority, or, at any rate, no such thing ascertainable and
> capable of being made use of; and that there is nothing but an infinite
> number of ideas . . . and suggestions of our natural taste for the bathos,
> pretty nearly equal in value, which are doomed either to an irreconcilable
> conflict, or else to a perpetual give and take; and that wisdom consists in
> choosing the give and take rather than the conflict, and in sticking to our
> choice with patience and good humour. And, on the other hand, we have
> another philosophical theory rife among us, to the effect that without
> the labour of perverting ourselves by custom or example to relish right
> reason, but by continuing all of us to follow freely our natural taste
> for the bathos, we shall, by the mercy of Providence, and by a kind of
> natural tendency of things, come in due time to relish and follow right
> reason.

Probably right and wrong cannot be determined absolutely (politics
and ethics are not, as Aristotle said, exact sciences) but they surely
can be determined approximately—by intuition, observation, analysis,
most important of all, by the faith that they *can* be known. The
analytical reason has yielded such melancholy results that it is certainly worth while to look for another instrument of intellectual discovery. Arnold evolves now the new instrument of *culture*.

Culture is not merely a method but an attitude of spirit contrived
to receive truth. It is a moral orientation, involving will, imagination, faith; all of these avowedly active elements body forth a universe that contains a truth which the intuition can grasp and the
analytical reason can scrutinize. Culture is reason involving the
whole personality; it is the whole personality in search of the truth.

It creates both a cosmology and a philosophy of history to assure its effectiveness. It is the escape, in short, from *Verstand* to *Vernunft,* from the mere understanding to the creative reason. Culture may best be described as religion with the critical intellect superadded.

Culture seeks (in Montesquieu's words) to "render an intelligent being yet more intelligent;" it is the love and study of perfection. But it "moves by the force, not merely or primarily of the scientific passion for pure knowledge, but also of the moral and social passion for doing good," and this is even its preeminent part: "the love of our neighbour, the impulse towards action, help, and beneficence, the desire for removing human error, clearing human confusion, and diminishing human misery." Arnold sums up its aims in the words of Bishop Wilson: "to make reason and the will of God prevail."

This is culture's first creation, *the will of God,* and by will of God Arnold means, more or less in the fashion of Spinoza, "the universal order which seems to be intended and aimed at in the world, and which it is man's happiness to go along with or his misery to go counter to." At one stroke, culture creates the certainty of the knowledge which it must apprehend and thus takes its advantage over the liberal method of thought. It affirms that truth exists and can be known, and it provides a test—happiness and misery—by which we know we have apprehended it.

And the analogy between religion and culture continues in that each conceives its perfection as an *inward* condition of the individual. Not that culture, Arnold makes clear, is what we would nowadays call "subjectivism;" it is concerned with the inner life, but never to the exclusion of the realities of the outer world. Arnold is concerned with a fundamental problem of human knowledge. Speaking, for instance, of the badness of a life judged by wealth, he says that what is important is "not only to say as a matter of words" that such a life is bad "but really to perceive and feel" that it is so. The difference may seem unimportant in the light of the difficulties he is undertaking to solve, or a merely pious emphasis;

actually it is considerably more, as anyone who has ever recognized the justice of a proverb or truism and then, after some experience to which it is relevant, looked at it again to find it vibrating with truth and meaning, or anyone who has "appreciated" and "understood" a poem, a picture or a piece of music and then suddenly had the revelation of its *"real"* meaning, will, upon comparing his former with his latter condition, bear witness to. Understanding is an ambivalent, even a contradictory, thing: we may understand and not understand at the same time; it exists at such varying degrees of intensity that there is actually a difference in kind. The breach between those who have a lesser degree and those who have a higher is perhaps one of the tragic problems of the race. The religious leader, the political thinker, the teacher, the artist everlastingly communicate their vision—their high intensity of understanding—and they win assent, but always at a lower level and consequently, therefore, to a different thing than they had intended. Their true vision, they know, the actuality of their passion, can never be truly reproduced; the result of their communication is inevitably a greater or less distortion. Arnold's concern with this problem is perhaps inevitable in the poet turned political philosopher; it is by no means a special one.*

The analogy of culture with religion draws to its conclusion: culture and religion are at one in their insistence on development: "Not a having and a resting, but a growing and a becoming, is the character of perfection as culture conceives it; and here, too, it coincides with religion." Arnold is speaking of the individual's personal development, not of the historical development of ideas.

And finally, religion and culture coincide in the conception of a general expansion. "Perfection, as culture conceives it, is not possible while the individual remains isolated. The individual is required, under pain of being stunted and enfeebled in his own development if he disobeys, to carry others along with him in his

---

* To Arnold's desire to make himself understood exactly as he wished may be ascribed his habit of exact repetition of his words, from work to work and in the same work—what Chesterton calls the manner of the patient master of an idiot school.

march towards perfection, to be continually doing all he can to enlarge and increase the volume of the human stream sweeping thitherward." "To promote the kingdom of God," as Bishop Wilson, speaking for religion, had said, "is to increase and hasten one's own happiness."

Here the similarity of culture to religion ends and we may understand how truly portentous the idea of culture was for Arnold since, profoundly as he admired religion, he yet insisted that culture went beyond it. Culture goes beyond religion in this: that it conceives perfection as the "harmonious expansion of *all* the powers which make the beauty and worth of human nature;" whereas religion, as it generally operates, puts an exclusive emphasis on merely a few powers or even on only one—the moral. It is not enough to do good Hebraistically, by *any* moral standard: the reasonable, the scientific part of culture refuses to take the intention for perfection: good must conform to the best notions of reason and these must involve all the human faculties, all that may be summarized as sweetness and light, beauty and reason. The strong moral fiber which religion implants is not sufficient; the English more than any other people desire to attain moral perfection, yet this desire, embodied in Puritanism and without the sweetness and light * of culture, has produced a religion of mere machinery which departs from the best ideal of religion itself. Even the language of religion has become a jargon and actually a betrayal, for where the truth lies in St. Paul's "Finally, be of one mind, united in feeling," Puritanism has raised the slogan of "The Dissidence of Dissent and the Protestantism of the Protestant religion," making of a negative thing a positive good. It is a consequence of this mechanical approach—typified by the literalism of

* This phrase has fallen into such disrepute, has come so much to mean a smirking, simpering flabbiness of attitude, a kind of Pollyanna hypocrisy, that it may be well to recall its origin in Swift. In *The Battle of the Books* the debate between the spider and the bee is an allegory of the struggle between the Moderns and Ancients. The bee has the best of it because he fills his hive "with honey and wax; thus furnishing mankind with the two noblest of things, which are sweetness and light." Arnold mentions his indebtedness and no doubt had a good deal of secret amusement in observing how well the spider, with his mathematics, engineering and rampant modernism, his self-appreciation and love of controversy, represented Liberalism.

the Puritan interpretation of the Bible—that the very doing of good has been defeated and that religion, fixed on morality, has, by its exclusion of intellect, failed to achieve even its moral end:

We are all of us included in some religious organisation or other; we all call ourselves, in the sublime and aspiring language of religion . . . *children of God*. Children of God;—it is an immense pretension!—and how are we to justify it? By the works which we do, and the words which we speak. And the work which we collective children of God do, our grand centre of life, our *city* which we have builded for us to dwell in, is London! London, with its unutterable external hideousness, and with its internal canker of *publicè egestas, privatim opulentia*,—to use the words which Sallust put into Cato's mouth about Rome,—unequalled in the world! The word, again, which we children of God speak, the voice which most hits our collective thought, the newspaper with the largest circulation in England, nay, with the largest circulation in the whole world, is the *Daily Telegraph!* I say that when our religious organisations, —which I admit to express the most considerable effort after perfection that our race has yet made,—land us in no better result than this, it is high time to examine carefully their idea of perfection, to see whether it does not leave out of account sides and forces of human nature which we might turn to great use; whether it would not be more operative if it were more complete. And I say that the English reliance on our religious organisations and on their ideas of human perfection just as they stand, is like our reliance on freedom, on muscular Christianity, on population, on coal, on wealth,—mere belief in machinery, and unfruitful . . .

The only salvation from this failure lies with culture, "bent on seeing things as they are, and on drawing the human race onwards to a more complete, a harmonious perfection."

How, then, does culture work? Culture begins with the realization "that the sweetness and light of the few must be imperfect until the raw and unkindled masses of humanity are touched with sweetness and light." It is a profound and simple perception and one which gives Arnold's idea of society and culture a basic validity. He had the democratic insight that a human value exists in the degree that it is shared, that a truth may exist but be unalive until it receives assent, that a good may have meaning but no reality until it is participated in. The very rewards which society bestows for virtue have their full reality only when bestowed by equals, and only the ungenerous mind finds satisfaction in receiving honor from inferiors. The artist has, in a certain sense, failed, though through no fault of his own, when his intention is not understood by reason of the inferior capabilities of his fellows and his very artistic existence depends on the nature of his society. The enlightened man must require a general development of his fellow-men, as an effort of self-salvation. "If I have not shrunk," says Arnold, "from saying that we must work for sweetness and light, so neither have I shrunk from saying that we must have a broad basis, must have sweetness and light for as many as possible. Again and again I have insisted how those are the happy moments of humanity, how those are the marking epochs of a people's life, how those are the flowering times for literature and art and all the creative power of genius, when there is a *national* glow of life and thought, when the whole of society is in the fullest measure permeated by thought, sensible to beauty, intelligent and alive."

But there is a warning in Arnold's last words as Professor of Poetry at Oxford:

Only it must be *real* thought and *real* beauty; *real* sweetness and *real* light. Plenty of people will try to give the masses, as they call them, an intellectual food prepared and adapted in the way they think proper for the actual condition of the masses. The ordinary popular literature is an example of this way of working on the masses. Plenty of people will try to indoctrinate the masses with the set of ideas and judgments constituting the creed of their own profession or party. Our religious and political organisations give an example of this way of working on the masses. I condemn neither way; but culture works differently. It does not try to teach down to the level of inferior classes; it does not try to win them for this or that sect of its own, with ready-made judgments and watchwords. It seeks to do away with classes; to make the best that has been thought and known in the world current everywhere; to make all men live in an atmosphere of sweetness and light, where they may use ideas, as it uses them itself, freely,—nourished and not bound by them.

This is the *social* idea; and the men of culture are the true apostles of equality. The great men of culture are those who have had a passion for diffusing, for making prevail, for carrying from one end of society to the other, the best knowledge, the best ideas of their time; who have laboured to divest knowledge of all that was harsh, uncouth, difficult, abstract, professional, exclusive; to humanise it, to make it efficient outside the clique of the cultivated and learned, yet still remaining the best knowledge and thought of the time, and a true source, therefore, of sweetness and light. Such a man was Abelard in the Middle Ages, in spite of all his imperfections; and thence the boundless emotion and enthusiasm which Abelard excited. Such were Lessing and Herder in Germany, at the end of the last century; and their services to Germany were in this way inestimably precious. Generations will pass, and literary monuments will accumulate, and works far more perfect than the works of Lessing and Herder will be produced in Germany; and yet the names of these two men will fill a German with a reverence and enthusiasm such as the names of the most gifted masters will hardly awaken. And why? Because they *humanised* knowledge; because they broadened the basis of life and intelligence; because they worked powerfully to diffuse sweetness and light, to make reason and the will of God prevail.

III

But to understand culture only in its attitude, its intention or its manner is not to understand it wholly. Culture is something more than any of these. It is a method of historical interpretation which leads to political action. The clue to the nature of its method and action lies in Arnold's explanation of why culture rejects "Jacobinism."

By Jacobinism Arnold did not mean what his father had meant, the preference of rights to duties; he meant rather the "violent indignation with the past, abstract systems of renovation applied wholesale, a new doctrine drawn up in black and white for elaborating down to the very smallest details a rational society for the future." Benthamism was Jacobinism, and Comtian positivism was Jacobinism, though Frederic Harrison pointed out that Comte was not in the least indignant with the past. Jacobinism, in short, is the bad, the mechanical aspect of the revolutionary tradition.

Behind Arnold's rejection of system-making there are important assumptions. Of these the first is the conception of the "order of the universe" which may also be called the "will of God." This is so far Spinozistic as to exclude personality from the deity, and it follows the Spinozism of the *Tractatus Politico-Theologicus* (though not of the *Ethics*) in making the moral order part of the natural order. Arnold, however, adds suggestions of evolutionism, so that the *order* is actually a *process*. This order or process is ascertainable through the kind of moral intuition Spinoza describes in the *Tractatus,* possessed by the lawgivers and prophets of mankind. Although not perfectly ascertainable, the order may be sufficiently known to establish the moral life on very firm ground, for the intuition by which it is apprehended is not a mystical and special one, but rather the exercise of all that is truly human in man—the suppression of what Arnold calls the *ordinary self* in favor of what he calls the *best self.*

It is the great error of Jacobinism, says Arnold, that, making systems, it ignores this world order. History is movement in a direction, but the direction is complex, certainly not a straight line, rather a confusion of currents in the stream of the universe, which veer now this way, now that—changeable, shifting, not easily charted. The work of culture is to ascertain the dominant current, the one which keeps most nearly to the course of the stream itself. What the dominant current of the next moment may be is not predictable, yet it must be ascertained; man's salvation is to move with it. The impracticability of any system lies in its negation of a moving current of history; it builds its house on the river bank, a static structure past which the living waters flow. Culture, on the other hand, seeks to navigate the flood by every trick of rudder and sail.

More than this, however, is implied by Arnold's rejection of systems, as the very use of the word "Jacobin" might hint: a reassertion of the political tradition of the English Romantics. The central political idea of Burke, Coleridge and Wordsworth was that society is of so organic a nature that it prohibits the interference of the

analytical intellect. One speculates about the breath one draws only
at the risk of interfering with the natural rhythm of breathing. Only
fiends or angels, said Coleridge, with his eye on Jacobinism, could
order their lives on the principles of abstract reason. And the most
notable part of Wordsworth's poetical life was devoted to the re-
statement of the causes of his revolt from Godwin and from all the
rationalist dissectors of society. He had learned to see conscious reason as the source of all cruelty, and habit, prejudice, custom—all
that was unconscious—as the beneficent ties which keep society together:

> The mild necessity of use compels
> To acts of love; and habit does the work
> Of reason; yet prepares that after-joy
> Which reason cherishes.

Burke was the political master of both poets, and Burke could
find no words too contemptuous for the men who projected social
systems: "metaphysical knights of the sorrowful countenance," "refining speculatists," "political aeronauts." As Wordsworth said,
Burke's conception of society

> Declares the vital power of social ties
> Endeared by Custom; and with high disdain,
> Exploding upstart Theory, insists
> Upon the allegiance to which men are born.

As Alfred Cobban puts it, Burke saw society "instinct with life
itself and throbbing with its rhythm, a cosmic harmony of myriad
men, more wonderful than the Newtonian universe or the music of
the spheres; a giant organism among whose leviathan bowels he
fears to probe with murderous scalpel." The world, Burke said, would
fall to ruins "if the practice of all moral duties, and the foundation
of society, rested upon having their reasons made clear and demon-
strative to every individual." Not abstract theory had built the social constitution and not abstract theory can test it. Society has grown
slowly, with a planlessness that is only apparent, for actually there

is a law at work which man cannot see, though man is its unconscious agent. For if *reason* has not made the social structure, *wisdom* has—what Burke calls the "Standing Wisdom of the country," the unconscious wisdom by which man fulfils his right destiny and the divine intention. If, therefore, change dictated by a group of presumptuous men is to be resisted, change in itself is not bad, provided it comes about as the inevitable, organic fruit of the past, the right development of all that has gone before. For at certain times, to paraphrase the passage by which Arnold set such store, the current of men's minds turns in a new direction and what has before been wise resistance becomes mere obstinacy.

Arnold, through all his earlier writing, had used an historical method learned from Burke, by which circumstantial rather than absolute morality determines the value of any social scheme or action. From Burke, too, he had learned the test of survival, by which the correctness of a social order is marked by its continuation and by which insufficiency is signalized by defeat. Thus, as we have seen, feudalism was right and necessary because it was the tendency which preserved society by centralizing it after the Roman Empire fell to pieces. And now, in the history of Hellenism: "if Hellenism was defeated, this shows that Hellenism was imperfect, and that its ascendancy at that moment would not have been for the world's good."

In short, there are the currents of history and it is for the "best self" to be sensitive to them, go along with them, further them. Culture has separated the best self from the ordinary self and culture will show the best self its method of action. Failing the action of the best self, the ordinary self will take the lead and this is a "contravention of the natural order," producing, "as such contravention always must produce, a certain confusion and false movement, of which we are now beginning to feel, in almost every direction, the inconvenience. In all directions our habitual courses of action seem to be losing efficaciousness, credit, and control, both with others and even with ourselves; everywhere we see the beginnings of confusion, and we want a clue to some sound order and authority. This we can only get by going back upon the actual instincts and forces which rule our life, seeing them as they really are, connecting them with other instincts and forces, and enlarging our whole view and rule of life."

Arnold published what was to be the first chapter of *Culture and Anarchy* in July, 1867. In November, the *Fortnightly Review* printed a brilliant satirical retort from the pen of Frederic Harrison, "Culture: A Dialogue," in which Harrison ironically assumed the rôle of expounder and defender of culture and assigned to Arnold's own Arminius of *Friendship's Garland* the task of savagely dismissing all the fine sentiments and the elegant, quasi-religious unction. The renegade Arminius attacked Arnold with the simple question of instrumentality—how is culture to work? With all that is to be done in the way of social amelioration, of what possible use can all this internality and personal enlargement and cool application of reason be? If it is anything more than a preachment for aristocratic good taste or a pleasantly devitalized religion, it must show what it can *do*. "Lieber Gott," cried Arminius, "I know not what this means. In your heathen, sottish, putrid cities . . . have I seen some *petit maître* preacher passing his white hands through his perfumed curls and simpering thus about the fringes of a stole. Come, . . . in the name of human woe, what Gospel does this offer to poor stricken men?"

Arnold was delighted with the satire; he wrote Lady Rothschild that he laughed over it until he cried. He did not use Socrates' reply to a question somewhat similar to Harrison's: "Then do not impose upon me the duty of exhibiting all our theory realized with precise accuracy in fact;" on the contrary, he undertook to demonstrate at once the practicability of his idea and to show how it might indeed be a Gospel.

Culture, said Arnold, has pointed out the condition of anarchy that exists in England and culture has pointed out that there must be a principle and center of authority. In theory this would receive everyone's assent but difficulty arises when the theory is applied. Then each class, deeming itself fit to provide the principle of authority and to act upon it, fears the principle and the action of each of the other classes and if the self-esteem of each class is not justified, its suspicion of the other classes is, for clearly no one class is fit to rule. But there is no need to rest in the dilemma: "what if we tried to rise above the idea of class to the idea of the whole community, *the State,* and to find our centre of light and authority there? Every one of us has the idea of country, as a sentiment; hardly any one of us has the idea of *the State,* as a working power." This failure is the result of living in the ordinary self. "But by our *best self* we are united, impersonal, at harmony. We are in no peril from giving authority to this, because it is the truest friend we all of us can have; and when anarchy is a danger to us, to this authority we may turn with sure trust. . . . We want an authority, and we find nothing but jealous classes, checks, and a deadlock; culture suggests the idea of *the State.* We find no basis for a firm State-power in our ordinary selves; culture suggests one to us in our *best self.*"

Class implies imperfection and any analysis of the three classes—the Barbarians, the Philistines and the Populace, as Arnold calls the aristocracy, the bourgeoisie, and the working class—inevitably discovers more faults than virtues. What, then, in actuality, is to make the State which is the best self? There are rare souls who have the talent for seeking perfection, men freed from the faults and prepossessions of their origins, led "not by their class spirit, but by a general *humane* spirit," yet such men as these, Arnold admits, are without power; they have a rough time of it in their lives and exercise their little influence only by "enfilading" the class with which they are ranked. They themselves must depend on the help they receive from things around them to increase their numbers or strengthen their virtue. It is not individuals, then, who can be thought of as the "best self." The national best self must be a greater concept; it must be the "national right reason" and the State must be founded on it.

But for so many centuries the world has lent its ear to the advice that it follow right reason rather than self-interest—has listened and done little—that for Arnold simply to repeat the advice yet again scarcely advances the constitution of the State which is truly everybody's State. In fact, his achievement at this point is, we must feel, a little like the magician who puts eggs into a hat and draws forth eggs. Perhaps, too, it is this vague and half-mystical retreat which, more directly than any other of Arnold's counsels, exposes him to the charge, preferred by competent critics, of apologizing for a reactionary if benevolent absolutism. The "spirituality" of Arnold's intention does not defend him from such a charge; the cat of "spirituality" may jump in too many directions. "The people is the body of the state," says Mussolini, for instance, "and the state is the spirit of the people." Or Carlyle's Hero is, in effect, the individualized "best self" of his nation, in touch with the purpose and movement of the universe, showing his countrymen how to fulfil their own best selves through his authority. Out of the belief that the best self, Hero or State, is in touch with the order of the universe, with right reason, with the will of God, may flow chauvinism, imperialism, Governor Eyre, the white man's burden—all the things which make us turn to Mill and skepticism, well-nigh willing to rest in "anarchy."

The reactionary possibilities of Arnold's vagueness are underscored by the time in which he formulated his theory—when the political power of the working class seems to have increased. Speaking of the workers' relation to the State, Arnold ignored or misrepresented the very real feeling for the State-idea which the proletariat possessed. Since the very beginning of the industrial revolution the workers had looked to Parliament for the amelioration of their lot; their innumerable petitions had, of course, been met with indignation or indifference.* Arnold speaks of a working class with so little

* Arnold's description of the nature of the State in England is misleading in that he represents it as quite functionless. But, as Th. Rothstein says in *From Chartism to Labourism*, there can be nothing more unfounded than the fiction that the State did

conception of the State that it prefers to hide in abandoned coal mines rather than be drafted for service in the Crimea, but he ignores a working class that had conceived the State as an instrument for international right-doing and had pressed the Crimean War as a kind of crusade against Russian despotism. Indeed, Arnold passes over the remarkable sense of *Europeanism* of the working class, which, until frightened by the Commune of 1871, was for many years the only class in England that held the idea of internationalism. And specifically he fails to mention that notable example of the abrogation of self-interest which the working class had supplied: the cotton operatives' support of the North in the American Civil War in the face of the North's blockade of cotton which threw the population of Birmingham and Manchester into unemployment and long distress—and this at a time when the upper classes of England were all for the South. For the struggles of the trade unions Arnold —now, though not later—has nothing but words of disapproval and contempt. Further, there stand against him the absurd, violent words which he quotes from his father—their absurdity struck him after the first edition of *Culture and Anarchy,* for he later excised them— "As for rioting, the old Roman way of dealing with *that* is always the right one; flog the rank and file, and fling the ringleaders from the Tarpeian Rock."

And finally to support the accusation that Arnold was at this time moving toward a reactionary position, there is the evidence of his intellectual tradition in politics which proves nothing but suggests

---

not interfere in English commercial and social life. "The interference of the State in the economic destinies and social relations of the countries on the Continent was mere child's play in comparison with the detailed and never-ending regulation of public and social life, the active policy of fostering, encouraging, planting, regulating, and prohibiting industrial and commercial activity, which had been practised by the 'mercantilist' Governments in England in the course of 150 years, beginning with the 'glorious Revolution' of 1688. . . . A perusal of the economic literature of that period or of any of the volumes of Hansard, will suffice to show at once how 'artificial' was the commercial, industrial and social development in England, how deliberately the State had been guiding the destinies of the British nation, and how the debates in Parliament were essentially concerned with economic policies." (pp. 10–11) Miss Gillespie, in Chapter V of her *Labor and Politics in England, 1850–1867,* records instances of the working class's appeal to the State shortly before the time Arnold was writing.

much. We have already spoken of his connection with the English romantic prophets of philosophical reaction, Burke, Coleridge and Wordsworth; the influence of Plato and Aristotle, clear enough throughout *Culture and Anarchy,* could scarcely make him a partisan of democratic hope. Arnold's own coupling of democracy with Protestantism and of Protestantism with anarchy suggests the reactionary Bonald, and his placing of authority in *reason,* though it might suggest nobler analogues, makes us at least glance at Cousin and the Doctrinaires who, in the dilemma of deciding whether to place authority in Louis XVIII or in the people, extricated themselves rather shabbily by compromising on this same "reason."

It is therefore not surprising that Leonard Woolf, defending liberal political theory in *After the Deluge,* makes Arnold his chief point of attack as the insidious proponent of a tyrannical authoritarianism; or that Ernest Barker finds the only logical conclusion of Arnold's theory in an absolute monarchy:

Where . . . authority may be found he will not decide; he lays his main emphasis on the duty of attaining self-perfection through culture in order to make such authority possible. But when he argues for an authoritative centre, like an Academy, in the field of literature; when he urges that representative government issues in pandering to the populace instead of the rule of right reason; when he praises the work done by an absolute monarchy in Prussia for the cause of education, his inclination seems clear. In the name of good taste or right reason he seeks an authority which will not pander to the bad taste of any class, and which must therefore, presumably, be non-representative; and it is difficult to see where such an authority can be found except in a sort of absolute monarchy. Arnold would have instantly denied that he sought anything of this order; he would have treated the idea with elusive and delicate irony; and yet this is the one logical issue of his teaching.*

---

* Not only *would* Arnold have denied that he meant anything of the sort but he *did* deny it. He had no illusions about Prussian monarchy; see Letter IV of *Friendship's Garland.* And, in "The Future of Liberalism," he spoke of the possibility of one class representing the interests of another as "the last of our illusions" and one that must quickly vanish. The instances of misinterpretation of Arnold might be multiplied. J. Dover Wilson speaks of Dr. Murray's *The English Social and Political Thinkers of*

But to rescue Arnold from the charges of reaction, we need only carry him out of the realm of metaphysico-political theory into the realm of practice (and this we shall do) to see that his practical recommendations are such as to make him, if a reactionary at all, a reactionary of a very strange kind. His defense in the terrain of theory must be undertaken first.

We recall that Arnold claimed to be continuing the work of the French Revolution; he had attacked the English system because it betrayed the Revolutionary ideals, and he had instituted his discussion of the State because, foreseeing a "revolution by due course of law," he wished to advance it. But if he did indeed desire a revolution, he did believe it could come by law: "great changes there must be, for a revolution cannot accomplish itself without great changes; yet order there must be, for without order a revolution cannot accomplish itself by due course of law." Yet Arnold, at the same time that he was in Burke's tradition of slow, almost imperceptible change, was also in the tradition of Rousseau—and for Burke Rousseau was the very essence of Revolution! The relation with Rousseau at once destroys the simplicity of the judgment which labels Arnold (with appropriate music from *Iolanthe*) an entirely obvious Liberal or else a palpable Conservative. Rousseau, prophet of the Revolution, never became a victim to the Revolution's prime mistake—simplicity. His *Social Contract* is commonly regarded as a paradox, beginning as it does, "Man is born free and is everywhere in chains," and going on to establish a rationale for authority. To examine Rousseau's theory of society and show how closely Arnold's own position approached it may not wholly explain Arnold but it at least makes clear the difficulties that the Revolution presented to a thinker and indicates the justification for Arnold's claim that he was in the Revolutionary line.

---

the *Nineteenth Century* as being "more at sea" than Dr. Barker's book. Mr. Wilson himself is as cogent on Arnold as he is on Shakespeare—*Culture and Anarchy* should be read in his edition—and his essay on Arnold's politics in *Social and Political Ideas of the Victorian Age* is in every way excellent.

Rousseau's theory had its logical beginning in the same problem that disturbed Arnold—the self in its relation to society. "The problem," said Rousseau, "is to find a form of association which will defend and protect with the whole common force the person and goods of each associate, and in which each, while uniting himself with all, may still obey himself alone, and remain as free as before." Rousseau found the beginning of the answer in the conception of what he calls the *general will* which must be distinguished from the *will of all*. The *will of all* is merely the sum of particular wills in the polity, each one concerned with its own private interest; it is, in effect, society as conceived by Mill. But the *general will* is concerned with the common interest, and indeed exists only when that common interest is truly served. As G. D. H. Cole says, *"There is no General Will unless the people wills the good. . . .* [The] term 'general' will means, in Rousseau, not so much 'will held by several persons,' as will having a general (universal) object." Or, as Bernard Bosanquet says in the *Philosophical Theory of the State,* "The General Will seems to be, in the last resort, the ineradicable impulse of an intelligent being to a good extending beyond itself, insofar as that good takes the form of a common good." In short, where Rousseau writes "general will," we may, with no violence to his idea or Arnold's, read "best self."

The formulation of the "general will" settles nothing, of course; it merely initiates the problem. "Of itself," Rousseau went on, "the people wills always the good, but of itself it by no means always sees it," and politics most often deals with a "blind multitude, which often does not know what it wills, because it rarely knows what is good for it." * The general will, then, "must be got to see objects as they are [we think of criticism and the task of education], and sometimes as they ought to appear to it [we think of the discussion of what reading-matter might be given to the little-instructed]; it must be shown the good road it is in search of, secured from the seductive in-

---

* Bosanquet calls the will acting with complete knowledge of the situation the *real will;* the will acting without this knowledge he calls the *apparent will.*

fluences of individual wills, taught to see times and spaces as a series, and made to weigh the attractions of present and sensible advantages against the danger of distant and hidden evils. The individuals see the good they reject; the public wills the good it does not see. All stand equally in need of guidance. The former must be compelled to bring their wills into conformity with their reason; the latter must be taught to know what it wills."

"This," Rousseau concludes, "makes a legislator necessary," and the peculiar power required of this lawgiver is nothing less than what Arnold conceived it to be—the power of the "best self:" the ability to know the will of God. "It would take gods to give men laws," says Rousseau; for what is needed is a "superior intelligence beholding all the passions of men without experiencing any of them," with a happiness independent of human happiness and with a vision of distant human glory, "working in one century, to be able to enjoy in the next." For consider his task:

He who dares to undertake the making of a people's institutions ought to feel himself capable, so to speak, of changing human nature, of transforming each individual, who is by himself a complete and solitary whole, into part of a greater whole from which he in a manner receives his life and being; of altering man's constitution for the purpose of strengthening it; and of substituting a partial and moral existence for the physical and independent existence nature has conferred on us all. He must, in a word, take away from man his own resources and give him instead new ones alien to him, and incapable of being made use of without the help of other men.

Rousseau, it is clear, set aside much of the liberalism and the libertarianism which were to form the French Revolution but he laid down the program of subsequent revolution and it is in this that Arnold followed him. Rousseau knew, however, that even his ideal legislator does not finally solve the problem of authority. For though the legislator may make the law he cannot enforce it, cannot make it the general will: only the free assent of the people can accomplish that. The problem, then, however urgent it be, appears an ultimate and insoluble one: "In the task of legislation we find to-gether two things which appear to be incompatible: an enterprise too difficult for human powers, and, for its execution, an authority that is no authority." As an absolute problem it can be solved only in absolute terms—in, for example, Karl Marx's ultimate anarchy when the State shall have withered away from lack of any need for it. And even were the barrier of the divergent interests of individual wills overthrown, there is, Rousseau knows, still another barrier created by the problem of reason and communication:

Wise men, if they try to speak their language to the common herd instead of its own, cannot possibly make themselves understood. There are a thousand kinds of ideas which it is impossible to translate into popular language. Conceptions that are too general and objects that are too remote are equally out of its range: each individual, having no taste for any other plan of government than that which suits his particular interest, finds it difficult to realise the advantages he might hope to draw from the continual privations good laws impose. For a young people to be able to relish sound principles of political theory and follow the fundamental rules of statecraft, the effect would have to become the cause; the social spirit, which should be created by these institutions, would have to preside over their very foundations; and men would have to be before law what they should become by means of law.

Arnold had said no more than this when he had written of Bishop Colenso and we must remember that Rousseau is the prophet of equality. Or again like Arnold, despairing of a mundane umpire for the bickerings of men, Rousseau turns to a transcendental judge, established, it is true, by a kind of pious fraud, but meant to serve the same end, actually meant to be the same imperative as that to which Arnold had appealed—the will of God or the order of the universe or ultimate reason. For the legislator, "being unable to appeal to either force or reason" must turn to an authority of a different order; he must "have recourse to divine intervention and credit the gods with . . . [his] own wisdom;" only thus will men obey freely and bear with docility the yoke of public happiness. Still, in the end, it is reason itself, not the pious fraud, which prevails:

But it is not anybody who can make the gods speak, or get himself believed when he proclaims himself their interpreter. The great soul of the legislator is the only miracle that can prove his mission. Any man may grave tablets of stone, or buy an oracle, or feign secret intercourse with some divinity, or train a bird to whisper in his ear, or find other vulgar ways of imposing on the people. He whose knowledge goes no further may perhaps gather round him a band of fools; but he will never found an empire, and his extravagances will quickly perish with him. Idle tricks form a passing tie; only wisdom can make it lasting.

The refinements and impasses into which the thinker falls who undertakes ultimately to reconcile reason and authority are inevitable; his conclusions must be either disturbing or sterile; yet if the merely immediate notions on which we act are to be refreshed and kept as nearly rational and universal as possible, the effort of reconciliation must be constantly made. Actually, the result of Rousseau's attempt was not wholly sterile, nor, when he curtails Liberty, does he depart from the expansive Revolutionary tradition. He diminished Liberty in the interests of what he thought more important— Equality and Fraternity; and Arnold does the same thing because he saw one word of the Revolutionary triumvirate living upon the other two words and harming all three of them.

And now, if we take Arnold out of the realm of theory into that of practice we see how very far indeed he was from reaction. One of the chapters of *Culture and Anarchy* ("Our Liberal Practitioners") is devoted to the analysis of middle class legislation. Of the four items which Arnold considers we may pass over two—the bill for the disestablishment of the Irish Church and the bill to permit marriage with a deceased wife's sister—as less relevant to the matter of this chapter, and consider only his discussion of the Real Estate Intestacy Bill and the question of Free Trade.

The Real Estate Intestacy Bill proposed to prevent the land of a man who died intestate from going to his eldest son, as by the existing law it did; instead, it was to be divided equally among all of his children. The bill was a timid expression of the manufacturing class's desire to break up the aristocracy's monopoly of land, because, according to the Ricardian doctrine, manufacturing profits were inversely proportional to land profits; the laws of primogeniture kept the great estates intact, thus maintaining the monopoly, preventing "free trade in land" and keeping land costs high. However, this soundly self-interested reason was not the one which the bill's supporters advanced. They preferred the high philosophic ground of natural law and natural right—the ground (as Arnold paraphrased Bright's expression of it) that "there is a kind of natural law or fitness of things which assigns to all a man's children a right to equal shares in the enjoyment of his property after his death; and that if, without depriving a man of an Englishman's prime privilege of doing what he likes by making what will he chooses,* you provide that when he makes none his land shall be divided among his family, then you give the sanction of the law to the natural fitness of things." For Arnold the theory of natural law and natural right had no meaning at all. But if he was attacking one of the strongholds of middle class liberalism by declaring that natural right was nonsense, he was standing in the direct line of Philosophical Radicalism, for Bentham's attack upon Blackstone had centered in this denial of natural right and John Austin had built his *Jurisprudence* on the same negation.

To be sure, at least one of Arnold's reasons for rejecting the theory is very clearly not of a Benthamite kind. "Now does any one," he asks, "if he simply and naturally reads his consciousness, discover that he has any rights at all? For my part, the deeper I go in my own consciousness, and the more simply I abandon myself to it, the more it seems to tell me that I have no rights at all, only duties; and that men get this notion of rights from a process of abstract reasoning, inferring that the obligations they are conscious of towards others, others must be conscious of towards them, and not from any direct witness of consciousness at all." This is a little finedrawn for practice, intended for people who prefer saintliness to

* Mill had defended the right of a man to make any will he chooses, no matter how silly it might be. (*On Liberty*, p. 126 n.). Arnold, without specific reference to Mill, had assailed that right in *Culture and Anarchy* (p. 78).

virtue; the impartial umpire, viewing the relations between two people, would naturally understand duties to imply rights and rights to imply duties—as much, perhaps, by the nature of language as of politics. However, this result of psychological research, though it was to interest Arnold more and more, is not the whole argument for the negation of natural right. Perhaps even more important is the Utilitarian judgment of morality. The "natural right" of children to share equally in their father's estate did not, Arnold points out, operate after the disintegration of the Roman Empire; at that time the centralization of property was necessary for organized society, and the small holding, whatever its virtues now may be (Arnold thinks them considerable) was then an evil. Yet the proponents of the theory of natural right would have it that the equal sharing of property is at all times an equal good.

Arnold does not argue against the breaking up of the monopoly of land; quite the contrary, he argues for it and his objection to the Real Estate Intestacy Bill is not to what it proposes but to what it dare not propose. He himself is actually willing to consider it an open question whether the very idea of private property constitutes a welfare and Utilitarianism could scarcely go further in its destruction of the old order than to formulate such a question. Toward the end of his life Arnold will speak more and more boldly on this point and adduce more and more instances where private ownership is not a public welfare; now, at least, he is perfectly willing to argue against the monopoly of land and not in the minimal way which is the method of the Liberals—not "with stock notions and mechanical action" but with living issues. The living issue here is that equality, or the tendency toward equality, of property is a clear social benefit and that inequality and the tendency to monopoly are clearly social evils.

It seems to me quite easy to show that a free disinterested play of thought on the Barbarians and their land-holding is a thousand times more really practical, a thousand times more likely to lead to some effective result, than an operation such as that of which we have been now speaking.

For if, casting aside the impediments of stock notions and mechanical action, we try to find the intelligible law of things respecting a great land-owning class such as we have in this country, does not our consciousness readily tell us that whether the perpetuation of such a class is for its own real good and for the real good of the community, depends on the actual circumstances of this class and of the community? Does it not readily tell us that wealth, power, and consideration are,—and above all when inherited and not earned,—in themselves trying and dangerous things? As Bishop Wilson excellently says: "Riches are almost always abused without a very extraordinary grace." But this extraordinary grace was in great measure supplied by the circumstances of the feudal epoch, out of which our land-holding class, with its rules of inheritance, sprang. The labour and contentions of a rude, nascent, and struggling society supplied it. These perpetually were trying, chastising, and forming the class whose predominance was then needed by society to give it points of cohesion, and was not so harmful to themselves because they were thus sharply tried and exercised. But in a luxurious, settled, and easy society, where wealth offers the means of enjoyment a thousand times more, and the temptation to abuse them is thus made a thousand times greater, the exercising discipline is at the same time taken away, and the feudal class is left exposed to the full operation of the natural law well put by the French moralist: *Pouvoir sans savoir est fort dangereux.* . . . Then, as to the effect upon the welfare of the community, how can that be salutary, if a class which, by the very possession of wealth, power and consideration, becomes a kind of ideal or standard for the rest of the community, is tried by ease and pleasure more than it can well bear, and almost irresistibly carried away from excellence and strenuous virtue?

A class such as this provides a false and deteriorating ideal for the Philistine, and for the populace this false ideal is "a stone which kills the desire before it can even arise," so impossible is it of attainment. In short, the real—the only sound—reason for the equalization of property has nothing to do with "natural right" but with the social human harm which is worked by monopoly, with the barrier that inequality offers to human expansion. And reasons such as these are the reasons raised by culture. This is Hellenizing. In a time when change is necessary, culture is also necessary for it "teaches us how gradually nature would have all profound changes brought about." It does more: sweetness and light can, in Arnold's opinion, even make a feudal class quietly and gradually drop its feudal habits.

And from the Real Estate Intestacy Bill, Arnold goes on to turn the free stream of thought upon the doctrine of free trade, to see it, too, "in reference to [a] firm intelligible law of things, to human life as a whole, and human happiness." The defense of free trade, Arnold admits, contains a simple enough justice: it is clearly right that the poor man should eat untaxed bread and that monopolies which favor one class alone should be abolished. But this is not at all the ground on which the Liberals defend free trade: rather, they press the argument that the policy has increased manufacture, business and population—which is to say, the welfare of the nation, of rich and poor alike. Yet here culture notes an anomaly which Liberalism ignores, that free trade has not so much made the already existing poor man's bread cheaper and more abundant, as it has created poor men to eat it, a result which Liberalism blindly believes to be a mark of social progress.

Liberals, he goes on, would argue that, other things being equal, the more the population increases, the more industrial production increases to keep pace with it, because the mere numbers of men create new activities and resources—in one another and in nature. They would argue, too, that though population always tends to equal the means of subsistence, the notion of the means of subsistence enlarges as civilization advances. But culture sees the object as it really is and is at pains to refute all this as fact; the enlarged conception of subsistence may be true, but enormous numbers of people barely attain the necessities; many fail to attain them: silk stockings may have cheapened since Queen Elizabeth's day but bread and bacon have not and one Englishman in every nineteen is now a pauper.

But what particularly concerns Arnold is the attitude of the Liberals toward their axioms—their reliance upon them "as if they were self-acting laws which will put themselves into operation without trouble or planning on our part." Against the dead necessitarianism of the Liberal philosophy, its passive acceptance of the cycles of prosperity and ruin, he sets the living fact. "There is no one to blame for this," says the *Times,* surveying the East End in the throes of economic depression, "it is the result of Nature's simplest laws!" What pitfalls are in that word Nature! as Arnold was later to say; he knows that it is not Nature but man that has created such squalor. Or he reads Robert Buchanan growing lyrical over the population growth which is providing the manufacturers with a cheap labor supply and a huge market for cheap goods: "Life, life, life,—faces gleaming, hearts beating, must fill every cranny. Not a corner is suffered to remain empty. The whole earth breeds, and God glories." But Arnold knows that the faces in the East End do not gleam but are dark with misery and he feels that by such desperation and suffering God is not glorified but blasphemed. Culture reminds him of the Revolution's word, Fraternity, tells him that "individual perfection is impossible so long as the rest of mankind are not perfected along with us." And perfection is a long way off with things as they are and with Liberal doctrines condoning and encouraging the increase of "vast, miserable, unmanageable masses of sunken people."

Against the deficiencies of Liberalism Hebraism is powerless. "Hebraism builds churches, indeed, for these masses, and sends missionaries among them; above all, it sets itself against the social necessitarianism of the *Times,* and refuses to accept their degradation as inevitable." But Hebraism is bound by its *own* necessitarianism. It interprets the Bible in its own fashion and repeats words spoken at a time when every child was a blessing to the depleted Jewish garrisons; it still says, "Be fruitful and multiply," and it still murmurs, "The poor shall never cease out of the land." No less than Liberalism, Hebraism regards the swarming children of the East End as "sent" and it has no instrument to help the misery save that of a pointless (under the circumstances) morality:

I remember, only the other day, a good man looking with me upon a multitude of children who were gathered before us in one of the most miserable regions of London,—children eaten up with disease, half-sized, half-fed, half-clothed, neglected by their parents, without health, without home, without hope,—said to me: "The one thing really needful is to teach these little ones to succour one another, if only with a cup of cold water; but now, from one end of the country to the other, one hears nothing but the cry for knowledge, knowledge, knowledge!" And yet surely, so long as these children are there in these festering masses, without health, without home, without hope, and so long as their multitude is perpetually swelling, charged with misery they must still be for themselves, charged with misery they must still be for us, whether they help one another with a cup of cold water or no; and the knowledge how to prevent their accumulating is necessary, even to give their moral life and growth a fair chance!

Nothing could cut more surgically into cant, whether of economic liberalism or of religion, than this. It illuminates the whole of Arnold's concept of culture and, rescuing it from the charge of vague and evasive religiosity, gives it sinew and bone. If you would have power, said the Christian Socialists to the depressed masses, learn first to govern yourselves, to check your own appetites. But Arnold knows that "moral life and growth" are not the result of an always-possible act of the will; he knows that they need "a fair chance." This is the outcome of the doctrine of culture and if in the evolution of that doctrine lapses of logic or of realism have appeared they are the lapses consequent upon most faiths. Arnold's own faith was a sound one:—that man by his wits and his virtue may perfect himself to become a whole human being.

It is interesting to observe where Arnold expected human wits, if not human virtue, to make their next important stand. On March 18, 1871, there was a revolutionary outbreak in Paris, heralding the establishment of the Commune. By now Arnold had lost much of his old love of France; French licentiousness—what he called Lubricity—had become a bugaboo for him and to it he attributed the French defeat in the just-concluded war. "One hardly knows what to wish," he writes, "except that the present generation of Frenchmen may pass clean away as soon as possible and be replaced by a better one:" his disgust is largely a moral one. Apparently he included the Communards in the present generation of Frenchmen even though he had always found the strength of France in its *people* as against the loose ruling classes. Nevertheless, he finds the only promise of French strength in a radical government: "One thing is certain, that miserable as it is for herself, there is no way by which France can make the rest of Europe so alarmed and uneasy as by a socialistic and red republic. It is a perpetual flag to the proletaire class everywhere—the class which makes all governments uneasy." And eight days later: "Paris does not make me so angry as it does many people, because I do not think well enough of Thiers and the French upper class generally to think it very important they should win. What is certain is that all the seriousness, clear-mindedness, and settled purpose is hitherto on the side of the Reds." And in May: "The Paris convulsion is an explosion of that fixed resolve of the working class to count for something and *live,* which is destined to make itself so much felt in the coming time, and to disturb so much which dreamed it would last for ever. It is the French working man's clearly putting his resolve before himself and acting upon it, while the working man elsewhere is in a haze about it, that makes France such a focus for the revolutionists of all Europe."

This was the new current in the history of Europe which culture had to perceive and navigate. But if the fixed resolve of the working class to count for something and to *live* was to be felt more and more in the future it could only be momentarily successful now. For however superior to its ruling class the French working class might be, still—"There is no person or thing . . . to give one any satisfaction when one regards France at present." "Nothing . . . that any of them [i.e., Frenchmen] now make can stand. There is not virtue enough amongst any of them to make what may really endure." What is lacking is righteousness, and, with religion fallen on evil days, this too must be supplied by culture.

Chapter Ten

⇉ ⇇

OBERMANN ONCE MORE

There is no other ethic for us than the heart of man, no other science or wisdom than the knowledge of its requirements, and the just estimation of the means of happiness! Leave useless knowledge, supernatural systems, and mysterious doctrines.—SENANCOUR

IN July of 1867, the month in which "Culture and its Enemies" appeared in *The Cornhill Magazine,* Arnold published his *New Poems.* To be sure, they were not wholly new. "St. Brandon," "A Southern Night," and "Thyrsis" had already appeared in periodicals between 1860 and 1866. At the instance of Browning's admiration, "Empedocles" was included—*published,* Arnold said, for the first time and "really the cause of the volume appearing at all," and six poems were lifted with "Empedocles" from the old suppressed volume of 1852. "Bacchanalia," according to Mrs. Humphry Ward, was a youthful piece and "Dover Beach," printed here for the first time, was probably composed many years before. What was new made but a small showing. With increasing years the "Progress of Poesy" went a hard way:

> Youth rambles on life's arid mount,
> And strikes the rock, and finds the vein,
> And brings the water from the fount,
> The fount which shall not flow again.
>
> The man mature with labour chops
> For the bright stream a channel grand,

And sees not that the sacred drops
Ran off and vanish'd out of hand.

And then the old man totters nigh
And feebly rakes among the stones.
The mount is mute, the channel dry;
And down he lays his weary bones.

The expression of the older poet has a rocklike quality; he adumbrates less than the younger; the conception of life has become crystallized, its limits defined. These new poems do not question but reply, do not hint but declare. A note of finality, even of dismissal, is here; not that values are dismissed, but the worry about them: "'That, or nothing, I believe,'" says the literal religionist of "Pis-Aller." "For God's sake, believe it then," is Arnold's almost brutally impatient answer. It is a volume of statements and the statements are acceptances.

Creep into thy narrow bed,
Creep, and let no more be said!
Vain thy onset! all stands fast;
Thou thyself must break at last.

Let the long contention cease!
Geese are swans, and swans are geese.
Let them have it how they will!
Thou art tired; best be still!

Charge once more, then, and be dumb!
Let the victors, when they come,
When the forts of folly fall,
Find thy body by the wall.

The old sense and fear of vanishing powers is still present and in such harsh directness that we might almost suspect Arnold had renounced his belief that poetry must be "fortifying." Horace's "For nature there is renovation, for man there is none," could scarcely match in negation Arnold's answer to his own question, "What is

it to grow old?" In clear, bitter, parsimonious phrases he tells us:
"It is to spend long days . . ." "It is to suffer this . . ."

> And feel but half, and feebly, what we feel.
> Deep in our hidden heart
> Festers the dull remembrance of a change,
> But no emotion—none.

Acceptance has not blunted the sense of life's anomalies and failures; "Empedocles" fits well into the volume and so do the old
"Lines Written by a Death-Bed," shortened, revised and retitled
"Youth and Calm;" after so many years the youthful perception
that "Calm's not life's crown, though calm is well" needs to be repeated. But the sense of frustration has been made to yield its fruit.
The advice of Empedocles to accept the world has been taken. The
nervous octosyllabic couplets and the machinery of perambulation of
"Resignation" are repeated by the "Epilogue to Lessing's Laocoön,"
but the almost bitter conception of the poet's function is now re-
solved; now it is not an unhappy brother and a romantic sister who
tramp the countryside but two mature men who walk through Hyde
Park, talking not of how to live but of aesthetics. Which, they ask
each other, is the perfect art—music, painting or poetry? And
Arnold, as might be expected, gives the crown to the poet, for his is
the most difficult task:

> . . . he must life's *movement* tell!
> The thread which binds it all in one,
> And not its separate parts alone!

The painter and the musician deal with perfection, but the poet's
glory is that he must wring beauty out of life's failure and distress:

> And many, many are the souls
> Life's movement fascinates, controls.
> It draws them on, they cannot save
> Their feet from its alluring wave;
> They cannot leave it, they must go

With its unconquerable flow.
But, ah, how few of all that try
This mighty march, do aught but die!
For ill prepared for such a way,
Ill found in strength, in wits, are they!
They faint, they stagger to and fro,
And wandering from the stream they go;
In pain, in terror, in distress,
They see, all round, a wilderness.
Sometimes a momentary gleam
They catch of the mysterious stream;
Sometimes, a second's space, their ear
The murmur of its waves doth hear.
That transient glimpse in song they say,
But not as painter can pourtray!
That transient sound in song they tell,
But not, as the musician, well!
And when at last these snatches cease,
And they are silent and at peace,
The stream of life's majestic whole
Hath ne'er been mirror'd on their soul.

Arnold has arrived at the Stoic affirmation. "Whatsoever is expedient unto thee, O World," said Marcus Aurelius, "is expedient unto me; nothing can either be unseasonable unto me, or out of date, which unto thee is seasonable. . . . O Nature! from thee are all things, in thee all things subsist, and to thee all tend. Could he say of Athens, Thou lovely city of Cecrops; and shalt not thou say of the world, Thou lovely city of God?" The poet's "Wish" for his own death-bed is that he should not be surrounded by gaping friends, that he be spared the physician and his "brother doctor of the soul" with "official breath," but that rather he be moved to the window to see

> The world which was ere I was born,
> The world which lasts when I am dead.
>
> Which never was the friend of *one*,
> Nor promised love it could not give,

But lit for all its generous sun,
And lived itself, and made us live.

Middle age has banished the sense of being a stranger in a strange land and it is possible at last "to feel the universe my home." A momentary departure from the Stoic calm to look with approval at the life of passion and sensuality makes the acceptance the more valid poetically and philosophically. For it means nothing to hear reconciliation preached by the man who has known no other way, but it means much when, like Arnold in the "Fragment of Chorus of a *Dejaneira*," he speaks of the good fortune of early death, yet goes on, in "Early Death and Fame:"

> But, when immature death
> Beckons too early the guest
> From the half-tried banquet of life,
> Young, in the bloom of his days;
> Leaves no leisure to press,
> Slow and surely, the sweets
> Of a tranquil life in the shade;
> Fuller for him be the hours!
> Give him emotion, though pain!
> Let him live, let him feel: *I have lived!*
> Heap up his moments with life,
> Triple his pulses with fame!

Nearly all the poems of the volume touch upon death; in the Stoic fashion, life is seen in the light of its end. It is Rachel dying whom the three sonnets make the symbol of modern Europe; it is his grave that calls forth the meditation on Heine. "Rugby Chapel" commemorates Dr. Arnold; "Stanzas at Carnac" and "A Summer Night" are memorials to Arnold's dead brother, William Delafield; the only considerable poem that appeared after 1867, "Westminster Abbey," is an elegy for Arthur Stanley;—and there is "Thyrsis." *

* This is not to mention the animal elegies: "Geist's Grave" and "Kaiser Dead," for dogs, and "Poor Matthias" for a canary.

Untimely death had indeed pressed Arnold close—father, brother, friend. His married life was to become "one long funeral;" in four years he was to carry three sons to their graves, two in the same year, 1868. Yet though death is omnipresent in the volume and though Arnold is at the point of beginning his specifically religious writing, the two themes are not apparently connected. Arnold is not brought to religion, as men so often are, by thoughts of death. The old dismay of Mycerinus is gone; he holds firm to naturalism and naturalism seems to give him comfort. The letters contain no expression of crazing grief at the death of his sons, no cry in the night. The intensest emotion seems to have gone into the hidden stream. "I saw Henry Coleridge for a few minutes; the first time for years," he wrote in December, 1872, two days before his fiftieth birthday. "I thought he would never let my hand go; at last he said—'Matt!!—I expected to see a white-headed old man.' I said that my white hairs were all internal."

The death of Clough left Arnold silent for many years. Clough had died in 1861 in Florence, whither he had gone in the effort to restore his shattered health. For eight years after his return from his abortive American adventure, he had drudged at his humble work in the Education Office, an appointment that had been procured for him by friends after much difficulty. Increased years, an exacting occupation which, with his love of detail, he did not greatly dislike even though it held little or no chance of advancement, the cares and pleasures of a felicitous domestic life and devotion to the work of his wife's cousin, Florence Nightingale, all tended to quiet the questions of conscience and intellect that had been his misery and his talent. But they quieted too, it would seem, the fine ebullience of his nature and perhaps they had also diminished his health. The sweetness of his temperament did not permit Clough to comment on it, perhaps did not even permit him to know it, but life had pushed him aside; from whatever combination of temperament and circumstance, he was now largely silent; apparently he avoided theoretical talk, and, in his poetry, disturbing subjects. His translations of Homer and his revision of the Dryden Plutarch attracted him more than creation; and though, when he set out to look for health, on a six months' leave of absence, he worked on the pleasant stories of *Mari Magno,* the problems of marriage and not of the soul were his theme. The matters of conscience that had literally wrecked his life were kept to the background. The illness which overtook him was ascribed by those close to him to the mental strain of his youth and to present overwork; it seems to have consisted largely of an affection of the nerves. In Florence he was seized by malarial fever; a paralysis followed; he died on the 13th of November, forty-two years old.

"Probably," wrote Arnold to Mrs. Clough, "you hardly know how very intimate we once were." The time of intimacy has gone; maturity had made much of the old fusion impossible. Clough died as Arnold was preparing his last Homeric lecture; he spoke of Clough in it, with tenderness and warmth, but with the constraint of the public occasion made the more difficult because, as he knew, the chief interest his friend had for people was that of a man who so conspicuously had not fulfilled the promise of youth. He would not write the notice for the *Daily News* that Mrs. Clough suggested. He even avoided writing a memoir for Mrs. Clough's edition of Arthur's prose pieces. Three years seem to have passed before Arnold's monody on his dead friend appeared to his mind, and five before "Thyrsis" appeared in print.

Memorial of a vanished youth and of a nearly vanished mood no less than of a vanished friend, "Thyrsis" is probably the last-composed of Arnold's great poems. Touching as it is, standing, where many have put it, with the three great English elegies—"Lycidas," "Adonais," and "In Memoriam"—it is in some ways a strange commemoration. Not that, as Professor Lowry says, it gives but one side of Clough, the troubled side, but that it celebrates the weakness of that side. Its theme is that "Thyrsis of his own will went away," unable to wait out the high winds of doctrine.

It irk'd him to be here, he could not rest.
He loved each simple joy the country yields,
  He loved his mates; but yet he could not keep,
For that a shadow lower'd on the fields,
  Here with the shepherds and the silly sheep.
    Some life of men unblest
He knew, which made him droop, and fill'd his head.
He went; his piping took a troubled sound
Of storms that rage outside our happy ground;
He could not wait their passing, he is dead!

Clough could not wait the passing of the storms: in many turns of phrase we sense Arnold's belief that his friend's despair and death were acts of surrender, an insight that was the more poignant because he felt the storms were passing. For in 1865 Arnold was in Switzerland and spoke with Obermann again, this time to receive a message not of despair but of hope. Nearly two decades had passed since he had bade "a last, a last farewell" to the unstrung will and broken heart of the Alpine recluse. His thought of emulating Senancour in his mountain withdrawal had been but a passing fiction; his dread of the world of 1852 had, however, been real enough. Twenty years have changed much; Arnold may disparage the New Age with the muted irony of "Bacchanalia," but he cannot escape its influence, its dominant note of optimism. The hysteria of the political events of 1867 could not fundamentally deny the feeling of security and the belief in progress. England is on the threshold of the lush and prosperous seventies. Europe, still to be shaken by the brief thunders of the French war and the new French revolution, is settling down to discreet quiet. And although we today may look back with posterity's small prerogative of irony and see that there was but little cause for complacency, understanding that Europe's settling into a routine of stable government was only the gathering of forces for the industrial and commercial drive which shattered peace and hope in 1914, to the men of the time commerce seems the sure preventative of war, science promises an earthly paradise, and reason, embodied in Parliaments yet to be educated, gives assurance that men will some day do only unselfish and sensible things. Arnold, to be sure, rejects much of this naivety. Yet in some way he can believe that the world has been sufficiently stabilized to allow reason to work its way, that Europe is entering on what he calls a period of expansion. If all is not good as the sixties draw to a close, all good is at least possible.

And so when Arnold is in the Alps again—but in fertile, quiet Glion this time, not, as before, on the wild Gemmi Pass—and again speaks with Obermann, even the shy recluse has learned to share the optimism of the day. Now it is not Arnold who pours out his misery to Obermann; Obermann approaches Arnold and his first words are a rebuke for despair. Living apart from the world as he does, says Obermann, he can see the world's course clearly, and he is astonished that the poet, who had gone back to life when it lay in gloom, should flee it in this propitious hour of hope.

> "And is it thou," he cried, "so long
> Held by the world which we
> Loved not, who turnest from the throng
> Back to thy youth and me?
>
> "And from thy world, with heart opprest,
> Choosest thou *now* to turn?—
> Ah me, we anchorites knew it best!
> Best can its course discern!
>
> "Thou fledd'st me when the ungenial earth,
> Thou soughtest, lay in gloom.
> Return'st thou in her hour of birth,
> Of hopes and hearts in bloom?"

And Obermann begins to trace through history the rise and fall of the power of faith—for it is new faith that is now bringing new hope. The Roman world, like the contemporary, was rich, clearheaded and unpausing in its activity, but its heart was stone and a disgusted *ennui* descended upon it; it thirsted for something to transcend the power and activity by which it tried to satisfy itself.

The East, which Rome had furiously conquered, spoke of the soul as a fountain from which flowed the cooling waters Rome sought. Rome turned from its worldly glory to Christ, who gave peace so long as men believed. But the saving quality of Christianity faded; men no longer believed.

> "Now he is dead. Far hence he lies
> In the lorn Syrian town,
> And on his grave, with shining eyes,
> The Syrian stars look down.
>
> "In vain men still, with hoping new,
> Regard his death-place dumb,
> And say the stone is not yet to,
> And wait for words to come."

And all that men hear is the word of their own loneliness and of the salvation that lies within one's self. The faith of the Middle Ages burgeoned—and withered, until of a living religion only a dead form remained; men longed for a storm to rive the dead bones and bring a new life into their world; the storm came—the fierce rationalism of the French Revolution. Yet the sun in the new-washed sky saw the race of man after the upheaval plying upon a chartless sea, clinging to remnants of their dead faith, the "blocks of the past, like icebergs high;" it is doubtful, indeed, that the destructive storm had been kind to man; it destroyed his poor spiritual habitation without bringing him another.

> "The past, its mask of union on,
> Had ceased to live and thrive.
> The past, its mask of union gone,
> Say, is it more alive?
>
> "Your creeds are dead, your rites are dead,
> Your social order too.
> Where tarries he, the power who said:
> *See, I make all things new?*"

"And he who sat upon the throne said, 'Behold, I make all things new.'" But like the promise of *Revelation,* the promise of revolution failed, and Obermann, despairing, must flee to his Alps.

But now? The time of destruction has passed and a new hour has come. A new sun has risen and the recluse bids the poet not to despair as he himself had despaired.

> "The world's great order dawns in sheen
> After long darkness rude,
> Divinelier imaged, clearer seen,
> With happier zeal pursued."

The millions "have such need of joy"—

> "And joy whose grounds are true!
> And joy that should all hearts employ
> As when the past was new!"

It is a *commonalty* of joy that is needed if the individual is to find happiness:

> "And who can be *alone* elate,
> While the world lies forlorn?"

But now the possibility of joy is again real; Obermann charges Arnold, though "shorn of the joy, the bloom, the power which best beseem its bard," to put the energies of his firmer manhood to the task of bringing hope "to a world new-made." And Arnold can end the colloquy on exactly the note of serene integration amid the peace of nature on which he had ended *Cromwell* so many years before: "the vision ended—"

> And glorious there, without a sound,
> Across the glimmering lake,
> High on the Valais depth profound,
> I saw the morning break.

The conclusion of *Cromwell* was a kind of self-dedication to life; the conclusion of "Obermann Once More" is also a dedication, but less vague, less purely personal. Its author is about to seek and set forth the roots of joy, cutting through theology and superstition, through metaphysics and bad temper, to what he believes are the inevitable grounds of faith. It is a work that is to occupy nearly ten years of his life. "Now I am within one year of papa's age when he ended his life," he wrote his mother the day before his forty-sixth birthday; "and how much he seems to have put into it, and to what ripeness of character he had attained! Everything has seemed to come together to make this year the beginning of a new time to me: the gradual settlement of my own thought, little Basil's death, and then my dear, dear Tommy's. And Tommy's death in particular was associated with several awakening and epoch-making things. The chapter for the day of his death was that great chapter, the 1st of Isaiah; the first Sunday after his death was Advent Sunday, with its glorious collect, and in the Epistle the passage [Romans xiii: 13] which converted St. Augustine. All these things point to a new beginning, yet it may well be that I am near my end, as papa was at my age, but without papa's ripeness, and that there will be little time to carry far the new beginning. But that is all the more reason for carrying it as far as one can, and as earnestly as one can, while one lives."

II

In 1888, England and indeed the whole literate world argued and wept over the affecting biography of a young man who, driven in many directions by the same winds that had carried Clough away, came at last to a secure new faith. Robert Elsmere was far more than the hero of an enormously successful novel; he was the protagonist in a great social and intellectual crisis that in one way or another involved all thinking people.

Elsmere, a youth of high talents, was the son of a younger son of a minor aristocratic family. His widowed mother, a gay and robust Irish lady, was good and charitable but she nursed a profound dislike of her late husband's clerical profession. She was not alone in such feelings; A. W. Benn, the historian of rationalism, tells us that between the forties and the sixties the clergy was coldly regarded by the intelligent upper and middle classes and attracted but few of the best young men at the universities. It was a source of great distress to Mrs. Elsmere that her son, whose gifts entitled him to look forward to a brilliant worldly career, should have followed in his father's footsteps by deciding at Oxford that he had a vocation to the Church.

The young man's decision was strange in the light of his Oxford associations. At the university Elsmere gave his especial allegiance and personal admiration to two men, Langham and Grey, neither of whom was of a temper calculated to influence an intelligent youth toward orthodoxy. Langham was Elsmere's tutor, a man of extensive learning and clear insight, who, after a short burst of remarkable critical and scholarly writing, had lapsed into literary silence. He had always been a great reader of Senancour and, for reasons that are necessarily obscure, he became very much like Obermann himself, a man of unstrung will; a student of religions rather than of religion, he conceived that all faiths were much alike and little more than mythologies, occasionally beautiful, sometimes harmless. Grey, on the other hand, was a man of force, cogency and bracing passion. He was of the school of Jowett and a scholar of widest learning and acute historical sense, whom doubts of the miraculous foundation of the Christian religion had turned from the intention of taking holy orders. Falling under the spell of Hegel, Grey had become the most eminent of the group of Oxford followers of that philosopher, compensating for his withdrawal from the Church by framing an attractive philosophy of anti-materialistic, anti-utilitarian social progress, a philosophy whose first premise was the free will of man. For him social progress was no mere figment of the philosopher's study; he shocked reserved Oxford and incurred the contempt of his colleagues by engaging in the political and social activity of the town and by being, unlike most idealistic philosophers, a firm believer in democracy. Yet religion, even a kind of pietism, ran through all his thought; the saint was ever his human ideal and it was therefore only natural that, though he himself was intransigent in maintaining his distance from the Church, the more philosophically advanced apologists of the Establishment should make use of his ideas to their own ends. Grey's dislike of controversy permitted these ecclesiastical perversions of his views.

Elsmere, whose love for Grey was profound, was one of the many who thus misinterpreted his master. For example, Grey delivered a lay sermon on St. Paul, preaching on the meaning of Paul's "Death unto sin and a new birth unto righteousness." He asked what precisely the apostle meant by death to sin and self, what were the precise ideas attached to the words "risen with Christ" and raised the question of whether this resurrection depended necessarily upon alleged historical events or whether they were not, to the mind of Paul, two aspects of a spiritual process perpetually reenacted in the soul of man, constituting the veritable revelation of God. And he went on to ask which was the stable and lasting witness of the Father: the spiritual history of the individual and the world, or the envelope of miracle to which mankind has attributed so much importance? It was a question calculated to awaken stirrings in the heart of an eager young man, but to the great disappointment of Grey, the sentiment it awakened in his pupil was not of the sort he had expected; it produced a yearning for the orthodox spiritual life. Nor did Elsmere doubt, despite Grey's hints, that he would be able to live that life in the Church.

The seventies in England witnessed a recoil from the rationalism which had so much dominated the two decades before; what may be called a religious romanticism had become increasingly appealing. Men discovered with a glad surprise that the last word about the universe had not been said by the rationalists and agnostics. Rationalism had been too starkly naked; it had no cloak to give its adherents. And religion, newly clad in the robes of idealistic philosophy and romantic poetry, was able to lend a traditional garment of a new cut. But our young man was not yet bothered with matters so complex. He entered the Church simply because he was "called" and for several years worked among the city poor until, like the pathetic John Sterling, he broke under the physical strain. When he recovered, marriage and a country living seemed to promise a less strenuous but no less spiritual existence.

But though Elsmere was in many ways most fortunate in his marriage, he found that it produced, in his religious life, a certain strain. His young wife, Catherine, was a woman of powerful though perhaps narrow intellect. Notable for every virtue save that of religious tolerance, she had the religious character usually attributed to the dissenting Puritan, but also not infrequently found in the Evangelical party of the Church. A stern and pious clerical father, whose memory young Mrs. Elsmere adored, had trained her to a loving but rigid virtue and framed her mind to the literal acceptance of an austere creed. Although the death of her husband was to soften Mrs. Elsmere's rigor, the doubt through which his soul was to pass alienated her from him and this separation was not the least of the young man's burdens.

Yet for a while the couple lived happily in their quiet parsonage in pleasant Surrey. Elsmere filled his days with that energetic activity for good which had marked his earlier and more strenuous life in the city. He organized men's clubs for the study of natural history, presided at story-circles, oversaw sanitation and distributed flannels—in a word, lived the life of so-called muscular Christianity which Charles Kingsley had preached, attempting to alleviate the misery, ignorance and boredom of the lower classes. There was little stimulus to thought and no time for it.

This life of pleasantly unalloyed action, however, did not last for long; Elsmere now found himself between the upper and nether millstones of Roger Wendover and the Reverend Mr. Newcome, his unreflecting peace quite gone. Newcome represented the High Church at its "highest" and, it must be said, at its most intolerant. About him there was more than a touch of the French "Black" and on more than one occasion he was open in his contempt for tolerance and for what he was pleased to call "a maudlin universal sympathy." For him the ideas of modernity were "lusts of the mind" to be crushed no less ruthlessly than the lusts of the body. But though Newcome added materially to the strain and bewilderment of the period into which Elsmere was now entering, he never managed to gain an ascendancy; Elsmere always continued to regard him with affection and with the admiration due the intensity of his religious passion, but the narrow fierceness of the older man's views were repellent to the younger.

But at the opposite pole from Newcome was Roger Wendover, the very embodiment of modern intellectual radicalism. Wendover, in his Oxford youth, had been a follower of Newman. He had become disillusioned with that religious genius and, by reaction, had gone over to the very investigation of the roots of religion and of its documents which Newman had so hated and in which German scholarship held the leadership. He had become an adept of this new scholarship, exhibiting his learning in the famous *Idols of the Market Place,* a vigorous and truculent examination of the foundations of religious belief. Now in old age he had confirmed himself in all his negative conclusions. Wendover was the magnate and squire of young Elsmere's parish and it was inevitable that the two men should meet—and clash. The first relationship, indeed, between the two men was even violent: the ardent young Elsmere was forced to hold Mr. Wendover responsible for the criminal neglect of sanitation which had caused a severe outbreak of diphtheria in his village, for Wendover, perhaps because his researches had thoroughly disillusioned him with the world, had learned an indifference for human life and even, it would seem, for his human duties, and Elsmere had gone so far as to tear down certain fatally squalid cottages. But after a period of intense anger at Elsmere's interference and scorn for his humanitarianism, Wendover developed an admiration and even a gruff love for the young man and the incongruous pair soon became fast friends.

Elsmere was by no means uninformed about modern ideas when he first met this intellectual radical. He had, for example, read Darwin's *Origin of Species*. Yet, as he once explained, "We used to take the thing half for granted, I remember, at Oxford, in a more or less modified sense." The mind has a great capacity to ingest and to "modify" and thus to tolerate matter which at first seems inimical to the organism, and many sincerely religious people of the time sincerely "accepted," as they said, the conclusions of science without being at all disturbed in their religious doctrine. Elsmere, even reading Darwin's work again some years after Oxford, found it, as he said to his old friend Langham, "a revelation"—to which Langham replied: "Yes, but it is a revelation, my friend, that has not always been held to square with other revelations." But Elsmere could not long be secure against Wendover's incessant logical questioning of the intellectual assumptions of his faith. Wendover was not especially concerned with the problems which physical science presented to religion; nor was physical science the only, or the chief cause of religious uneasiness to many thinking people of the time. Ruskin might write, "If only the geologists would let me alone I could do very well, but those dreadful hammers! I hear the clink of them at the end of every cadence of the Bible phrases;" Lyell might do great damage; Baden Powell, himself a clergyman, might insist that the findings of science must be faced and not shirked with vague phrases like "the law behind the law of nature;" the nebular hypothesis, the theory of the conservation of energy, might make men revise their basic notions of the universe and therefore of God; but it was historical criticism far more than science which jarred the foundations of orthodoxy. And in historical criticism Wendover was a master.

The great religious question of the time was ferociously simple: did the biblical miracles occur or did they not? Here lay the nub of religious faith, for, as Gladstone said, "if you sweep away miracles, you sweep away *the Resurrection!*" And the tendency of all modern biblical scholarship was to deny miracles. By 1867 Ruskin could tell his honest working man that there were four possible theories respecting the Bible "and four only:"

The first is that of the comparatively illiterate modern religious world, namely, that every word of the book known to them as "The Bible" was dictated by the Supreme Being, and is in every syllable of it His "Word." The second theory is, that although admitting verbal error, the substance of the whole collection of books called the Bible is absolutely true, and furnished to man by Divine inspiration of the speakers and writers of it. The third theory is that the group of books which we call the Bible were neither written nor collected under any Divine guidance and that they contain, like all other human writings, false statements mixed with true, and erring thoughts mixed with just thoughts; but that they nevertheless relate, on the whole, faithfully, the dealings of the one God with the first races of man, and His dealings with them in aftertime through Christ; that they record true miracles, and bear true witness to the resurrection of the dead, and the life of the world to come. The fourth, and last possible theory is that the mass of religious Scripture contains merely the best efforts which we hitherto know to have been made by any of the races of men towards the discovery of some relations with the spiritual world; that they are only trustworthy as expressions of the enthusiastic visions or beliefs of earnest men oppressed by the world's darkness and have no more authoritative claim on our faith than the religious speculations and histories of the Egyptians, Greeks, Persians, and Indians; but are, in common with all these, to be reverently studied, as containing the best wisdom which human intellect, earnestly seeking for help from God, has hitherto been able to gather between birth and death.

The first theory, Ruskin said, was tenable by no well-educated person; the second was held by "most good and upright clergymen," and the better class of the professedly religious laity; the third by "many of the active leaders of modern thought in England;" the fourth by the "leading scholars and thinkers of Europe." To be sure, there was yet a fifth position, but this for Ruskin was an infidelity "which merely indicates a natural incapacity for receiving certain emotions:" this is "the incredulity . . . of inspiration in any sense, or of help given by any Divine power to the thoughts of men." And it was this position, militantly held, that Roger Wendover occupied and to which he tried to bring Robert Elsmere.

For a while Elsmere attempted to flee from the squire's logic. "I am perfectly conscious," he said, "that my own mental experience of the last two years has made it necessary to re-examine some of these intellectual foundations of faith. But as to the faith itself, that is its own witness. It does not depend, after all, upon anything external, but upon the living voice of the Eternal in the soul of man!" But though this will do very well for a religious but unchurched man, it defended no dogmas. Elsmere was the priest of a Church with dogmas to defend. At last and at the cost of much misery he was forced to believe the Church supererogatory and himself unable to remain within it.

Desperate, he made a flying trip to Oxford to visit Grey, his old friend and teacher; Grey advised that he withdraw from the Church. And so Elsmere gave up his living and settled in London. *"Do I believe in Christ?"* he said. "Yes,—in the teacher, the martyr, the symbol to us Westerns of all things heavenly and abiding, the image and pledge of the invisible life of the spirit,—with all my soul and all my mind! *But in the Man-God,* the Word from Eternity, —in a wonder-working Christ, in a risen and ascended Jesus, in the living Intercessor and Mediator for the lives of His doomed brethren"—in this he can no longer believe. He rests for a while in a theism which assures him of the moral order of the world and of the existence of a guiding spirit. "What I conceive to be the vital difference between Theism and Christianity," he wrote, "is that as an explanation of things *Theism can never be disproved.*"

But so energetic and so essentially religious-spirited a man as Elsmere could scarcely rest in this negative state of mind. Inevitably he began to think of an unassailable religion rising upon the broad and certain base of Theism. And not merely the cravings of his own heart dictated the need for such a religion but the political condi-

tion of the world. "In the period of social struggle which undeniably lies before us," he wrote, "both in the old and the new world,
are we then to witness a war of classes, unsoftened by the ideal
hopes, the ideal law, of faith? It looks like it. What does the artisan
class, what does the town democracy throughout Europe, care any
longer for Christian checks or Christian sanctions as they have
been taught to understand them? Superstition, in certain parts of
rural Europe, there is in plenty, but wherever you get intelligence
and therefore movement, you get at once either indifference to, or
a passionate break with, Christianity. And consider what it means,
what it will mean, this Atheism of the great democracies which are
to be our masters! The world has never seen anything like it; such
spiritual anarchy and poverty combined with such material power
and resource. Every society—Christian and non-Christian—has always till now had its ideal, of greater or less ethical value, its appeal
to something beyond man. Has Christianity brought us to this:
that the Christian nations are to be the first in the world's history to
try the experiment of a life without faith—that life which you and
I, at any rate, are agreed in thinking a life worthy only of the brute?"
Has Christianity brought us to this? In short, Christian *dogma*
based on miracle had disillusioned the working classes with Christian *faith* and Christian *ethics*. And Elsmere came to believe that
one had but to cut away the miraculous dogma to leave the faith
and ethics standing clear, beautiful and effective. He accepted the
opportunity offered by a schismatic Unitarian group to do mission
work among the better-paid working class. He found conditions
prevailing which even the Church was forced to admit: religion had
no hold on the workers of England. "Eight hundred thousand people in South London, of whom the enormous proportion belong to
the working class, and among them, Church and Dissent nowhere
—*Christianity not in possession.*" Indifference accounted for some
defection, but a reasoned distrust accounted for more. Elsmere
learned that parsons were actively disliked and suspected, just as

many years later and despite the efforts of many sincere and hard-working men of Elsmere's own kind, it was found by Bakke that in the same stratum of society the same feeling still existed.

Elsmere entered this wilderness and undertook to cultivate it. He found that many of the workers of the district had acquired fair educations and that they were making a cult of their hostility to religion. Great readers of Paine and Ingersoll and *The Freethinker*, they regularly attended their rationalist clubs. But against even so formidable a foe, the strength and sweetness of Elsmere's personality prevailed and in time he overcame the often sour and uncouth rationalism of the working men. He began with stories and with lectures on science. In no long time he had so won the confidence of the men that, when he lectured on Jesus according to the new interpretation, the men listened with genuine sympathy, with the negligible exception of a couple of Socialists who wanted to do without "any cultus whatsoever" and who feared that the new church at which Elsmere hinted "would only be a fresh instrument in the hands of the *bourgeoisie*."

Elsmere called his lecture "The Claim of Jesus on Modern Life." "I want simply, if I can," he said, "to transfer to their minds that image of Jesus of Nazareth which thought, and love, and reading have left upon my own. I want to make them realise for themselves the historical character, so far as it can be realised." At this time not the least of Elsmere's burdens was Mrs. Elsmere's resistance to his religious development. "How can that help them?" she said to him on this occasion of his lecture. "Your historical Christ, Robert, will never win souls. If he was God, every word you speak will insult him. If he was man, he was not a good man!" But though disturbed by this lack of domestic sympathy, Elsmere succeeded astonishingly with his audience. "He dwelt," we are told, "on the magic, the permanence, the expansiveness, of the young Nazarene's central conception—the spiritualised, universalised 'Kingdom of God.'" He said: "The world has grown since Jesus preached in Galilee and Judaea. We cannot learn the *whole* of God's lesson from him now

—nay, we could not then! But all that is most essential to man—
all that saves the soul, all that purifies the heart—that he has still
for you and me, as he had it for the men and women of his own
time." Then he pleaded with his audience to protect the true Jesus
from the secularist slanders, telling them that Christ can indeed be
risen "in a wiser reverence and a more reasonable love; risen in new
forms of social help inspired by his memory."

In Elsmere's own circle only one voice—beside that of his wife—
was raised against his new work: Wendover's. "You and Grey between you," said the great rationalist, "call yourselves Liberals, and
imagine yourselves reformers, and all the while you are doing nothing but playing into the hands of the Blacks. All this theistic philosophy of yours only means so much grist to their mill in the end."
Yet there were many to feel that the miserable insanity in which
the old man died was in part the result of his inability to find a
refuge in faith—or that his insane death was the symbol of what
happens to intellect when it is not guided by religion. Elsmere, un-
deterred by Wendover's gibes, went forward to the foundation of
his "New Brotherhood of Christ," whose communicants wore a
silver badge with the head of Jesus, believed in an undefined but
beneficent God, partook of a simple and undogmatic but highly
emotional service of praise and love and said grace in their homes
with a more pious fervor than any the older churches could now inspire. He saw his Brotherhood as "a new compelling force in man
and in society." He believed that it would prove an instrument to
mitigate what he called the class struggle. "What are you economists
and sociologists of the new type always pining for?" he wrote. "Why,
for that diminution of the self in a man which is to enable the individual to see the *world's* ends clearly, and to care not only for his
own but for his neighbour's interest, which is to make the rich devote themselves to the poor, and the poor bear with the rich."

But not long after the foundation of the Brotherhood Elsmere
died, worn out by the strain of his work, a prey to tuberculosis. He
died strong in his new faith, refusing to call upon the Christ who

was a sacrifice and an atonement, even though it was his beloved wife who pleaded with him to do so. He refused, even on his death-bed, the comfort of a personal God: "No," he said, "we cannot real-ise Him in words—we can only live in Him, and die to Him!"

This, then, is the story of Robert Elsmere as written by Mrs. Humphry Ward, the daughter of the younger Thomas Arnold whose mercurial religious sense twice led him from Anglicanism to Catholicism and back again, the niece of Matthew Arnold. Her novel appeared in 1888 and few books have had so wide an appeal. Its sale soon reached the million mark; its readers must have num-bered twice or three times this. When, more than two decades after its first appearance, it was reissued in a cheap edition, it sold 50,000 copies in two weeks and 100,000 in a year. It was translated into in-numerable languages; its success in America was as great as in England.

The popularity of the book is evidence of the intense concern with religion which its contemporaries felt. Not, to be sure, that its theme alone accounted for the book's reception; the enthusiasm of Walter Pater and Henry James is testimony to its literary quality; Taine praised it, and not only out of friendship for its author, for it is a sophisticated, civilized book, full of personal insight, often amusing, frequently imaginative. But its chief interest surely lay in the skill and completeness with which it recorded the movement of liberal-ized religion of its time. Its relevance is attested to by the response of the aged Gladstone who felt the bite of the book so keenly that he took time from his political duties to write a long essay in the *Nineteenth Century* defending orthodox Christianity from its conclusions.

Mary Arnold Ward knew whereof she spoke. As the daughter of her father and the niece of her uncle, as the wife of an Oxford don, she was in close contact with both the progressive and the conservative religious leaders of her time. She herself became a proficient student of history and of the historical problems of religion; she published not a little on the latter. She dedicated her novel to T. H. Green, her friend and teacher and the model for the very literal portrait of "Grey;" it is the gist of Green's own sermon on St. Paul which constitutes Grey's sermon that is misinterpreted by Elsmere.* And we may be sure that the other portraits, if not so literal, are at least as accurate.

When the Reverend John Wordsworth delivered his first Bampton lecture in 1881, he spoke of modernism and the roots of doubt, of Christ's connection of unbelief with sin; he ascribed doubt to prejudice, to the desire to avoid the severe claims of religion and to the intellectual faults of indolence, coldness, recklessness, pride and avarice. The granddaughter of Thomas Arnold was furious with the grandnephew of William Wordsworth—the years had increased the theological breach between the two families—and at this slur upon the "patient scholars and thinkers of the Liberal host," she says, "my heart burned within me; and it sprang into my mind that the only way to show England what was in truth going on in its midst, was to try and express it concretely,—in terms of actual life and conduct. Who and what were the persons who had either provoked the present unsettlement of religion, or were suffering under its effects? What was their history? How had their thoughts and doubts come to be? and what was the effect of them on conduct?" She succeeded admirably in the expression.

Robert Elsmere appeared in 1888, the year in which Matthew Arnold died; he wrote it down in his list of books to be read that year but he read only the first of the three volumes; he liked it but did not comment on it critically. "I doubt very much whether the second and third volumes would have appealed to him," says Mrs. Ward. "He had little sympathy with people who 'went out.'" But

---

* In retailing the career of "Grey" I have included some material from the life of Green himself, not spoken of in the novel—Green's democratic feelings, for instance.

the intellectual world in which Elsmere lived was Arnold's world, the religious ferment which so stirred England moved Arnold too and was increased by him. Above all, Elsmere's intention was Arnold's—to preserve faith through the demolition of dogma, to the end that ethics might emerge and fraternity prevail.

Chapter Eleven

⇛⇚

JOY WHOSE GROUNDS ARE TRUE

*I am indeed persuaded, said PHILO, that the best
and indeed the only method of bringing every one
to a due sense of religion, is by just representations
of the misery and wickedness of men. And for that
purpose a talent of eloquence and strong imagery
is more requisite than that of reasoning and argument. For is it necessary to prove, what every one
feels within himself? 'Tis only necessary to make
us feel it, if possible, more intimately and sensibly.*
—HUME

ARNOLD'S ten-year concern with the problems of religion was
forced upon him by four important considerations. He had
attacked the religion of Dissent as a source of political discord and he must now show, on grounds of doctrine and of ecclesiastical polity, why Puritanism need no longer be schismatic from the
national Church. He had spoken—"in a hasty moment," says T. S.
Eliot—of the will of God which is the ultimate sanction of the idea
of the State and now he must demonstrate the existence and nature
of that God and that will. He had based government on the "possible Socrates" in each man's breast and he must show how that
Socrates might be educed, put in control of the self and into fruitful communication with his Socrates-neighbors. And last, he had
not yet settled scores with his youthful cosmological problems. Although his earlier conflicts had not issued in commitment to a ma-
terialist atheism, they had at best tended to a Stoic or Spinozistic
naturalism which was not cheerful; life had in no small degree been
diminished and cooled, emotion checked, thought made uncertain,

317

morality threatened with becoming mere duty; and the demand for a world that was palpitant and alive, that took some cognizance of man and his ideals—a world of meaning, in short—was still present. The need to rescue the world from the cheerless conclusions of science and to establish Joy was the fourth motive of Arnold's religious investigations, and perhaps the most important.

If, said Arnold in effect, one could cut beneath all the overgrowths of religion, if one could get to the basic and even minimal in religion, one might find that an irrefragable truth existed which would at once be safe from all the falsifications of dogmatic theology and popular superstition on the one hand, and from the further meddling of science on the other. If, he continued, one could be concerned only with the mind and nature of man and cast aside all cosmological pretensions, would one not come to a religion which, while claiming far less for itself than orthodoxy, could still be important and effective? And need religion, rightly viewed, be occupied at all with the nature of the universe in its physical aspects, is not its proper sphere man only, and not man in his search for knowledge, but man insofar as he acts—with the right way of human action, with *conduct?* But man can act best when he believes in a universe which in some way is acting with him, when he has the notion of a friend, a Paraclete, a helper in the scheme of things. And since man's mind is of such sort that it tends to imagine this helper, since it can even be proved that man acts more effectively when he cultivates the belief in this aid, surely he does well to have faith in its existence and to conceive of a world with meaning, that meaning being moral. Such an act of faith, indeed, is even, by some descriptions of science, not unscientific: Hume had shown that the notion of cause and effect is not logically "necessary" but a matter of habit and convenience, and Arnold, ignoring the tendency of the physical science of his own time to declare the absolute truth of scientific laws, thinking as he does of science as empirical and classificatory rather than as experimental and generalizing, finds it easy to conclude that that which helps us to act better certainly exists because we see its effects. True, in the way of science, nothing beyond existence may be predicated of such a force: it is not a "thing," nor a "person," nor a "gas." Nevertheless, it is a law, just as we speak of the law of gravitation, which is not thing nor person nor gas. "God is real since he produces real effects" was the doctrine of William James. It is also the doctrine of Arnold, and had James not read Arnold, we might have said that Arnold had read James, for the earlier writer argued the pragmatic position with which the name of the later is more intimately associated.

Arnold spoke of his religious work as "an attempt conservative and an attempt religious." He was therefore not surprised that the Continental critics attacked him as a traitor to the liberal cause, who, by recasting religion, helped prevent its destruction. He answered these critics in part, that so far as liberal politics went he was rather their defender than their betrayer inasmuch as anti-religious activity seemed to bring periods of black reaction in its wake. But he was puzzled and hurt that the orthodox opinion of England saw his "attempt religious" as wholly subversive. For Arnold, religion was simply the connection of the imagination with conduct; "the whole work of again cementing the alliance between the imagination and conduct remains to be effected," he said. But for the orthodox the kind of imagination he offered was not the right kind; they had long lived with an imagination which claimed to be no imagination at all but *knowledge,* and scientific rather than moral knowledge, and what Arnold offered them was on the one hand poetic and, on the other, scientific in only the empirical way. For Arnold poetry and science meet on the common ground they have of experience, and *experience* is the key-word to Arnold's religious discussion. He had attacked the doctrine of natural rights because of its *a priori* character; a relation of man to man is not good because it has been everlastingly decreed or abstractly determined, but only insofar as experience shows it useful to man's nature and necessary to his development. True religion may have its revelation, but it can be only this: that "that in us which is really natural is, in truth, *revealed*."

But "natural" means "good" and good can only be judged by human
experience. Whatever part of religion is based on *ought* Arnold
does not seek to defend; he defends, or thinks he defends, only that
part which rests on empirical trial and human judgment. Why is
righteousness to be followed? Because righteousness produces certain good effects. How do we know? Experience, not revelation or
authority, verifies it as a fact. Defenders of religion have argued in
this way before and after Arnold but it is not religion's traditional
and characteristic method—nor perhaps its safest.

Arnold, distressed as he might be by the response of orthodoxy,
believed that he was performing a life-saving surgery upon religion.
He knew that the religious way of thought about religious things
was losing its force. He was the spiritual son of Goethe, and the
Zeitgeist, Goethe's *Zeitgeist,* had brought the reign of science which,
admitting that it could not disprove revelation in miracle and prophecy, yet refused to accept the supernatural as the ground for the
validity of any idea. Goethe had taught men to ask, "But is it so, is
it so for me?" Religious thought could not answer the questions that
followed, but scientific thought, itself the source of the questions,
could. "What essentially characterises a religious teacher," said Arnold, "and gives him his permanent worth and vitality, is, after all, just
the scientific value of his teaching, its correspondence with important
facts, and the light it throws on them." Science, the modern *Zeitgeist,* could be shown to be actually the ally of religion if only religion would limit itself to the realm of morality.

Orthodoxy, thinking for the moment pragmatically, will perhaps
admit with Arnold that the problem of all religious teaching is not
so much one of truth as of effectiveness, but then it will want to
know whether the kind of imagination Arnold wants is—in James's
word—"thick" enough to *enforce* morality. Orthodoxy knows that
as the mind of man is constituted, "thickness" is the mark of reality and that with a "thick" religion men may indeed be deceived or
made fantastic or fanatic, but that with a "thin" religion, however
conformable to fact, they may do nothing religious though they may,

in the way of conduct (and like men with no religion at all), do much that is good. Will men build Chartres to a "power not ourselves that makes for righteousness?" Will they, murmuring *"Aberglaube,"* paint Annunciations or write *The Divine Comedy?* Will even *The Temple* spring from a mind taught to think of prayer as "an energy of aspiration"? Is it not true of religion as of poetry that, as T. S. Eliot said in a famous footnote, the "spirit killeth, but the letter giveth life"? In short, might not Arnold's religion—by no means contemptible, so often appealing, probably incapable of leading anyone into an extreme error of conduct—only be one of the forces which, in the words of the French secularist, Guyau, guide "faith to the ultimate point beyond which nothing remains but to break definitively with the past and its texts and dogmas"?

To answer questions such as these it is necessary to use Arnold's own criterion of experience, and in a most difficult matter. On the whole, it may be said that for the mass of men conceptions such as Arnold's are likely to be "thin" and therefore ineffective, although in the case of men of greater sophistication, they may be said to have "thickness" enough—as much "thickness," say, as a philosophical idea. The idea of "history," for example, is no more firmly based in fact than the idea of "meaning" in the universe, yet it can condition men's actions profoundly. And so, for Aldous Huxley, the idea of moral meaning in the universe can make all the difference between active morality and passive negation, and flood his life, as he tells us, with meaning and energy. Or for Julian Huxley too—Arnold is justified in his grandnephews!—a similar conception is socially, if not personally, necessary and quite tenable.

However, there is another, more formal, and therefore more fundamental, point of attack to be used against Arnold. When his position does more than *allow* man's values to have all the cosmic meaning he wants to give them—when it is more than merely permissive and goes on to assert that values exist in things—it becomes illegitimate and denies its own premises. Materialistic science had said, in effect: "You do not taste the tang of the wine because what is really happening is the action of certain molecules in the liquid which affects the molecules in the taste-buds,"—had said that human meaning is not meaning at all but mere opinion. This is an absurd position, but it cannot properly be answered by saying: "I taste the tang of the wine because the tang is *in* the wine and in the molecules." Nevertheless, Arnold, in spite of his whole program, and tempted perhaps by the exigencies of polemic, takes this very position and at times affirms the value of morality by asserting that the moral law is, as it were, graven on the face of the universe, that meaning is preexistent to man. But the idea of "tang" and of "taste" —the idea of meaning—is what is added to the raw activity of molecules by human mind and experience: the material given, the mind derives meaning; the meaning itself is not *given,* as Arnold, departing from pragmatism, can sometimes suppose.

Arnold is confused, there can be no doubt, but let us look behind the confusions and try to understand his essential—what he himself would call his "primary"—idea. If we imagine him to speak as follows, perhaps we have a fair perception of it: "Suppose we agree to think of the world almost exclusively as a theater of man and his morality. Granted that it is something more, for purposes of living it is best to consider it in this way: after all, what conceivable difference does the physical universe make beyond providing man with himself and his opponent, beyond giving him the material for action and morality? Let us quite frankly make man the measure of all things and put out of our minds the notions of infinities and absolutes which haunt us. Let us, for purposes of action, put into a subordinate place all that seems to make man unimportant in the universe: our power, our joy, our very sense of humanity are diminished when we do not do this. What then becomes the most desirable thing? Is it not the moral perfection of man, however we might define it? Of the things that make for unhappiness, we can control physical nature up to a certain point—but only up to that point; there remain our relations to each other and to ourselves and this is the greater part, and with infinite possibility of control. Do not our hopes tend toward it, is it not the whole of our best aspiration? The possibility of its attainment exists: forces in men drive toward it as much as away from it; forces in nature permit and even aid it as well as hinder it. These forces in man and nature, this possibility of moral perfection, are what we most adore. Then why not call this concatenation of forces and possibilities *God* and fix our attention on it in religion and by thus fixing our attention on it make actual what is possible?"

II

Arnold's campaign to revise modern religion was in a sense made easier by what seemed to him to be religion's most sterile aspect—the ideology of Protestantism. Bibliolatry was the Palladium of Puritan theology; if it could be reached and taken the whole perverse structure would collapse and Arnold set out to capture it by reinterpretation. The Bible was the word of God, ran the Protestant argument, and almost the chief crime of the Catholic Church (to be offset by George Borrow and the London Bible Society) was its concealment of this word from its communicants; but the Protestant had only to read his Scriptures by the light of his own understanding and he would have the truth. Arnold, however, knew what every critic and every teacher knows, that it is impossible to expect most readers to read any book aright, let alone so complex a one as the Bible. The failure of the Bible as a source of authority had become notorious. As Coleridge had pointed out, the sects so multiplied and grew, each sect justifying itself by its own interpretation of Scripture, that the Bible had become a schismatic rather than a unifying agent.

Arnold had read widely in the liberal biblical scholarship of his day; he preferred, however, not to rely on it, for he found it too often insensitive or puerile, or falsely scientific, or too high-flown, or irrelevant to the nature of religion. His own guides to interpretation were rather two men who had in many other ways influenced his thought: Spinoza and Coleridge. Both Spinoza and Coleridge used a method not rationalistic, nor primarily philological or historical, but literary and intuitive.

We have already seen how closely Arnold identified his own aims and methods with those of Spinoza and the part played by the *Tractatus Theologico-Politicus* in Arnold's first foray into the religious field. Spinoza, undertaking to answer the questions, "What is prophecy? in what sense did God reveal Himself to the prophets, and why were these particular men chosen by Him?" had determined "to examine the Bible afresh in a careful, impartial, and unfettered spirit, making no assumptions concerning it, and attributing to it no doctrines, which [he did] not find clearly therein set down." He concluded that the prophets were not chosen on account of any high philosophical attainments nor because of the value of their thoughts on Deity or nature, but solely by reason of their piety; "the authority of the prophets," he therefore concluded, "has weight only in matters of morality . . . their speculative doctrines affect us little." He made, that is, a sharp dichotomy between two spheres of human knowledge, the speculative and the moral.

The difference between the two kinds of knowledge, Spinoza said, is that the speculative may be tested by its mathematical certainty, but moral knowledge can be subjected to no such test; between philosophy, or science, and faith, or theology, there can be no valid relationship, he declared, because the former is the product of the intellect, the latter of the imagination. But faith, though it cannot be proved, can—indeed, must—be acted upon, for to reject it would be "as though we should admit nothing as true, or as a wise rule of life, which could ever, in any possible way, be called in question."

The God of Spinoza's *Ethics* is the deity of a universe of certain knowledge. But the God of his *Tractate,* framed for men of relatively weak intelligence who cannot accept the rigors of the philosophic life of the *Ethics,* is a deity whose word is written in our hearts, whose worship involves no dogma, obedience to whom consists only of the practice of justice and love towards one's neighbor. But even though the word of this God is written in all hearts, there have been some who have understood it better than others and such men were the prophets. Their superiority consisted not in their unusually perfect minds but in their unusually lively imaginations, for by methods of apprehension not scientific but intuitive, they grasped the truth in metaphor, parable and allegory. From these men, then, we learn nothing of natural or intellectual phenomena but from their poetic insights we may derive a profound knowledge of morality.

But though we understand the nature of the knowledge of the prophets, Spinoza continues, we must keep in mind that they were individual human beings conditioned by accidents of personal temper and also that they were men of their time and place, marked by the prejudices of their civilization and conditioned by the mentality of their contemporary audience. Further, all language is basically figurative, the Hebrew tongue even more figurative than most languages, and the knowledge of the imagination cannot express itself save in the allegorical or metaphorical way. Thus we see that we must be extremely suspicious of all literal interpretations of the Bible; the interpretation of Scripture must be made in such a way that we do not confound the mind of the Holy Spirit with the mind of the prophet or historian.

When we have read the Bible in the light of these considerations, Spinoza says, we find that what we call the natural law and what we call the help of God are necessarily the same thing: "Now since the power in nature is identical with the power of God, by which alone all things happen and are determined, it follows that whatsoever man, as a part of nature, provides himself with to aid and preserve his existence, or whatsoever nature affords him without his help, is given to him solely by the Divine power, acting either through human nature or through external circumstance. So whatever human nature can furnish itself with by its own efforts to preserve its existence, may be fitly called the inward aid of God, whereas whatever else accrues to man's profit from outward causes may be called the external aid of God." This understood, we may comprehend the language of the Bible—why, for example, the Jews were called a *chosen* nation. They were chosen in a perfectly naturalistic sense, in that, having a superior government and laws, they had the reward of these in temporal happiness and freedom.

And just as the Divine power may be equated with human best action, so the Divine law may be equated with natural reason. The Divine law does not depend on any historical narrative but is naturally known to the human mind. The Bible is essentially a simple book teaching a simple idea, a book which has always sought to adapt itself to the intelligence not of the learned but of the masses of men in every age and of every race. It does not bind us to believe anything that is not necessary for the fulfilment of its main precept—which is that we have a knowledge of the justice and charity of God and this is not a knowledge necessary for scientific accuracy but for obedience. Speculative matters which have no bearing on the obedience to God in the love of our neighbors do not concern religion, and the intellectual knowledge of God has nothing whatever to do with conduct. For the masses, it is true, a notion of God's physical nature seems necessary because of their weaker imaginations, but it would be wrong to suppose that these notions have any philosophical dignity. They are a matter of theology, which is the organization of the reasons for faith, and "faith does not demand that dogmas should be true as that they should be pious—that is, such as will stir up the heart to obey."

It is for this reason that philosophy must not encroach upon theology and that theology must not presume to be philosophical. It is a cool and apparently equitable arrangement, and in its time a largely useful one. It provided, as Sir Frederick Pollock says, a euthanasia for theology, but this was a deed of mercy for which religion has not been very grateful: and understandably, for all that religion had left when Spinoza finished with it was the truth that morality is the will of God—a truth to be respected by philosophy, as, say, the British respect the languages and customs of India.

Spinoza's influence on Coleridge was very great; the romantic poet, so profoundly concerned with the idea of inspiration, gladly took up Spinoza's conception of the word of God in the heart of man. The Bible, said Coleridge, was to be read like any other book, with the same literary and historical criteria. It was, to be sure, inspired, but the nature of its inspiration had been misunderstood by readers who had confounded the Revealing Word with the Inspiring Spirit. At a few—but only at a few—points, the Scriptures declare themselves to be inspired and at these points they must be taken literally. But in general, the Revealing Word does not fully encompass and express the Inspiring Spirit; where it does there is a test: "Whatever *finds* me, bears witness for itself that it has proceeded from a Holy Spirit." This would seem to be the essence of the very Protestantism Coleridge so fears; but he saves himself by declaring that "as a Christian, I can not,—must not,—stand alone." In short, for Coleridge the proof of Christianity lies not so much in the historical testimony but rather in its experiential correspondence to human nature: "The truth revealed through Christ has its evidence in itself, and the proof of its divine authority in its fitness to our nature and needs;—the clearness and cogency of this proof being proportioned to the degree of self-knowledge in each individual hearer."

Coleridge will not go so far as to say that belief in the literal inspiration of the Bible is impossible, but it has, he insists, this disadvantage, that it "petrifies at once the whole body of Holy Writ with all its harmonies and symmetrical gradations,—the flexile and the rigid,—the supporting hard and the clothing soft,—the blood *which is the life*," and makes the living organism a "colossal Memnon's head, a hollow passage for a voice, a voice that mocks the voices of many men, and speaks in their names, and yet is but one voice, and the same;—and no man uttered it, and never in a human heart was it conceived." The literal interpretation of the Bible has for Coleridge yet another disadvantage: it denies the conception of religious *development* which was so important for him. The books of the Bible, he believes, "were composed in different and widely distant ages, under the greatest diversity of circumstances, and degrees of light and information" and he maintains that this is a necessary hypothesis not only to explain biblical discrepancies but to defend freedom of the will: by the theory of literal inspiration man becomes the mere puppet of a divine "Ventriloquist."

It is one thing, then, to say, "The Bible contains the religion revealed by God," and quite another to say, "Whatever is contained in the Bible is religion, and was revealed by God." If the latter be accepted, metaphor and allegory become literal statements and the errors and absurdities of bibliolatry follow.* Such an interpretation results in the cruelties of the Catholic oppression; it has resulted in the Protestant disunion, making infidels of good and learned men. For "every sentence found in a canonical Book, rightly interpreted, contains the *dictum* of an infallible Mind;—but what the right interpretation is,—or whether the very words now extant are corrupt or genuine—must be determined by the industry and understanding of fallible, and alas! more or less prejudiced theologians." The right understanding of the Bible requires a flow of knowledge to be directed upon what we read, yet the doctrine of literal interpretation would permit "every man that can but read . . . to sit down to the consecutive and connected perusal of the Bible under the expectation and assurance that the whole is within his comprehension, and that, unaided by note or comment, catechism or liturgical preparation, he is to find out for himself what he is bound to believe and practise, and that whatever he conscientiously understands by what he reads, is to be *his* religion. For he has found it in his Bible, and the Bible is the Religion of Protestants!"

Arnold wrote *St. Paul and Protestantism* (it appeared first in *The Cornhill Magazine* in 1869) to demonstrate the illegitimacy of the Protestant theology. Every Protestant doctrine rests ultimately upon

---

* And an unacceptable morality: the speeches of Job's friends—actually "the hollow truisms, the unsufficing half-truths, the false assumptions and malignant insinuations of the supercilious bigots, who corruptly defended the truth"—must be understood, by a literal reading, to be the truth itself.

a Pauline text and Spinoza and Coleridge had undertaken to show how falsely the texts had been used. Their method had been none other than the method of Arnold's *culture*. Protestantism's Paul was theurgic and cosmological; culture's Paul was moral, psychological, humanistic, basing his ideas everlastingly on experience. And out of Paul's living insights, Protestantism had woven the web of a dead system. But if culture's Paul could be shown to be the true one, Protestantism would have nothing to stand on and Paul himself would be shown to be not at all, as Renan had called him, the doctor of Protestantism; freed of his illegitimate followers he would be rehabilitated for all men.

The Paul whom culture sees is concerned primarily with one thing: morality. His whole religion is a means of coming to true righteousness. If it seems strange, says Arnold, that so great and complex a thing as religion should be taken up with so simple a thing as conduct, we may remember that the greater part of life is conduct; Arnold makes great statistical play to determine just how much and arrives at three-fourths as a conservative estimate. For conduct is taken up with the exercise of the instincts of self-preservation and reproduction: "eating, drinking, ease, pleasure, money, the intercourse of the sexes, the giving free swing to one's temper and instincts." And with nothing else is religion concerned; all that appears in it which is irrelevant to this end is but inessential accretion to be treated with varying degrees of tolerance.

To be sure, Arnold says, Paul is a mystic and "nothing is so natural to the mystic as in rich single words, such as faith, light, love, to sum up and take for granted, without specially enumerating them, all good moral principles and habits." But even mysticism did not turn Paul from moral realism; he specified again and again what he meant by morality; he had the instant awareness of what he calls the "bowels of mercy," by which he meant meekness, humbleness of mind, gentleness, forbearance; he had, too, a great sense of what moderns call the "solidarity of man"—the "joint interest . . . which binds humanity together, the duty of respecting everyone's part in life, and of doing justice to his efforts to fulfil that part."

Protestantism deals with complete but unverifiable cosmic systems, but Paul deals with verifiable moral facts. How, then, did Paul, this student of the spirit of man, become the theurgist of Protestant theology? The answer must lie in Protestantism's ignorance of the literary nature of Scripture and of the nature of man, in its violation of all the rules that Spinoza had formulated. Nothing could be easier than to make a Calvinistic Paul—if we forget that morality was Paul's primary concern; if we believe that the discredited science, metaphysics and legend of his day, by means of which he expressed himself, were his primary interest and that we must take these literally; if we are insensitive to his metaphor; if we forget the limitations of his speech and thought—that as an Oriental he uses language hyperbolically, that as a Jew he uses the Old Testament talismanically. But the truth is that Paul was motivated by one thing alone: the desire for righteousness, and righteousness uses the language of literature, a language emotive, not exact, whereas Protestantism, assuming the very opposite, reads Paul as a scientist —and therefore does not read Paul at all.

Once we have understood this mistaken assumption of Protestantism, says Arnold, it is easy to see how Paul's words of "justification" and "election," the intent of which was to make the problems of morality more lively, should have come to be the crowning ideas of a system in which God, a "sort of magnified and non-natural man" decreed all things to come, gave, out of his free grace and love, to certain men and angels, everlasting life, no matter what their deeds, created Adam and Eve and made a contract with them which they broke and thus became his enemies, made another contract, of redemption, which he had previously agreed on with God the Son in the Council of the Trinity before the world began, according to which, if the son humbled himself—and so on, through the sordid "machinery of covenants, conditions, bargains, and parties-contractors, such as could have proceeded from no one but the born

Anglo-Saxon man of business." Such a system is surely not to be found in Paul; in fact, it is directly contrary to Paul's whole intention. Neither Calvinism nor Methodism is primarily concerned with morality; the one is motivated chiefly by the desire to "flee from the wrath to come," the other is motivated chiefly by the desire for eternal bliss. Man is almost entirely passive in both and all the activity is of God, whereas for Paul morality is an everlasting effort, and its achievement is possible to all men.

Again, says Arnold, the beliefs of neither Calvinism nor Methodism can be accepted by modern science, for neither fear, which is the basis of Calvinist belief, nor hope, which is the basis of Methodist belief, nor revelation—but only experience—can affirm the truth of an idea. Where Paul, indeed, takes his advantage over the Protestantism that misrepresents him, is that he begins in science, he *starts* with experience and "appeals to a rational conception which is a part, and perhaps the chief part, of our experience; the conception of the law of *righteousness,* the very law and ground of human nature so far as this nature is moral . . . [and] when Paul starts with affirming the grandeur and necessity of the law of righteousness, science has no difficulty in going along with him." Science, in other words, is willing and able, in Arnold's opinion, not only to affirm the *necessity* of the law of righteousness (surely an act of supererogation) but also its *grandeur*. And if we should object that science cannot deal with values and that Arnold's use of the word "science" implies that science is nothing more than criticized experience, Arnold would doubtless reply that this definition is accurate and that the mark of a scientific truth, like that of a moral truth, is that great teachers the most unlike are in agreement on the matter. We recall his scientific conclusions on "race."

But of equal importance with Arnold's idea of the moral essence of all religion, is his conception of religion's developmental or evolutionary nature, a dominant theme of *Literature and Dogma,* the volume that, in 1873, followed *St. Paul and Protestantism*. We have seen that Spinoza had implied and Coleridge had asserted that religion could not be thought of as static because it was growing and ever-changing; there were a host of other, inescapable, influences to confirm Arnold in this belief, among them Protestantism itself, and particularly contemporary German Protestantism with its complex historical method. However, though there might be a general agreement that religion was not static, the formulation of the idea produced fundamental divergence. Thus Newman, himself a developmentalist, characterized the German Protestant formulation as follows: "it considers [Christianity] a syncretism of various opinions springing up in time and place and forming such combinations one with another as their respective characters admitted; it considers it as the religion of the childhood of the human mind, and curious to the philosopher as a phenomenon." And against this conception of development, Newman offered a conception of religion as an Idea originally and completely given; not the Idea itself, he said, but the human understanding of it grows and exfoliates. "From the nature of the human mind, time is necessary for the full comprehension and perfection of great ideas; . . . the highest and most wonderful truths, though communicated to the world once for all by inspired teachers [cannot] be comprehended all at once by the recipients, but, as received and transmitted by minds not inspired and through media which were human, have required only the longer time and deeper thought for their full elucidation." By a process of sorting, comparing and shifting, a process wholly human but infallible of the truth, humanity establishes systems of government or of ethics or of ritual which "will after all be only the adequate representation of the original idea, being nothing else than what that very idea *meant* from the first."

In 1871–2 there was an exchange of letters between Arnold and the aged Cardinal in which Arnold gracefully acknowledged Newman's influence: "We are all of us," he wrote, "carried in ways not of our own making or choosing, but nothing can ever do away the effect you have produced upon me, for it consists in a general disposition of mind rather than in a particular set of ideas. In all the conflicts I have with modern Liberalism and Dissent, and with their pretensions and shortcomings, I recognize your work; and I can truly say that no praise gives me so much pleasure as to be told (which sometimes happens) that a thing I have said reminds people, either in manner or matter, of you." And a chief part of the disposition of Arnold's mind was his *acceptance* of human history, which prevented him from the Protestant and Liberal readiness to stamp much or all of what had gone before as error, pure and simple. But though, like Burke, Arnold was attracted to the Catholicism of the Anglican Church rather than to its Protestantism, he was, after all, an Anglican, and Newman's theory was intended to justify the present and future state of the Roman Church. Development, for Newman, was therefore in a relatively straight line; for Arnold it was undulant, now rising, now falling, as various aspects of the human spirit asserted themselves in response to the conditions of the times. His method of understanding, then, required that he track the course of the human spirit and undertake a research in psychology and anthropology.

In a great many of its aspects, Arnold's method had been anticipated by Ludwig Feuerbach—the teacher and later the philosophical opponent of Marx and Engels—whose *Essence of Christianity* had been translated by George Eliot in 1854. Feuerbach, the enemy of orthodox theology, was the friend of religion; if he sought to dissolve theology by a genetic account of the nature and function of religion, he nevertheless believed that religion, in that it fulfilled a real need, commanded respect. And piercing behind the veil of theology, the product of cognitive thought, pushing aside all that was intellectual and theoretical, he came to that in religion which was practical—that is, to what was purely emotional. "For Feuerbach," says Sidney Hook,* "philosophy must not begin with abstractions but with something which in the first instance is not even philosophical—with life, in all its concrete wants and needs." So, too,

---

* Professor Hook's chapter on Feuerbach in his *From Hegel to Marx* (1936) may be consulted for a summary of Feuerbach's position.

Arnold began—in sensory practical experience, and like Feuerbach probed "for the psychological roots out of which flowered the whole of human culture." Both Feuerbach and Arnold started with assumptions: first, that religion insofar as it is rooted in human emotion cannot be dismissed or destroyed; and, second, that every religious concept has some grain of truth because created by human need. Theology may pervert or hide the truth in trying to express it, but the genetic, historical analysis rediscovers it. As for the basic question of theology, the existence of God, "the question," said Feuerbach, "concerning the existence or non-existence of God is for me nothing but the question concerning the existence or non-existence of man," and Arnold, in effect, agrees.

Arnold felt that by taking the emphasis off theology, off the cognitive and intellectual, and by putting it on the emotional and imaginative, he was taking religion off its apex where it had been standing and putting it on its base where it belonged; *Literature and Dogma* is in large part the history of the religious idea, both in this inversion and in its true and healthy growth.

Before Jesus, says Arnold, and up to the time of the classical Jewish faith, religion was a clear development of the idea of righteousness which is the pure stuff, the *datum,* "religion given." The central notion of early Jewish literature was that righteousness tendeth to life, and that God is the power which ensures this. No metaphysics beclouded this simple idea, no system was needed to prove it. It was a fact, simply and directly experienced. But in course of time this classical perception was modified, both for good and ill. The strong optimism of the earlier Psalms gave way to the pessimism of the later ones; the skepticism of Job and the despair of Ecclesiastes emerged. Israel's fundamental idea, that righteousness tendeth to life and that he who pursueth evil pursueth it to his own death, suffered the shocks of social conditions changed for the worse; the connection between justice and life was no longer sure. Job explored the problem—it had become a problem—but could come to no conclusion, yet the religious feeling was still strong enough to keep him silent before the insoluble. Ecclesiastes, despite his skepticism, reached out blindly to a faith in the old connection between justice and life. And Malachi, oppressed by the same question, living in a time of political and social disintegration, "with a Persian governor lording it in Jerusalem, with resources light and taxes heavy, with the cancer of poverty eating into the mass of the people, with the rich estranged from the poor and from the national traditions, with the priesthood slack, insincere, and worthless," had to reconcile his indestructible faith in righteousness with all that seemed to contradict it and consequently put the emphasis on the human shortcomings that produced the degeneration; he spoke of the future, counseled repentance, "change of the inner man," to meet the day that was to come.

From this ground of hope there grew the Messianic idea, an *Aberglaube,* or "extra-belief," which means not so much superstition as a vault of the imagination to reach an idea not easily grasped. The Messianic idea, for the Jews of the post-prophetic time, was almost wholly political—implying a Prince who would restore the worldly dominion of Israel; all the hopes and imagination of a stricken people centered in this idea. It was, says Arnold, certainly natural and probably salutary; it *carried,* as it were, the truth. But it was dangerous because confusing: *"Extra-belief,* that which we hope, augur, imagine, is the poetry of life, and has the rights of poetry. But it is not science; and yet it tends always to imagine itself science, to substitute itself for science, to make itself the ground of the very science out of which it has grown. The Messianic ideas, which were the poetry of life to Israel in the age when Jesus Christ came, did this; and it is the more important to mark that they did it because similar ideas have so signally done the same thing with popular Christianity."

But Jesus, when he came, offered no fulfilment of the political *Aberglaube;* he did not bring political renovation. On the other hand, he did not bring only poetry: he brought new *fact*—and with him religion was "new given." For, Arnold says, "judgment and justice themselves, as Israel in general conceived them, have something exterior in them; now, what was wanted was more *inwardness,* more *feeling*. This was given by adding *mercy* and *humbleness* to judgment and justice." The religion of the Old Testament had been chiefly a matter of national and social conduct; the new datum of religion that Jesus brought was personal.

. . . Righteousness had by Jesus Christ's time lost, in great measure, the mighty impulse which emotion gives; and in losing this, had lost also the mighty sanction which happiness gives. "The whole head was sick and the whole heart faint;" the glad and immediate sense of being in the right way, in the way of peace, was gone; the sense of being wrong and astray, of sin, and of helplessness under sin, was oppressive. The thing was, by giving a fuller idea of righteousness, to reapply *emotion* to it, and by thus reapplying emotion, to disperse the feeling of being amiss and helpless, to give the sense of being right and effective; to restore, in short, to righteousness the sanction of *happiness*.

Happiness, no longer a material thing but emotional and psychological, was to be won by the *method* and the *secret* which Jesus brought. The method was repentance, "the setting up a great unceasing inward movement of attention and verification" in matters of conduct, and the inducement to repentance was the secret: "joy and peace, missed on every other line, [but] to be reached on this."

But since both the method and the secret of Jesus, says Arnold, might become excessive, Jesus brought *epieikeia*—his sweet reasonableness—to protect them. For "what are the method of inwardness and the secret of self-renouncement without the sure balance of Jesus, without his *epieikeia?* Much, but very far indeed from what he showed or what he meant; they come to be used blindly, used mechanically, used amiss, and lead to the strangest aberrations. St. Simeon Stylites on his column, Pascal girdled with spikes, Lacordaire flogging himself on his death-bed, are what the *secret* by itself produces. The *method* by itself gives us our political Dissenter, pluming himself on some irrational 'conscientious objections' and not knowing, that with conscience he has done nothing until he has got to the bottom of conscience, and made it tell him *right*."

This, then, is the new-given religion of Jesus. And Jesus may properly be called the Son of God, because God is the author of righteousness and the way of Jesus is the only way to righteousness.* "It *is* so!" says Arnold. "Try, and you will find it to be so! Try all the ways to righteousness you can think of, and you will find that no way brings you to it except the way of Jesus."

But a new *Aberglaube* develops about the truth of Jesus. Just as the old *Aberglaube* "carried" the Messianic idea of righteousness, this new *Aberglaube* carried the idea of Jesus. The old *Aberglaube* had been omnipresent; Jesus had used it to illustrate his intuitions; Paul, who understood Jesus perfectly, used it in the same way. But with the passing of the Apostolic age the Christian community took literally this use of the old *Aberglaube* and constructed a new. The literal acceptance of the words of Jesus and Paul did indeed give Christianity its fervor; it produced the martyrs and accelerated Christianity's conquest of the world. However, "it was already an evidence of failure, in some sort, to follow the mind of Jesus and the teaching of his greatest apostles." The Jesus legend was embodied in the so-called Apostle's Creed, the "popular science of Christianity." The educated classes were converted in course of time: the Nicene Creed embodies the learned science of Christianity. The Athanasian creed followed—"learned science with a strong dash of violent and vindictive temper." And all three creeds, "and with them the whole of our so-called orthodox theology, are founded upon words which Jesus in all probability never uttered;" the whole Patristic interpretation of the Bible sprang from a culture which lacked the proper conditions for true criticism.

* William Johnson Cory's comment on Arnold's view of Jesus is suggestive of the orthodox feeling of the time: "I never could relish Matthew Arnold's prose, except the preface to *Merope* and the Homer Lectures; but I have not even looked at a tithe of his prose. I suppose he was driven to patronizing Jesus Christ as the only way of earning cash. It is a mean way of getting a livelihood . . ." *Extracts from the Letters and Journals of William Johnson Cory,* p. 532.

And yet with this popular science of religion, with miracle and prophecy, Arnold is disposed to be gentle. "What we reach but by hope and presentiment may yet be true; and he would be a narrow reasoner who denied, for instance, all validity to the idea of immortality, because this idea rests on presentiment mainly, and does not admit of certain demonstration. . . . The object of religion is conduct; and if a man helps himself in his conduct by taking an object of hope and presentiment as if it were an object of certainty, he may even be said to gain thereby an advantage." Nevertheless *"He pays for it.* The time comes when he discovers that it is *not* certain; and then the whole certainty of religion seems discredited, and the basis of conduct gone."

So, at the behest of his scientific *Zeitgeist,* firmly, if gently, Arnold must reject both miracle and prophecy. And not so gently, indeed with mockery and scorn, he must attack the God of metaphysics and theology. There remains the task of establishing the validity of religion and deity—on the "shadowy Throne" of the human mind.

III

By detaching Paul from the cosmological system of Protestantism Arnold had destroyed the theology of the orthodox, but however necessary this work might be it was still only a negative accomplishment; he had expelled the clergyman Thwackum but he was still left with the philosopher Square. Thwackum's dogmatic religion might be undesirable but surely Square's rationalistic morality, whether as advanced by Bishop Butler or by John Stuart Mill, was no better. It seemed to Arnold that the Squares of the world were on the increase, that all utilitarian and all revolutionary morality was the insufficient morality of Square. The positive work that was yet to be done, Arnold felt, was to fill the wide emotional gap that rationalism had been content to leave.

It was necessary, first, to show that religion as taught by Paul was, though primarily moral, something more than moral and that the *more* could not be dispensed with. In Arnold's opinion, the real problem of conduct was not to know the rules: these are easy to know and everybody knows them: the real problem was to put the rules into practice, an enormously difficult task. And Paul's great accomplishment, says Arnold, was that he had shown how the rules may be carried out: by the new-given religion of Jesus, "by giving a fuller idea of righteousness, to reapply *emotion* to it, and thus by reapplying emotion, to disperse the feeling of being amiss and help-less, to give the sense of being right and effective; to restore, in short, to righteousness the sanction of *happiness*." Paul's contribution, in other words, was a psychological one and since religion's basis and method are psychological, since religion "means simply either a binding to righteousness, or else a serious attending to righteousness and dwelling upon it," the true definition of religion is "not simply *morality,* but *morality touched by emotion*." It was a definition that gave Arnold great satisfaction and attained considerable vogue in liberal religious circles.

Yet Arnold's words had not been long current when F. H. Brad-ley, with an irony even more deadly than Arnold's own, quite blasted them. Mill says that all men are either Benthamites or Coleridgeans and Bradley had this in common with Arnold, that in all matters of morality they both scorned the Benthamite "advanced thinkers," as Bradley liked to call them. Bradley, too, like Arnold, was concerned to establish religion and, like Arnold, thought of religion "as es-sentially a doing, and a doing which is moral." But this similarity of aim in no way softened the brilliant logician's contempt for Arnold's powers of reason. The morality which characterizes reli-gion, Bradley insisted, gives us no right to say that religion *is* morality, or even that religion is morality touched by emotion. In-deed the fine phrase means absolutely nothing, for "*all* morality," says Bradley, "is, in one sense or another, 'touched by emotion.' Most emotions, high or low, can go with and 'touch' morality; and the moment we leave our phrase-making, and begin to reflect, we see all that is meant is that morality 'touched' by *religious* emotion is religious; and so, as answer to the question What is religion? all that we have said is, 'It is religion when with morality you have—religion.'" He adds: "I do not think we learn a very great deal from this."

Bradley is clearly right: Arnold is advancing a tautology. When he compares the *dogmata* of mere morality with those of religion—when he puts the Greek maxim, "We all want to live honestly, but cannot," against Paul's "O wretched man that I am, who shall deliver me from the body of this death!" or when he contrasts Cicero's "Hold off from sensuality, for, if you have given yourself up to it, you will find yourself unable to think of anything else," with Jesus Christ's "Blessed are the pure in heart, for they shall see God"—clearly it is not *any* emotion that touches morality and translates it into religion but specifically an emotion about an outside and transcendent force, or help, or criterion, referred to as "who" or "God" or "eternal life" or "the kingdom of heaven." It is the emotion about this external reference which constitutes religion for Arnold—as for anyone else; not joy at having done a good deed, not pleasure in thwarting evil, nor satisfaction simply, but the fact that these results have reference to an outside power is what constitutes the emotion of religion.

But Arnold ignores what logically cannot be ignored to go on to the problem—his most difficult one—of establishing his transcendent power in the language of naturalism. Spinoza had given him a hint by saying that whatever man makes use of to aid and preserve his existence, whether external or internal, is a gift of the divine power. At a later time, in *Literature and Dogma,* Arnold will be emboldened to establish God in the external world, but first, in *St. Paul and Protestantism,** he turns to an exposition of God as an internal aid, to God as a psychological fact.

* To avoid the confusion which might result from not having followed the chronological order of Arnold's religious work it may be well to have that order clear: *St. Paul and Protestantism:* in *The Cornhill Magazine,* October and November 1869, in book form, 1870; "Puritanism and the Church of England:" *Cornhill,* February, 1870, reprinted in *St. Paul and Protestantism; Literature and Dogma,* in part in the *Cornhill.*

Socrates had spoken of his *daimon,* Marcus Aurelius of the "mistress part" of reason, Bishop Butler of the principle of reflection or conscience: in one way or another each of these men had found some element of man which is in direct relation with the whole of the universe as the rest of man is not. And we have seen how Arnold, whatever else he had doubted of divinity in his unsettled period, never doubted the divine nature of morality, and how often he recurred to the idea of a "clue," as he calls it, or of some instinct which drives the personality aright. This may once have been a poetic metaphor; it now becomes the statement of a working fact. There is in us, says Arnold, a "central moral tendency," a "central clue in our moral being which unites us to the universal order." But not only is the central moral tendency our link with the universal order, it is also bound to be right: moral *knowledge* (though not moral performance) is perfectly easy for it.*

This theory of the moral clue inevitably involves the dualism of Stoicism and Christianity—of the contemptible flesh and the potentially perfect spirit. Arnold himself disclaims any desire to find "evil inherent in the flesh and its working;" he believes that all the forces and tendencies in us are in themselves beneficent, but he maintains that those of the flesh are diverse in their workings and unharmonized and that "the evil which flows from these diverse workings is

---

July and October, 1871, complete in book form 1873; "A Persian Passion Play" in the *Cornhill* of December, 1871, reprinted in the third edition, 1875, of *Essays in Criticism I* and therefore often thought of as belonging to an earlier period; "Review of Objections to 'Literature and Dogma,' " *The Contemporary Review,* October and November, 1874 and January, March, May, July, September, 1875, reprinted as *God and the Bible,* 1875; "Bishop Butler and the Zeit-Geist," *The Contemporary Review,* February and March, 1876; "The Church of England," *Macmillan's Magazine,* April, 1876; "A Last Word on the Burials Bill," *Macmillan's,* July, 1876; "A Psychological Parallel," *Contemporary,* November, 1876. The last four were reprinted, with an important preface, as *Last Essays on Church and Religion,* 1877.

* Bradley tells us much the same thing when he declares that moral judgments are never discursive: "we know what is right in a particular case by what we may call an immediate judgment, or an intuitive subsumption;" we know what is right by the intuition of the just man, and he is one "who has identified his will with the moral spirit of the community, and judges accordingly. If an immoral course be suggested to him, he 'feels' or 'sees' at once that the act is not in harmony with a good will, and he does not do this by saying, 'this is a breach of rule A, *therefore* &c.'; but the first thing he is aware of is that he 'does not like it.' "

undeniable." It is the central moral tendency which harmonizes them, however, and makes their beneficence appear.

Arnold, as we have said, is concerned with establishing a Christian kind of conduct as against (what, for the sake of shortness, we may call) a revolutionary kind. The essential difference between the two may be seen in Joubert's attack upon Rousseau for making morality positive rather than negative. No doubt with Socrates' *daimon* in mind, which never urged but often forbade, Joubert had said, "Morality is formed only to repress and constrain; . . . morality is a bridle and not a spur." For to make morality a spur is to admit the natural goodness of man; to call it a bridle is to declare man's essential badness. And it is the essence of revolutionary theory to insist on man's natural goodness. For Arnold, too, morality is essentially a check, a bridle, a renunciation:

That an opposition there is, in all matter of what we call *conduct,* between a man's first impulses and what he ultimately finds to be the real law of his being; that a man accomplishes his right function as a man, fulfils his end, hits the mark, in giving effect to the real law of his being . . . all good observers report. No statement of this general experience can be simpler or more faithful than one given us by that great naturalist, Aristotle. "In all wholes made up of parts," says he, "there is a ruler and a ruled; throughout nature this is so; we see it even in things without life, they have their *harmony* or *law*. The living being is composed of soul and body, whereof the one is naturally ruler and the other ruled. Now what is natural we are to learn from what fulfils the law of its nature most, and not from what is depraved. So we ought to take the man who has the best disposition of body and soul; and in him we shall find that this is so; for in people that are grievous both to others and to themselves the body may often appear ruling the soul, because such people are poor creatures and false to nature." And Aristotle goes on to distinguish between the *body,* over which, he says, the rule of the soul is absolute, and the *movement of thought and desire,* over which reason has, says he, "a constitutional rule," in words which exactly recall St. Paul's phrase for our double enemy: "The *flesh* and the *current thoughts*." So entirely are we here on ground of general experience. And if we go on and take this maxim from Stobæus: "All fine acquirement implies a foregoing *effort* of *self-control;*" or this from Horace: "*Rule* your current self or it will rule *you!* bridle it in and chain it down!" or this from Goethe's autobiography: "Everything cries out to us that we must *renounce;*" or still more this from his *Faust:* "Thou must *go without, go without!* this is the everlasting song which every hour, all our life through, hoarsely sings to us!" then we have testimony not only to the necessity of this natural law of rule and suppression, but also to the strain and labour and suffering which attend it.

It is this frank and simple dualism which made Arnold in part congenial to the Humanism of Irving Babbitt and Paul Elmer More.*

Now it is perhaps a matter of dispute only for theologians *manqués,* whether man, in his impulses and instincts, is naturally good or bad. Simplification on either side makes falsification; observation shows us that men are both hideous in their cruelty and superb in their generosity, and which is the product of "nature" and which of "morality" depends on what one means by nature and how natural one thinks society. Impulse produces both evil and good; no less ambivalent are the results of self-control, which may make the most admirable martyrs and the most repulsive oppressors. Since, however, we face Arnold's *parti pris,* we may rather recall the benefits of impulse—how the moral act, the subordination of members to mind, may be done by the man for whom the part of passion is the far harder part, so that what the world sees as self-control is scarcely a moral act at all but almost one of self-indulgence. The systematic moralist does not help us here; we must rather turn to the novelist and find the truth in such a character as Sonya in *War and Peace*

* Compare, for example, these statements from More's "Definitions of Dualism":
"Beside the flux of life there is also that within man which displays itself intermittently as an inhibition upon this or that impulse, preventing its prolongation in activity, and making a pause or eddy, so to speak, in the stream. This negation of the flux we call the inner check. It is not the mere blocking of one impulse by another, which is a quality of the confusion of the flux itself, but a restraint upon the flux exercised by a force contrary to it.

"In the repeated exercise of the inner check we are conscious of two elements of our being—the inner check itself and the stream of impulses—as coexistent and coöperative, yet essentially irreconcilable, forces. What, if anything, lies behind the inner check, what it is, why and how it acts or neglects to act, we cannot express in rational terms. Of the ultimate source of desires and impressions, and of the relation of the resulting flux of impulses to the inner check in that union which we call ourselves, we are darkly ignorant. These are the final elements of self-knowledge—on the one hand multiplicity of impulses, on the other hand unity and *cupiditatum oblivio, alta rerum quies.*"—*The Drift of Romanticism* (1913), pp. 247–8.

who reminds us that natures which live by abnegation alone may become warped and scarcely trustworthy. We often find that the best morality, that which interferes least, demands least, bullies least, is that which is simply the overflow of a generous nature and that the moral act may be done with scarcely any more thought than the perception of the good that will result, involving no struggle of self-control because it is a kind of self-expression. Arnold speaks of the two instincts of life which require control—the instinct of self-preservation and the reproductive instinct. But the first is not so fierce as systems make out; there are many who, by the very law of their members, as it were, prefer the preservation of others above their own. The instinct of reproduction—even when we call it by the more direct name of the sexual instinct—does sometimes make for cruel acts of aggression and possession but at least as much for acts of tenderness and generosity. Or again, often the moral problem of the highly developed man is not one of right and wrong but of right and right. One does not, to be sure, dismiss morality by citing the differences of moral ideals in different times and cultures. But the agreement of moral teachers which Arnold offers as the core of morality does not solve problems of allegiance and of the clash of cultural ideals—the problems eternally typified in the dilemmas of Antigone or Orestes. Too often the moral problem may resolve itself into a conflict between the *new kind of right* and the old.* In short, the dualistic morality of the spirit and the members turns out to be far too simple.

It is interesting at this point to note how great a part in Arnold's morality is played by sex. Indeed, in Arnold's calculation, sex is half

---

* Arnold never touches on this problem, surely a serious flaw in a moralist. The solutions which have been offered by three moralists of different political stripe make an interesting contrast. For Bradley, to deal with a new kind of right, to set up to be better than the social world around you, was *per se* an immorality. Fitzjames Stephen, a little to the left of Bradley as a kind of conservative utilitarian, believed that one had a right to appeal to a new and better morality but that society also was justified in killing one for it and then adopting it at leisure. George Mead, a democrat and progressive, believed that a new morality might sanction what was contrary to the old.

the matter of conduct—the other half being concerned with the drives of self-preservation. "Kindness and pureness, charity and chastity . . . ," he says, "if any virtues could stand for the whole of Christianity, these might." The sexual concern is often almost central to Arnold's morality. Even in the 1870's "one may hear many doubts thrown, in the name of science and reason, on the truth and validity of the Christian idea of pureness" and to Arnold this phenomenon is not isolated; it is clearly linked, he believes, with revolutionary theory; France for him is now far less the home of lucidity than of lubricity, and France is the home of natural rights. *L'homme sensuel moyen* and natural rights are sprung from the same stem: France "develops the senses, the apparent self, all round, in good faith, without misgivings, without violence, she has much reasonableness and clearness in all her notions and arrangements; a sort of balance even in conduct; as much art and science, and it is not a little, as goes with the idea of *l'homme sensuel moyen*. And from her ideal of the average sensual man France had deduced her famous gospel of the Rights of Man, which she preaches with such an infinite crowing and self-admiration." The French defeat in the Prussian war was retribution for a personal lubricity resulting in political confusion.

The Goddess Aselgeia—Lubricity—which Arnold supposes to preside over the French pantheon becomes well-nigh obsessive with him. Renan is said to be in her service because he questions whether Nature had much regard to chastity and because he wrote *The Abbess of Jouarre,* an interesting play of—to us—no indelicacy whatever. Zola comes into Arnold's ken, but chiefly as a purveyor of the repulsive. Now, whatever Arnold finds admirable in Shelley and Keats, he finds their sexuality repulsive. The whole and final comment on all speculations about love and marriage is the sentence from *Proverbs* on the "Strange Woman:" "He knows not that the dead are there, and that her guests are in the depths of hell"—to be repeated like a litanic charm to banish whoredom. The modern temper will feel that this is all quite unacceptable and—not without justice this time—will look to Arnold's biography to explain it.*

However, though the overemphasis on sex in Arnold's theory of morality exemplifies the too great stress which Arnold put on the most personal aspects of morality, we cannot either dismiss the questions of personal morality or believe that Arnold is being only simple in speaking of them. Perhaps it is not until we look attentively at his writing about Jesus and the "intuition" that we begin to suspect that Arnold, when he becomes insistent and reiterative, does not really mean morality or righteousness or even holiness so much as what, for lack of a clearer word, we may call *innocence*. This is something with which, again, the writers of ethical treatises can scarcely be concerned. Here, too, is the province of the novelist, for the novelist explores the realm beyond conscious motivation and knows far better than the moralist that an act or a conscious intention may be good at the same time that there is behind it a lack of innocence or an element of self-assertion which, because it is not expressed, makes the act of virtue either issue in badness or fail of subjective worth. Into this realm law can never penetrate, articulate social judgment cannot go, nor even religion. This is the province of Dostoievsky and Tolstoy, of Henry James, D. H. Lawrence and E. M. Forster, of George Santayana and Aldous Huxley, of all the writers of fiction who are concerned with the question of *style* in morality.

It is the very difficulty of the moral life, Arnold believes, the difficulty of self-knowledge and of performance, that makes religion humanly—psychologically—necessary. The question is "how to find the energy and power to bring all those self-seeking tendencies of the flesh, those multitudinous, swarming, eager, and incessant impulses, into obedience to the central tendency." With a brilliant insight Arnold insists that merely to *command* them to obey is not only

---

* We must note, however, that so remarkable an exponent of the modern spirit as Aldous Huxley, has turned back to his granduncle and found, like him, a strong connection between erotic libertarianism on the one hand and political revolution, cosmic meaninglessness and the fall of nations on the other.

insufficient but even harmful, for command "only irritates opposition in the desires it tries to control." Paul, when he passed into
religion, was doing nothing more than solving this problem and it
is Paul's great virtue that his religion came by experience and not
a priori, scientifically and not theologically, for he saw that sin was
"not a monster to be mused on, but an impotence to be got rid of;"
religion is his handmaiden of morality. Yet while Arnold is explaining the pyschological soundness of Paul's religion, the camel of theology puts its head into his tent. Until now, Arnold has been willing
to find God first in the law of things fulfilling themselves, then in
the moral order. But neither of these notions of deity is very com-
pulsive; indeed, they are rather dreary, the kind of thing that so
depresses one in Marcus Aurelius. Arnold therefore attributes to
Paul the Hebrew conception of God as "not merely . . . in conscience, the righteous judge," but as "God in the world and the
workings of the world, the eternal and divine power from which all
life and wholesome energy proceed . . . [the] element in which we
live and move and have our being, which stretches around and beyond the strictly moral element in us, around and beyond the finite
sphere of what is originated, measured, and controlled by our own
understanding and will."

In other words, it has never been enough to have only the movement of man toward the order of the universe; what is needed is
also a movement of the universe toward man. And at the risk of
impugning the Aristotelian definition, which makes morality an act
of consciousness, will and habit, Arnold introduces a power from
without so that the moral play of man and universe may be recipro-
cal. The universe is conceived to be generating and emanating morality, as it emanates other forces which we experience. "By this
element," says Arnold, "we are receptive and influenced, not origina-
tive and influencing; now, we all of us receive far more than we
originate. Our pleasure from a spring day we do not make; our
pleasure, even, from an approving conscience we do not make. And
yet we feel that both the one pleasure and the other can, and often

do, work with us in a wonderful way for our good." We have good emotions—then we may objectify their source as God, and, says Arnold, the greater men are, the more natural it is for them to have this objective reference for their feelings. "Great men like Sylla and Napoleon have loved to attribute their success to their fortune, their star; religious great men have loved to say that their sufficiency was of God." But all people recognize the *sense of influence* that Arnold speaks of; they put it high in the hierarchy of their emotions, however, not outside it. As a theological argument, the fond phantasm of Napoleon's self-love is certainly not convincing. If we may derive God from the sense of influence, we may derive a blind bowboy from our experience of love or a Muse from our experience of that flattering integration of faculties which suddenly makes the words flow where a moment before they had halted. The fact that we say we have been "hard hit" in the one case or "inspired" in the other, does not permit us to believe that there is actually a Cupidon or a Muse. And what is at work when the spring day gives no pleasure or when the conscience approves and no happiness results? Must we not be Manicheans when, from no cause discernible to ourselves, black and maleficent moods descend on us? Arnold met this last objection by saying that we have no rights in this world, only duties; we have no right to *expect* the good and if it comes we may deify it, though we may not deify evil as Satan.

In short, the objective existence of the generator of the sense of influence is Arnold's own *Aberglaube* of morality. Different temperaments will, of course, respond differently to its assertion. William James, for example, is perfectly at one with Arnold on the matter of objectification and is willing to defend its non-rationality: *

Now, what is called "extradition" is quite as characteristic of our emotions as of our senses: both point to an object as the cause of the present feeling. . . . An enraptured man and a dreary-feeling man are not simply aware

* James, we may remember, is in the tradition of the men of the 19th century who had well-nigh intolerable emotional struggles with the problem of the freedom of the will. The problem formed the intellectual content of James' neurosis which he describes so well in his letters and in *The Varieties of Religious Experience*.

of their subjective state; if they were, the force of their feelings would all evaporate. Both believe there is outward cause why they should feel as they do: either, "It is a glad world! how good life is!" or, "What a loathesome tedium is existence!" Any philosophy which annihilates the validity of the reference by explaining away its objects or translating them into terms of no emotional pertinency, leaves the mind with little to care or act for.

The *Aberglaube* of "extradition" is for James "absolutely indispensable" and must be treated tolerantly so long as it is not intolerant itself. Yet one must wonder in how far this gives sanction to delusion and hallucination.

In *St. Paul and Protestantism,* however, Arnold is not so much concerned with this God of cosmological certainty as with the God of psychological fact with which Paul worked to make morality operative. Indeed, once he feels that he has suggested God as the Creator and as the Eternal Order, he shows Paul in relation not with this God but with Jesus. Paul, says Arnold, conceived Christ as divine because he was free from sin and wholly in conformity with the divine order, an experimental foundation for faith in Jesus and therefore superior to Calvinism's, by which the sinlessness of Christ is established by his divinity. The whole of Paul's religion was his passionate attachment to Jesus by which he received strength for righteousness. It was as natural a thing as the love of man for woman, for "everyone knows how being in love changes for the time a man's spiritual atmosphere, and makes animation and buoyancy where before there was flatness and dulness." Arnold might have made an illuminating comparison between the way Paul's love for Christ aided virtue and the part played by Plato's "passionate and spirited element" of the soul in allying itself with reason to control the desires.

To this simple idea that the love of Jesus gives us strength for righteousness, there are, says Arnold, ideas which are truly sequential and ideas that are merely incidental. He calls the first "primary;" they are the ideas which, he says, science will confirm, such as that

Jesus is the perfect follower of the natural order, or the idea of "faith," by which Paul secures his attachment to Jesus. By "faith" Paul usually means *fidelity,* the "power of holding fast to an unseen power of goodness;" it is identification with Christ by dying with him. And this concept of *necrosis* is also primary, at once mystic and rational; *necrosis* is Paul's central doctrine and he meant by it "to die with Christ to the law of the flesh, to live with Christ to the law of the mind." *

Ideas "secondary" in Paul's thought are those which science can neither affirm nor deny. Among these are the metaphysics according to which Jesus was the Logos; theology according to which Jesus was the Messiah; the occasional use of "faith," in the sense of "belief"—the sense in which Protestantism contrasts it with "works"—rather than of "fidelity;" ideas of the belief in the physical resurrection of Christ and of men; the acceptance of the eschatology of his time—the end of the world, Satan, angels, trumpets and the judgment; the notion of predestined grace or election or calling; the doctrine of appeasement.

In short, all that is conceptual in Paul, all that is theoretical, all that touches the realm of science, is unscientific, secondary and to be passed over. All that is emotional, all that is experiential, is primary and in conformity with science.

It was upon the basis of what was primary in Paul that Arnold appealed for religious union. He had tried to cut all dogmatic ground from under Protestantism and thus to make religion ac-

---

* "How can the human-divine ideal ever be my will?" asks Bradley. "The answer is, Your will it never can be as the will of your private self, so that your private self should become wholly good. To that self you must die, and by faith be made one with the ideal. You must resolve to give up your will, as the mere will of this or that man, and you must put your whole self, your entire will, into the will of the divine. That must be your one self, as it is your true self; that you must hold to both with thought and will, and all other you must renounce; you must both refuse to recognize it as yours, and practically with your whole self deny it. You must believe that you too really are one with the divine, and must act as if you believed it. In short, you must be justified not by works but solely by faith. This doctrine, which Protestantism, to its eternal glory, has made its own and sealed with its blood, is the very center of Christianity; and where you have not this in one form or another, there Christianity is nothing but a name."

ceptable to men of the scientific *Zeitgeist*. And the very conception of Paul's religion implied union. The idea of faith, said Arnold, does not apply only to the individual man's relation to Christ. It implies the ideal of the State, the cooperative ideal. "Whoever identifies himself with Christ, identifies himself with Christ's idea of the solidarity of man. The whole race is conceived as one body . . . forming by the joint action of its regenerate members the mystical body of Christ." Therefore "my neighbour is merely an extension of myself, [and] deceiving my neighbour is the same as deceiving myself." It is with this conception of unity in Christ that Arnold finds his way to solve the dilemma of community and assent in politics. For each man may discover the Socrates in his own breast by the religious act of "dying to himself," by dissolving his lower nature in the act of *necrosis* and finding accord with his fellows in Christ.

IV

In his *Non-Religion of the Future,* Guyau speaks of the 19th century attempts at radical religious redefinition as being "without myth, without dogma, without cult, without rite," and as "resolvable into a system of metaphysical hypotheses." This is scarcely an adequate description of many of the religious redefinitions of the time and it certainly does not tell the truth about Arnold's. For whatever Arnold did with religion, he did not resolve it into a system of metaphysical hypotheses; if he banished dogma, he defended myth, cult and rite. If his conception of religion is in the line of Kant and Ritschl and points to morality, it is no less in the line of Schleiermacher and based in emotional subjectivism. We may ask the man listening to his phonograph how he knows there is music playing and he will surely answer that he knows not only because there is sound but because he gets certain pleasant emotions. If we then reply that we also hear sound but see no reason to call it music inasmuch as we get no emotions, or only unpleasant ones, our friend can reply that we simply have no ear—it is a lack which he pities in us. So for Arnold and others of the collateral lineage of Schleier-macher, the sense of God was proof enough of his existence; or nearly.

The aesthetic analogy is not figure merely: the establishment of God was necessary as a guarantee of the aesthetic of life. People who did not need it for metaphysical completeness needed it for Joy. Whatever of sense and reason Benthamism and Communism might bring, they did not, it seemed to Arnold, bring the sense of Joy, of wonder, of pleasure at being alive, of a world illuminated and burst-ing to tell a secret—that sense for which G. K. Chesterton in our own day is the spokesman and for which he went to Catholicism, and for which William James was willing to admit the value of any popular religion, especially its *Aberglaube.* "The sense of *life,* of being truly *alive,"* said Arnold, was the reward of right conduct, but it could not be had merely by the performance of duty; it could only be assured by religion and religion implies a God.

A God is necessary, but the old God can no longer be accepted—the God who was a "non-natural and magnified man in the next street," who, in theology, turned out to be a collocation of three as-pects of Lord Shaftesbury (the seventh earl, of course, who was the philanthropist, not the third earl, who was the chancellor and Deist philosopher) standing in strange familial and metaphysical relations with each other—

a sort of infinitely magnified and improved Lord Shaftesbury, with a race of vile offenders to deal with, whom his natural goodness would in-cline him to let off, only his sense of justice will not allow it; then a younger Lord Shaftesbury, on the scale of his father and very dear to him, who might live in grandeur and splendour if he liked, but who pre-fers to leave his home, to go and live among the race of offenders, and to be put to an ignominious death, on condition that his merits shall be counted against their demerits, and that his father's goodness shall be re-strained no longer from taking effect, but any offender shall be admitted to the benefit of it on simply pleading the satisfaction made by the son;— and then, finally, a third Lord Shaftesbury, still on the same high scale, who keeps very much in the background, and works in a very occult man-

ner, but very efficaciously nevertheless, and who is busy in applying everywhere the benefits of the son's satisfaction and the father's goodness. . . .

Arnold will not say that this is a "degrading superstition," though
he hints that it is somewhat ignoble; what is chiefly wrong with it
or any similar doctrine, like that of the Mass, is that it is not *verifiable*. "Is it *sure?* can what is here assumed be *verified?*" Clearly not,
by any scientific standard of verification, and here, says Arnold, lies
the danger of quasi-scientific theology—it may fail the believer and
then all the good that attaches to it may vanish with it.

What then shall we mean by God—since there must be a sub-
stratum of meaning which everyone assumes? Theology is no help:
it evolved the three Lords Shaftesbury and similar unacceptable notions. Metaphysics is no help: it involves us in subtle and tautological
arguments about being. A translation of the word into value is somewhat useful: Luther wanted it to mean the best that man knows or
can know, but this, while it is attractive, has the disadvantage of
not telling us what the best is and everyone's notion of the best differs.
Philology is of some help: it tells us that the original meaning of
the word God was quite vague, that Deus and Diva originally meant
nothing more than "shining," and lack of precision is exactly what
Arnold wants for his definition of God. But in science truly conceived we find our best answer: science tells us that God is *"the
stream of tendency by which all things fulfil the law of their being;"*
Arnold rests temporarily upon this formulation. Why science, having
discovered that "all things fulfil the law of their being," should not
stay content with this axiomatic *petitio principii* (for such it is: it
says no more than "all things act as they act") instead of going back
of it to say that this happens by the movement of "a stream of tendency," thus suggesting that things fulfil the law of their being only
approximately, surely a fatal assumption for science, is a consideration that does not disturb him. And for Arnold science does another
thing not in its character—it violates its principle of economy by
calling the stream of tendency "God," nomenclature which, however

aptly it may serve morality, adds nothing to the functioning of science.

Spinoza—and Arnold himself—had drawn a line between science and morality; now, by ignoring this line, Arnold steps into the world of physics and metaphysics and becomes subject to the God of the *Ethics,* the morally neutral God. By declaring that man, too, has a law of being and that the law of man's being is morality, he makes an unhappy confusion of two realms of knowledge. For in the sense of science, morality is not the law of man's being. Whatever happens to a stone is the fulfilment of the law of its being; if it be thrown, rolled, crushed, builded with, it fulfils that law. And in the same context of science the same is true of man; to be dismembered, impaled, eaten with cancer, or to be cruel or gentle, to win a race or to lose it, to be contented or miserable are equally "necessary" and equally the fulfilment of man's nature. It is only in a purely moral context that we may say that man's cruelty is "unnatural" or his misery a "shame."

Men will not, after all, rest in the validity of their emotions merely; perhaps it is only the observer and philosopher who can regard these, with a hint of patronage, as sufficient. James's description of the process by which men come to assert that their beliefs rest on more than "extradition" is well known: "[the individual] becomes conscious that this higher part is conterminous and continuous with a *more* of the same quality, which is operative in the universe outside of him, and which he can keep in working touch with, and in a fashion get on board of and save himself when all his lower being has gone to pieces in the wreck." But at some point it is necessary not only to believe but to prove the *more.* "Is such a 'more' merely our own notion, or does it really exist? If so, in what shape does it exist? Does it act, as well as exist?" It must, as Arnold said, be a *not ourselves,* whatever else it be. Arnold was making a religion for people whose minds were dyed in science, theological or physical. He may reduce predication about God to a minimum but he cannot entirely get rid of it. At some point he must pass from a judgment of value to a judgment of existence. He must at least show that God implies power and explain how this power works. He wants the word God and he wants some reality behind the word, however minimal: "No one," he says, "will say, that it is admittedly certain and verifiable, that there is a personal first cause, the moral and intelligent governor of the universe, whom we may call *God* if we will. But that all things seem to us to have what we call a law of their being, and to tend to fulfil it, is certain and admitted; though whether we will call this *God* or not, is a matter of choice. Suppose, however, we call it *God,* we then give the name of *God* to a certain and admitted reality."

There is something almost touching about this reasoning. It is as if a once mighty empire had been shorn of power by its enemies and forbidden to maintain even the remnants of its shattered but once invincible Grand Imperial Army. Its conquered rulers recall that in the past nothing gave them greater pleasure or more self-esteem than the existence of their Grand Imperial Army. They therefore say, "We could, of course, continue to talk of our Grand Imperial Army, though not a single squadron remains to convince us of its reality. However, our conquerors permit us to maintain a police-force, small but sufficient to keep order. This we know does exist, we see it every day, and we might call this the Grand Imperial Army. Suppose we do call it the Grand Imperial Army; we then give the name of the Grand Imperial Army to a certain and admitted reality."

Once Arnold has established a word and a reality and linked the two, he declares with the strongest emphasis that we must say nothing further about them. He himself, as we shall at once see, will not be able to obey his own injunction; to refrain from all predication about God, however, is of the essence of his teaching on religion. Precisely, runs his argument, because an idea is enormous and complex we can say little about it. Anciently and properly, the word God was not by any means "a term of science or exact knowledge, but a term of poetry and eloquence, a term *thrown out,* so to speak, at a not fully grasped object of the speaker's consciousness, a *literary* term, in short; and mankind mean different things by it as their consciousness differs." Here is the crux of Arnold's exposition and it is momentous in denying almost completely the centuries of Christian intellectual tradition, from Augustine to Aquinas and beyond. He goes back of all Christianity, for his theology, to the God of the Old Testament Jews. Originally, he says, Elohim, the Mighty, was not a specifically religious conception, but Elohim became Jehovah, the Eternal; "the Eternal *what?* The Eternal *Cause?* Alas, these poor people were not Archbishops of York. They meant the Eternal *righteous,* who loveth righteousness." To the Jews—the people who had the greatest talent for righteousness and religion—God meant, in the best period of their history, *"The power not ourselves that makes for righteousness."* Arnold has told us we may not with safety say anything about God beyond that he is the stream of tendency by which all things fulfil the law of their being; he has not heeded his own warning and within a few lines has himself gone a long and assumptive way.

The drive to predication indeed is not lightly to be dismissed; it is far more compelling than Arnold in theory admitted. In *Reason and Nature,* Morris Cohen puts the matter well: "One may say: I hold these truths and the faith in them strengthens my life. But such assertions cannot keep out the lurking doubt that it is the psychologic attitude rather than the truth of what is assumed that produces the practical effects. The pragmatic glorification of belief contains the deep poison of scepticism as to what really exists, and this like a Nessus shirt will destroy any religious belief that puts it on. Religion may begin in ritual and conduct, but it inevitably goes on to reflective belief that must submit to the canons of logic. The popular and superficial contrast between religion and theology ignores the fact that where a diversity of religion exists it is impossible to stop a process of reflection as to which of two conflicting claims is true. In such a society, religious creed or theology (including the possibility of a negative or atheistic theory) becomes inescapable. Hazy talk about religious experience will not adequately meet the difficulties."

In *St. Paul and Protestantism* Arnold had been content to speak of the moral "element" rather vaguely, as a kind of Paraclete or Helper of man in his moral struggle; although he had, to be sure, spoken as if it were external, he had emphasized chiefly its psychological genesis, what James calls the "hither side" of the "more." In *Literature and Dogma* he is tempted to speak fully of the "farther side"—of the actual working of the "power." Now we learn that the power is the creative source of morality itself; man does not create and perfect morality; rather, he obeys with increasing exactness an absolute morality which is preexistent. Arnold is most literal and explicit about this: "Who first, amid the loose solicitations of [sexual] sense, obeyed (for create it he did not) the mighty *not ourselves* which makes for moral order, the stream of tendency which was here carrying him, and our embryo race along with him, towards the fulfilment of the true law of their being?—became aware of it, and obeyed it?"

For create it he did not: the phrase is not a comforting one; it brings Arnold into the dangerous tradition of absolute moralists, of Bonald, Newman, and Carlyle, all of whom argued against a rationalistic conception of morality on the ground of an *a priori* morality intuitively perceived, a conception intended to check moral questioning, reform and certainly revolution. In Arnold, to be sure, the belief in an *a priori* morality is not perfectly central to his thought; it did not, as we shall see, operate in his later political ideas. It did, however, severely limit the scope of his ethical notions.

Arnold keeps moving further and further from his start in emotion and as he does he falls into extravagances of statement beside which the "license of affirmation" which he so condemned in the theologians sometimes seems the soul of sobriety. "We did not make ourselves and our nature, or conduct as the object of three-fourths of that nature," he says; "we did not provide that happiness should follow conduct, as it undeniably does." The sentence unleashed all Bradley's thunder: "If what is meant be this, that what is ordinarily called virtue does always lead to and go with what is ordinarily called happiness, then so far is this from being 'verifiable' in every-day experience, that its opposite is so; it is not a fact, either that to be virtuous is always to be happy, or that happiness must always come from virtue. Everybody knows this, Mr. Arnold must know this, and yet he gives it, because it suits his purpose, or because the public, or a large body of the public, desire it; and this is clap-trap."

But the difficulty of proving his proposition positively only led Arnold to attempt it negatively; if he cannot prove that righteousness leads to happiness, he can at least prove that unrighteousness leads to unhappiness. "Nations and men," he cries, "whoever is shipwrecked, is shipwrecked on *conduct.*" "Down they come, one after another; Assyria falls, Babylon, Greece. Rome." Upon them the power not ourselves, apparently unable to make for righteousness, works its revenge. But—how long does this power permit unrighteousness to flourish? what, by this theory, is to be thought about those who, themselves righteous, suffer under unrighteousness? have we an example of a righteous nation, which did flourish because of righteousness, to use as a "control"?—those questions Arnold does not stop to answer. "We hear the word 'verifiable' from Mr. Arnold pretty often," says Bradley. "What is it to verify? Has Mr. Arnold put 'such a tyro's question' to himself?"

Bradley's question indicates the root of all of Arnold's difficulties: he is basically confused about the nature of fact and verification. He wants apodictic certainty of God but he wants it according to an empirical notion of science, a science which is experience purely, nothing more than organized common-sense, in which the content of any scientific law is only the account of the order of our sensations. For vigor, exactness, universality and system he has no respect; indeed, it is his old hatred of "system" that betrays him. His dismissal of metaphysics in *God and the Bible* is based on the contention that all abstract ideas are merely the illegitimate inflation of concrete experiences, that Descartes was obtuse not to see that the question of *being* was really reducible to the knowledge that *being* comes from the word meaning *breathe* which in turn comes from the word meaning *grow*—that, in short, *essence* is rightly a concern of the perfumer alone and *being* a

matter for the physiologist. But if one is committed to a method of
science purely empirical—and not very strict—one can have no apodictic proofs. And to such a method of science Arnold was committed.
His statement of it in "A Liverpool Address" of 1882 is interesting:

> Long ago, when I was occupying myself with things which seem now
> much out of my line, and when I had even thoughts of studying medicine,
> I fell in with two sentences of two eminent men in high honour with all
> surgeons and physicians, which made a deep impression upon me, which
> I carefully wrote down, and have never forgotten. One is an exhortation
> by Sir Astley Cooper to a young student: "That, sir, is the way to learn
> your business; *look for yourself,* never mind what other people may say;
> no opinion or theories can interfere with information acquired from dis-
> section." The other is a saying, more brief, of the great John Hunter:
> "*Don't think;* try and be patient."
>
> I cannot easily say for how much light and help I feel myself indebted
> to those two sentences. Sir Astley Cooper's words are words to stand for
> ever before the mind of a man setting himself to see things as they really
> are—to stand for ever before his mind to save him from doubt and dis-
> couragement. And the brief and profound saying of John Hunter points
> to the simplicity of truth, the simplicity with which things are seen when
> they are seen as they really are. We labour at words and systems, and
> fancy that we are labouring at the things for the sake of which those exist.
> But in truth we are often only labouring at the artificial and difficult forms
> under which we choose to try to think things, and the things themselves
> must be seen simply if we are to see them at all.

It is surely significant that Hume, not only as a religious skeptic but
as the father of skeptical empirical science, suggested a formulation of
religion very similar to Arnold's, beginning in emotion and, eschew-
ing all precise definition, staying in emotion. But Arnold, at the last
and in the face of his own warnings, refuses to stay in emotion; he
wants a certainty that his experience of emotion and his conception of
science will not grant. And he falls back on a juggling both with facts
and with terminology—and into unreality.*

---

* Bradley, having denied Arnold's facts, exposes his terminological juggling with
irresistible ferocity and suggests that "the habit of washing ourselves might be termed
'the Eternal not ourselves that makes for cleanliness,' or 'Early to bed and early to rise,'
the 'Eternal not ourselves that makes for longevity,' and so on."

V

In *Science and Poetry*, I. A. Richards distinguishes between what he calls "statement" and "pseudo-statement." "A pseudo-statement is a form of words which is justified entirely by its effect in releasing or organising our impulses and attitudes (due regard being had for the better or worse organisation of these *inter se*); a statement, on the other hand, is justified by its truth, *i.e.,* its correspondence, in a highly technical sense, with the fact to which it points." This says, of course, only what Arnold said when he contrasted scientific with literary language, but perhaps the new words add a new light. In his theoretical religious writing Arnold seems quite unable to keep his two kinds of propositions distinct. In his practical plans for religion, however, he never confuses them.

Arnold conceived the Church to be nothing more than "a great national society for the promotion of what is commonly called goodness"—a society for organizing impulses and attitudes to the end that the Best Self may be educed and the idea of the State fulfilled.

That the established Church was the true one for England seemed to Arnold proved by its history—particularly by its long resistance to tight formularies, to "statements." The *via media* which had incurred the scorn of both Dissent and Catholicism was, for Arnold, the proof and guarantee of the Church's flexibility and powers of growth. In the religious struggles of the 17th century the Church had resisted Calvinism's demand for a rigid doctrine of predestination, sensing not only its moral harmfulness but the danger of any strict definition. In short, the Church had rested in pseudo-statement and its reward was its power of growth. And the Church, for Arnold, must always stay in pseudo-statement; it is not a corporation for "speculative" purposes, but for purposes of "moral growth and of practice;" it can only reflect the speculation of its age, cannot be intellectually better than its *Zeitgeist* and must always be forgiven its intellectual failures. True that "terms like *God, creation, will, evil, propitiation, immortality,* evoke . . . and must evoke, sooner or later, a philosophy; but to evoke this was the accident and not the essence of Christianity." The whole future of Christianity, then, depends on its ability to disengage itself from its speculative accretions of "statement" and to engage in "pseudo-statement" solely. By doing this the Church will be able to solve its relation with three important groups—with Dissent, with the men who have given themselves to the scientific *Zeitgeist* and with the working masses.

Arnold's feeling about the relation of Establishment with Dissent was almost entirely that of his father. In the matter of doctrine he believed that the Bible, together with John Smith's "great discourse," *On the Excellency and Nobleness of True Religion,* and Reuss' *History of Christian Theology at the Time of the Apostles* were sufficient preparation for clerical ordination within an Establishment that would comprehend all sects. Tillotson's proposals for comprehension (1689) seemed to him right in spirit, emphasizing as they did a looseness of formulation and a broad tolerance. The latitude which Arnold allowed in ritual was wide but, interestingly enough, not so wide as the latitude he allowed in doctrine. If organized religion is pseudo-statement, ritual is indeed its very essence; and style is the very essence of ritual. Arnold believed in the profound importance of keeping services in (what Hobbes called) "words and phrases, not sudden, nor light nor Plebeian; but beautiful and well-composed; For else we do not God as much honour as we can." "Suddenness" was especially prized by many Nonconformist sects, and individual spontaneity, Arnold felt, was likely to lead to the "Plebeian." When he considered the Burials Bill of 1876 by which the Dissenters were to be granted the right to be buried in the consecrated ground of the parish churchyard, but with their own ministers and their own services, Arnold, although he admits the national character of the churchyards and the right of the Dissenters to bury there, will not admit their right to use the public domain for their private preference in aesthetics.

What is the intention of all forms of public ceremonial and ministration? It is, that what is done and said in a public place, and bears with it a public character, should be done and said worthily. The public is respon-

sible for it. The public gets credit and advantage from it if it is done
worthily, is compromised and harmed by it if it is done unworthily. The
mode, therefore, of performing public functions in places invested with a
public character is not left to the will and pleasure of chance individuals.
It is expressly designed to rise above the level which would be thence
given. If there is a sort of ignobleness and vulgarity (*was uns alle bändigt,
das Gemeine*) which comes out in the crude performance of the mass of
mankind left to themselves, public forms, in a higher strain and of recognised worth, are designed to take the place of such crude performance.
They are a kind of schooling, which may educate gradually such performance into something better, and meanwhile may prevent it from standing
forth, to its own discredit and to that of all of us, as public and representative. This, I say, is evidently the design of all forms for public use on serious and solemn occasions. No one will say that the common Englishman
glides off-hand and by nature into a strain pure, noble, and elevated. On
the contrary, he falls with great ease into vulgarity. But no people has
shown more attachment than the English to old and dignified forms calculated to save us from it.

The relation of the Church with the scientific-minded was far more
delicate. There were many, it seemed, who would enter the Church
as ministers, in the belief that the Church was "a national society for
the promotion of goodness," if they did not find themselves compelled
to declare their belief in what one of them called, in a letter to Arnold,
"a quantity of things which every intelligent man rejects." In "A
Psychological Parallel" Arnold undertook to resolve this problem.
He offered the examples of Justice Hale and John Smith, the one
noted for his humanity and his intellectual acumen in the law, the
other for his clear and tender insight into the human spirit. Yet Hale
is no less admirable for his legal work and Smith no less exact in his
perception of the natural truth of religion because both held and the
former acted on the 17th century belief in witchcraft. Their acceptance
of witchcraft was simply an inescapable manifestation of the time in
which they lived. In much the same way Paul's belief in Christ's
miraculous physical resurrection does not invalidate his belief in the
general idea of a moral resurrection, nor do the formularies of the
Church invalidate the real truth the Church holds. A man could

scarcely, Arnold admits, take orders while holding the view of religion set forth in *Literature and Dogma*—"for the Church of England presents as science, and as necessary to salvation, what it is the very object of that book to show to be *not* science and *not* necessary to salvation." Yet the man who has already taken orders has the articles behind him and never has to rehearse them again; and what he deals with in his prayers and services is in part the literal rendering of what he believes and in part an approximate rendering. It is "language *thrown out* by other men, in other times, at immense objects which deeply engaged their affections and awe, and which deeply engage his also; objects concerning which, moreover, adequate statement is impossible. To him, therefore, this approximative part of the prayers and services which he rehearses will be poetry. It is a great error to think that whatever is thus perceived to be poetry ceases to be available in religion. The noblest races are those which know how to make the most serious use of poetry."

Yet will righteousness, as our experience widens, seek the rational language of science? Arnold of course cannot think so. Habit and tradition have great force; the poetry of religion (and even the illegitimate science of Christianity is, in the phrase Arnold borrows from Schopenhauer, the "scholastic poetry" of religion) has power: "something in us vibrates" to the phrases of the old concepts. It is, one feels, an intensely difficult task that Arnold sets for the rightly religious man: he must "vibrate" intensely to the old words "while at the same time to purge and raise [his] view of that ideal at which they are aimed, should be [his] incessant endeavour. Else the use of them is mere dilettanteism."

Dilettanteism is exactly the charge which Santayana levels at the whole movement from which Arnold's thought proceeds. The modernist, says Santayana (he means especially the Catholic modernist but this does not limit the judgment), "has ceased to be a Christian to become an amateur, or if you will a connoisseur of Christianity. . . . Modernism is accordingly an ambiguous and unstable thing. It is the love of all Christianity in those who perceive that it is all a fable."

The very motive, he continues, that attaches the modernists to Christianity is worldly and un-Christian. "They wish to preserve the continuity of moral traditions; they wish the poetry of life to flow down to them uninterruptedly and copiously from all the ages. It is an amiable and wise desire; but it shows that they are men of the Renaissance, pagan and pantheistic in their profounder sentiment, to whom the hard and narrow realism of official Christianity is offensive just because it presupposes that Christianity is true." That Christianity is true: that is, after all, the one thing that Arnold cannot really say. That Christianity contains the highest moral law, that Christianity is natural, that Christianity is lovely, that Christianity provides a poetry serving the highest good, that Christianity *contains* the truth —anything but that *Christianity is true*. When Gretchen questions Faust on his belief in God, he utterly rejects her suggestion that he does not believe and launches into an enraptured description of the "sacred Whole" which is everlastingly about us filling our breasts with its mystery—who can name it?

> Joy, Love, Felicity, God;
> There is no name that I dare give;
> Feeling is all—the heart by which we live.
> The name is sound and smoke
> Clouding the light of heaven.

And Gretchen is for a moment convinced; it sounds much like what the priest said—"though he spoke Not quite as you do." And Faust:

> It's what all hearts say
> In every land where sun and starlight shine,
> All in their several languages; then may
> Not I say so in mine?

But Gretchen's simple sense asserts itself:

> Ah, as you put it, that sounds fine;
> But there's a twist in it all the same;
> You're not a Christian except in name.

Feeling is all, says Faust. But Gretchen knows what neither Faust nor Arnold knew, that feeling is *not* all in poetry and religion. The language, she knows, *is* the feeling, the language *is* the idea. We cannot have one kind of word for another kind of emotion. We cannot think modernly in ancient words; we betray either the one time or the other. The act of translation which Arnold makes the basis of so much of religious activity is an interesting cultural device, the device of the critic concerned for human continuities. Professor Saurat, for example, translates Milton's Calvinism into a most realistic philosophy, and the perceptive critic can translate almost any idea into rational and useful terms. But still the act of translation and "purification" is anything but a religious act, or it is religious only in the sense in which Professor McGiffert says that anything disinterested is religious. The emotions which a sensitive non-believer experiences from a well-sung requiem mass or any other elaborate ritual may have much in common with the religious emotion; they are clearly not religious. Here is poetic experience merely, and however much the poetic experience may order our lives, however much pseudo-statement may organize our emotions, its effect is not so great as that of "statement" or what we firmly believe to be statement. To keep in mind, as Arnold recommends, that all the language of prayer is the result of a great but charming mistake about the nature of a fundamental reality is, for the religious person, scarcely fortifying; for the non-religious person, it is scarcely persuasive to faith.

VI

One other relation of the Church remained to be solved—that with the advanced and religiously unattached section of the working class. It was of the utmost importance, if only because the working class, now enfranchised, had the power of pushing the disestablishment of the Church. The very phenomenon of a disaffected working class was, says Arnold, new in the Church's experience, for in the Renaissance only men of intellect and education had revolted against religion while the masses had stood firm in simple piety. The cause of the present disaffection was, to be sure, in some part intellectual but Arnold knew that it was more than this. He had learned from his father as well as from observation how far the Church was removed from the working class ideal. The aims of the proletariat had developed since his father's day, until now they were formulated as "a future on earth, not up in the sky," a future "which shall profoundly change and ameliorate things for them; an immense social progress, nay, a social transformation."

Against such an ideal for the future, the Church was popularly supposed to have set its face; it was considered as an appendage to the propertied and satisfied classes, "favouring immobility, preaching submission, and reserving transformation in general for the other side of the grave." And such a Church, Arnold said in "The Church of England," an address to a clerical audience at Zion College, cannot possibly nowadays hope to attach the working classes or incur anything but disfavor.

Yet Arnold will not admit that there inheres in the Christian religion "a superstitious worship of existing social facts, a devoted obsequiousness to the landed and propertied and satisfied classes." Indeed, he was willing to take up the spreading notion (carried by such popular books as Mrs. Lynn Linton's novel, *The True History of Joshua Davidson* and Seeley's life of Christ, *Ecce Homo*) that the Bible teaches Communism. To be sure, Communists are fierce, violent and insurrectionary people, and the Bible condemns all violence, revolt, fierceness and self-assertion; but when this is understood it may then be said that there is indeed Communism in the Bible, for "the Bible enjoins endless self-sacrifice all round; and to any one who has grasped this idea, the superstitious worship of property, the reverent devotedness to the propertied and satisfied classes is impossible." And Arnold goes on to speak of the fundamentally healthy attitude of the Church in matters of property.

Nevertheless he seems to have entertained the gravest private doubts, not only of the Church's social action, but of its social theory. For in 1871 he wrote to Newman:

The other question relates to your remarks on Lamennais at the bottom of p. 121 in the first volume of your Essays, and again in p. 123. It is this: Do not you think that what is Tory and anti-democratic in the Church of England (and undoubtedly her Tory, anti-democratic, and even squire-archical character is very marked) is one of her great dangers at the present time; and a danger from which the Catholic Church, with its Gregories and Innocents of whom you speak, is much more exempt? I mean, though the R. Catholic Church may in fact have been anti-democratic in modern times on the Continent, there seems nothing in her nature to make her so; but in the nature of the English Church there does; and is not this an additional peril, at the present day, for the English Church?

Arnold saw clearly that all the parochial labors of the clergy with the working class, the work done by many men like John Sterling, who gave up his life to it, men touched with the ideas of Maurice, were not enough. What was needed, he said, was "a positive sympathy with popular ideals. And the great popular ideal is . . . an immense renovation and transformation of things, a far better and happier society in the future than ours is now." It is true that he felt the working class ideal was often "mixed with all manner of alloy and false notions" yet in itself, he said, "it is precious, it is true. And let me observe, it is also the ideal of our religion. It is the business of our religion to make us believe in this very ideal; it is the business of the clergy to profess and to preach it." * He is sure that it is what Jesus

---

* This position may be interestingly compared with that of the Introduction to *God and the Bible* in which Arnold attacks a "revolutionary Deism, hostile to all which is old, traditional, established and secure; favourable to a clean sweep and a new stage, with the classes now in the background for chief actors." True religion, he goes on to say, has "nothing to do with the gospel of the rights of man, of the natural claim of every man to a certain share of enjoyment. Political science may create rights for a man and maintain them, may seek to apportion the means of enjoyment. Such is not the function of the Christian religion. Man sincere, man before conscience, man as Jesus put him, finds laid down for himself no rights; nothing but an infinite dying, and in that dying is life." The two views need not, of course, be taken as diametrically opposed, yet the shift in emphasis is significant.

preached—a kingdom of earth, not of heaven only, not established by the violent processes of Fifth Monarchy men or German Anabaptists or of French Communists: but established. The modification is a familiar one but it is not what Arnold emphasized. He is chiefly concerned to show that "righteousness" itself is not enough: "It is a contracted and insufficient conception of the gospel which takes into view only the establishment of *righteousness,* and does not also take into view the establishment of the *kingdom.*"

Chapter Twelve

※≫ ≪※

RESOLUTION

What must be said, may well be said twice o'er.
—THE FRAGMENTS OF EMPEDOCLES

W HEN a man begins his career in personal confusion and lyric poetry, progresses through literary and political criticism, and arrives at the affirmations of religion, all the charms of symmetry suggest that his work is complete. And in a sense the design of Arnold's work is indeed finished; at least there are no new themes to be added. But the eleven years left to him after the last of the religious work form a coda quite as interesting as anything that had come before and in some ways more vigorous.

Arnold's whole career had been spent in evaluating the French Revolution and if this seems small distinction in a century whose whole effort was to accommodate itself to that event, it is nevertheless true that Arnold worried the problem more constantly and explicitly than his contemporaries and was least satisfied with the simple answers. He had denied much of the Revolution, had translated Liberty to mean order, had affirmed Fraternity only after reestablishing religion, had controverted the theory of natural rights. He had, to be sure, defended much, yet the greater weight of his judgment had fallen to the anti-revolutionary side. But now he tells us that Liberty is *not* order but a great deal more, that Equality is the most precious of social principles, not civil equality merely but economic and social equality, and— going beyond 1789—that the denial of natural rights may be applied to what he calls the "metaphysical phantom of property." True, he

369

does not quite throw his cap over the Red mill: we hear much of the faults of the French which the Revolution had confirmed, of the merely negative nature of French lucidity, and again and always of the French lack of "conduct:" "You know the French;—a little more Biblism . . . would do them no harm." However, the feeling of these last years is clearly with the Revolutionary philosophy.

Still, Arnold had formed his entire religious theory to supply the lacks of the French Revolution and he had to continue his fight against the Revolution's moral and psychological assumptions even while he fought for its social principles; he had expressly forsworn further writing about religion but literary criticism was as good a field for the battle. The literary criticism of his last period is thought to be almost the most memorable of all his writing; certainly his last political writing has been far less influential. But political and social subjects occupied the much greater part of his effort; not merely the number of political essays which were collected into *Mixed Essays* and *Irish Essays* but the laborious pieces, not reprinted, which were devoted to examining the achievements of a Parliamentary session or to some small corner of the Irish Question, make it difficult not to believe that, however joyously Arnold may have cast off the burden of religious polemic for literature, literature was by now really posterior to social theory. Indeed he himself, in the preface to *Mixed Essays,* said what amounts to as much:

Whoever seriously occupies himself with literature will soon perceive its vital connection with other agencies. Suppose a man to be ever so much convinced that literature is, as indisputably it is, a powerful agency for benefiting the world and for civilising it, such a man cannot but see that there are many obstacles preventing what is salutary in literature from gaining general admission, and from producing due effect. Undoubtedly, literature can of itself do something towards removing those obstacles, and towards making straight its own way. But it cannot do all. In other words, literature is a part of civilisation; it is not the whole.

His literary theory at this time is in no essential way different from that of his first critical period except in the emphasis it puts upon literature as an *agency,* depending upon and supplementing other social agencies. It falls now into two parts, related but distinct, of which one, enunciated in "Literature and Science," is the affirmation of the French Revolution, the other, set forth in "The Study of Poetry," the statement of what must be added to the Revolution to make it wholly acceptable.

"Literature and Science" is perhaps the classic defense of the humanistic tradition against the attacks of positivism and science. The tradition had been long under assault but perhaps never so dangerously as at T. H. Huxley's hands. Huxley had said that literature should and inevitably would step down from its old high place in education, for science and not "culture" supplied the practical knowledge of a practical age and even the very basis of its ethical assumptions. Arnold's reply could not have been simpler or more effective. He denied that by culture he or any other sensible person had ever meant the elegant study of *belles lettres;* the culture of a nation, he said, includes its whole intellectual activity. On the other hand, he conceded that the early ascendancy of the non-scientific and non-practical disciplines had expressed an aristocratic point of view which could no longer be effective in a working society. But this did not mean, he continued, that science could ever take the place of the humanistic studies, because such a change would leave out of account the powers "which go to the building up of human life, . . . the power of conduct, the power of intellect and knowledge, the power of beauty, and the power of social life and manners." Science relates only to intellect and knowledge whereas culture relates to them all and connects each to the others. Though culture can and must relate science to the other powers, actually the true knowledge of how to live depends on no special or correct knowledge of the universe. It was always available to the men of the past even when they held the most grotesque scientific ideas. And the student trained in literature will inevitably study science; the question is whether the student of science according to the newly projected school programs will study letters. If he does not, says Arnold, he will be incomplete. With a reminiscence of his father, who had said that a man might be ever so good an engineer or chemist yet not know how to exercise the elective franchise, he brings his defense to a close with the example of the Member of Parliament, a mining engineer, who came back from America with the certainty that what the United States needed was an hereditary monarchy and an aristocracy.

Among the modern poets of England no one better than Byron exemplified for Arnold this conception that the aim of literature is understanding and action. The attraction to Byron was an old one; Byron had haunted Arnold's youth, helped shape his poetry, put before him the problems of sexual conduct, symbolized passion and action—and then had come, for a time, to seem merely vulgar. Again and again Arnold had revised his opinion: but his last word is praise. He is quite sure that Byron, as a man, is in many ways inferior to Shelley and—strange comparison!—inferior in all ways to Raphael. But it is significant that however severely Arnold holds Keats and Shelley to account for their sexual lives, he is perfectly indifferent to Byron's. He will admit that Keats is really a man of iron character but not until he has had a severe and snobbish word about the affair with Fanny Brawne; and if Shelley steps outside respectability only amazement (and French) can do justice to the disgust: "What a set! what a world!"—a *sale* world; there follows an astonishing comparison of the Shelley set with the old Oxford set of Copleston, the Kebles and Hawkins. But of Byron's sexuality he says nothing—perhaps because Byron did not theorize about love like Shelley nor allow it to "enervate" him like Keats. Indeed, for Arnold, Byron, in all his offenses against respectability, was only doing the positive work of attacking Philistinism. Attracted to politics though he was, Byron had been temperamentally unable to make his way as a Liberal peer by fawning on the respectable Philistines who had established themselves on the wave of English reaction against the Revolution. Instead, he turned and attacked them in his poetry and continued what was salutary in the Revolution:

Unfitted for such politics, he threw himself upon poetry as his organ; and in poetry his topics were not Queen Mab, and the Witch of Atlas, and the Sensitive Plant—they were the upholders of the old order, George the Third and Lord Castlereagh and the Duke of Wellington and Southey, and they were the canters and tramplers of the great world, and they were his enemies and himself.

As a poet, Arnold admits, Byron was neither precise nor delicate, and Goethe was right in saying that, when he thought, Byron was a mere child; yet Goethe was no less right when he insisted that Byron's influence was formative and good. Of the whole Byronic legend Arnold will make little: "whoever stops at the theatrical preludings does not know him." And beside Byron, Shelley is but the beautiful and *ineffectual* angel beating his luminous wings in vain; even Wordsworth, in some ways superior, is in other ways inferior to Byron as a poetic force. The summation of Arnold's praise is superb:

His own aristocratic class, whose cynical make-believe drove him to fury; the great middle-class, on whose impregnable Philistinism he shattered himself to pieces,—how little have either of these felt Byron's vital influence! As the inevitable break-up of the old order comes, as the English middle-class slowly awakens from its intellectual sleep of two centuries, as our actual present world, to which this sleep has condemned us, shows itself more clearly,—our world of an aristocracy materialised and null, a middle-class purblind and hideous, a lower class crude and brutal,—we shall turn our eyes again, and to more purpose, upon this passionate and dauntless soldier of a forlorn hope, who, ignorant of the future and unconsoled by its promises, nevertheless waged against the conservation of the old impossible world so fiery battle; waged it till he fell,—waged it with such splendid and imperishable excellence of sincerity and strength.

If Byron is the hero of "Literature and Science," Wordsworth is the hero of "The Study of Poetry." For where Wordsworth eventually takes his superiority over Byron is in his power of joy and consolation—in his religious power. The theme of "The Study of Poetry" is that poetry will, as things are going, eventually take the place of religion. Never, perhaps, has such a tremendous burden been placed on secular poetry: "Without poetry, our science will appear incomplete; and most of what now passes with us for religion and philosophy will be replaced by poetry." And what follows is quite inevitable: if poetry is to take the place of religion it must become religious. But Arnold does not say this in so many words: he simply finds poetry's greatest power to be that of "consolation and stay," and tells us that this power will be in proportion to the truth and seriousness of its criticism of life; by truth and seriousness he means a purely transcendental thing. Longinus-fashion, Arnold will convey the quality of the greatest poetry only by what he calls the "touchstones" of greatness. "The specimens I have quoted," * Ar-

* The touchstones are: the lines in which Helen speaks of her brothers as though they were alive, not knowing that they were long since buried in Lacedaemon (*Iliad*, iii, 243, 244); the address of Zeus to the horses of Peleus (*Iliad*, xvii, 443–445); and the line in which Achilles speaks of Priam's ancient happiness (*Iliad*, xxiv, 543). From Dante:

> Io no piangeva; sì dentro impietrai
> Piangevan elli . . .

I wailed not, so of stone grew I within;—*they* wailed.—*Inferno*, xxxiii, 39–40 and

> Io son fatta da Dio, sua mercè, tale,
> Che la vostra miseria non mi tange,
> Nè fiamma d'esto incendio non m'assale . . .

Of such sort hath God, thanked be His mercy, made me, that your misery toucheth me not, neither doth the flame of this fire strike me.—*Inferno*, ii, 91–93 and

> In la sua volontade è nostra pace.

In His will is our peace.—*Paradiso*, iii, 85.
From Shakespeare:

> Wilt thou upon the high and giddy mast
> Seal up the ship-boy's eyes, and rock his brains
> In cradle of the rude imperious surge . . .

and

> If thou didst ever hold me in thy heart,
> Absent thee from felicity awhile,
> And in this harsh world draw thy breath in pain
> To tell my story . . .

From Milton:

> Darken'd so, yet shone
> Above them all the archangel; but his face
> Deep scars of thunder had intrench'd, and care
> Sat on his faded cheek . . .

and

> And courage never to submit or yield
> And what is else not to be overcome . . .

nold says, "differ widely from one another, but they have in common this: the possession of the very highest poetical quality." By the highest poetical quality he seems to mean, from the examples he quotes, poetry in the "grand style;" grimness or sadness or melancholy or resignation seem to be its essence.

How little we ought to be willing to agree with this appears when Arnold goes on to rate the English poets and tells us that Chaucer is not really in the first rank—because he has not the accent of Dante in *"In la sua volontade è nostra pace."* Chaucer, he says, may be large, free, simple, clear, shrewd, kindly, but he is not really serious. And we see at once that Arnold does not really mean seriousness at all. He means solemnity; he means the knowledge of how to be "sick or sorry" and for this reason he says that Villon at his "best"— i.e., his regretful—moments has more seriousness than all of Chaucer. But if Chaucer is not serious, then Mozart is not serious and Molière is not serious and seriousness becomes a matter of pince-nez glasses and a sepia print of the Parthenon over the bookshelf. Many will feel that an excellent case might be made for Chaucer's being in some ways more serious than Wordsworth in that he saw more of the press and actuality of life than Wordsworth did, more of its confusion, the literalness of its sadness, the truth of its laughter. If to be sad is to be serious then are we not sad because life is not as Arnold thinks Chaucer represents it—gay and free? One must indeed have a strange notion of laughter to make it a bar to seriousness —as Arnold does when he excludes Rabelais, Molière and Voltaire from the company of Sophocles, Homer, Vergil, Horace and Dante.

That Molière was a serious *man* Arnold is perfectly sure; but that Molière was not a serious poet in the way that Shakespeare was he is quite as sure. The point for him admits no argument: Molière wrote comedy and Shakespeare tragedy. Yet looking at the matter without Arnold's preconception, all we can say is that Shakespeare often

---

and "the exquisite close to the loss of Proserpine," the loss
. . . which cost Ceres all that pain
To seek her through the world.

(though of course not always) used more awe-inspiring subjects; but awe is not a necessary adjunct of seriousness; Lear's scenes on the heath with their terrible pessimism are, perhaps, more *moving* than a discussion by Molière of education or custom: but not more serious. Arnold, however, is certain that tragedy is necessarily superior to comedy in every moral way: ". . . Only by breasting in full the storm and cloud of life, breasting it and passing through it and above it, can the dramatist who feels the weight of mortal things liberate himself from the pressure, and rise, as all seek to rise, to content and joy. Tragedy breasts the pressure of life. Comedy eludes it, half liberates itself from it by irony." But irony is as much the adjunct of tragedy as of comedy (see *Oedipus*); and perhaps if the question of evasiveness be raised, tragedy is, if anything, the more evasive of the two. Bernard Shaw has suggested that Shakespeare shuffles out of many a dilemma with a purple passage and perhaps insofar as one of the functions of tragedy is to create the illusion of finality and solution its sweeping pall may hide our vision. After all, no one is ever taken in by the happy ending, but we are often divinely fuddled by the implications of the tragic curtain. This *sense* of reconciliation, however, is exactly what Arnold wants.

Arnold insists that Molière would have written tragedy if he could; * and for Arnold the failure is not personal but national. Molière, he says, despite all his seriousness and depth of nature, could not write tragedy because in France the proper poetic form for tragedy did not exist: "and this is only another way of saying that for the highest tasks in poetry the genius of his nation appears to have not power."

Here, in brief, is the fault of the French Revolution—it was too *French* a revolution. In some way the sense of the transcendent and the supernal, lacking in the French, must be added to it. What Arnold

---

* It is interesting to note that Goethe called Molière's plays *tragic*. "[Molière] is a man by himself," he said to Eckermann (May 12, 1825), "his pieces border on tragedy. . . . His *Miser,* where the vice destroys all the natural piety between father and son, is especially great, and in a high sense tragic."

wanted cannot be called mysticism: "Let me be candid," he said in an essay on John Tauler. "I love the mystics, but what I find best in them is their golden single sentences, not the whole conduct of their argument and the result of their work." He mocked the maunderings of Amiel about infinity and the Double Zero and found him interesting only when he spoke of social and literary actualities; he deprecated the hazinesses of Emerson. But the sense of the supernal which Wordsworth conveyed, with which, indeed, Wordsworth had expressly sought to bring comfort to souls sterilized by the Revolution, was what Arnold sought in the highest poetry. Wordsworth spoke of imagination but always of imagination as against critical intellect and always of imagination that carried the imaginer to meaning, to awe, to union. Neither French poetry nor the English poetry of the 18th century, so much influenced by France, had, in Arnold's opinion, imagination.

To deprecate the charm and value of Wordsworth's great moments and of the quality which Arnold called the highest poetical quality, would be either obtuse or perverse. And, knowing how a poetic school seems never able to establish itself save on its rejection of its predecessors, we may forgive the early romantic rejection of the poetry of the 18th century. It is, however, not so easy to forgive Arnold for continuing the rejection, for declaring that Dryden and Pope are not real poets at all but only great writers of prose in verse, or for insisting that French poetry had—necessarily, as it were—always failed of greatness. Arnold's perfectly indiscriminate rejection of French poetry had been made as far back as his essay on Heine, but now, beginning with his explanation of why Molière could not be serious, we have it in its full illegitimacy. Just how fallacious it is Émile Legouis has shown in detail in his *Défense De La Poésie Française À L'Usage Des Lecteurs Anglais* and the demonstration need not be repeated. Professor Legouis not only accuses Arnold of being the most insensitive of men in respect to French poetry (and his own sensitivity to English poetry gives him the right to so downright a statement) but even an unfair and sophistical critic, basing his adverse judgments on few and atypical passages and utterly ignoring all that might the most readily appeal to English taste.

The difference that Arnold finds between French poetry and the greatest poetry is on the whole the same that he finds between "genuine poetry" and the poetry of Dryden, Pope and all their school: "their poetry is conceived and composed in their wits, genuine poetry is conceived and composed in the soul." And on this, Mark Van Doren's comment is salutary:

. . . A poem 'conceived in the soul' suggests [for Arnold] a poem conceived in spiritual pain. Arnold's touchstones, if not sentimental, did deal in pain, sad old memories, and death, an atmosphere which Dryden could hardly expect to survive. If there were to be no touchstones ringing with malice, disdain, or merriment, Dryden could lay no claim to a soul. . . . He had written to please hard-headed men of the world; he had labored to satisfy critics of poetry, not critics of soul. He had written genuine poetry, but he was not a Dante.

One wonders why Byron's admiration of Pope did not mean more to Arnold and check him in his headlong career of rejecting the 18th century poets. Byron's defense of Pope has been called a mere perversity but it was no more perverse than his Missolonghi adventure or his attempts to approximate the Greek dramatic form. Like these, it was the manifestation of something very important in him, the thing, indeed, that made Arnold so respect him, the feeling for society and social unity. A similar feeling had animated the great masters of 18th century verse. The common sense for which they strove is often juxtaposed to a nobler and more aspiring vaunt of man's nature, and even characterized as something low and downright cynical. But it had its own aspiration, a social, even a kind of democratic aspiration; the *common* was the *general* sense as against the sense of the mere individual. It was a sense that all qualified men were able to contribute to and understand, and it implied that agreement could be reached by the curtailment and subordination of merely private observation and feelings.

It was, in short, what Arnold, when he had been less cordial to Elizabethan and romantic verse, had so constantly asked for, what he was glad to find in the 18th century even now—but he will not call it poetry. Leslie Stephen, in connection with the dispute whether or no Swift is a poet, called such a problem simply "a question of classification" * but Arnold makes it a question of definition; poetry is what gives Joy. And what *does* give Joy is, of course, a matter of temperament. Proust's dying Bergotte can find the justification of life in a patch of yellow wall in a painting; for others the saying of a small thing well may make human speech and human life important. One suspects that it is not the mark of the greatest sensitivity to see grandeur only in the grand style, that it is a dull solemnity that has called Watteau trivial, that a kind of insensitivity attaches to requiring that all the stops of the transcendental organ be opened before we can be wholly stirred.

Arnold's concern with the greatness of poetry's function, the function of substituting for religion and even for philosophy, made him insist upon the importance of ascertaining the "true rank" of famous writers. Surely literature has become dogma when it becomes as important to grade writers as to make a scriptural canon. Nor can it be a true hierarchy of human values that excludes Rabelais and Molière from the company of Horace and Vergil and Dante; if ranking is to be undertaken it is strange that the roll of the great English poets does not include such names as Marlowe, Jonson, Donne, Marvell, Herbert, Vaughan and Blake.† At the same time it must not be thought that Arnold had no sense of anything else

* The phrase is quoted by Edmund Wilson in a review of Swift's poetry in *The New Republic* of December 8, 1937, a piece which is valuable as showing the high quality of Swift's poetry and interesting as a demonstration of the change of taste since Arnold's day, for Arnold would never have even considered whether Swift was a poet whereas Wilson takes for granted that he is.

† Arnold's roll of "our chief poetical names" is worth repeating as much for what it does include as for what it excludes: Shakespeare, Milton, Spenser, Dryden, Pope, Gray, Goldsmith, Cowper, Burns, Coleridge, Scott, Campbell, Moore, Byron, Shelley, Keats. Arnold seems to be speaking of the degree of establishment and reputation which the poets have achieved rather than his own personal preferences. In a letter of his middle years he had paid his respects to both Vaughan and Herbert.

in poetry than the transcendental tone. He suggests Burns as a corrective to Shelley, rejecting the moralizing Burns for the poet of Tam o' Shanter and the carefree songs. He admires Heine and much else that is racy and comic. He will not, however, "rank" them high; the highest place is reserved for that which is at once the sense of mystery in life and high personal energy—the quality Gray had been deprived of by his *Zeitgeist,* by his living in the age of Pope and not in the age of Elizabeth or of the Revolution, which would have made him one of the greatest of English classics instead of what Arnold says he now is, the "scantiest and frailest."

But Arnold's most heartfelt praise at this period goes not to Byron and not to Wordsworth (nor to Milton, model of the grand style in English) but to George Sand—and perhaps for the very reason that in her he finds the perfect combination of the themes of "Literature and Science" and "The Study of Poetry." As with Byron, there is no thought of George Sand's sexual vagaries; Frederic Harrison might be wearied by her "unwomanly proneness to idealise lust" but Arnold has no word of objection, perhaps only because it could scarcely be polite to impugn the morals of a lady whose guest he had been—or, more likely, because her virtues so far overtopped her vices. More than thirty years after he had seen her at Nohant her memory vibrates through his pages and he writes of her with a full heart. Of the three principal elements of her life, he says, two were of the French Revolution: "the cry of agony and revolt" and "the aspiration towards a purged and renewed human society;" but between the two comes a third and it is what Arnold wanted to add to the Revolution, what he calls here "the trust in nature and beauty." George Sand, almost alone among French writers, had a feeling for nature and "she regarded nature and beauty, not with the selfish and solitary joy of the artist who but seeks to appropriate them for his own purposes, she regarded them as a treasure of immense and hitherto unknown application, as a vast power of healing and delight for all." Even more important, her religion was at one with Arnold's. Having lost all faith in the God of the popular creeds she believes that the loss "is no loss of the religious sense . . . it is quite the contrary, it is a restitution of allegiance to the true Divinity. It is a step made in the direction of this Divinity, it is an abjuration of the dogmas which did him dishonour." Nor, Arnold explains, does she seek to be more precise about this Divinity than Wordsworth had been when he spoke of a "presence that disturbs me with the joy of elevated thoughts."

George Sand had begun her life in revolt—against stupidity, against prudence, convention, aridity. Revolt passed away but not the sentiment that had always animated her: "the sentiment of the ideal life, which is none other than man's normal life as we shall some day know it." If, with this sentiment, George Sand had fired Arnold's youth, with it she also fortified his age. Her passionate idealism, her concern "not with death, but with life," her devotion to bringing about a "social new-birth," her belief that only by the principle of *association* could man live, her faith in the Revolution, her certainty that social change was a religious duty: these affirmations Arnold found, on the occasion of her death, as valid as they had ever been; they were, he said, "the large utterance of the early gods."

And one especial theme of George Sand's Arnold now picked up and made his own. Commenting on a passage in which she spoke of love as the basis of the good social life, Arnold says, "So long as love is thus spoken of in the general, the ordinary serious Englishman will have no difficulty in inclining himself with respect while Madame Sand speaks of it. But when he finds that love implies, with her, social equality, he will begin to be staggered." Against the English fear of equality Arnold now directs the greater part of his philosophic-political effort.

What, he asks, is civilization? and answers: "Civilisation is the humanisation of man in society." Of the means by which man is brought to his humanity the first is what he calls *expansion*. There follow "the power of conduct, the power of intellect and knowledge, the power of beauty, the power of social life and manners." But expansion is first and it consists of Liberty and Equality, against which may be brought many arguments of expedience but which may always be defended by one great fact: that their absence "thwarts a vital instinct, and being thus against nature, is against our humanisation." In his lecture "Equality," before the Royal Institute, he said: "Our present [social] organisation has been an appointed stage in our growth; it has been of good use, and has enabled us to do great things. But the use is at an end, and the stage is over. Ask yourselves if you do not sometimes feel in yourselves a sense, that in spite of the strenuous efforts for good of so many excellent persons amongst us, we begin somehow to flounder and to beat the air; that we seem to be finding ourselves stopped on this line of advance and on that, and to be threatened with a sort of standstill. It is that we are trying to live on with a social organisation of which the day is over. Certainly equality will never of itself alone give us a perfect civilisation. But with such inequality as ours, a perfect civilisation is impossible."

It was no light thing to say in England among the upper classes in 1878, for, as Arnold himself admitted, the preponderance of formulated theory was on the side of inequality and one had but to point to France, her recurrent revolutions and recent defeat, to show the dangers and horrors of equality. Arnold, of course, has his own opinion of the real root of the French troubles: it is not equality but lack of conduct ("You know the French . . ."). Indeed, whatever good there is in France springs from the motivation of the Revolution—which was not philanthropy on the one hand nor envy on the other, but "the spirit of society" which is in effect the spirit of equality; without equality the homogeneity of a society cannot exist and there can be no unembarrassed intercourse among people. The well-being of the many becomes, he says, necessary not only for the happiness of the noble man but necessary for the security of even the ignoble.

With this theme pressed home in almost every piece of writing that could accommodate the idea, it was inevitable that Arnold should turn to the question of property, and with a sharply critical eye. With property as such, Arnold insisted he had no quarrel; he even asserted that its growth and defense had served a necessary end. But with property as a natural right he had no patience whatever; following Sir Henry Maine and John Stuart Mill, he insisted that it was the mere creation of law for the good of the whole. However, the good of the whole, he went on, at the time in which the great accumulations of property had been made, was not the same as the good of the whole now. He had no doubt that inequality of property might, conveniently to the whole, continue; but that the inequality should be enormous "or that the degree of inequality admitted at one time should be admitted *always*" he was certain was not right. And the present degree of inequality of property could only corrupt and materialize the upper class, which enjoyed wealth without function; shutting off the middle and lower classes from the good influences of a free and graceful life, it resulted in a vulgarized middle class and a brutalized lower class.

Yet in some ways Arnold's ideas of equality were rather limited. George Sand's passionate belief in the Revolution was the result of her passionate love for the new French peasant class created by the Revolution. The peasant alone, she believed, had kept his head in the trying days after the war and through the new Empire; she defended him zealously against her liberal Republican friends who blamed him for the abandonment of the war and the establishment of the Empire. Despite the peasant's mistakes she thought him the soundest element in France, far sounder than the liberal parties. And Arnold thought so too—had always thought the French *people* the most alive and the soundest class in France and Europe. The Commune and Zola had brought the "proletaire" class to his notice and it had won his qualified admiration, but France, after all, was still an agricultural and not a manufacturing country; the French working class was still unformed; the class of small holders and small shopkeepers was still, and with some reason, most important in Arnold's eyes.

He brought to his consideration of England this Revolutionary ideal of the small holder, to combat the long tendency toward the amalgamation of the small freehold into great estates. When Arnold spoke of property concentrated in a few hands he usually meant the aristocratic holding of land, the condition that the Real Estate Intestacy Bill had so inadequately attempted to ameliorate. But the property problem that was becoming central to England was no longer so much the land problem as the factory problem, a fact that Arnold does not quite see. Or rather, seeing it, he was kept by his political program from giving it greater importance. With what must be felt to be disinterestedness, Arnold held that the immediate future lay not with the working class but with the middle class. "The master-thought by which my politics are governed," he said, "is . . . this,—the thought of the bad civilisation of the English middle class;" and again: "The great work to be done in this country, and at this hour, is not with the lower class but with the middle." If he defends the working class ideal he has no immediate hope of its realization; if he desires the enlargement of working class life he believes that it depends on the previous enlargement of middle class life and he is perfectly willing to say so to a working class audience. In "Ecce, Convertimur ad Gentes" he explains to his proletarian listeners that the hopes of their class are in every way justified but can be gained only by the middle class developing a civilization into which the workers can "grow." He urges upon them that they undertake to support a policy of State interference in middle class secondary education. That the workers themselves do not possess a secondary education at all is not to the point; they have at least the principle of State interference in their own educational system, however limited the scope of the system may be, and the establishment of the State in middle class schooling will not only create a more enlightened middle class but have the schools ready against the day when more and more workers will take advantage of them. In short, neither the working class nor the middle class is now really fit to bear rule and it is for the working class to legislate the middle class's spiritual reform in order to insure its own spiritual future.

The idea has its quixotic charm, yet we must remember the nature of the schools provided by the State for the lower classes in the late 1870's. H. G. Wells, in *Experiment in Autobiography,* reminds us not only of their low standards but of their strict class character:

He [i. e., Geoffrey West, Wells' biographer] probably considers the National Schools were "democratic" schools, like the common schools of the United States, "all class" schools, but that is a mistaken view. In spirit, form and intention they were inferior schools, and to send one's children to them in those days, as my mother understood perfectly well, was a definite and final acceptance of social inferiority. The Education Act of 1871 was not an Act for a common universal education, it was an Act to educate the lower classes for employment on lower-class lines, and with specially trained, inferior teachers who had no university quality.

Mr. Wells also gives us a description of the middle class academy he had previously attended; it was pretty bad, an enlightening supplement to the example of Dotheboys Hall which for Arnold was a fair enough representation of the level of middle class training. But Mr. Wells, with realistic understanding of class disabilities, preferred it to the National Schools. "The more ancient middle-class schools, whatever their faults, were saturated with the spirit of individual self-reliance and individual dignity . . . I think it was a very lucky thing for me personally that I acquired this much class feeling."

But certainly, though Arnold might put off the working class future it was not out of admiration for the middle class. If Dotheboys Hall and Mr. Creakle represented middle class education, Mr. Murdstone and Miss Murdstone represented the middle class culture, religion and way of life, and to them Arnold had no idea of trusting anyone's future. He knew perfectly well that one of the last English illusions is that "one class is capable of properly speaking for another." He knew too that "free political institutions do not guarantee the well-being of the toiling class." He knew that with the

Murdstone-class of manufacturers rested the moral responsibility for the creation of the "hell-holes" of the manufacturing towns, the responsibility for the overproduction of cheap stuff and the subsequent abandonment of the enterprises, the sudden unemployment, the privation. His conception of the whole process is perfectly realistic: "And perhaps," he says, "these capitalists have had time to make their fortunes; but meanwhile they have not made the fortunes of the clusters of men and women whom they have called into being to produce for them, and whom they have . . . as good as begotten."

And upon the righteous Puritanism of the Murdstones and upon the conception of the human mind framed by Creakle he places the responsibility for much of the English policy in regard to Ireland. The Irish problem fascinated him, as it had his father, and as well it might with the Home Rule question stirring Parliament yearly and his own brother-in-law, William Forster, going out to Ireland as Chief Secretary and serving none too successfully in a post in which success was clearly impossible, but being rather more of a failure than necessary because he based his action on the belief that all the trouble was being caused by a few "village ruffians" whom time and police could quell. Arnold had profounder views than "K's" husband. The Murdstones and Creakles, he knew, had to be shown that nothing was to be gained by their perpetual religious antagonism to the Irish, their refusal to provide proper education for fear it might be turned to Catholic account. But he believed that the basic problem of Ireland was to be solved economically and only by the creation of a class of freeholding farmers through the gradual expropriation of the great estates, the better landlords to be bought out over a long period, the worse over a punitively shorter period. With a superb carelessness he brushes aside the indignation such a suggestion raises. No one, he said, looks with horror on the English confiscation of Irish lands in the first place, and the landowners of England regard with the greatest complacency Henry VIII's expropriation of the monastic orders. Both acts are accepted now as having been done for reasons of state, and it is mere "pedantry" not to see that a present expropriation is justifiable for the same reason. "Let us beware," he says in the essay, "Copyright," in which he finds the whole copyright situation anomalous but in which nothing is more anomalous than the argument offered by those who would revise the law, that an author has a natural right to, and a property in, his work,—"Let us beware of this metaphysical phantom of property in itself, which, like other metaphysical phantoms, is hollow and leads us to delusion. Property is the creation of law."

He found the justification of his position on property in the teachings of religion. "In this practical country of ours, where possessing property and estate is so loved, and losing them so hated, the opposition to [Christian charity] is almost as strong as that to Christian purity in France. The *Saturday Review* is in general respectful to religion, intelligent and decorous, in matters of literary and scientific criticism reasonable. But let it imagine property and privilege threatened, and instantly what a change! There seems to rise before one's mind's eye a sort of vision of an elderly demoniac, surrounded by a troop of younger demoniacs of whom he is the owner and guide, all of them suddenly foaming at the mouth and crying out horribly. The attachment to property and privilege is so strong, the fear of losing them so agitating." And against this frenzied imagination of frenzy, Arnold sets the teachings of Jesus on riches.

He called himself a Liberal but he stipulated "Liberal of the future." The distinction for him was chiefly in the positive and creative quality that the Liberalism of the future must have; the Liberalism of his conception might have for its motto Ruskin's "There is no wealth but life." Life, he believed, must be affirmative, interesting, complete, human. He thought that Carlyle's prescription to substitute "blessedness" for happiness was a mere eccentricity, just as he thought that Bishop Butler's conception of freedom from pain as the end of human life was a mere formalism; the true fulfilment of life was Joy. He knows that the days of aristocracy and conservatism are over; he can praise the simple loyalty of the young officer who died in a Zulu war but he knows that the future does not belong to simplicity, loyalty and faith but to knowledge, intelligence and lucidity; he knows that disasters as well as victories have been prepared on the playing fields of Eton. He knows too, what in *Culture and Anarchy* one was not sure he knew, that Order is not Liberty: "Order is a most excellent thing, and true liberty is impossible without it; but order is not itself liberty, and an appeal to the love of order is not a direct appeal to the love of liberty, to the instinct for expansion." And to Liberalism he looks for the satisfaction of the instinct of expansion but only to a Liberalism which can perceive and understand *all* the parts and powers of expansion and serve them all.

II

He loved passionately all growing things. The bearing of his fruit trees, the flowering of his roses, were the family's great events. Whether in the meadows near Harrow or in the Italian woods or in an American swamp, he sought for and found the leaves and roots he was always reading about, and his letters are filled with their names: pellitory, tansy, pennywort, mugwort, wild parsnip, sheep's parsley, *Ruta muraria, Helianthus giganteus, Phytolacca, Monotropa Uniflora*. The heavy fall of snow that weighed down his evergreens or the gale that ripped his cork trees and twisted his hollies were domestic disasters. With less passion and more warmth he loved animals; poor Matthias, the canary, and Geist, the dachshund, were celebrated in elegies; Geist's place was taken by Max and Kaiser, "the dear men," the "dear, dear little boy." Atossa, named out of Aeschylus, was the Persian cat; there was also a Rover and a sudden, straying affection for a little French dog, Patou, presumably superior to the rest of his race in being a model of conduct. Lola was the pony who died of old age; "there was something in her character which I particularly liked and admired."

Fishing was a passion too, partly for the paraphernalia but mostly

for the solitude and the success. He could get rid of a cold by taking off his shoes and wading five hours in the cold stream as he
fished. Shooting was not quite so successful and it brought certain
compunctions. He played lawn tennis for his children's sake and
skated for his own; when, after sixty, his heart began to tell on
him and he suffered severe pains across his chest, he gave up cutting
figures and skating backward but whenever the ice was good he
skated forward. He liked champagne and found it doleful to be put
by his physician on a small glass of brandy-and-water a day.

He rose with the daylight but when the light came too late he
rose at six and used the gas. He worked on his Hebrew continually,
made a point of reading half an hour of Greek before dinner and in
freer times went through five pages a day of the Greek Anthology,
looking up all the words he did not know: "this is what I shall
always understand by *education,* and it does me good, and gives me
great pleasure." He continued to make New Year's resolutions and
until his death set down in his pocket diary a curriculum of reading
for the year. To finish a piece of writing, he might sit up until
after five in the morning.

The old sense of passing time does not leave him: so much to be
done and will it ever be done? But after sixty, he said, he regarded
each year as it ended as something to the good and beyond what he
could naturally have expected. Confronted with the pessimism of
Vergil on old age, he turned to the fortification of Wordsworth.

In 1873, his mother died, aged eighty-two. She had gone along
with her husband in his religious views and made every effort to go
along with her son in his. "It will be a long time," Arnold wrote to
his sister Fan, "before you feel of your grief, as you look out on the
hills and the fern and the trees and the waters,

> It seems an idle thing, which could not live
> Where meditation was—

and yet that is undoubtedly the right thing to feel, and that the
thought of dearest mamma should be simply a happy memory and

not a gnawing regret. But one cannot say that dear old Wordsworth succeeded in complying with his own teaching when he lost Dora. Perhaps he was too old and had not his strength and spirits enough left to him. But he was right in his preaching for all that, and not in his practice."

Carlyle died in 1881: "I never much liked Carlyle." In the same year Arthur Stanley died; the living connections with his past were vanishing. "Westminster Abbey" appeared in 1882, Arnold's last-published poem; many called it, as they had "Thyrsis," but a cold memorial. "However, one can only do these things in one's own way."

He is more and more at home with himself and his nation. In middle life he believes that his poetical turn will come, as Browning's and Tennyson's came; for his poetry, he believes, represents "the main movement of mind of the last quarter of a century," and he thinks that if he has less poetical sentiment than Tennyson and less intellectual vigor than Browning, he has more of the fusion of the two. And he is right in his prediction; he tinkers with new editions, puts off Swinburne, who wants "The New Sirens" restored to the canon—best wait for a posthumous edition—and people find, as George Eliot did, that his poetry grows on them. In 1878 he can note that the public is taking his poetry to its bosom. Oxford honors him with a D.C.L. though he will not allow himself to be called Dr. Arnold; he is offered a magistracy for the county of Middlesex and refuses, is offered the Lord Rectorship of St. Andrew's University and refuses; a new term as Professor of Poetry is urged upon him in 1877, and, fearing a religious squabble and believing a younger man should have the chance, he refuses. The suggestion is repeated in 1885, with a memorial from the undergraduates and another from the heads and tutors: "Everyone is very kind as one grows old."

More and more his sense of his own influence grows. Disraeli flatters him with quotations from his work, and Arnold, despite himself, consents to be flattered by the praise of a man who is still a dandy. Gladstone is angry at the author of *Literature and Dogma* but even Gladstone grows cordial. "I am really surprised myself at the testimonies I continually receive to the influence which my writings are gaining." John Morley may be a Liberal but he "has certainly learnt something from me, and knows it." He is everywhere quoted in the daily and religious press; he is parodied by Mallock and less skillful hands; he is caricatured. Royalty on the Continent attends to him; Princess Alice of Darmstadt learns by heart whole passages of *Culture and Anarchy;* on the other hand, Vicky, Princess of Prussia, has no patience with Mr. Arnold. His name might be dangerous among some sects and among the most rigorously orthodox of the Church, but a man like Andrew Carnegie makes him his guide in religion as Herbert Spencer was his guide in philosophy. It is a "gratifying marvel, considering what things I have published," but he dines with the Archbishop of Canterbury. He speaks, he says, for the "quiet and simple" people; why should he not make his way?

Yet however much the quiet and simple people may read his books they do not buy them sufficiently to keep him from money worries. In 1870 the Income Tax Commission assessed him 1000 pounds on book profits. "You see before you, gentlemen," he said to the Commissioners, "what you have often heard of, *an unpopular author.*" The assessment was cut to 200 pounds; Arnold said that he would have to write a great many more articles to meet even that; the Chairman bowed and said, "Then the public will have reason to be much obliged to us." In 1882 he speaks of an income of 1000 pounds from the school system but he has daughters, and he wants to retire. True, the grind of inspecting has been made bearable by taking the problems of education into the very heart of his thought; in time he got what he called the perfect district: the teachers subordinate to him loved him and, after all, he said, in what other country would a Minister have exhorted his subordinate to write more poetry, as A. J. Mundella * exhorted him? Still—"I have no

* The Vice-President of the Committee of Council on Education.

wish to execute the Dance of Death in an elementary school," he writes to John Morley and subscribes himself "Ever yours, till the execution of the D. of D." He believed Gladstone would never promote the author of *Literature and Dogma*. To be sure, in 1883 Gladstone did offer (perhaps at the instance of Morley) a pension of 250 pounds as a "public recognition of service to the poetry and literature of England;" Arnold hesitated until the insistence of his friends prevailed. But even the pension did not sufficiently augment an income that would be considerably reduced by retirement. In 1883 he considered and agreed to a lecture tour of America.

It was a dramatic decision for Arnold, and for America. He was to be one of the many foreigners who, dropped into the uneasy brew of American culture, could make it boil and seethe and precipitate strange things. Interest in his work had been of slow growth on the other side of the Atlantic; Henry James had been almost his only passionate admirer, surely a guarantee of his countrymen's indifference. And it was not until Arnold's foray into theology that America's attention was attracted to his poetical, his critical and his political work; by 1883, however, America was ready for him.

Arnold had always been ready for America: almost too ready. America had been for him a symbol and at times an obsession. Say what he might about the dangers of judging from a distance, say what he might about the necessity for discounting the absolute tone of Tocqueville, he knew what America was—raw and conceited and vulgar and grasping and dull and commercial and Philistine and prostrate before bunkum. He knew many things that were true and collected them into a courteous essay, "A Word about America" (1882); he knew that the hold of dissenting and eccentric religion was strong; he had learned from a book by a Miss Bird that the pioneer life, so frequently romanticized, might be a long, depressed misery, engendering ill-temper and intolerance; he knew from the novels of Howells and from the novels and conversation of James that the Philistine was strong in the land; that the "class of gentlemen" (which had brought so much credit to the English in

India) was lacking; that education, though widespread, was more pretentious than effective. But he also thought that the humor of Mark Twain was the humor of Quinion, Murdstone's agent, and the lighter side of Philistinism. Even after he met Mark Twain and fell under his spell, he asked, "But is he *never* serious?" He had to be told, "Mr. Arnold, he is the most serious man in the world." With Mark Twain closed off from him, there was surely much of America he could never see.* For Arnold America was, or should be, the America of Crèvecoeur's letters and Thomas Jefferson's dream, the America of the small holder and cultivator. Americans, he insisted, were "the English on the other side of the Atlantic." Even after his visit, the idea of speaking of an *American* literature was for him an absurd provincialism, almost a blasphemy.

But just as Arnold knew what America was—or should be—so America knew what Arnold was—or should be. He was culture, and he was suspicion of democracy; he was amenity, urbanity, the Church of England and aristocratic manners. Whitman's America, Mark Twain's America, Howells' and Norton's and Holmes' America, Artemus Ward's and Josh Billings' America, all the James' America, James Whitcomb Riley's America, Carnegie's and Vanderbilt's and Grant's America—they wanted this prophet of culture and lay in wait for him. They lusted for the best of Europe at the same time they despised it. Cambridge, Concord, all the college towns of New England; New York with its exclusive clubs and great crowds; the Middle West with its state universities and land-grant colleges,

---

* Speaking, in "A Word about America," about the Quinonian humor and undertaking to show how it is not specifically American but Philistine, he quotes from an Australian paper the following description of an Italian opera singer: "Barring his stomach, he is the finest-looking artist I have seen on the stage for years; and if he don't slide into the affections or break the gizzards of half our Sydney girls, it's a pretty certain sign there's a scarcity of balm in Gilead." Arnold comments: "This is not Mark Twain, not an American humorist at all. . . ." But who that knew Mark Twain's manner could suppose that this wordy pointlessness was his humor?

However, it must be remembered that Mark Twain's reputation had been made by *Innocents Abroad,* a book undeniably and intentionally "Philistine." Still, *Roughing It,* the first half of *Life on the Mississippi,* and *Tom Sawyer* had appeared when Arnold wrote and one suspects that even *Huckleberry Finn* would not have appeased Arnold. What he would have thought of Oxford's conferring of the Litt. D. degree on Mark Twain in 1907 makes amusing conjecture.

with its stockyards and river cities; Richmond with its poverty and its vestiges of English customs: all these were the America that awaited the English writer. But which America was the real America and how did one speak to it? Both during his visit and after, the visitor comported himself with poise, dignity and friendliness. Yet, after one has been understood by the sensible people, how should one not be made rather ridiculous, with Maggie pulling one way and Jiggs the other? *

With his wife and his daughter Lucy, Arnold sailed from Liverpool in October on the Cunard liner, *Servia,* and was met at the New York pier by Andrew Carnegie and his secretary. The first few days were exhilarating and exhausting. There were interviews with the press, the American press that Arnold came so to despise and with such good personal reason. † Carnegie gave a party at which General Grant, Theodore Dwight and Dr. Damrosch were

* Dr. Chilson Leonard—to whose admirable *Matthew Arnold in America,* a manuscript dissertation in the Sterling Memorial Library of Yale University, I am indebted for much of the material of this section—quotes (from the *Jersey City Journal* of December 31, 1883) an account of the meeting of the Jersey City Aesthetic Club which admirably illustrates the Maggie aspect of American culture. After Mrs. Smith, the president, had opened the meeting with an address, the Meigs Sisters, quartet, sang "God Save the King," Miss Henrietta Markstein rendered a piano solo—"Old Black Joe" with variations—and "not a sound or movement in the audience until the last note had died away." Then Arnold was introduced as the "most distinguished aesthetician of the age." Mr. Arnold delivered his lecture. Mrs. Studwell sang "The Star-Spangled Banner," the audience joining; Chief Justice Shea of New York was introduced and made a neat speech in which he referred to meeting Mr. Arnold in Oxford. Mrs. Studwell sang "Within a Mile of Edinburgh Town." Mr. Arnold left. The Meigs Sisters sang "Little Jack Horner;" Miss Markstein played "Pretty Girl Milking Cow" and "The Girl I Left Behind Me" (both with variations). Mr. Lincoln did imitations of Mr. Irving and Miss Terry, showing how each would play the Tragedy of Cock Robin. "There were present during the afternoon many people who stand high in the New York world of letters, art and music."

† Dr. Leonard's study makes very clear how restrained was Arnold's response to the American press. There were, to be sure, many instances of journalistic kindness but also a great deal of brash ungenerosity. The climax came after Arnold's departure, with the New York *Tribune's* hoax of the Chicago *Tribune* in revenge for the latter's stealing the former's cable dispatches. The New York paper trapped its Chicago namesake by printing a special edition in which it published a summary—with "quotations"— of an essay by Arnold which severely criticized Chicago. Arnold had written no such essay, which was the point of the hoax, for the Chicago *Tribune* took the bait, reported the "essay," which it could have known only through the New York *Tribune,* and denounced Arnold ferociously. Arnold, of course, denied authorship of the "essay" and the case of the New York *Tribune* was proved. The Chicago *Tribune* sought to brazen it out and carried headlines: "Arnold denies; Mr. Medill [the editor and an

present. What seems first to have interested Americans on meeting this English prophet of culture was his lack of refinement. John Burroughs records the impression of a "large, coarse, but pure mouth" —"in fact, a much coarser looking man than you would expect." H. C. Bunner found Arnold downright common,—like a bricklayer or perhaps the leader of a strikers' delegation; one of the chief difficulties was with Arnold's trousers, baggy in the fashion of Lincoln. The note of coarseness is heard again and again; there is a certain beef-eating quality in this man Arnold, or perhaps a certain Jewish strain—? If Oscar Wilde is culture, can this redfaced man be culture too?

As Arnold toured the country on his gruelling one-night stands, the feeling grew that here was Europe in America's toil-worn, honest clutches; and perhaps Europe was not so much after all; surely she was fair game. Arnold became both a fad and a myth. It scarcely mattered what he said or was: here was something for the rugged virtues of America to test themselves upon. New England might take him to its heart (and thus increase the interest and hostility of the West) but even New England was not wholly pleased. Miss Emerson found nothing painful in the Emerson lecture, which sought to establish Emerson by giving up "to envious Time as much of Emerson as Time can fairly expect ever to obtain," but there were many who resented this certain condescension in the foreigner. The American feeling that criticism implies hostility asserted itself; there grew up a legend of Arnold's bad manners: it was a simple and cheap revenge.

Everyone has heard the story of Arnold's pointing to a plate of pancakes and saying to his wife, "Do try one, my dear, they are not nearly so nasty as they look." But Dr. Leonard has found the story told, as at first hand, by a score of hostesses and he concludes that it is apocryphal. Dr. Leonard also cites the tale of Arnold's being

---

acquaintance of Arnold's] refuses to accept Arnold's disclaimer; says Arnold is a cur." Arnold refers to the incident in his "Civilization in the United States," and Dr. Leonard gives it in detail in his *Matthew Arnold in America.*

given an honorary degree by the University of Pennsylvania and refusing to utter a public word in reply until paid. "But where is the honorarium?" he asked, and the cash had to be raised. But as Dr. Leonard points out, Arnold never received a degree from the University, did not speak there until his second visit to America, and was then paid, in regular course, by regular arrangement, a check for a hundred dollars which he acknowledged in a gracious note. Still, it was increasingly whispered about that Arnold was a difficult and arrogant guest.* America, proud of having culture, proud of having no culture, watched him with sharp eyes; his whiskers, his eyeglass, his clothes, his accent, his complexion, all came under scrutiny and comment. The knowledge that he had come to the country to make money gave a handle to irritation—that handle by which America can always lay hold of the foreign lecturer who comes to talk about things of the spirit; the attitude of Arnold's managers, apparently no more than business-like, added to the irritation. James Whitcomb Riley met Arnold on the train to Binghamton, N. Y. and found significant the care with which Arnold stowed away his 2¢ change from a 3¢ newspaper; he admits that Arnold is poor but he finds the gesture distressing enough to make him say, " 'Tis very good to be an American."

And Arnold was cold; one wanted, said the Detroit *News,* to poke him in the ribs and say, "Hello Matt! Won't you have suthin'?" This friendly desire was perhaps what Arnold reprobated in democracy, its fear of distinction and its loss of the discipline of respect. But there was something else implied for Americans by Arnold and Walt Whitman stated it.

Not that it carries perfect conviction, even as Whitman stated it. For one thing, Whitman overstated it. Arnold, said the American poet, was "one of the dudes of literature;" he brought coals to New-

* When, after Arnold's death, the publication of his letters brought to light his belief that he had breakfasted at Andover on, among other and more reasonable things, hashed veal and mince pie, Andover, believing that it was being slandered, denied categorically the veal and pie and was very angry. "Andover is still angry," says Dr. Leonard.

castle, for the world "is rich, hefted, lousy, reeking, with delicacy, refinement, elegance, prettiness, propriety, criticism, analysis: all of them things which threaten to overwhelm us." "Vellum?" said Whitman, refusing that material for the binding of a new edition, "pshaw! hangings, curtains, finger-bowls, chinaware, Matthew Arnold!" The essay on Heine was the only one of Arnold's writings he could stomach; for the rest, "I accept the world—most of the world—but somehow draw the line somewhere on some of those fellows;" those fellows were the "great army of critics, parlor apostles, worshippers of hangings, laces, and so forth and so forth—they never have anything properly at first hand," and Arnold led them. For another thing, Whitman was probably personal in his animosity. For when W. D. O'Connor, his fiery friend, tried to make a cause of Whitman's dismissal from the Indian Department for the publication of *Leaves of Grass*, he had sent Whitman's volumes, together with his own pamphlet, *The Good Gray Poet*, to leading writers of America and Europe, to Arnold among them. But Arnold refused to be exercised over the dismissal. "I have read your statement with interest," he wrote, "and I do not contest Mr. Walt Whitman's powers and originality. I doubt, however, whether here, too, or in France, or in Germany, a public functionary would not have had to pay for the pleasure of being so outspoken the same penalty which your friend has paid in America." Whitman might have forgiven this, but not this:

As to the general question of Mr. Walt Whitman's poetical achievements, you will think that it savours of our decrepit old Europe when I add that while you think it his highest merit that he is so unlike anyone else, to me this seems to be his demerit; no one can afford in literature to trade merely on his own bottom and to take no account of what the other ages and nations have acquired: a great original literature America will never get in this way, and her intellect must inevitably consent to come, in a considerable measure, into the European movement. That she may do this and yet be an independent intellectual power, not merely as you say an intellectual colony of Europe, I cannot doubt; and it is on her doing this, and not on her displaying an eccentric and violent originality that wise Americans should in my opinion set their desires.

It is therefore not surprising that Whitman, the perfect Bohemian, saw Arnold as—the perfect Philistine! Yet apart from the misconceptions and the exaggerations that inhere in his estimate, Whitman saw something that had to be seen. In part he stated it in an article in *The Critic* in which he warned Arnold (and Lord Coleridge, who was in America at the same time) that not in the institutional and the polite would he see the truth about America, but in the factories and foundries and crowds. One of his outbursts to Traubel carried the truth a little further: "Arnold always gives you the notion that he hates to touch the dirt—the dirt is so dirty! But everything comes out of the dirt—everything: everything comes out of the people, the everyday people, the people as you find them and leave them: not university people, not F.F.V. people: people, people, just people!" Discount as much as we will of Whitman's "optimism," as he calls it, about democracy, there is point in the accusation. It was the *just people* aspect of life that Arnold could never get; he missed the right perception of that world which has always existed and perhaps always will exist, which no Utopia, no State, no culture, no rule of superior intelligence, no progress, will—or should—ever get rid of: life warm, mistaken, silly, but the "dirt" out of which things grow. Arnold, baffled by that life in Shakespeare, had never truly learned the nature of tragedy, just as, essentially indifferent to it in Chaucer, Molière and Rabelais, he had never truly learned the nature of comedy.

Arnold had come to America armed with three lectures, a rewritten and expanded version of the Rede Lecture, "Literature and Science," which he had delivered at Cambridge in 1882; "Emerson" which gave him great difficulty and which he did not finish until after his arrival; and "Numbers." It was by these three lectures, collected in *Discourses in America,* that Arnold said he wished to be remembered. "Numbers" was the first lecture delivered in New York and it was not a success. Chickering Hall was larger than any auditorium Arnold had ever spoken in and he could not be heard; the audience, unused to the British intonation and perhaps distracted by the eyeglass, could not make out what he was saying. There were cries of "Can't hear you," and "Louder," and after a while people began to leave, General Grant among them, disappointed that a British lion should roar so inaudibly. Mrs. Carnegie told Arnold that his voice was too ministerial, Mr. Carnegie suggested instruction in elocution. The problem of audibility was present through most of the tour, though after some coaching, by an Andover professor, in the trick of keeping his voice up, Arnold felt that he had improved.

The lecture itself was in many ways a curious performance, intended both to flatter American self-esteem and to make it question itself. Its subtitle is "The Majority and the Remnant" and its thesis is that while neither the propertied classes nor the intellectual classes can be trusted to be sound and while it is good and educative for the people to legislate for itself, yet the majority cannot be the hope of the nation; that hope inevitably lies only in the righteous "remnant." And, by a strange mathematics, Arnold goes on to show how remnants have hitherto been powerless because too small, but that in America the great numbers of the population may produce a greater remnant than history has yet known; the question of proportion does not disturb him:

It is said that the Athenian State had in all but 350,000 inhabitants. It is calculated that the population of the kingdom of Judah did not exceed a million and a quarter. The scale of things, I say, is here too small, the numbers are too scanty, to give us a remnant capable of saving and perpetuating the community. . . . [But] how different is the scale of things in the modern States to which we belong, how far greater are the numbers! It is impossible to overrate the importance of the new element introduced into our calculations by increasing the size of the remnant. And in our great modern States, where the scale of things is so large, it does seem as if the remnant might be so increased as to become an actual power, even though the majority be unsound.

America, Arnold continues, has the right to great hopes because of its English Puritan tradition. He points to France, lying prostrate before the Goddess Aselgeia, the average sensual man dominant, his grandiloquence exemplified by Victor Hugo, his "going near the ground" exemplified by Zola; and there is Renan being chaste for no better reasons than those of personal delicacy, believing as he did that moral lightness does not become one who has been bred up a priest, but denying too that nature has any regard for chastity, not remembering what Plato had said about lubricity, not knowing that "hardness and insolence come in its train; an insolence which grows until it ends by exasperating and alienating everybody; a hardness which grows until the man can at last scarcely take pleasure in anything, outside the service of his goddess, except cupidity and greed, and cannot be touched with emotion by any language except fustian. Such are the fruits of the worship of the great goddess Aselgeia." Of course, what chiefly caught America was the questioning of the rightness of the majority; the more or less subtle modulations of the lecture were largely overlooked. Nevertheless Barnum was convinced that he wanted to be of the remnant and invited Arnold to stop with him when he lectured at Bridgeport; Arnold accepted.

From New York Arnold went on to Boston, to which by tradition, temperament and old association he felt much closer. Oliver Wendell Holmes, who presided at his first Boston lecture, Charles Eliot Norton, Emerson's family, all represented old ties and a reflection of his own culture. He toured the small cities and the college towns of New England which gave him his best audiences.

He had missed Howells in Boston but found him in Hartford, visiting Mark Twain. "Oh, but he doesn't like *that* sort of thing, does he?" Arnold had asked when he had been told where Howells might be reached. And he had been answered, presumably with some asperity, "He likes Mr. Clemens very much, and he thinks him one of the greatest men he ever knew." Howells and Clemens went to meet Arnold at the reception given for him. "Who—who in the world is that?" Arnold asked, indicating a red head, streaked with gray. "Oh, that is Mark Twain," Howells replied, and reports that when the two men were introduced, Arnold stayed, fascinated, by Clemens' side all evening and the next night was at his house for dinner.

Boston was invaded again, then Brooklyn, Princeton, New Haven and more college towns. At Cambridge it was found that Sanders Theatre could not be used for money-making purposes; the admissions were turned back and instead of lecturing, Arnold read his poems; it was not a very successful performance and many students left. Young Gamaliel Bradford, introduced by Dr. Holmes, called on Arnold at Shady Hill, Norton's home. The meeting was amusing and eventually touching. Bradford was one of the many whom Arnold was always to haunt; for some years before he had been a devoted admirer. The interview, as Bradford recorded it in his journal that night, went nicely; Bradford advised against giving the Emerson lecture in Concord; Arnold was "English in manner, but exceedingly cordial, and with that sort of deference to your opinions which is always delightful, and which I did not expect from him." There is, to be sure, a slight reservation; meeting Arnold now, Bradford says, does not mean quite as much as it would have meant when he was younger (he is twenty); but many years later, Bradford faced the truth of that interview. He writes to discourage a young man from seeking personal meetings with celebrities: "I remember many, many years ago, when I was much younger than you are, getting an introduction to Matthew Arnold, whom I had read and adored for a number of years. Our talk amounted to nothing. He did not get at me and I was disillusioned with him. When I finally left him, he patted my shoulder and remarked paternally, 'What is the age?' Matthew Arnold has never meant so much to me since."

From New England Arnold went on to tour the upper South and the Midwest. In Washington he was entertained by Henry Adams and he dined with the historian Bancroft; his lecture was unceremoniously turned into a debate by a couple of legislative spirits. He

liked Richmond; the old English customs were still to be found and
he had always wanted the South to secede, much as he had reprobated the Southern cause, because he had disliked the Northern culture and thought that a rival nation might purify it; he found the
segregation of Negro children in the public schools distressing. The
Midwest was inclined to resist him; he had a relatively unhappy
time and in Cleveland John Hay, unknown to Arnold, bought out
the unsold tickets and distributed them; Arnold was impressed by
the size of his audience. From Cleveland he went to Toronto, and,
touring Canada, found that he would rather be a poor priest in
Quebec than a rich hog-merchant in Chicago. He angered the Catholics of Montreal by asking them to acquire a greater liberalism.

Arnold sailed from America on March 9, 1884. He had made some
$6,000, not quite all he had anticipated, but enough. His last days
in New York had been made very pleasant; people warmed to him
and his speech at the Author's Club touched everyone who heard it.
His daughter's engagement to an American had created new ties
with America and on the whole he was inclined to regard the trip as
a pleasant and instructive one. Politically he had found America
more admirable than he had expected. The American institutions
seemed so efficient that he retracted his early characterization of all
institutions as "machinery." He found the division between the
Federal government and the government of the various states an excellent device, proving the possibility of a larger measure of local
self-government for England and Ireland, a reform which, in his
view, should supplement and mitigate the centralization of the
strong State. He thought the homogeneity of the American people
the chief source of their strength; the absence of sharply distinguished classes made the danger of revolution almost non-existent.
He believed that wealth did not constitute class in America (Andrew
Carnegie could not but have convinced him of this) and he was
sure that wealth did not breed hatred as it did in France, not only
because the condition of men was less fixed, but because the Americans did not worship the Goddess Lubricity. "Wealth excites the

most savage enmity [in France]," he said, "because it is conceived as a means for gratifying appetites of the most selfish and vile kind. . . . Wealth [in America] is no more conceived as the minister to the pleasures of a class of rakes, than as the minister to the magnificence of a class of nobles [as in England]. It is conceived as a thing which almost any American may attain, and which almost every American will use respectably. Its possession, therefore, does not inspire hatred." *

The homogeneity of the egalitarian Americans supported Arnold's old belief in the evils of inequality and of an aristocracy; here perhaps Carnegie's influence was felt again, for Carnegie loved to rail at the British monarchy and aristocracy (which privately he liked). At any rate, Arnold returned to England to tell his countrymen that the British government would never be clear-sighted until it was purged of its titles; he suggested that, without confiscation or expropriation, all titles end at the death of the present holder, but he knew there was no likelihood of the proposal being taken seriously.

Yet, if America had solved the political problem, it was, Arnold believed, far from having solved the human problem. He had found, for one thing, that America was not at all comfortable for the class of gentlemen, for the people with incomes of 300–400 pounds to 1500 pounds a year. All luxuries were dear, cabs and tailors, for example, and almost everything except ice, fruit (which was inferior to the English) and oysters. Yet working clothes and plain food were cheaper than in England and the American working man could afford ice and fruit. He had liked the social equality, had liked the universal use of "Mr." and the indifference to the meaningless medi-

* Charles and Mary Beard agree with Arnold that class feeling in America in the 1880's was not acrimonious; see *The Rise of American Civilization*, vol. II, p. 395. However, if Arnold's "respectably" is to be an accurate word, it must be interpreted in the very narrowest sense of sexual respectability. The Beards' account of the habits and manners of American wealth toward the end of the last century, or a more detailed history such as Dixon Wecter's *The Saga of American Society: A Record of Social Aspirations, 1607–1937*, presents a picture of conspicuous consumption, costly snobbery and vulgarity which make open sexual debauch preferable as a more living thing. And surely the political and economic conduct of the financial barons was far from "respectable."

eval "frippery" of the invidious *Esquire:* "I only hope they will persevere, and not be seduced by *Esquire* being 'so English, you know.' " He had liked the natural manners of the American women, which he attributed to the lack of the aristocracy which makes English women of the middle class self-conscious.*

Still, he could not find American civilization interesting: it lacked, he said, distinction and beauty. The lack of the sense of beauty, he thought, came chiefly from the restlessness of the people which drew them from their homes and kept them from sinking deep roots into the soil and from giving to rural life the sense of tradition and permanence which is its charm. "If we in England were without the cathedrals, parish churches, and castles of the catholic and feudal age, and without the houses of the Elizabethan age, but had only the towns and buildings which the rise of our middle class has created in the modern age, we should be in much the same case as the Americans. We should be living with much the same absence of training for the sense of beauty through the eye, from the aspect of outward things." This had been a great part of the complaint of Henry James. The very names of the American towns—the Briggsvilles and Higginsvilles on the one hand, the Uticas and Syracuses on the other—he noted and loathed, but his ear was not caught by the great sonorous names which have delighted American poets: Susquehanna, Shenandoah, Monongahela.

The lack of "distinction" he attributed in large part to the American newspapers which destroyed the nation's "discipline of awe and respect." He speaks in a letter of the craving for publicity that characterized Americans, even some of the best of them. He can find in

---

* But Arnold cites a Parisian doctor who had isolated a nervous disease of wealthy or comfortable American women, occasioned by their worries over their servant problems. The former Mrs. Harry Lehr, in *"King Lehr" and the Gilded Age,* tells us that Mrs. Stuyvesant Fish "never had time for anything; it was her constant cry. She was always quoting [Arnold's] lines:
'Her life was turning, turning,
In mazes of heat and sound,
But for peace her soul was yearning
And now peace laps her round.'
Her husband had them inscribed on her gravestone." (p. 162).

American history few men fit to inspire respect by their natural distinction—Hamilton and Washington, perhaps, but they were pre-American; * not Lincoln, despite all his shrewdness, sagacity, humor, honesty, courage and firmness. The ubiquitous praise of "the average man," the adulation of the "funny man"—that "national misfortune"—were fatal to distinction.

Arnold returned to England, to work and to "horrid pains across my chest." He is dieted, he gives up hills and lawn-tennis but not fishing. The pains do not go away. "I cannot get rid of the ache across my chest when I walk; imagine my having to stop half a dozen times in going up to Pains Hill! † What a mortifying change. But so one draws to one's end." The strain of the American trip, the accumulated strain of years of hard traveling have begun to tell on him. But in October 1885 he was asked to visit Berlin and Paris to get information about free schools, and he was delighted to go. His German was rusty and in Berlin he brushed up with lessons from an "excellent old man (born in the same year as myself)." The Crown Prince and Princess of Prussia invited him to call and at Dresden he had an interview with the King of Saxony. Perhaps more interesting was the meeting with Mommsen, who, he reported, was "in manner, mode of speech, and intellectual quality something between Voltaire and Newman," surely a difficult and fascinating state of being. He returned to Cobham for Christmas, skated and had no pain and went back to Germany. He heard *Tristan and Isolde:* saw it, he says; he found Wagner's stories interesting but the music meant little to him and he believed that he had managed the Tristan story better. In Hamburg he had great pleasure from the Burgomeister, "who has really and truly the title of 'Your Magnificence' . . . I am really quite glad to have called a man 'Your Magnificence' and to have been asked to dinner by him;" in America he had been righteously rebuked by Mr. Carnegie because he wanted to meet Mr.

* It is interesting, in view of Arnold's early admiration for Benjamin Franklin, that he does not find "distinction" in him.

† Pains Hill Cottage, Cobham, Surrey, was Arnold's home from the time of his removal from Harrow after his son William's death until his own death.

Vanderbilt, but he had stuck to it that the richest man in the world was a person to see.

The birth in America of his daughter Lucy's child gave him great joy, offset though it was by the death of his brother-in-law, William Forster. The new granddaughter tempted him to America again in 1886; his wife was already there and he found the separation from her insupportable. But the climate was too much for his heart and he was glad to come home. He retired that year from his school post, with many tokens of affection from his teachers. His health is somewhat restored; he returns to skating again. As far back as 1882 he had written to Lord Coleridge that he wanted to give up writing: "One or two promises I have still to fulfil, but then I mean to keep silence, and endeavor to collect myself a little before my final disappearance." But he was writing till the last. On February 13, 1888, he delivered his Milton address on the occasion of the unveiling of a memorial window, the gift of an American, to Milton's "late espoused saint," in St. Margaret's Church, Westminster.

On the 14th of April he went to meet his daughter and granddaughter at Liverpool on their way from America. "In his joy and lightness of heart at the prospect of seeing [them] so soon," wrote the wife of his old college mate, Sellar, "he leapt over a low fence, and, alas! dropped down dead." In the little diary note-book which contained the *dogmata* he loved to meditate on he had written texts for the next two weeks, both from *Ecclesiasticus*—for April 15, "Weep bitterly over the dead," for April 22, "When the dead is at rest let his remembrance rest." John Morley, who, though a Liberal, had learned something from Arnold and knew it, said "a word or two in the House of Commons on this bright ornament, and much more than ornament, of our day and the recognition of his loss was well taken by members of both sides."

REFERENCES

⋙ ⋘

The following notes refer almost entirely to quoted material although, in a few instances, they document indirect quotations or salient statements of fact. In the case of quotations, the catchwords used below are always the last words of the passage to be documented. In the case of indirect quotations or statements of fact, either proper names or words central to the idea are used as catchwords.

Editions of certain of the writings of Matthew and Thomas Arnold which are frequently cited in these notes are abbreviated as follows:

C A and F G   *Culture & Anarchy: An Essay In Political And Social Criticism* and *Friendship's Garland, Being the Conversations, Letters, And Opinions Of the Late Arminius, Baron Von Thunder-Ten-Tronckh. Collected and Edited, With A Dedicatory Letter to Adolescens Leo, Esq., Of "The Daily Telegraph,"* New York, 1924.

C and A   *Culture and Anarchy,* ed. J. Dover Wilson, Cambridge, 1932.

Celtic and Homer   *On the Study of Celtic Literature* and *On Translating Homer,* New York, 1924.

Essays Crit. I   *Essays in Criticism: First Series,* New York, 1924.

Essays Crit. II   *Essays in Criticism: Second Series,* New York, 1935.

Essays Crit. III   *Essays in Criticism: Third Series,* ed. E. J. O'Brien, Boston, 1910.

Essays Oxf.   *Essays by Matthew Arnold, Including Essays in Criticism, 1865, On Translating Homer (With F. W. Newman's Reply) and Five Other Essays Now For The First Time Collected,* Oxford, 1919.

Letters   *Letters of Matthew Arnold, 1848–1888,* ed. G. W. E. Russell, two vols. in one, New York and London, 1900.

Letters to Clough   *The Letters of Matthew Arnold to Arthur Hugh Clough,* ed. with an introductory study by Howard Foster Lowry, London and New York, 1932.

Life of T. A.   *The Life and Correspondence of Thomas Arnold, D.D.,* by Arthur Penrhyn Stanley, 13th ed., 2 vols., London, 1882.

Lit. and Dog.   *Literature & Dogma: An Essay Towards a Better Ap-*
prehension of the Bible, New York, 1924.

Misc.   *Miscellaneous Works of Thomas Arnold, D.D., First Ameri-*
can Edition, with Nine Additional Essays not Included in
the English Collection, New York and Philadelphia, 1845.

Mixed   *Mixed Essays, Irish Essays, And Others,* New York, 1924.

Poems   *The Poems of Matthew Arnold, 1840–1867,* London, 1930.

St. P.   *St. Paul & Protestantism, With An Essay On Puritanism &*
The Church Of England and *Last Essays on Church &*
Religion, New York, 1924.

Unpub. Letters   *Unpublished Letters of Matthew Arnold,* ed. Arnold Whitridge, New Haven, 1923.

INTRODUCTORY NOTE

Page

x   of Montaigne. *Celtic and Homer,* p. 245.

xi   catastrophe? E. M. Forster, *Abinger Harvest,* p. 75.

to formulate. Quoted by E. M. Forster, *Goldsworthy Lowes Dickinson,*
New York, 1934, p. 112.

xii   reach the truth. *The New York Times,* June 30, 1936.

xiii   Eliot tells us. T. S. Eliot, *The Use of Poetry and the Use of Criticism,*
p. 95.

Eliot yet again. *Ibid.,* p. 98.

xiv   and eternal. "Democracy," *Mixed,* p. 35.

CHAPTER ONE

15   high spirits. *Correspondence of Henry Crabb Robinson with the Words-*
worth Circle, II, 743.

16   looked for. Mrs. H. Ward, *A Writer's Recollections,* I, 59.

voyageant. *Letters,* II, 151.

voiceless night. *Poems,* p. 22.

17   cradles of freedom. *Ibid.,* p. 27 ("Synopsis of *Cromwell*").

child began. *Ibid.,* p. 28, ll. 45–46.

gleaming flood. *Ibid.,* p. 33, ll. 234–240.

18   Citizen. E. H. Coleridge, *Life and Correspondence of John Duke Lord*
Coleridge, I, 121.

wild eyes. Wordsworth, "Lines Composed a Few Miles Above Tintern
Abbey," ll. 118–119.

live poet. Thomas Arnold [the younger], *Passages in a Wandering Life,*
p. 45.

twinkling expression. Mrs. Ward, *op. cit.,* I, 70.

Page
19 fame for himself. J. C. Shairp, "Balliol Scholars," in *Glen Desseray and Other Poems*, p. 218.
to be working. Clough, *Prose Remains*, p. 95.
20 my keeper. E. H. Coleridge, *op. cit.*, I, 129.
chapel *once*. *Letters to Clough*, p. 25. From a previously unpublished letter of· Clough to J. C. Shairp.
hounds again. Margaret Woods, "Matthew Arnold," p. 8.
21 suggested '——'. *Letters to Clough*, p. 55.
ways to go. *Ibid.*, p. 56.
satisfaction. *Ibid.*, p. 56.
22 mean too much. E. H. Coleridge, *op. cit.*, I, 145.
23 invigorating. *Letters to Clough*, p. 86.
making anything. *Unpub. Letters*, p. 17.
being an *artist*. *Letters to Clough*, p. 66.
24 express himself. *Ibid.*, p. 99.
inert mass. *Unpublished Letters of S. T. Coleridge*, I, 170.
without Images. *Ibid.*, I, 163.
in poetry. *Letters to Clough*, p. 81.
never "natural." *Ibid.*, p. 98.
25 and knowledge. *Ibid.*, p. 71.
subjective, you. *Letters to Clough*, p. 89.
before the mind." *The Philosophy of Schopenhauer*, ed. Edman, Modern Library, New York, 1928, p. 156.
the proud. "Dejection: An Ode."
Gita before that date. See W. P. D. Hill's translation of and commentary on *The Bhagavadgītā*, Oxford, 1928, pp. 274-275.
26 ineffable tale. "Alastor."
power of joy. "Tintern Abbey."
on his pulses. In a letter, p. 301 of the Cambridge ed. of his poems and letters.
in equipoise. Quoted by I. A. Richards, *Coleridge on Imagination*, p. 150, footnote 2. Mr. Richards quotes from E. H. Coleridge's "The Lake Poets in Somerset," *Transactions of the Royal Society of Literature*, Vol. XX.
that light. "Dejection: An Ode."
the Poetry. *Unpublished Letters of S. T. Coleridge*, I, 215.
27 advancing [him]. *Letters to Clough*, p. 129.
my rudder. *Ibid.*, p. 146.
might be. *Ibid.*, p. 130.
his misery. *Poems* ("Self Dependence"), p. 165.
28 preserve oneself. *Ethics*, p. 157.
deeply regret. E. H. Coleridge, *op. cit.*, I, 126.
der Stille. Goethe, *Torquato Tasso*, Act I, Scene ii.
29 Zeit Geist. *Letters to Clough*, p. 95.

Page
29 acquaintance. *Ibid.*, p. 59.
   Exhibition. *Ibid.*, p. 59.
30 typed spirit. *Ibid.*, p. 59.
   effect as mind. *Ibid.*, p. 101.
   moral desperado. *Ibid.*, p. 111.
   write Job? *Ibid.*, p. 75.
   as an emotion. *Ethics*, p. 152.
31 a grand style. *Letters to Clough*, p. 100.
   dogmas at all. *Ibid.*, p. 143.
   painted shell. *Ibid.*, p. 63.
   into prose. *Poetry and Truth from My Own Life*, II, 41.
   its *contents*. *Letters to Clough*, p. 124.
   on your age. *Ibid.*, p. 65.
   every century. *Ibid.*, p. 65.
   and curiously. *Ibid.*, p. 65.
32 much for him. *Ibid.*, p. 65.
   unite matter. . . . *Ibid.*, p. 65.
   magister vitae. *Ibid.*, p. 124.
   to the whole. *Ibid.*, p. 124.
   and images. *Ibid.*, p. 124.
33 multitudinousness. *Ibid.*, p. 97.
   d—d Elizabethan poets. *Ibid.*, p. 97.
   see to it. *Ibid.*, p. 97.
   consider desirable. *Ibid.*, p. 118.
34 is all over. *Ibid.*, p. 120.
   experiencing it! *Ibid.*, p. 125.
   Gosse tells us. R. Garnett & E. Gosse, *English Literature, An Illustrated Record*, 4 vols., New York, 1905, IV, 308.
   personality. *Letters of Benjamin Jowett*, p. 223.
   iced over. *Letters to Clough*, p. 128.
   my hair. E. M. Sellar, *Recollections and Impressions*, p. 152.
35 been ourselves. *Poems*, p. 170.
   gone away. Epigraph to "New Poems," *Poems*, p. 393.
   the power. *Ibid.*, p. 441.

CHAPTER TWO

37 make it better. Quoted by P. A. Brown, *The French Revolution in English History*, p. 98.
40 in their company. *Life of T. A.*, II, 232.
41 of objections. *Ibid.*, I, 20.
   textual authority. *Ibid.*, I, 18–19.
   sacerdotal sophistries. *Miscellanies*, p. 68.

Page
42 it was given. *Life of T. A.*, I, 311.
    historical Staines. *Letters*, I, 3.
43 absolute play. *Life of T. A.*, I, 82.
    was—a man. *Miscellanies*, p. 94.
    men alive. *Life of T. A.*, I, 31.
    for command. Quoted by H. W. Garrod, *Wordsworth*, p. 38.
    aut nullus. *Life of T. A.*, I, 32.
44 surprises everyone. *Correspondence of H. C. Robinson with the Words-worth Circle*, II, 815.
45 schools of England. *Life of T. A.*, I, 49.
46 or die. *Ibid.*, I, 169.
47 economic hegemony. See R. W. Church, *The Oxford Movement*, p. 1, p. 102.
    its developments. *Apologia Pro Vita Sua*, p. 67.
48 an opinion. See H. L. Steward, *A Century of Anglo-Catholicism*, pp. 9-10.
49 and Ministers. "The Church of England," *Misc.*, p. 233.
    of conformity. *Ibid.*, p. 227.
    its own ministers. See *Ibid.*, pp. 224–232.
    more reforming. *Life of T. A.*, I, 77.
    stand aghast. *Ibid.*, II, 167.
    in America. *Ibid.*, I, 249.
50 ignorant system. "The Christian Duty of Conceding the R. C. Claims," *Misc.*, p. 163.
    of his child. "The Social Progress of States," *Misc.*, p. 312.
    peculiar disorders. *Ibid.*, p. 306.
    of numbers. *Ibid.*, p. 325.
51 Vico demonstrates. In the account of Vico's system I have relied largely on the summary by Flint in *Vico* (pp. 166–229) which is held by modern scholars to be a reliable work though lacking in a conception of Vico's place in the thought of his time; also on Michelet's *Principes de la Philosophie de l'Histoire, traduits de la Scienza Nuova*, on Croce's *The Philosophy of Giambattista Vico*, and on H. P. Adams' *The Life and Writings of Giambattista Vico*. Arnold speaks of Vico in "The Social Progress of States."
    God alone. T. Arnold, *Introductory Lectures on Modern History*, p. 161.
52 and a conquered. "The Social Progress of States," *Misc.*, p. 307.
53 earthly thing. *Life of T. A.*, II, 81.
    earthly control. "The State and the Church," *Misc.*, p. 458.
    evil principle. T. Arnold, *Intro. Lects. on Mod. Hist.*, p. 32.
54 hearts and heads. "Social Condition of the Operative Classes," *Misc.*, p. 430.
    spiritual condition. *Ibid.*, p. 434.
    without duties. Quoted by A. Cobban, *Edmund Burke and the Revolt against the Eighteenth Century*, p. 168.

Page
54 White Jacobinism. *Life of T. A.*, II, 142.
eternal progress. *Ibid.*, I, 249.
55 not to improve. *Ibid.*, I, 249.
Consumption. *Ibid.*, II, 104.
unjust restraint. "Discipline of Public Schools," *Misc.*, p. 355.
of a slave. *Life of T. A.*, II, 158.
national benefit. *Ibid.*, I, 66.
56 *Church of England.* "Principles of Church Reform," *Misc.*, p. 115.
embodiment of Truth. Hegel, *Lectures on the Philosophy of History*,
   p. 440.
actual world. *Ibid.*, p. 434.
57 and moral. "[Fragment on] The Church," *Misc.*, p. 18.
devil worship. "Faith and Reason," *Misc.*, p. 266.
primitive antiquity. "Tradition," *Misc.*, p. 272.
58 revealed will. *Life of T. A.*, II, 75–76.
moral nature. *Ibid.*, II, 193.
bond of union. *Ibid.*, I, 343.
power of society. "Principles of Church Reform," *Misc.*, p. 127.
59 with impunity. "Christian Politics: The State and the Church," *Misc.*,
   p. 458.
at the altar. "Principles of Church Reform," *Misc.*, p. 127.
kind of person. *Ibid.*, pp. 77–78.
and Christian. *Life of T. A.*, I, 333.
minus the clergy. *Ibid.*, I, 196.
oppression on the earth. Quoted by Denis Saurat, *Milton: Man and
   Thinker*, New York, 1925, p. 88.
60 pays taxes. *Life of T. A.*, I, 330.
61 and mischievous. *Ibid.*, II, 41.
62 unity of the Christian Church. *Anglicanism*, p. 256.
be fulfilled. *Ibid.*, p. 258.
63 great empire. *Life of T. A.*, I, 87.
64 school in itself. *Ibid.*, I, 95.
answer to it. *Ibid.*, II, 37.
65 just or reasonable. *Ibid.*, II, 38.
67 their practice. *Ibid.*, I, 75.
Calvinistic. A. Whitridge, *Dr. Arnold of Rugby*, p. 94.
amongst them. *Life of T. A.*, I, 75.
not a baby. *The Letters of D. H. Lawrence*, New York, 1932, p. 623.
body or mind. *Life of T. A.*, I, 99.
68 and Nickleby. *Ibid.*, II, 137.
69 why preach? *Poetical Works of A. H. Clough*, pp. 167–169. The passage
   is much condensed.
in Puseyism. *Ibid.*, p. 169.

Page
69 premature men. R. L. Archer, *Secondary Education in the Nineteenth Century*, pp. 93–94.
70 of Attica. E. F. Benson, *As We Were*, pp. 133–134.
71 and Romans. Aldous Huxley, *Texts and Pretexts*, London, 1935, p. 157.
'pretty.' *Life of T. A.*, II, 303–304.
Bill calls for. "The Education of the Middle Class," *Misc.*, p. 375.
prime Wisdom. *Paradise Lost*, Bk. VIII, ll. 191–194.
72 elective franchise. "The Education of the Middle Class," *Misc.*, p. 375.
right and expedient. L. Trotter, *Hodson of Hodson's Horse*, *passim*.
73 them brutes. W. D. Arnold, *Oakfield; or, Fellowship in the East*, pp. 12, 111, 332.
so welcome. T. Arnold, *Intro. Lects. on Mod. Hist.*, p. 50.
74 mere opinion. *Life of T. A.*, II, 238.
75 through Jesus Christ. *Ibid.*, II, 273.
'Vixi.' *Ibid.*, II, 281.
bear it. *Ibid.*, II, 285.
afraid it is. *Ibid.*, II, 284.
76 just as before. *Ibid.*, II, 264n.

CHAPTER THREE

77 poetry displayed. *The Germ*, no. 2, February 1850, p. 84 *et seq.*
and "Tristram." Swinburne, *Essays and Studies*, pp. 124–126.
78 modern themes. *Times*, November 4, 1853, p. 5.
modern age. *North British Review*, August 1854, vol. 21, pp. 503–504.
more particularly. *The English Review*, March 1850, vol. 13, p. 211.
nineteenth century. *Fraser's Magazine*, May 1849, vol. 39, no. 233, p. 575.
the scimitar. *Blackwood's Magazine*, March 1854, vol. 75, p. 309.
Goldwin Smith. E. H. Coleridge, *Life and Corr. of J. D. Lord Coleridge*, I, 211.
79 his verses. *Blackwood's Magazine*, September 1849, vol. 66, p. 346.
80 my weakness. *Unpub. Letters*, p. 18.
81 was given. *Poems*, p. 37, l. 20.
Necessity? *Ibid.*, p. 37, l. 42.
82 our doom. *Ibid.*, p. 38, ll. 49–54.
sustain'd. *Ibid.*, p. 39, ll. 107–111.
to be human. "Arnold and Browning," in *Characters and Events*, I, 8.
83 spiritual life. T. S. Eliot, intro. to Charles Baudelaire, *Intimate Journals*, trans. Ch. Isherwood, London, 1930, p. 14.
84 answered, 'No!' *Autobiography*, pp. 94–107.
live for. *Ibid.*, *loc. cit.*
85 *existing not? Obermann*, p. 361.
unstrung will! *Poems*, p. 179, l. 183.

Page
85 luminous view. *Ibid.*, p. 176, ll. 77–80.
    direct it. *Obermann*, p. 207.
86 fatherly character. *Poetry and Truth from My Own Life*, I, 20.
    vos adorations. Alfred de Vigny, "La Maison de Berger," ll. 292–294.
    suffering easily. *Poems*, p. 107, ll. 272–281.
    for their use. *Ethics*, p. 31.
87 kill the man. *Ibid.*, p. 33.
    ignorance. *Ibid.*, p. 33.
    founder'd bark. *Poems*, p. 107, ll. 257–261.
    our mould. *Ibid.*, p. 104, l. 186.
    false powers. *Ibid.*, p. 106, ll. 222–226.
88 keep chime. *Ibid.*, p. 105, l. 196.
    Denominator! *Sartor Resartus*, p. 168 (Bk. II, Chapt. IX).
    moderate desire. *Poems*, p. 110, l. 386.
89 word Nature! *Lit. and Dog.*, p. 321.
    of thee. *Poems*, p. 36, l. 1.
    her slave! *Ibid.*, p. 60, l. 14.
    live by hers. *Ibid.*, p. 62, l. 14.
90 holy secret. *Ibid.*, p. 62, l. 9.
    breast of God. *Ibid.*, p. 193, ll. 31–36 *et ante.*
    the two possibilities. *Ibid.*, pp. 85–86.
    read him. *The History of English Rationalism in the Nineteenth Century.*
        II, 55.
91 and ear. "Tintern Abbey," ll. 105–106.
92 Blümlisalp! *Letters to Clough*, p. 110.
93 and element! "Dejection: An Ode."
    to discern? *Poems*, p. 187, ll. 59–74.
    of the world." *Ibid.*, p. 188, ll. 79–86.
94 and joy. *Ibid.*, p. 189, ll. 131–132.
    can feel. *Ibid.*, p. 190, ll. 28–37.
95 is miserable. *Pensées*, p. 107, # 397.
    to live. *Poems*, p. 78, ll. 39–40.
    deposed king. *Pensées*, p. 107, # 398.
96 grief again. *Poems*, p. 78, ll. 53–56; ll. 65–68.
    omnipotence. *Ibid.*, p. 84, ll. 17–24.
97 what we sing. *Ibid.*, p. 47, ll. 232–234.
98 Iacchus. *Ibid.*, p. 48, ll. 270–281.
    my soul! *Ibid.*, p. 48, ll. 282–297.
99 same experience. *Movements of Thought in the Nineteenth Century.*
        p. 63.
    the others. *Ibid.*, p. 63.
    his imagination. *Ibid.*, p. 63.
    uncravingly. *Poems*, p. 90, l. 161.

Page
99 beings in Self. W. P. D. Hill (trans.), *The Bhagavadgītā*, p. 160.
100 lucidity of soul. *Poems*, pp. 90–91, ll. 186–198.
101 general Life. *Ibid.*, p. 92, ll. 245–250.
    infects the world. *Ibid.*, p. 93, ll. 273–276.
102 weariness. *Letters to Clough*, p. 106.
    break it. *Poems*, p. 74, ll. 32–40.
    and Control. *Ibid.*, p. 59, ll. 1–2.
    mental stream. *Principles of Psychology*, 2 vols., New York, 1918, I, 196.
103 human nature. *St. P.*, p. 275.
    to live. *Ibid.*, p. 279.
    and misery. *Ibid.*, p. 276.
    majestic unity. *Poems*, p. 59, ll. 5–8.
104 unswerv'd-from law. *Ibid.*, p. 48, l. 8.
    ties of blood. *Ibid.*, p. 49, l. 31.
    endure. *Ibid.*, p. 49, ll. 17–22.
105 *sake of punishment. Ethical Studies*, p. 26.
106 sense of all. *Complete Poetical Works of William Wordsworth* (Cambridge ed.), p. 763, Sonnet IX.
    after thaw. *Poems*, p. 59, l. 5.
107 we deem. *Ibid.*, p. 62, ll. 5–8.
    human nod. *Ibid.*, p. 62, l. 9.
    aspire. *Ibid.*, p. 272, ll. 68–70.
108 their side. *Ibid.*, p. 272, ll. 85–90.
    remain. *Ibid.*, p. 273, l. 132.
    than then? *Ibid.*, p. 273, ll. 127–130.
109 its peace!" *Ibid.*, p. 275, ll. 199–210.
    may gain? *Ibid.*, p. 138, l. 28.

CHAPTER FOUR

111 contriving head. *Poems*, p. 116, ll. 90–91.
    invincible. *Ibid.*, p. 116, ll. 92–94.
    alone. Ibid., p. 135, l. 4.
    scattered. *The State*, p. v.
112 restless mind. *Poems*, p. 122, l. 330.
    for rest. *Ibid.*, p. 236, ll. 221–223.
113 no more. *Ibid.*, p. 122, l. 328.
    like ours. *Ibid.*, p. 236, ll. 224–230.
    individualism. *Some Aspects of the Greek Genius*, p. 53.
114 prosperous. *The History of England*, Chapt. III, paragraph 2.
    definite object. Quoted by Jean Carrère, *Degeneration in the French Masters* [*Les Mauvais Maîtres*], trans. J. McCabe, New York, 1922, p. 80.
    unreal City. "The Waste Land," *Poems, 1909–1925*, London, 1926, p. 67.

Page
114 with cities. *Poems*, p. 229, ll. 35–36.
115 their breast. *Ibid.*, p. 167, ll. 37–46.
     impotence. *The State*, p. 243.
116 Catholic revival. *Cousin Betty*, 2 vols., trans. J. Waring and C. Bell,
     Philadelphia, 1901, II, 419. The passage is condensed.
     the Pleiads. *The Pleiads*, trans. J. F. Scanlan, New York and London, 1928,
     pp. 241–242. The passage is condensed.
117 virtue of life. *Military Servitude and Grandeur*, trans. F. W. Huard, New
     York, 1919, pp. 313–317. The passage is condensed.
118 perish. *Obermann*, p. 97.
     truly burns. *Poems*, p. 185, ll. 21–24.
     and to live. *Obermann*, p. 152.
119 roaring reefs. *Faust*, trans. G. M. Cookson, p. 77.
     God of the Prologue. *Ibid.*, p. 16. "Through every dim and dark and
     dubious aim, etc." See *Goethes Werke* (Knaur, Berlin, circ. 1930), Erster
     Band, p. 618:
              Ein guter Mensch, in seinem dunklen Drange,
              Ist sich des rechten Weges wohl bewusst.
     thy *Goethe*. *Sartor Resartus*, p. 168 ("The Everlasting Yea").
120 from everything. *Literature and Criticism*, vol. 9 of *Complete Writings of
     Alfred de Musset*, 10 vols., New York, 1905, p. 126.
     flight from it. *Main Currents in Nineteenth Century Literature*, II, 19.
121 were at hand. *Confessions of a Child of the Century*, vol. 8 of *Complete
     Writings of A. de M.*, p. 39.
     extinction. Quoted from Sainte-Beuve's *Correspondence* by W. F. Giese,
     Sainte-Beuve: A Literary Portrait, p. 84.
     of the race. The translation is by E. H. Coleridge; it appears in I, 212,
     footnote 2, of his *Life and Corr. of J. D. Lord Coleridge*.
     of impiety. *Confessions of a Child of the Century*, vol. 8 of *Complete Writ-
     ings of A. de M.*, p. 332.
122 actual love affair. See Chambers, *Matthew Arnold*, p. 7; also Kingsmill,
     Matthew Arnold, p. 166; Mr. Kingsmill indirectly quotes the statement
     of Arnold's daughter, Lady Sandhurst, that Arnold always insisted
     Marguerite was imaginary.
     poetical figment. *Letters to Clough*, pp. 91, 93.
123 that experience. *Poetry and the Criticism of Life*, pp. 38–39.
     another girl. Kingsmill, *op. cit.*, pp. 73–74.
     and chin. *Matthew Arnold and France: The Poet*, p. 100, etc.
124 unallay'd Desire. *Poems*, p. 134.
     art, alone. *Ibid.*, p. 281, l. 30.
     despatched. *Letters to Clough*, p. 93.
     from them. *Ibid.*, p. 93.
     be love. Baudelaire, *Intimate Journals*, ed. cit., p. 117.

Page
125 or sorry. "Pagan and Mediæval Religious Sentiment," *Essays Crit. I*, p. 209.
positive, happy. *Ibid.*, p. 219.
of pleasure. *Ibid.*, p. 216.
of sorrow. *Ibid.*, p. 219.
o'erlabour'd heart. *Poems*, p. 127, l. 17.
control. *Ibid.*, p. 272, l. 96.
mocking. *Ibid.*, p. 126, ll. 5, 6.
126 than they are. *Ibid.*, p. 127, ll. 1–8.
universe. *Ibid.*, p. 128, ll. 21–24.
by night. *Ibid.*, p. 402, ll. 29–37.
127 and care. *Ibid.*, p. 128, l. 14.
bliss within. *Ibid.*, p. 129, l. 26.
that breast. *Ibid.*, p. 133, ll. 63–70.
durability. *Ibid.*, p. 403, l. 43.
thy hair? *Ibid.*, p. 403, ll. 17–24.
128 them through. *Ibid.*, p. 127, l. 12.
no fear. *Ibid.*, p. 172, ll. 29–36.
129 of soul. *Ibid.*, p. 164, l. 10, l. 12.
vulgarity. *Letters to Clough*, p. 92: "that furiously flaring, bethiefed rush-light, the vulgar Byron."
hadst thine. *Poems*, pp. 164–165, ll. 17–24.
singt. Quoted so by Arnold in *Lit. and Dog.*, p. 187, though with different punctuation. Arnold omits a third line, "Der jedem an die Ohren klingt." See *Goethes Werke*, I, 646. The translation is Arnold's.
130 withdraw. *Poems*, p. 164, ll. 1–4.
make upon themselves. *Poetry and Truth*, II, 125.
131 supremacy. J. Dewey and J. H. Tufts, *Ethics*, New York, 1908, p. 210.
misery. *Poems*, p. 166, ll. 31–32.
heavenly Friend. *Ibid.*, p. 135, l. 5, l. 2.
132 keep company! *Ibid.*, p. 136, ll. 7–12.
chance's fool. *Ibid.*, p. 136, l. 18.
seem stale. *Ibid.*, pp. 158–159, ll. 112–126.
133 generous fire. *Ibid.*, p. 137, l. 12.
Garrod believes. *Poetry and the Criticism of Life*, p. 38.
and youth? *Poems*, p. 139, ll. 21–22.
side death. *Ibid.*, p. 139, ll. 32–35.
calm is well. *Ibid.*, p. 139, l. 39.
134 emotion—none. *Ibid.*, p. 409, ll. 21–30.
delightful world. *Ibid.*, p. 218, ll. 854–856.
wanderer. *Ibid.*, p. 219, l. 888.
135 fixity. *Letters*, I, 66.
Tüchtigkeit. Letters to Clough, p. 146.
to *guide* it?' *Ibid.*, p. 84.

Page
136 not true. *Poems*, p. 170, ll. 59–66.
137 our day. *Ibid.*, p. 170, ll. 72–76.
138 surprise of morning. *Some Aspects of the Greek Genius*, p. 246.
     corded bales. *Poems*, pp. 236–237, ll. 232–250.
139 Eliot calls him. *The Use of Poetry and the Use of Criticism*, p. 97.
140 always bad. Spinoza, *Ethics*, p. 171.
     fast losing. *Letters to Clough*, p. 146.
     such like. *Ibid.*, p. 126.
     unpoetrylessness. Ibid., p. 126.
     and increases. *Ibid.*, p. 116.
     my situation. *Ibid.*, p. 126.
     but for wisdom. *Rousseau and Romanticism*, p. 308.
141 my poetics. *Letters to Clough*, p. 146.

CHAPTER FIVE

142 than Kant. *Times*, November 4, 1853, p. 5.
     in his manner. *Blackwood's Magazine*, September 1849, vol. 66, p. 343.
     Tennyson. This was the "influence" most frequently observed: *Blackwood's*, vol. 66, p. 344; *English Review*, March 1850, p. 212; Rossetti in *The Germ*, February 1850, p. 90; and there are many others.
143 and metric. For example, *The Eclectic Review*, March 1855, p. 281.
     of the conscience? Quoted by A. Symons, *The Letters of Baudelaire*, New York, 1927, p. viii.
     of the present. *New Poems*, New York, 1920, p. ii.
     recitative. *Essays in Literary Criticism*, p. 332.
     Lowell spoke of him. Quoted by S. T. Williams, *Studies in Victorian Literature*, New York, 1923, p. 160.
144 colorless. *Editorials*, ed. C. W. Hutson, Boston and New York, 1926, p. 215.
     educated versifier. *The Pleasures of Poetry*, London, 1930–1932, Series 3, p. 48; Series 2, p. 4.
146 true-love knots. Coleridge, "On Donne's Poetry."
     Athens, Rome. *Poems*, p. 395, l. 12.
     my mind? *Ibid.*, p. 40, l. 1.
     I think so. *Letters to Clough*, p. 136.
147 and lifelike. Clough, *Prose Remains*, p. 358.
     of industry. *Ibid., loc. cit.*
     Castaly. *Ibid.*, p. 359.
148 plain rules. *Ibid.*, pp. 372–373.
     way of poetry. *Poems*, p. 8.
149 from the other. W. E. Aytoun, *Firmilian*, in *The Book of Ballads*, p. vi.
     self-contemplation. *Apologia Pro Vita Sua*, p. 154.
     and similes. Clough, *Prose Remains*, p. 374.

Page
150   to Joy. *Poems*, p. 2.
      with itself. *Ibid.*, p. 1.
      more terrible. *Ibid.*, p. 2.
      to be done. *Ibid.*, pp. 2–3.
152   affected by them. *Ibid.*, pp. 13–14.
153   poetry of Arnold. *Journal*, p. 353.
154   newspapers ebbed. *Abinger Harvest*, p. 89.
      course of fate. Poems, p. 304 (Preface to *Merope*).
      anything else. *Ibid.*, p. 283.
155   of impression. *Ibid.*, p. 303.
      severest form. *Ibid.*, p. 305.
156   Oxford woman. *National Review*, April 1858, vol. 6, no. xii, p. 274.
157   of the Law.' *Letters*, I, 66.
      with dignity. *Ibid.*, I, 69.
      turn critic. Indirectly quoted by Giese, *Sainte-Beuve*, p. 112.
      rightly interpreted. Quoted by L. F. Mott, *Sainte-Beuve*, p. 225.
158   Huxley believes. *Texts and Pretexts*, London, 1935, p. 294.
      interest in it. *Unpub. Letters*, pp. 31–32.
      life to poetry. *Letters*, I, 72.
159   practical life. *Essays Oxf.*, pp. 465–466.
161   and complex. *Ibid.*, pp. 455–456.
      . . . comprehension. *Ibid.*, p. 456.
      deliverance. *Ibid.*, p. 455.
      our comprehension. *Ibid.*, p. 456.
163   refined classes. Matthew Arnold, *England and the Italian Question*, p. 22.
      adventurous. *Ibid.*, pp. 27–28.
      resistance. *Ibid.*, p. 30.
      Mohammedan fury. *Ibid.*, p. 29.
      and ideas. *Ibid.*, p. 31.
164   their countrymen. *Ibid.*, p. 45.
      culminating epoch. *Essays Oxf.*, p. 457.
165   intelligible to us. *Ibid.*, p. 456.
      of his age. *Ibid.*, p. 469.
166   not interpretative. *Ibid.*, p. 472.
      Charakter. Goethe, *Torquato Tasso*, Act I, Scene ii.

CHAPTER SIX

168   grand style. *Celtic and Homer*, p. 183.
      blessed *yea*. J. W. Cross, *George Eliot's Life as Related in her Letters and Journals*, 3 vols., Edinburgh and London, 1885, I, 193–194.
      pious enthusiasm. Carlyle, *The Life of John Sterling*, p. 184.
169   under authority. *The Literature of the Victorian Era*, p. 117.

Page
169 and copulate. . . . *Letters to Clough*, p. 115.
170 anti-everything. I. G. Sieveking, *Memoir and Letters of Francis W. Newman*, p. 26.

ward it off. *Ibid.*, p. 84.

of civilization. *Ibid.*, p. 267. Throughout my account of Francis Newman I have drawn freely upon Sieveking's *Memoir*.
171 be his people. *Hebrew Theism, &c.*, p. 2.

purely temporary. Sieveking, *op. cit.*, p. 339.

Brother Jonathan. See Sieveking, *op. cit.*, portraits facing p. 114, p. 126, p. 128.
172 into being. *Ibid.*, pp. 257–258.
173 English literature. *Celtic and Homer*, p. 198.

know it not. *Ibid.*, p. 264.

serious subject. Ibid., p. 265.

I owe them. E. H. Coleridge, *Life and Corr. of J. D. Lord Coleridge*, II, 160.

general ideas. Reynolds, *Fifteen Discourses Delivered in the Royal Academy*, p. 40.

heroic suffering. *Ibid.*, pp. 40–41.
174 to atoms. *Ibid.*, p. 66.

and appreciate. *Letters to Clough*, p. 122.
175 love of truth. Tocqueville, *Democracy in America*, II, 51.

we can find. Joubert, *Pensées and Letters*, p. 188.

Keble believed him. *Keble's Lectures on Poetry*, I, 239–260.
176 last century. *Celtic and Homer*, p. 157.
177 wishing for it. *Ibid.*, pp. 245–246.

incredible jargon. *Ibid.*, p. 177.

for *vigorous*. F. W. Newman, *The Iliad of Homer*, pp. xxi–xxii.

kick the beam. *Introductory Lecture*, New York and Cambridge, 1937, pp. 24–25.
178 it is mean. F. W. Newman, *op. cit.*, p. iv; quoted by Arnold, *Celtic and Homer*, p. 171.
180 *regarded as true.* From the extract in E. Burns (ed.), *A Handbook of Marxism*, New York, 1935, p. 225.
181 better his condition. Adam Smith, *An Inquiry into the Nature and Causes of the Wealth of Nations*, 2 vols., Everyman ed., I, 306.
183 Disinterested students. See, for example, C. Birchenough, *History of Elementary Education in England and Wales*, pp. 74–87; or J. W. Adamson, *English Education, 1789–1902*, Chapt. V. On the other hand, these writers feel that the rivalry between the groups had its stimulating effects.
185 Reign of Terror. Matthew Arnold, *The Popular Education of France with Notices of that of Holland and Switzerland*, p. 10.

of the State. *Ibid.*, pp. 10–11.

Page
185   its own equity. *Ibid.*, p. 149.
national sentiment. *Ibid.*, p. 166.
186   above them. *Ibid.*, p. 169.
corporate character. *Mixed*, p. 31.
187   nation then? *Ibid.*, p. 20.
can trust. *Ibid.*, p. 31.
hand of the State. Matthew Arnold, *A French Eton; or, Middle Class Education and the State*, p. 86.
188   purged away. *Ibid.*, p. 117.
perfected itself. *Ibid.*, p. 117.
189   and eternal. *Mixed*, p. 35.

CHAPTER SEVEN

190   Arnold tradition. F. O. Matthiessen, *The Achievement of T. S. Eliot*, Boston and New York, 1935, p. 2.
and F. W. H. Myers. T. S. Eliot, *The Use of Poetry and the Use of Criticism*, p. 115.
by his votaries. R. A. Scott-James, *The Making of Literature*, New York, n. d., p. 262.
191   Oxford prose. See Ludwig Lewisohn, *The Sewanee Review*, April 1902, vol. x, no. 2, p. 143. Mr. Lewisohn quotes a letter of Saintsbury to Professor L. M. Harris of the College of Charleston.
192   *criticism of life. Essays Crit. I*, p. 303.
scientific manner. Renan, *The Future of Science*, p. 19.
of humanity. *Ibid.*, p. 18.
spiritual reality. *Lectures on the Philosophy of History*, p. 466.
194   imaginative reason. *Essays Crit. I*, p. 220.
dream dreams. *Characters and Events*, I, 17.
195   a bad one. *The Profession of Poetry*, p. 263.
brazen world. Sir Philip Sidney, "An Apology for Poetry," *English Critical Essays, 16th, 17th, 18th Centuries*, ed. Jones, Oxford, 1922, p. 8.
experience of poetry. *The Sacred Wood*, p. ix.
best order. S. T. Coleridge, *Table Talk and Omniana*, p. 54.
and confused. *Principles of Literary Criticism*, pp. 61–62.
196   them, in short. *Essays Crit. I*, p. 5.
natural world. *Ibid.*, pp. 106–107.
whole man. *Ibid.*, p. 82.
that Nature. *Ibid.*, p. 107.
197   relations with them. *Ibid.*, p. 81.
short-lived affair. *Ibid.*, p. 6.
literary work. *Goethe's Literary Essays*, p. 83.
198   is *energy. Essays Crit. I*, p. 50.

Page

198   saying things. *Ibid.*, p. 161.

199   to no law. *Main Currents in Nineteenth Century Literature*, II, 40.

200   what has she? *Recollections of the Table Talk of Samuel Rogers, &c.*, New York, 1856, pp. 99–100.

as we do. Quoted by Carl Van Doren, *Swift*, New York, 1930, p. 133.

organic unity. *The Civilization of France*, p. 45.

201   too busy there. *Essays Crit. I*, p. 62.

202   tom-fool. In the Morgan Library. The letter is dated 1858.

as it really is. Arnold first uses the phrase in *On Translating Homer* (*Celtic and Homer*, p. 199). He quotes himself in the first paragraph of "The Function of Criticism at the Present Time."

designated. Hegel, *Lectures on the Philosophy of History*, p. 448.

204   and obstinate. Quoted in *Essays Crit. I*, p. 15.

any literature. *Ibid.*, p. 15.

given to them. *Ibid.*, pp. 18–19.

205   of the reason. *Ibid.*, pp. 11–12.

withdraw from them. *Ibid.*, p. 34.

beneficent. *Ibid.*, p. 34.

206   acridity. *Ibid.*, p. 160.

awakening of the modern spirit. *Ibid.*, p. 159.

and seventeenth. *Ibid.*, p. 160.

of good sense. *Ibid.*, p. 160.

power of working. *Ibid.*, p. 160.

dissolvents of it. *Ibid.*, p. 160.

207   routine thinking. *Ibid.*, p. 161.

most deeply. *Ibid.*, p. 161.

clair de lune. *Letters*, I, 10–11.

208   and character. *Essays Crit. I*, p. 193.

209   *historically true.* J. W. Colenso, *The Pentateuch and Book of Joshua Critically Examined*, Part I, p. xix. My account summarizes Colenso's own in the Preface to Part I of his work.

and death. *Ibid.*, p. xxxii.

state of things. *Ibid.*, p. xxiv.

211   little-instructed. "The Bishop and the Philosopher," *Macmillan's Magazine*, January 1863, vol. vii, no. 39, p. 242.

educated Europe. *Ibid.*, p. 241.

212   proclaiming this. *Ibid.*, pp. 242–243.

convulsing it. *Ibid.*, p. 243.

213   composing it. *A Discourse on the Origin of Inequality* in *The Social Contract*, p. 200.

214   of speculation. *Macmillan's Magazine, loc. cit.*, p. 252.

be withheld. *Tractatus Theologico-Politicus*, p. 1.

215   and charity. *Ibid.*, p. 9.

Page
215 and hazard. *Ibid.*, p. 197.
216 right is ready.) *Essays Crit. I*, p. 12.
     legitimate ruler. *Ibid.*, p. 12.
     to an end. Pascal, *Pensées*, pp. 84–85.
     strong just. *Ibid.*, p. 85.
217 and practice. *Essays Crit. I*, p. 12.
     be resisted. *Ibid.*, pp. 12–13.
218 of expansion. *Ibid.*, p. 17.
     secure liberty. *Ibid.*, pp. 300–301.
219 best it may. *Pensées and Letters*, p. 39.
     to my star. *Ibid.*, p. 211.
     in all this. *Essays Crit. I*, p. 285.
     his livery. *Pensées and Letters*, p. 81.
     not a spur. *Ibid.*, p. 78.
220 own lamp! *Ibid.*, p. 113.
     work [of art]. *Ibid.*, p. 156.
     hurting me.' *Ibid.*, p. 156.
     certain amenity. *Ibid.*, p. 129.
     and color. "Self-Reliance," *Essays: First Series.*
221 as laws. *Essays Crit. I*, p. 346.
     he can bear. *Ibid.*, p. 346.
     it at all. *Ibid.*, p. 346.

CHAPTER EIGHT

223 shabby motives, Karl Marx, *The Story of the Life of Lord Palmerston,*
     p. 10.
     Whiggism. *Ibid.*, p. 9.
     generosity. *Ibid.*, p. 9.
     running away. *Ibid.*, p. 9.
225 in its body. Karl Marx, *Capital*, I, 189.
226 rural life. "The Communist Manifesto," in Burns (ed.), *A Handbook of
     Marxism*, New York, 1935, p. 27.
     has no master.' *Capital*, I, 131n.
     colored labor. *Religion and the Rise of Capitalism*, p. 269.
     for existence. *Ibid.*, p. 271.
227 with business. "My Countrymen," *CA and FG*, p. 340.
     calling. M. Weber, *The Protestant Ethic and the Spirit of Capitalism*, p. 80.
228 ridiculous. "My Countrymen," *CA and FG*, p. 328.
229 second Holland. *Ibid.*, p. 351.
     and rational. *Ibid.*, p. 333.
     their people. *Ibid.*, p. 334.
230 taken care of. *Ibid.*, p. 339.

Page
230 unenviable? *Ibid.*, p. 340.
    want of both. *Ibid.*, p. 342.
231 the life there. *Ibid.*, p. 343.
    destination. *Ibid.*, p. 344.
    and prejudice. *CA and FG*, pp. 224–225.
232 historical wave. "My Countrymen," *CA and FG*, p. 356.
233 dependent upon race. *Anthropology and Modern Life*, p. 59.
    are concerned. *We Europeans*, p. 18.
234 can be true. *Race: A Study in Modern Superstition*, p. 11.
    created things. *Ibid.*, p. 299.
    natural differences. *Principles of Political Economy*, I, 390. See also *Auto-biography*, p. 192.
235 on his back. Referred to by F. H. Hankins, "Race as a Factor in Political Theory," in Merriam and Barnes (eds.), *A History of Political Theories, Recent Times*, p. 525.
    tell upon it. *Celtic and Homer*, pp. 90–91.
    governess theory. *Experiment in Autobiography*, New York, 1934, p. 658.
    anecdotal. *We Europeans*, p. 161.
236 Celtic question. *The Racial Basis of Civilization*, p. 143.
    correctly. *The Lion and the Fox*, pp. 302–326.
237 feel impressions. *Celtic and Homer*, p. 76.
    personality. *Ibid.*, p. 76.
    to sorrow. *Ibid.*, p. 76.
    to be up. *Ibid.*, p. 77.
    eloquent. *Ibid.*, p. 77.
    of fact. Ibid., p. 77. Arnold quotes from H. Martin's *Histoire de France*.
    investing it all. *Ibid.*, p. 79.
    Celt's grasp. *Ibid.*, p. 81.
238 amusing to him. *Man and Superman*, New York, 1903, p. xv.
    passion and melancholy. *Celtic and Homer*, p. 115.
239 superstructure. *Ibid.*, p. 64.
    Latin civilisation. *Ibid.*, p. 85.
240 Latin spirit. *Ibid.*, p. 87.
    empêtré. Ibid., p. 100.
    English basis. *Ibid.*, p. 98.
241 to promise. *Ibid.*, p. 105.
    Welsh Border. *A Study of British Genius*, pp. 37–50.
242 ethnologists. *Celtic and Homer*, p. 15.
    distinguishing marks. *Ibid.*, p. 15.
243 is going. *Ibid.*, p. 132.
    by storm. *Ibid.*, pp. 136–137.
246 come armed. *Autobiography*, p. 203. It is difficult to get at the true nature of the Hyde Park affair. J. H. Park has a good account in *The English*

Page
246   *Reform Bill of 1867*, pp. 102–105; Spencer Walpole in his *History of Twenty-Five Years*, II, 169 *et seq.* gives what is perhaps the "classic" account, though he is a little too concerned with defending the quite honorable part which his father, the Home Secretary, played. G. M. Trevelyan's *The Life of John Bright* (pp. 360–362) gives a good summary of the incident and of its political effects.

     accomplish one. *Autobiography*, p. 204.

     July 30. S. Walpole, *A History of Twenty-Five Years*, II, 176.

247   destruction. Quoted by J. H. Park, *The English Reform Bill of 1867*, pp. 111–112.

     Honour Bright. Trevelyan, *Life of John Bright*, p. 362n.

     such offers. *Ibid.*, p. 365.

248   the reality. Quoted, *ibid.*, p. 365.

     them altogether. Park, *op. cit.*, pp. 145–146.

     old parties. *Labor and Politics in England, 1850–1867*, p. 289.

249   E. W. Bakke. *The Unemployed Man*, New York, 1934, pp. 9–10.

250   our generation. *Essays and Leaves from a Note-Book*, p. 262. The passage is condensed.

     Human Society. "Shooting Niagara," in *Scottish and Other Miscellanies*, p. 308.

     this last. *Ibid.*, p. 317.

251   a victory. *Letters*, I, 390.

     smouldering. *Ibid.*, I, 390.

CHAPTER NINE

252   Socrates. *C and A*, p. 211.

253   best self. *Ibid.*, p. 95.

255   to face. *Voltaire*, London, 1935, p. 115.

257   this death. *C and A*, p. 136.

258   moral perfection. *Ibid.*, p. 55.

     to the activities. *Nichomachean Ethics*, trans. J. E. C. Welldon, London, 1920, p. 1.

259   inoffensive way. *Letters*, I, 111.

260   consistent whole. *The Sphere and Duties of Government*, p. 11.

261   atheism. *C and A*, pp. 120–121.

262   *Banner* low. *Ibid.*, pp. 110–111.

263   to individuals. *On Liberty* in *Utilitarianism, Liberty and Representative Government*, pp. 70–71.

     the deed is forgivable. See "Marcus Aurelius," *Essays Crit. I*, pp. 358–363.

     with error. *On Liberty*, p. 79.

264   these years!' *C and A*, p. 21.

     sufficient warrant. *On Liberty*, pp. 72–73.

Page
265 follow right reason. *C and A*, p. 120.
266 more intelligent. *Ibid.*, p. 44.
doing good. *Ibid.*, p. 45.
human misery. *Ibid.*, p. 44.
God prevail. *Ibid.*, p. 45.
counter to. *Ibid.*, p. 46.
and feel. *Ibid.*, p. 51.
267 coincides with religion. *Ibid.*, p. 48.
268 thitherward. *Ibid.*, p. 48.
one's own happiness. *Ibid.*, p. 48.
human nature. *Ibid.*, p. 48.
269 and unfruitful. . . . *Ibid.*, p. 59.
harmonious perfection. *Ibid.*, p. 60.
and light. *Ibid.*, p. 69.
270 and alive. *Ibid.*, p. 69.
271 God prevail. *Ibid.*, pp. 70–71.
for the future. *Ibid.*, pp. 65–66.
273 said Coleridge. Quoted by A. Cobban, *Edmund Burke and the Revolt against the Eighteenth Century*, p. 165.
reason cherishes. Wordsworth, "The Old Cumberland Beggar," ll. 99–102.
aeronauts. Quoted by R. H. Murray, *Edmund Burke*, p. 28.
are born. "The Prelude," Book VII, ll. 527–530.
scalpel. Cobban, *op. cit.*, p. 88.
every individual. Quoted by Murray, *op. cit.*, p. 67.
274 of the country. Quoted by Cobban, *op. cit.*, p. 79.
world's good. *C and A*, pp. 142–143.
275 rule of life. *Ibid.*, pp. 143–144.
stricken men? F. Harrison, *The Choice of Books*, p. 113.
276 working power. *C and A*, p. 94.
best self. *Ibid.*, pp. 95–96.
humane spirit. *Ibid.*, p. 109.
277 of the people. Quoted by H. W. Schneider, *The Fascist Government of Italy*, New York, 1936, p. 32.
278 struggles of the trade unions. *C and A*, pp. 107–108.
Tarpeian Rock. *Ibid.*, p. 203.
279 his teaching. *Political Thought in England from Herbert Spencer to the Present Day*, pp. 198–199.
280 course of law. *C and A*, p. 97.
in chains. *Social Contract*, p. 5.
281 free as before. *Ibid.*, p. 14.
will of all. *Ibid.*, p. 25.
(universal) object. G. D. H. Cole, Introduction to *Social Contract*, p. xl.
common good. *The Philosophical Theory of the State*, p. 102.

Page
281 good for it. *Social Contract*, p. 34.
282 what it wills. *Ibid.*, p. 34.
legislator necessary. *Ibid.*, p. 34.
in the next. *Ibid.*, p. 35.
of other men. *Ibid.*, p. 35.
283 is no authority. *Ibid.*, p. 37.
by means of law. *Ibid.*, p. 37.
[his] own wisdom. *Ibid.*, pp. 37–38.
284 it lasting. *Ibid.*, p. 38.
285 fitness of things. *C and A*, pp. 174–175.
consciousness at all. *Ibid.*, p. 175.
286 mechanical action. *Ibid.*, p. 177.
287 strenuous virtue? *Ibid.*, pp. 177–178.
even arise. *Ibid.*, p. 179.
288 brought about. *Ibid.*, p. 180.
human happiness. *Ibid.*, p. 180.
289 on our part. *Ibid.*, p. 188.
simplest laws! *Ibid.*, p. 190.
God glories. *Ibid.*, p. 191.
along with us. *Ibid.*, p. 192.
sunken people. *Ibid.*, p. 193.
as inevitable. *Ibid.*, p. 193.
290 a fair chance! *Ibid.*, pp. 194–195.
291 a better one. *Letters*, II, 60.
uneasy. *Ibid.*, II, 60.
of the Reds. *Ibid.*, II, 62.
of all Europe. *Ibid.*, II, 65–66.
at present. *Ibid.*, II, 66.
really endure. *Ibid.*, II, 62.

CHAPTER TEN

292 appearing at all. *Letters*, I, 431.
a youthful piece. Mrs. H. Ward, *A Writer's Recollections*, II, 86.
293 weary bones. *Poems*, pp. 409–410.
believe it then. *Ibid.*, p. 413, ll. 11–12.
by the wall. *Ibid.*, p. 410, ll. 1–8 and p. 411, ll. 13–16.
294 emotion—none. *Ibid.*, p. 409, ll. 26–30.
calm is well. *Ibid.*, p. 408, l. 23.
parts alone! *Ibid.*, pp. 416–417, ll. 140–142.
295 on their soul. *Ibid.*, pp. 417–418, ll. 163–188.
city of God? *Meditations*, trans. Meric Casaubon, Everyman ed., p. 33.
296 made us live. *Poems*, p. 412, ll. 35–40.

Page

296 my home. *Ibid.*, p. 412, l. 43.
    with fame! *Ibid.*, p. 407, ll. 8–19.

297 long funeral. *Ibid.*, p. 75, l. 10.
    all internal. *Letters*, II, 104.

298 we once were. *Letters to Clough*, p. 159.
    as Professor Lowry says. *Ibid.*, pp. 21–22.
    went away. *Poems*, p. 387, l. 40.
    he is dead! *Ibid.*, p. 387, ll. 41–50.

299 last farewell. *Ibid.*, p. 179, l. 184.

300 in bloom?" *Ibid.*, p. 435, ll. 69–80.

301 words to come." *Ibid.*, p. 438, ll. 173–180.
    all things new?" *Ibid.*, p. 439, ll. 225–232.

302 *all things new.'* *Revelation*, 21.5.
    zeal pursued." *Poems*, p. 441, ll. 289–292.
    was new!" *Ibid.*, p. 440, ll. 238–240.
    lies forlorn?" *Ibid.*, p. 440, ll. 247–248.
    beseem its bard. *Ibid.*, p. 441, ll. 299–300.
    new-made. *Ibid.*, p. 441, l. 308.
    morning break. *Ibid.*, p. 442, ll. 341–344.

303 while one lives. *Letters*, I, 466.

304 A. W. Benn. *The History of English Rationalism in the Nineteenth Century*, II, 4, 113–114.

307 of the mind. Mrs. H. Ward, *Robert Elsmere*, I, 299.

308 modified sense. *Ibid.*, I, 307.
    other revelations. *Ibid.*, I, 307.
    Bible phrases. Quoted by Amabel Williams-Ellis, *The Exquisite Tragedy*, New York, 1929, p. 129.
    the Resurrection! "Conversation with Mr. Gladstone on *Robert Elsmere*, April 8, 1888," Appendix I of *Robert Elsmere*, II, 566.

309 birth and death. *Time and Tide*, pp. 31–32. The passage is condensed.
    of Europe. *Ibid.*, pp. 31–32.

310 thoughts of men. *Ibid.*, p. 32.
    soul of man! *Robert Elsmere*, II, 44.
    doomed brethren. *Ibid.*, II, 84.
    be disproved. Ibid., II, 203.

311 of the brute? *Ibid.*, II, 205–206.
    not in possession. Ibid., II, 315.

312 by Bakke. E. W. Bakke, *The Unemployed Man*, New York, 1924, pp. 202–222.
    bourgeoisie. Robert Elsmere, II, 365–366.
    be realised. *Ibid.*, II, 329.
    a good man! *Ibid.*, II, 329.
    Kingdom of God.' *Ibid.*, II, 361.

Page

313 his own time. *Ibid.*, II, 361–362.

by his memory. *Ibid.*, II, 364.

in the end. *Ibid.*, II, 378–379.

in society. *Ibid.*, II, 499.

with the rich. *Ibid.*, II, 499.

314 die to Him! *Ibid.*, II, 556.

its conclusions. W. E. Gladstone, *"Robert Elsmere" and The Battle of Belief.*

315 on conduct? *Robert Elsmere*, I, xxiv.

books to be read. *Matthew Arnold's Note-Books*, p. 137.

who 'went out.' Mrs. H. Ward, *A Writer's Recollections*, II, 74.

CHAPTER ELEVEN

317 hasty moment. T. S. Eliot, *Selected Essays, 1917–1932*, p. 366.

319 nor a "gas." Matthew Arnold, *God and the Bible: A Review of Objections to "Literature and Dogma,"* pp. 84, 78.

real effects. W. James, *The Varieties of Religious Experience*, p. 517.

attempt religious. *God and the Bible*, p. xli.

to be effected. *Ibid.*, p. x.

in truth, *revealed*. *Lit. and Dog.*, p. 45.

320 throws on them. *St. P.*, p. 6.

321 giveth life? *For Lancelot Andrewes*, p. 94.

texts and dogmas. *The Non-Religion of the Future*, p. 180.

for Aldous Huxley. *Ends and Means*, London and New York, 1937, Chapt. XIV.

for Julian Huxley. *What Dare I Think?*, London, 1931, Chapts. VI and VII.

324 therein set down. Spinoza, *Tractatus Theologico-Politicus*, p. 8.

affect us little. *Ibid.*, p. 8.

in question. *Ibid.*, p. 197.

325 aid of God. *Ibid.*, p. 45.

326 heart to obey. *Ibid.*, p. 185.

Pollock says. *Spinoza, his Life and Philosophy*, p. 155.

327 Holy Spirit. S. T. Coleridge, *"Confessions of an Inquiring Spirit," Complete Works of S. T. Coleridge*, V, 580.

stand alone. *Ibid.*, V, 580.

individual hearer. *Ibid.*, V, 605.

is the life. *Ibid.*, V, 591.

was it conceived. *Ibid.*, V, 591.

328 Ventriloquist. *Ibid.*, V, 591 and 593.

was revealed by God. *Ibid.*, V, 597.

theologians. *Ibid.*, V, 602.

Page

328 of Protestants! *Ibid.,* V, 618.
defended the truth. *Ibid.,* V, 593.

329 and instincts. *Lit. and Dog.,* p. 14.
and habits. *St. P.,* p. 30.

330 fulfil that part. *Ibid.,* pp. 31–32.
non-natural man. *Ibid.,* p. 9.

331 man of business. *Ibid.,* p. 14.
wrath to come. *Ibid.,* p. 22.
along with him. *Ibid.,* pp. 37–38.
teachers the most unlike. *Ibid.,* p. 38.

332 phenomenon. *An Essay on the Development of Christian Doctrine,* p. 12.
elucidation. *Ibid.,* p. 19.
from the first. *Ibid.,* p. 23.

333 matter, of you. *Unpub. Letters,* p. 56.
wants and needs. S. Hook, *From Hegel to Marx,* p. 229.

334 human culture. *Ibid.,* p. 225.
non-existence of man. Quoted by Hook, *op. cit.,* p. 223, from Feuerbach,
    Sämmtliche Werke, 1846, I, xiv–xv.

335 and worthless. *Lit. and Dog.,* p. 62.
inner man. *Ibid.,* p. 66.
popular Christianity. *Ibid.,* p. 70.

336 and justice. *Ibid.,* p. 74.
sanction of *happiness. Ibid.,* pp. 76–77.
verification. *Ibid.,* p. 177.
reached on this. *Ibid.,* p. 177.

337 tell him *right. Ibid.,* p. 195.
way of Jesus. *Ibid.,* p. 300.
greatest apostles. *Ibid.,* p. 248.
science of Christianity. *Ibid.,* p. 250.
vindictive temper. *Ibid.,* p. 253.
never uttered. *Ibid.,* p. 255.

338 an advantage. *Ibid.,* pp. 97–98.
conduct gone. *Ibid.,* p. 98.

339 sanction of *happiness. Ibid.,* p. 77.
dwelling upon it. *Ibid.,* p. 17.
touched by emotion. Ibid., p. 18.
which is moral. F. H. Bradley, *Ethical Studies,* p. 281.

340 deal from this. *Ibid.,* p. 281.
shall see God. *Lit. and Dog.,* p. 20.

341 central moral tendency. *St. P.,* p. 40.
universal order. *Ibid.,* p. 39.
its working. *Ibid.,* p. 39.
'does not like it.' *Ethical Studies,* p. 175, p. 177.

Page
342   is undeniable. *St. P.*, p. 39.
     not a spur. *Pensées and Letters*, p. 78.
343   which attend it. *Lit. and Dog.*, pp. 185–187.
345   these might. *St. P.*, p. 169.
     idea of pureness. *Ibid.*, p. 170.
     self-admiration. *Lit. and Dog.*, pp. 322–323.
     Jouarre. Letters, II, 414.
     Zola. *Mixed*, p. 254.
     depths of hell. *God and the Bible*, p. 130 *et seq.*
346   central tendency. *St. P.*, p. 40.
     spirit as Aldous Huxley. *Ends and Means*, London and New York, 1937,
       p. 360 *et seq.*
347   to control. *St. P.*, p. 40.
     got rid of. *Ibid.*, p. 46.
     understanding and will. *Ibid.*, pp. 48–49.
348   for our good. *Ibid.*, p. 49.
     was of God. *Ibid.*, p. 49.
349   or act for. "The Sentiment of Rationality," in *Selected Papers on Philos-
      ophy*, p. 142.
     indispensable. *The Varieties of Religious Experience*, p. 515.
     and dulness. *St. P.*, p. 50.
350   power of goodness. *Ibid.*, p. 59.
     law of the mind. *Ibid.*, p. 64.
     but a name. *Ethical Studies*, p. 290.
351   body of Christ. *St. P.*, p. 66.
     deceiving myself. *Ibid.*, pp. 67–68.
     metaphysical hypotheses. *The Non-Religion of the Future*, p. 10.
352   truly *alive*. *Lit. and Dog.*, p. 341.
353   father's goodness. . . . *Ibid.*, p. 278.
     be *verified? Ibid.*, p. 279.
     their being. Ibid., p. 37.
354   in the wreck. *The Varieties of Religious Experience*, p. 508.
     as exist? *Ibid.*, p. 510.
355   admitted reality. *Lit. and Dog.*, p. 38.
356   consciousness differs. *Ibid.*, pp. 10–11.
     loveth righteousness. *Ibid.*, p. 28.
     difficulties. *Reason and Nature*, p. 455.
357   the "more." *The Varieties of Religious Experience*, p. 512.
     and obeyed it? *God and the Bible*, p. 129.
     undeniably does. *Lit. and Dog.*, pp. 24–25.
358   clap-trap. *Ethical Studies*, p. 283.
     on *Conduct. Lit. and Dog.*, p. 317.
     Greece, Rome. *Ibid.*, p. 317.

Page
358 to himself? *Ethical Studies*, p. 283n.
359 see them at all. "A Liverpool Address," *Nineteenth Century*, Nov. 1882,
         vol. XII, no. 69, p. 716.
       and so on. *Ethical Studies*, p. 283.
360 it points. *Science and Poetry*, pp. 70–71.
       called goodness. *St. P.*, p. 312.
       and of practice. *Ibid.*, p. 131.
361 essence of Christianity. *Ibid.*, pp. 131–132.
       as we can. Hobbes, *Leviathan*, Everyman ed., p. 195.
362 save us from it. *St. P.*, p. 348.
       man rejects. *Ibid.*, p. 209.
363 to salvation. *Ibid.*, p. 210.
       use of poetry. *Ibid.*, p. 213.
       us vibrates. *Ibid.*, p. 218.
       dilettanteism. *Ibid.*, p. 227.
       all a fable. *Winds of Doctrine*, p. 49.
364 Christianity is true. *Ibid.*, p. 54.
       except in name. *Faust*, trans. Cookson, pp. 160–161.
365 McGiffert says. *The Rise of Modern Religious Ideas*, p. 79.
366 social transformation. *St. P.*, p. 321.
       of the grave. *Ibid.*, p. 321.
       satisfied classes. *Ibid.*, p. 322.
       is impossible. *Ibid.*, p. 322.
367 English Church. *Unpub. Letters*, pp. 57–58.
       ours is now. *St. P.*, p. 327.
       to preach it. *Ibid.*, pp. 327–328.
       chief actors. *God and the Bible*, p. 6.
       dying is life. *Ibid.*, p. 8.
368 of the kingdom. *St. P.*, p. 330.

CHAPTER TWELVE

369 phantom of property. *Mixed*, p. 465.
370 no harm. *Ibid.*, p. 58.
       not the whole. *Ibid.*, p. vii.
371 Huxley had said. See "Science and Culture" in Vol. III of *Selected Works
         of Thomas H. Huxley*.
       life and manners. *Mixed*, p. x and *Discourses in America*, p. 101.
372 what a world! *Essays Crit. II*, p. 167.
373 and himself. *Ibid.*, p. 138.
       not know him. *Ibid.*, p. 139.
       and strength. *Ibid.*, pp. 142–143.
374 replaced by poetry. *Ibid.*, p. 2.

Page
374 and stay. *Ibid.*, p. 4.
375 poetical quality. *Ibid.*, p. 14.
Horace and Dante. *Mixed*, p. 207.
376 by irony. *Ibid.*, p. 440.
to have not power. *Ibid.*, p. 441.
377 of their work. *Essays Crit. III*, p. 239.
Professor Legouis. *Défense de la Poésie Française*, pp. 16–25.
378 in the soul. *Essays Crit. II*, p. 68.
not a Dante. *John Dryden*, New York, 1920, p. 323.
379 chief poetical names. *Essays Crit. II*, p. 94.
380 and frailest. *Ibid.*, p. 30.
idealise lust. *Choice of Books*, p. 69.
nature and beauty. *Mixed*, p. 241.
delight for all. *Ibid.*, pp. 248–249.
381 him dishonour. *Ibid.*, p. 251.
some day know it. *Ibid.*, p. 240.
with life. *Ibid.*, p. 249.
new-birth. *Ibid.*, p. 251.
early gods. *Ibid.*, p. 260.
staggered. *Ibid.*, p. 253.
man in society. *Ibid.*, p. viii.
and manners. *Ibid.*, p. x.
382 our humanisation. *Ibid.*, p. ix.
is impossible. *Ibid.*, pp. 70–71.
383 admitted *always*. *Ibid.*, pp. 46–47.
384 English middle class. *Ibid.*, p. 379.
with the middle. *Ibid.*, p. 105.
385 university quality. *Experiment in Autobiography*, New York, 1934, pp. 67–68.
class feeling. *Ibid.*, p. 68.
for another. *Mixed*, pp. 383–384.
toiling class. *Ibid.*, p. 391. Quoted by Arnold from John Morley's quotation of a unionist workingman.
386 begotten. *Ibid.*, p. 391.
387 creation of law. *Ibid.*, p. 465.
so agitating. "A Comment on Christmas," *Contemporary Review*, April 1885, vol. 47, p. 471.
of the future. *Mixed*, p. 381.
388 for expansion. *Ibid.*, pp. 386–387.
and admired. *Letters*, II, 372.
389 great pleasure. *Ibid.*, II, 368.
390 his practice. *Ibid.*, II, 126.
liked Carlyle. *Ibid.*, II, 222.

Page
390 one's own way. *Ibid.*, II, 229.
of a century. *Ibid.*, II, 10.
grows old. *Ibid.*, II, 338.
391 are gaining. *Ibid.*, II, 20.
and knows it. *Ibid.*, II, 59.
have published. *Ibid.*, II, 326.
and simple. *Mixed*, p. 277.
obliged to us. *Letters*, II, 54.
392 the D. of D. *Ibid.*, II, 241.
of England. *Ibid.*, II, 250.
393 in the world. Albert Bigelow Paine, *Mark Twain*, 4 vols., New York,
1912, II, 759.
of the Atlantic. Matthew Arnold, *Civilization in the United States*, p. 71.
395 you would expect. Quoted by C. H. Leonard, *Arnold in America*, p. 80.
H. C. Bunner. *Ibid.*, p. 82.
ever to obtain. Matthew Arnold, *Discourses in America*, p. 178.
is apocryphal. Leonard, *op. cit.*, p. 156 *et seq.*
396 gracious note. *Ibid.*, pp. 191–192.
be an American. Quoted, *ibid.*, p. 188.
have suthin'? Quoted, *ibid.*, p. 209.
dudes of literature. Traubel, *With Walt Whitman in Camden*, I, 45.
397 overwhelm us. *Ibid.*, III, 400.
chinaware, Matthew Arnold! *Ibid.*, III, 532.
those fellows, *Ibid.*, II, 204.
at first hand. *Ibid.*, I, 23.
paid in America. B. Perry, *Walt Whitman*, p. 178.
398 set their desires. *Ibid.*, p. 178.
foundries and crowds. Quoted by Leonard, *op. cit.*, p. 114.
just people! Traubel, *op. cit.*, I, 232.
399 roar so inaudibly. Leonard, *op. cit.*, p. 87.
be unsound. *Discourses in America*, pp. 23–24 and pp. 25–26.
400 goddess Aselgeia. *Ibid.*, pp. 59–60.
401 that is Mark Twain. William Dean Howells, *My Mark Twain*, New York,
1910, p. 28.
expect from him. G. Bradford, *Journal*, pp. 43–44.
to me since. *Letters of Gamaliel Bradford*, p. 286.
402 unsold tickets. W. R. Thayer, *Life of John Hay*, 2 vols., New York and
Boston, 1908, II, 70.
$6000. Leonard, *op. cit.*, p. 247.
at the Author's Club. *Ibid.*, p. 240.
403 inspire hatred. *Civilization in the United States*, pp. 125–126.
404 'so English, you know.' *Ibid.*, p. 168.
outward things. *Ibid.*, p. 173.

Page
404   Henry James. See, for example, his *Hawthorne*.
     awe and respect. *Civilization in the United States*, p. 176.
405   national misfortune. *Ibid.*, p. 177.
     pains across my chest. *Letters*, II, 324.
     to one's end. *Ibid.*, II, 326.
     year as myself). *Ibid.*, II, 354.
     and Newman. *Ibid.*, II, 362.
     dinner by him. *Ibid.*, II, 378.
406   final disappearance. E. H. Coleridge, *Life and Corr. of J. D. Lord Coleridge*, II, 310.
     down dead. E. M. Sellar, *Recollections and Impressions*, p. 158.
     both sides. Morley, *Recollections*, I, 129.

BIBLIOGRAPHY

»» ««

WORKS OF MATTHEW ARNOLD

The following list, arranged alphabetically, includes only those editions of the works of Matthew Arnold which have been used in this book. For a complete Matthew Arnold bibliography the reader should consult Thomas Burnett Smart, *Bibliography of Matthew Arnold*, London, 1892.

"Address to the Wordsworth Society," *Macmillan's Magazine*, June 1883, vol. xlviii, no. 284, pp. 154–155.

"The Bishop and the Philosopher," *Macmillan's Magazine*, Jan. 1863, vol. vii, no. 39, pp. 241–256.

Civilization in the United States: First and Last Impressions of America, Boston, 1888.

"A Comment on Christmas," *Contemporary Review*, April 1885, vol. xlvii, pp. 457–472.

Culture & Anarchy: An Essay In Political And Social Criticism and *Friendship's Garland, Being The Conversations, Letters, And Opinions Of The Late Arminius, Baron Von Thunder-Ten-Tronckh. Collected And Edited, With A Dedicatory Letter To Adolescens Leo, Esq., Of "The Daily Telegraph,"* New York, 1924.

Culture and Anarchy, ed. with an intro. [and notes] by J. Dover Wilson, Cambridge, 1932.

Discourses in America, New York, 1924.

"Disestablishment in Wales," *National Review*, Mar. 1888, vol. xi, no. 61, pp. 1–13.

England and the Italian Question, London, 1859.

Essays by Matthew Arnold, Including Essays In Criticism, 1865, On Translating Homer (With F. W. Newman's Reply) And Five Other Essays Now For The First Time Collected, Oxford, 1919.

Essays in Criticism: First Series, New York, 1924.

Essays in Criticism: Second Series, New York, 1935.

Essays in Criticism: Third Series, ed. E. J. O'Brien, Boston, 1910.

A French Eton; or, Middle Class Education and the State, London and Cambridge, 1864.

436

"From Easter to August," *Nineteenth Century,* Sept. 1887, vol. xxii, no. 127, pp. 310–324.

God & The Bible: A Review Of Objections To "Literature & Dogma," New York, 1924.

"Italian Art and Literature before Giotto and Dante," *Macmillan's Magazine,* Jan. 1876, vol. xxxiii, no. 195, p. 228.

Letters of an Old Playgoer, ed. with an intro. by Brander Matthews, New York, 1919.

Literature & Dogma: An Essay Towards A Better Apprehension Of The Bible, New York, 1924.

"A Liverpool Address," *Nineteenth Century,* Nov. 1882, vol. xii, no. 69, pp. 710–720.

Mixed Essays, Irish Essays, And Others, New York, 1924.

"The Nadir of Liberalism," *Nineteenth Century,* May 1886, vol. xix, no. 111, pp. 645–663.

On the Study of Celtic Literature and *On Translating Homer,* New York, 1924.

The Poems of Matthew Arnold, 1840–1867, with an intro. by Sir A. T. Quiller-Couch, London, 1930.

The Popular Education of France with Notices of that of Holland and Switzerland, London, 1861.

Reports on Elementary Schools, 1852–1882, by Matthew Arnold . . . , ed. Sir Francis Sanford, London and New York, 1889.

St. Paul & Protestantism, With An Essay On Puritanism & The Church of England and *Last Essays on Church & Religion,* New York, 1924.

Schools and Universities on the Continent, London, 1868.

Special Report on Certain Points Connected With Elementary Education in Germany, Switzerland, and France, London, 1888.

"A Speech at Westminster," *Macmillan's Magazine,* Feb. 1874, vol. xxix, no. 172, pp. 361–366.

Thoughts on Education Chosen from the Writings of Matthew Arnold, ed. Leonard Huxley, London, 1912.

"Up to Easter," *Nineteenth Century,* May 1887, vol. xxi, no. 123, pp. 629–643.

"The Zenith of Conservatism," *Nineteenth Century,* Jan. 1887, vol. xxi, no. 119, pp. 148–164.

WORKS EDITED BY MATTHEW ARNOLD

A Bible-Reading for Schools. The Great Prophecy of Israel's Restoration, London, 1872.

Isaiah of Jerusalem in the Authorized English Version with an Introduction, Corrections, and Notes, London, 1883.

Letters, Speeches and Tracts on Irish Affairs by Edmund Burke, London, 1881.

Poems of Wordsworth, London, 1879.

Poetry of Byron, London, 1881.
The Six Chief Lives from Johnson's "Lives of the Poets," with Macaulay's "Life of Johnson," London, 1878.

LETTERS AND NOTEBOOKS OF MATTHEW ARNOLD

Letters from Matthew Arnold to Churton Collins, London, 1910 ("Edition limited to 20 copies").
Letters of Matthew Arnold, 1848-1888, collected and arranged by G. W. E. Russell, two vols. in one, New York and London, 1900.
The Letters of Matthew Arnold to Arthur Hugh Clough, ed. with an introductory study by Howard Foster Lowry, London and New York, 1932.
Matthew Arnold's Notebooks, New York, 1902.
Unpublished Letters of Matthew Arnold, ed. Arnold Whitridge, New Haven, 1923.

WORKS OF THOMAS ARNOLD

The Christian Life: Its Course, its Hindrances, and its Helps, London, 1845.
The Christian Life: Its Hopes, its Fears, and its Close, London, 1845.
Fragment on the Church, London, 1844.
History of Rome, 3 vols., London, 1840-43.
Introductory Lectures on Modern History, New York, 1845.
Miscellaneous Works, First American Edition, with Nine Additional Essays not Included in the English Collection, New York and Philadelphia, 1845.
Principles of Church Reform, 4th ed. with a postscript, London, 1833.
Sermons preached in the Chapel of Rugby School, with an address before confirmation, London, 1845.
Sermons: To which is added a new edition of two sermons on the interpretation of prophecy, London, 1834-44.

GENERAL BIBLIOGRAPHY

※》》 《《

For a full list of the now very extensive writings on Matthew Arnold, see Smart's bibliography, mentioned above, which covers the period up to 1891 and T. G. Ehrsam, R. H. Deily and R. M. Smith, *Bibliographies of Twelve Victorian Authors,* New York, 1936, which, including the material in Smart though in less convenient form, continues the list up to 1934.

The following bibliography lists the works which have been most useful to the author or which, in his opinion, are likely to be most useful or interesting to the reader. It excludes many books referred to in the text, such as novels, classical writings in philosophy, standard poetical works, modern essays. However, when any book not mentioned in this bibliography has been directly quoted from, the necessary bibliographical information will be found either in the text itself or in the reference notes.

Adams, H., *The Life and Writings of Giambattista Vico,* London, 1935.

Adamson, J. W., *English Education: 1789–1902,* Cambridge, 1930.

Archer, R. L., *Secondary Education in the Nineteenth Century,* Cambridge, 1921.

Arnold, Thomas [the younger], *Passages in a Wandering Life,* London, 1900.

Arnold, William Delafield, *Oakfield; or, Fellowship in the East,* Boston, 1855.

Aytoun, Wm. Edmondstoune, *The Book of Ballads, edited by Bon Gaultier (Professor Aytoun and Theodore Martin) and Firmilian, A Spasmodic Tragedy by T. Percy Jones (W. E. Aytoun),* New York, 1867.

Babbitt, Irving, *The Masters of Modern French Criticism,* Boston and New York, 1912.

Rousseau and Romanticism, Boston and New York, 1919.

Baddeley, M. J. B., *The English District,* London, 1922.

Balleine, G. R., *A History of the Evangelical Party in the Church of England,* New York, 1933.

Barker, Ernest, *Political Thought in England from Herbert Spencer to the Present Day,* New York and London, n.d.

Political Thought of Plato and Aristotle, New York, 1906.

Barzun, Jacques, *Race: A Study in Modern Superstition*, New York, 1937.

Beach, Joseph Warren, *The Concept of Nature in Nineteenth Century English Poetry*, New York, 1936.

Beard, Charles A. and Mary R., *The Rise of American Civilization*, two vols. in one, New York, 1930.

Becker, Carl, *The Heavenly City of the Eighteenth Century Philosophers*, New Haven, 1932.

Benn, A. W., *The History of English Rationalism in the Nineteenth Century*, 2 vols., London and New York, 1906.

Benson, E. F., *As We Were*, New York, 1930.

Birchenough, C., *History of Elementary Education in England and Wales from 1800 to the Present Day*, London, 1914.

Boas, Franz, *Anthropology and Modern Life*, New York, 1928.

Bonnerot, L., "La Jeunesse de Matthew Arnold," *Revue Anglo-Américaine*, August 1930, Année 7, pp. 520–537.

Bosanquet, Bernard, *The Philosophical Theory of the State*, London, 1920.

Bradford, Gamaliel, *The Journal of Gamaliel Bradford*, ed. Van Wyck Brooks, Boston and New York, 1933.
　The Letters of Gamaliel Bradford, 1918–1931, ed. Van Wyck Brooks, Boston and New York, 1934.

Bradley, Andrew Cecil, *A Miscellany*, London, 1929.

Bradley, Francis Herbert, *Ethical Studies*, New York, 1911.

Brandes, Georg, *Main Currents in Nineteenth Century Literature*, 6 vols., New York and London, 1924.

Brinton, Crane, *The Political Ideas of the English Romanticists*, Oxford, 1926.

Brooks, Van Wyck, *The Malady of the Ideal*, London, 1913.

Brown, E. K., *Studies in the Text of Matthew Arnold's Prose Works*, Paris, 1935.

Brown, Philip Anthony, *The French Revolution in English History*, London, 1918.

Burke, Edmund, *Writings and Speeches of Edmund Burke*, Beaconsfield edition, 12 vols., Boston, 1901.

Bury, J. B., *The Idea of Progress*, London, 1920.
　A History of the Freedom of Thought, London and New York, 1913.

Butcher, S. H., *Some Aspects of the Greek Genius*, London, 1916.

Carlyle, Thomas, *The Life of John Sterling*, New York [Scribner], n.d.
　Sartor Resartus, New York, 1893.
　Scottish and Other Miscellanies, Everyman edition.

Carnegie, Andrew, *Autobiography*, Boston and New York, 1920.

Chambers, Sir Edmund K., *Matthew Arnold*, reprinted from *The Proceedings of the British Academy*, vol. xviii, London, 1932.

Cheyne, T. K., *Founders of Old Testament Criticism*, New York, 1893.

Church, R. W., *The Oxford Movement*, London, 1922.

Clifford, W. K., *Lectures and Essays*, ed. Leslie Stephen and Sir Frederick Pollock, 2 vols., London, 1901.

Clough, Arthur Hugh, *The Emerson-Clough Letters,* ed. H. F. Lowry and R. L. Rusk, Cleveland, 1934.

    Poetical Works, ed. C. Whibley, London, 1920.

    Prose Remains, ed. by his Wife [Blanche (Smith) Clough], London, 1888.

Cobban, Alfred, *Edmund Burke and the Revolt against the Eighteenth Century,* London, 1929.

Cohen, Morris, *Reason and Nature,* New York, 1931.

Colenso, John Wm., *The Pentateuch and Book of Joshua Critically Examined,* Part I, 6th ed., London, 1873.

Coleridge, Ernest Hartley, *Life and Correspondence of John Duke Lord Coleridge,* 2 vols., London, 1904.

Coleridge, J. T., *A Memoir of the Rev. John Keble, M.A.,* 2 vols., New York, 1869.

Coleridge, Samuel Taylor, *The Complete Works of S. T. Coleridge,* ed. Shedd, 7 vols., vol. v, *Confessions of an Inquiring Spirit;* vol. vi, *On the Constitution of the Church and State, According to the Idea of Each,* New York, 1853–4.

    Table Talk and Omniana, ed. T. Ashe, London, 1923.

    Unpublished Letters of S. T. Coleridge, ed. E. L. Griggs, 2 vols., New Haven, 1933.

Collinwood, W. G., *Lake District History,* London, 1925.

Cornish, F. W., *The English Church in the Nineteenth Century,* 2 vols., London, 1910.

Craik, Henry, *The State and Education,* London, 1884.

Croce, Benedetto, *The Philosophy of Giambattista Vico,* trans. R. G. Collingwood, New York, 1913.

Curtius, Ernst Robert, *The Civilization of France,* trans. O. Wyan, New York, 1932.

Dallas, Eneas Sweetland, *The Gay Science,* London, 1866.

Dewey, John, *Characters and Events,* ed. Joseph Ratner, 2 vols., New York, 1929.

Dicey, A. V., *Lectures on the Relation between Law and Opinion in England during the Nineteenth Century,* London, 1920.

Dobbs, A. E., *Education and Social Movements,* London, 1919.

Drinkwater, John, "Some Letters from Matthew Arnold to Robert Browning," *Cornhill Magazine,* December 1923, n.s., vol. 55, pp. 654–664.

Edman, Irwin, *The Mind of Paul,* New York, 1935.

Elias, Otto, *Matthew Arnolds Politische Grundanschauungen,* Leipzig, 1931.

Eliot, George, *Essays and Leaves from a Note-Book,* New York, 1884.

Eliot, T. S., *For Lancelot Andrewes,* New York, 1929.

    The Sacred Wood, 2nd ed., London, 1928.

    Selected Essays, 1917–1932, New York, 1932.

    The Use of Poetry and the Use of Criticism, Cambridge, Mass., 1933.

Ellis, Havelock, *A Study of British Genius,* Boston and New York, 1926.

Estève, Edmond, *Alfred de Vigny: Sa Pensée et Son Art,* Paris, 1923.

Fairchild, Hoxie Neale, *The Romantic Quest,* New York, 1931.

Faulkner, H. V., *Chartism and the Churches,* New York, 1916.

Fitch, Sir Joshua, *Thomas and Matthew Arnold and Their Influence on English Education,* New York, 1899.

Flint, Robert, *Vico,* Edinburgh and London, 1884.

Foakes-Jackson, F. J., *The Life of St. Paul: The Man and the Apostle,* London, 1933.

Foerster, Norman, "Matthew Arnold and American Letters Today," *Sewanee Review,* July 1922, vol. 30, pp. 298–306.

Forster, E. M., *Abinger Harvest,* New York, 1936.

Furrer, Paul, *Der Einfluss Sainte-Beuves auf die Kritik Matthew Arnolds,* Zurich, 1920.

Garrod, H. W., *Wordsworth,* 2nd ed., Oxford, 1927.
  The Profession of Poetry, Oxford, 1929.
  Poetry and the Criticism of Life, Cambridge, Mass., 1931.

Giese, Wm. Fred., *Sainte-Beuve: A Literary Portrait,* Madison, Wis., 1931.

Gillespie, Frances E., *Labor and Politics in England, 1850–1867,* Durham, N. C., 1927.

Gladstone, W. E., *"Robert Elsmere" and the Battle of Belief* (*Reprinted from "The Nineteenth Century," May, 1888*), New York, n.d.

Glover, T. R., *Paul of Tarsus,* New York, 1930.

Goethe, J. W. von, *Conversations with Eckermann,* Everyman edition.
  Faust: Part One, trans. G. M. Cookson, London [Routledge], n.d.
  Goethes Werke, 2 vols., Berlin [Knaur], [1932?].
  Literary Essays, ed. and trans. J. E. Spingarn, New York, 1921.
  Poetry and Truth from My Own Life, trans. M. S. Smith, 2 vols., London, 1913.

Gooch, G. P., *History and Historians in the Nineteenth Century,* London, 1913.

Green, Thomas Hill, *Works of Thomas Hill Green,* ed. R. L. Nettleship, 3 vols., New York and London, 1885–8.

Gretton, R. H., *The English Middle Class,* London, 1917.

Grierson, H. J. C., *The Background of English Literature,* New York, 1921.

Guedalla, Philip, *Palmerston: 1784–1865,* New York and London, 1927.

Guérin, Maurice de, *From Centaur to Cross,* trans. H. Bedford Jones, New York, 1929.

Guyau, Marie Jean, *The Non-Religion of the Future: A Sociological Study,* London, 1897.

Haigh, Arthur Elam, *The Attic Theatre,* 3rd ed., Oxford, 1907.

Halévy, Elie, *Histoire du Peuple Anglais aux XIX Siècle,* 3 vols., Paris, 1912–23.
  La Formation du Radicalisme Philosophique, 3 vols., Paris, 1901–04.

Hall, Walter Phelps, "The Three Arnolds and Their Bible," *Essays in Intellectual History Dedicated to James Harvey Robinson,* New York, 1929.

Hankins, Frank H., *The Racial Basis of Civilization,* New York and London, 1926.

Harrison, Frederic, *The Choice of Books,* London, 1886.

Tennyson, Ruskin, Mill and other Literary Estimates, New York and London, 1900.

Hearnshaw, F. J. C. (ed.), *The Social and Political Ideas of some Representative Thinkers of the Age of Reaction and Reconstruction, 1815–1865,* London, 1932.

The Social and Political Ideas of some Representative Thinkers of the Victorian Age, London, 1933.

Hegel, G. W. F., *Lectures on the Philosophy of History,* trans. J. Sibree, London, 1872.

The Philosophy of Right, trans. S. W. Dyde, London, 1896.

Henson, Herbert Hensley (Bishop of Durham), *Anglicanism,* London, 1921.

Herford, R. Travers, *The Pharisees,* New York, 1924.

Hill, W. Douglas P. (trans. and ed.), *The Bhagavadgītā,* Oxford, 1928.

Höffding, Harald, *A History of Modern Philosophy,* trans. from the German ed. by B. E. Meyer, 2 vols., London, 1920.

Hook, Sidney, *From Hegel to Marx,* New York, 1936.

Hughes, Thomas, *Tom Brown's School-days,* Everyman edition.

Humboldt, Wilhelm von, *The Sphere and Duties of Government,* trans. Joseph Coulthard, London, 1854.

Hutton, Lawrence, *Literary Landmarks of Oxford,* New York, 1903.

Hutton, R. H., *Essays in Literary Criticism,* 3rd ed., London, 1888.

Essays on Some of the Modern Guides of English Thought in Matters of Faith, London, 1883.

Huxley, Julian S. and Haddon, A. C., *We Europeans: A Survey of "Racial" Problems,* London, 1935.

Huxley, T. H., *Selected Works of T. H. Huxley,* 6 vols., vol. iii, *Science and Education,* New York, n.d.

James, Henry, *Views and Reviews,* Boston, 1908.

James, William, *Selected Papers on Philosophy,* Everyman edition.

The Varieties of Religious Experience, New York, 1903.

Joubert, Joseph, *Pensées and Letters,* trans. H. P. Collins, London, 1928.

Jowett, Benjamin, *Letters of Benjamin Jowett,* ed. E. Abbott and L. Campbell, London, 1899.

Keble, John, *Keble's Lectures on Poetry,* trans. Edward Kershaw Francis, 2 vols., Oxford, 1912.

Kingsmill, Hugh, *Matthew Arnold,* New York, 1928.

Klineberg, Otto, *Race Differences,* New York, 1935.

Knickerbocker, Wm. S., *Creative Oxford,* Syracuse, N. Y., 1925.

"Matthew Arnold at Oxford: The Natural History of a Father and Son," *Sewanee Review,* Oct.–Dec. 1927, vol. 35, pp. 399–418.

"Semaphore: Arnold and Clough," *Sewanee Review,* April 1933, vol. 41, pp. 152–174.

Lake, Kirsopp, *Paul: His Heritage and Legacy,* New York, 1934.

Laski, Harold, *Authority in the Modern State,* New Haven, 1919.

The Rise of Liberalism, New York, 1936.

The State in Theory and Practice, New York, 1935.

Legouis, Émile, *Défense De La Poésie Française À L'Usage Des Lecteurs Anglais*, Paris, 1912.

Leonard, Chilson Hathaway, *Arnold in America: A Study of Matthew Arnold's Literary Relations with America and of his Visits to this Country in 1883 and 1886*, New Haven, 1932. (Unpublished doctoral dissertation in the Sterling Memorial Library, Yale University.)

Leonard, W. E. (trans.), *The Fragments of Empedocles*, Chicago, 1908.

Leopardi, Giacomo, *Poems*, ed. and trans. Geoffrey L. Bickersteth, Cambridge, 1923.

Lewis, Wyndham, *The Lion and the Fox*, London, 1927.

Lewisohn, Ludwig, "A Study of Matthew Arnold," *Sewanee Review*, Oct. 1901, vol. 9, pp. 442–456; April–July 1902, vol. 10, pp. 143–159, pp. 302–319.

Lippincott, B. E., *Victorian Critics of Democracy*, Minneapolis, 1938.

"Longinus," *On the Sublime*, trans. W. Hamilton Fyfe, London and New York, 1927.

MacCunn, John, *Political Philosophy of Edmund Burke*, London, 1913.

McGiffert, Arthur Cushman, *A History of Christian Thought*, 2 vols., New York, 1932.

The Rise of Modern Religious Ideas, New York, 1925.

Mallock, W. H., *The New Republic*, London, n.d.

Martineau, James, *Miscellanies*, Boston and New York, 1852.

Marx, Karl, *Capital*, trans. Eden and Cedar Paul, 2 vols., Everyman edition.

The Story of the Life of Lord Palmerston, ed. Eleanor Marx Aveling, London, 1899.

Mead, George H., *Movements of Thought in the Nineteenth Century*, ed. Merritt H. Moore, Chicago, 1936.

Merriam, C. E. and Barnes, H. E. (eds.), *A History of Political Theories: Recent Times*, New York, 1924.

Meusel, Alfred, "The Middle Class," *Encyclopedia of the Social Sciences*, vol. x, New York, 1933.

Michelet, Jules, *Principes de la Philosophie de L'Histoire, traduits de la Scienza Nuova de J. B. Vico, &c.*, Brussels, 1835.

Mill, John Stuart, *Autobiography*, New York, 1924.

Principles of Political Economy, 3rd ed., 2 vols., London, 1852.

Utilitarianism, Liberty & Representative Government, Everyman edition.

Montmorency, J. E. G., *State Intervention in English Education*, Cambridge, 1902.

Moore, George Foot, *Judaism in the First Centuries of the Christian Era*, 2 vols., Cambridge, Mass., 1927–30.

More, Paul Elmer, *The Drift of Romanticism*, Boston and New York, 1913.

Morley, John, *Recollections*, 2 vols., New York, 1917.

Mott, Louis Freeman, "Renan and Matthew Arnold," *Modern Language Notes*, Feb. 1918, vol. xxxiii, no. 2.

Sainte-Beuve, New York, 1925.

Muirhead, J. H., *Coleridge as Philosopher*, London, 1930.

Murray, R. H., *Edmund Burke*, Oxford, 1931.

Neff, Emery E., *Carlyle and Mill*, 2nd ed., New York, 1926.

Newman, Francis W., *Hebrew Theism: The Common Basis of Judaism, Christianity, and Mohammedism*, London, 1874.

The *Iliad of Homer faithfully translated into Unrhymed English Metre*, London, 1856.

Newman, John Henry (Cardinal), *An Essay on The Development of Christian Doctrine*, New York, 1845.

Apologia Pro Vita Sua, Everyman edition.

Tract I in *Tracts for the Times, by members of the University of Oxford*, vol. i for 1833-4, London, 1834.

Oakesmith, John, *Race and Nationality*, London, 1919.

Omond, T. S., "Arnold and Homer," *Essays and Studies by Members of the English Association*, vol. iii, Oxford, 1912.

Oppenheimer, Franz, *The State*, trans. J. M. Gitterman, New York, 1926.

Orrick, James Bentley, *Matthew Arnold and Goethe*, Publications of the English Goethe Society, London, 1928.

Osborne, J. I., *Arthur Hugh Clough*, London, 1920.

Park, Joseph H., *The English Reform Bill of 1867*, New York, 1920. (A Columbia University doctoral dissertation published by the author.)

Pascal, Blaise, *Pensées*, trans., W. F. Trotter, intro. T. S. Eliot, Everyman edition.

Patterson, M. W., *A History of the Church of England*, London, 1925.

Perry, Bliss, *Walt Whitman*, Boston and New York, 1906.

Perry, G. G., *Student's History of the Church of England*, 2nd ed., 3 vols., London, 1890.

Pollock, Sir Frederick, *Spinoza: His Life and Philosophy*, 2nd ed., London, 1899.

Powell, A. Fryer, "Sainte-Beuve and Matthew Arnold," *The French Quarterly*, vol. iii, Sept. 1921.

Prothero, R. E., *The Life and Correspondence of Arthur Penrhyn Stanley*, 2 vols., New York, 1894.

Randall, John Herman, *The Making of the Modern Mind*, New York, 1926.

Reid, Wemyss, *Life of W. E. Forster*, 2 vols., London, 1888.

Renan, Ernest, *Recollections of my Youth*, trans. C. G. Pitman, London, 1929.

The Future of Science, London, 1891.

Reynolds, Sir Joshua, *Fifteen Discourses Delivered in the Royal Academy*, Everyman edition.

Richards, I. A., *Coleridge on Imagination*, New York, 1935.

Principles of Literary Criticism, New York, 1928.

Science and Poetry, New York, 1926.

Richardson, Bessie Ellen, *Old Age Among the Ancient Greeks*, Baltimore, 1933.

Robertson, J. M., *A History of Free Thought*, 2 vols., New York, 1930.

Robinson, Henry Crabb, *Correspondence of H.C.R. with the Wordsworth Circle*, ed. Edith J. Morley, 2 vols., Oxford, 1927.

Rothstein, Th., *From Chartism to Labourism*, New York, 1929.

Rousseau, Jean Jacques, *Émile*, Everyman edition.

    The Social Contract, intro. G. D. H. Cole, Everyman edition.

Routh, H. V., *Towards the Twentieth Century*, New York, 1937.

Ruskin, John, *Time and Tide*, New York, 1928.

Sainte-Beuve, C. A., *Chateaubriand et son groupe littéraire*, Paris, 1861.

    Étude sur Virgile, Paris, 1857.

Saintsbury, George, *A History of Criticism and Literary Taste*, 3 vols., New York, 1904.

    Matthew Arnold, London, 1899.

Santayana, George, *Winds of Doctrine*, London and New York, 1913.

Scherer, Edmond, *Essays on English Literature*, trans. George Saintsbury, New York, 1891.

    Études sur la Littérature Contemporaine, 6 vols., Paris, 1886.

Schweitzer, Albert, *The Mysticism of Paul the Apostle*, trans. William Montgomery, New York, 1931.

Sellar, E. M. (Mrs.), *Recollections and Impressions*, Edinburgh and London, 1907.

Sells, Iris Esther, *Matthew Arnold and France: The Poet*, Cambridge, 1935.

Senancour, Étienne Pivert de, *Obermann*, avec un Préface de Sainte-Beuve, Paris, 1833.

    Obermann, trans. A. E. Waite, New York, 1903.

Shafer, Robert, *Christianity and Naturalism*, New Haven, 1926.

Shairp, John Campbell, *Glen Desseray and Other Poems*, London, 1888.

Sherman, Stuart, *Matthew Arnold, How to Know Him*, Indianapolis, 1917.

    Shaping Men and Women, ed. J. Zeitlin, New York, 1932.

Sieveking, I. Giberne, *Memoir and Letters of Francis W. Newman*, London, 1909.

Sikes, E. E., *The Greek View of Poetry*, New York, 1931.

Smith, Alexander, *City Poems*, Cambridge, 1857.

    A Life Drama and other Poems, Boston, 1865.

    Poems, 4th ed., London, 1856.

Spencer, Herbert, *The Man versus the State*, New York, 1916.

Spinoza, Benedict de, *Ethics*, trans. A. Boyle, intro. G. Santayana, Everyman edition.

    Tractatus Theologico-Politicus in *The Chief Works of Benedict de Spinoza*, trans. R. H. M. Elwes, 2 vols., London, 1905.

Stanley, Arthur Penrhyn, *The Life and Correspondence of Thomas Arnold, D.D.*, 13th ed., 2 vols., London, 1882.

Stephen, James Fitzjames, *Liberty, Equality, Fraternity*, London, 1873.

Stephen, Leslie, *The Life of Sir James Fitzjames Stephen*, London, 1895.

    The English Utilitarians, 3 vols., London, 1900.

    Studies of a Biographer, vol. ii, London, 1898.

Stewart, H. L., *A Century of Anglo-Catholicism*, New York, 1929.
Swinburne, A. C., *Essays and Studies*, London, 1901.
Tawney, R. H., *Equality*, New York, 1931.
  Religion and the Rise of Capitalism, New York, 1926.
Thorndike, Ashley H., *Literature in a Changing Age*, New York, 1920.
Tinker, Chauncey Brewster, "Arnold's Poetical Plans," *Yale Review*, n.s., June 1933, vol. 22, pp. 782–793.
Tocqueville, Alexis de, *Democracy in America*, trans. Reeve and Bowen, 2 vols., Boston, 1882.
Traubel, Horace, *With Walt Whitman in Camden*, 3 vols., New York, 1914–5.
Trevelyan, George Macaulay, *British History in the Nineteenth Century*, London, 1930.
  The Life of John Bright, Boston and New York, 1925.
Trotter, Lionel, *Hodson of Hodson's Horse*, Everyman edition.
Wagner, Donald O., *The Church of England and Social Reform Since 1854*, New York, 1930.
Walker, Hugh, *The Literature of the Victorian Era*, London, 1921.
Walpole, Spencer, *The History of Twenty-Five Years*, 4 vols., London, 1904.
Ward, Mrs. Humphry, *Robert Elsmere*, Westmoreland ed., 2 vols., London, 1911.
  A Writer's Recollections, 2 vols., New York, 1918.
Webb, Clement, *A Study of Religious Thought in England from 1850*, Oxford, 1933.
Weber, Max, *The Protestant Ethic and the Spirit of Capitalism*, trans. T. Parsons, New York, 1930.
White, Andrew Dickson, *A History of the Warfare of Science with Theology in Christendom*, 2 vols., New York and London, 1910.
Whitridge, Arnold, *Dr. Arnold of Rugby*, New York, 1928.
Woods, Margaret, "Matthew Arnold" in *Essays and Studies of the English Association*, vol. xv, Oxford, 1929.
Woolf, Leonard, *After the Deluge*, London, 1931.

Contemporary Reviews Referred To

Blackwood's Magazine, Sept. 1849, vol. 66, pp. 340–346; Mar. 1854, vol. 75, pp. 303–314.
The Eclectic Review, n.s., Mar. 1855, vol. 9, pp. 276–284.
The English Review, Mar. 1850, vol. 13, pp. 211–213.
The Fortnightly Review, n.s., Oct. 1867, vol. 2, pp. 414–445.
Fraser's Magazine, May 1849, vol. 39, pp. 570–586.
The Germ, Feb. 1850, no. 2, pp. 84–96.
The National Review, April 1858, vol. 6, pp. 259–279.
The North British Review, Aug. 1854, vol. 21, pp. 493–504.
The Times, Nov. 4, 1853, no. 21, 577, p. 5.

ACKNOWLEDGMENTS

➤➤➤ ◄◄◄

The following have generously permitted me to quote from works of which they hold the copyright: George Allen and Unwin, Ltd.; D. Appleton-Century Company; G. Bell and Sons; Coward McCann; Dodd, Mead and Company; Doubleday, Doran and Company; Duke University Press; E. P. Dutton and Company; Harcourt, Brace and Company; Harper and Brothers; the President and Fellows of Harvard College; Henry Holt and Company; Houghton Mifflin Company; International Publishers Company; Mr. Mitchell Kennerley; Alfred A. Knopf; *The Living Age;* Longmans, Green and Company; The Macmillan Company; *The Menorah Journal;* The Morgan Library; John Murray; Oxford University Press; Eric S. Pinker and Adrienne Morrison Incorporated; Random House; George Routledge and Sons; Charles Scribner's Sons; The University of Chicago Press; The Viking Press; Mr. H. G. Wells; Yale University Press.

INDEX

>>> <<<